ADVANCED ANS COBOL
WITH STRUCTURED PROGRAMMING

Advanced
ANS COBOL

WITH STRUCTURED
PROGRAMMING

Gary D. Brown

A Wiley-Interscience Publication

JOHN WILEY & SONS

New York · Chichester · Brisbane · Toronto · Singapore

To my daughter Lindsay

Library of Congress Cataloging in Publication Data:

Brown, Gary DeWard.
   Advanced ANS COBOL with structured programming.

   "A Wiley-Interscience publication."
   1. COBOL (Computer program language).   2. Structured
programming.   I. Title.
QA76.73.C25B76   001.6'424   76-55706
ISBN 0-471-10642-9

Printed in the United States of America

20 19 18 17 16 15

preface

A typical classified section of the *Sunday Los Angeles Times* contains perhaps 50 ads for programmer jobs that mention COBOL, 5 that mention FORTRAN, and 1 that mentions PL/I, with seldom any mention of ALGOL, BASIC, or APL. This is especially significant because Los Angeles is the heart of the aerospace industry where scientific languages such as FORTRAN, PL/I, and APL should be used the most. Certainly COBOL is not so widely used because of indoctrination; universities usually teach FORTRAN, frequently PL/I, ALGOL, BASIC, and APL, but rarely COBOL. COBOL is widely used because it is better suited to the type of applications to which the computing industry has moved, and most graduates must learn COBOL outside of the universities in order to get jobs in programming. This book is intended to help them. It will also be useful for those who already know COBOL, but who wish to become more skilled and familiar with all its features and with a wider range of programming techniques.

COBOL was intended to be easy to learn and use, but over time it has so evolved that it has some of the most complex statements to be found in any programming language. Some statements take pages to describe and are rarely utilized because of their complexity, but they can be of service if they are made easier to understand. To make their use simple and familiar, they are described in this book with many short examples. This method of describing COBOL should be especially appreciated by the reader who is a little impatient and would rather see a few simple examples than a long, wordy explanation.

This volume described ANS COBOL, with emphasis on System/370 COBOL. It differs from a beginning text in that it covers the more advanced COBOL features rather than introducing the reader to the fundamentals of programming. Experienced COBOL programmers will find the book equally useful in learning these advanced features, as a basis for establishing programming standards, and for developing criterion for good programming.

At first I had some reservations when I titled the book *Advanced* COBOL: the word *advanced* might lead readers to believe that they will be dragged through a collection of clever coding tricks, but that is not the intent. Reduced to a single word, the essence of this book would be to *simplify*. I decided to retain the word *advanced* because I believe that we should accept as advanced programming that which is the simplest and clearest.

The book also describes *structured* programming. Although structured programming itself may boil down to a narrow set of programming constructs, it is arousing interest in the whole spectrum of programming techniques. Perhaps its most significant contribution is to change the primary emphasis in programming from efficiency to clarity. This emphasis is carried throughout the book, even where it conflicts with the rules of structured programming.

The current interest in structured programming can lead to new and unexpected benefits. For example, the COBOL report writer is often neglected and has nothing to do with structured programming. But if you step back to consider what other things contribute to program simplicity and clarity as is done in Chapter 2, it becomes apparent that the report writer is a useful feature. Perhaps the most interesting part of the book is Chapter 2, where I attempt to replace subjective judgments about programming techniques ("The report writer didn't work in Version 16.86 and so forget it!") with an objective set of criteria ("It is easier to make programming changes in the data and data descriptions than in the executable statements, and the report writer does just this.")

A description of COBOL cannot be complete without the interfaces to the computer's operating system and input/output devices. This interface in System/370 is the Job Control Language, and it too is described.

In using this book, you may discover that some of the COBOL features are not supported in the compiler you use, or are supported but contain errors, or are inefficient. This is especially likely to be true of the advanced COBOL features, because they are not often used. Problems can also be harder to solve because your coworkers may be unfamiliar with the advanced features. There are so many different COBOL compilers that nothing lasting can be said about any specific one. Nonetheless, most COBOL statements do work properly in most compilers, and this book argues that it is more productive to concentrate on how you code in COBOL than on the compiler implementation.

My special thanks to Susan Kachner who reviewed the text and made many suggestions, and to Richard Tracy from whom I learned many of the COBOL programming techniques.

GARY DeWARD BROWN

November 1976
Los Angeles, California

acknowledgment

The following acknowledgment is reprinted from *American National Standard Programming Language COBOL*, X3.23-1974, published by the American National Standards Institute, Inc.

Any organization interested in reproducing the COBOL standard and specifications in whole or in part, using ideas from this document as the basis for an instruction manual or for any other purpose, is free to do so. However, all such organizations are requested to reproduce the following acknowledgment paragraphs in their entirety as part of the preface to any such publication (any organization using a short passage from this document, such as in a book review, is requested to mention "COBOL" in acknowledgment of the source, but need not quote the acknowledgment):

COBOL is an industry language and is not the property of any company or group of companies, or of any organization or group of organizations.

No warranty, expressed or implied, is made by any contributor or by the CODASYL Programming Language Committee as to the accuracy and functioning of the programming system and language. Moreover, no responsibility is assumed by any contributor, or by the committee, in connection therewith.

The authors and copyright holders of the copyrighted material used herein

FLOW-MATIC (trademark of Sperry Rand Corporation), Programming for the UNIVAC® I and II, Data Automation Systems copyrighted 1958, 1959, by Sperry Rand Corporation; IBM Commercial Translator Form No. F 28-8013, copyrighted 1959 by IBM; FACT, DSI 27A5260-2760, copyrighted 1960 by Minneapolis-Honeywell

have specifically authorized the use of this material in whole or in part, in the COBOL specifications. Such authorization extends to the reproduction and use of COBOL specifications in programming manuals or similar publications.

contents

one

INTRODUCTION

More and more people learn COBOL each year, adding to the number of active COBOL programmers. Having advanced beyond the introductory programming manual, they need a book that touches only lightly on the basics of computing, and goes into detail on both advanced programming techniques and advanced COBOL statements. This book begins where introductory programming manuals leave off. The reader is assumed to be familiar with computers, computer applications, and a programming language, preferably COBOL, although the book describes the COBOL statements in enough detail to enable an experienced programmer to learn COBOL.

The book is intended to make the programmer a master of COBOL programming skills. This may help to solve some of his or her programming problems, but not all of them. The book cannot help in the difficult problems of dealing with an uncooperative customer, in fighting an unreliable computer system, or in designing a computer solution to a problem that is not worth a solution. But the book should give the reader a confidence in his or her technical programming skills, making it possible to face the other more difficult problems with this confidence.

In addition to the advanced COBOL features such as the SORT verb, the report writer, tables, subroutines, character-string manipulation, and teleprocessing, the book describes advanced programming techniques, including structured programming. Advanced programming does not imply that programming be clever, obscure, or difficult. On the contrary, it implies that it be simple, concise, and clear. Programming style can also

1

contribute to simplicity, conciseness, and clarity. Although style is partly a matter of personal taste, Chapter 2 develops a set of objective criteria that lead to the style used throughout this book.

This book is based on the 1974 version of the American National Standard (ANS) Programming Language COBOL, ANSI X3.23-1974,[1] and the IBM System/370 COBOL compilers, particularly the Versions 3,[2,3] 4,[4] and OS/VS[5] compilers. This causes some problems because System/370 COBOL is based on the 1968 ANS Standard, not the 1974 Standard. There are a few significant differences between the two and many minor ones. The major differences are explained, but many of the minor differences result from a relaxation of some of the rules and do not represent significant functional changes. This book takes the lowest common denominator between the two so that where there are nonessential differences, a single form is used that will work for both. For example, ANS COBOL no longer requires a space before the left parenthesis [A(I) is legal] whereas System/370 does [A (I) must be coded]. Since there is no difference in function, the latter is used in this book because it will work in both ANS and System/370 COBOL.

Parts of the ANS Standard and System/370 COBOL are incompatible. The 1974 ANS Standard contains 42 changes to the previous standard that could impact existing programs. Some statements, such as the NOTE, REMARKS, and EXAMINE, have been replaced by new forms, and this book explains both forms. Other parts of the new ANS Standard contradict the previous Standard, as, for example, the meaning of the NOT in implied logical operations. In these instances, the reader is generally urged to avoid the construct altogether and use another form. All of these changes place the compiler manufacturers in a quandary that may take some time to resolve.

Where the book must deal with a specific implementation, IBM System/370 COBOL and the System/370 operating systems are assumed. The book also includes information from the IBM COBOL *Programmer's Guide*[6] at the appropriate places in the text, combining the language reference descriptions with the *Programmer's Guide*. An introduction to System/370 Job Control Language[7] is also included because it is essential to System/370 COBOL. The System/370 implementation is described because it is the most widely used operating system. The readers not using System/370 will find the parts of the book dealing with the System/370 operating system less useful, but COBOL programmers must deal with the operating system, and this interface, which is outside of the ANS Standard, constitutes much of the difficulty in COBOL.

I. USE OF THIS BOOK

The language features are described by giving examples of their use; not long examples illustrating applications, but short examples illustrating language features. Applications are important, but as examples they are too long and involved to hold the reader's interest. A few complete programs are included, but they are intended more to show how all the COBOL statements look when they are put together in a complete program than to be read in detail.

Criteria are first developed to evaluate programming techniques and language features. The basic COBOL statements are then presented, and structured programming is introduced. The advanced COBOL features follow, organized into chapters. When used as a textbook, the chapters should be read in sequence and the exercises performed at the end of each chapter. The experienced programmer may wish to choose selected chapters after reading Chapters 2 through 5.

Although the standard COBOL notation shows optional clauses with braces and brackets, this makes it difficult to tell how to code the statement. Consequently, the book indicates how each statement is actually written. If there are several forms or options, each form is shown so that the reader can see how it is coded without the distraction of braces and brackets. A dashed line indicates that one of several items may be coded, and the items are listed above the dashed lines. Parenthetic comments that describe the statements are set off in brackets. Language statements are written in typewriter type in uppercase letters; lowercase type denotes generic terms such as *name* or *value*.

```
        OUTPUT
        INPUT
OPEN _ _ _ _ file-name.          [Any explanation is set in this typeface.
                                  This statement could be coded in two
                                  ways.]

OPEN OUTPUT file-name.    [Or:]        OPEN INPUT file-name.
```

The COBOL vocabulary differs from that in other languages such as FORTRAN and PL/I. This book generally tries to avoid any specialized vocabulary, but the following COBOL terms are used throughout the book.

* *alphanumeric literal.* A character-string bounded by quotation marks. It is also termed a nonnumeric literal in COBOL and sometimes a character literal in other languages.

- *data item.* A character or set of contiguous characters (excluding in either case literals) defined as a unit of data by the COBOL program.
- *data name.* A user-defined word that names a data item described in a data description entry in the Data Division. When used in the general formats, data name represents a word that can be neither subscripted, indexed, nor qualified unless specifically permitted by the rules of the format.
- *elementary item.* A data item that is described as not being further logically subdivided.
- *identifier.* A data name, followed as required, by the syntactically correct combination of qualifiers, subscripts, and indices necessary to make unique reference to a data item. An identifier is often termed a variable in other languages.
- *numeric literal.* A literal composed of one or more numeric characters that also may contain either a decimal point or an algebraic sign, or both. The decimal point must not be the rightmost character. The algebraic sign, if present, must be the leftmost character. A numeric literal is often termed a constant in other languages.
- *table.* A set of logically consecutive items of data that are defined in the Data Division by means of the OCCURS clause. A table is also termed an array in other languages.

The term *item* is used within this book to describe an item that may be either a literal or identifier of a data type appropriate to the context. Hence the general form of a statement may be given as:

```
MOVE item TO identifier.
```

The following MOVE statements are then valid.

```
MOVE 2 TO X.

MOVE 'A' TO Y.

MOVE W TO Z.
```

But the following statement is invalid.

```
MOVE W TO 2.
```

The reader will notice that many examples use short, meaningless names, such as ADD Y TO X, despite urging the readers themselves to use meaningful names. The reason for this apparent contradiction is to emphasize the statement rather than the data. A statement such as ADD 2 TO CITY-POPULATION might evoke thoughts about cities and their populations, distracting from the operation of the ADD.

In both ANS and System/370 COBOL, there may be several alternative ways to code the same thing, such as A OF B or A IN B. This book generally describes only one of the forms. Additionally, COBOL has several optional words that may be omitted, such as (A IS = B) or (A = B), and some optional words are ignored. These omissions are made to simplify the descriptions of the language by giving the reader one form for coding the language statements that will work. Because the complete features of neither ANS COBOL nor System/370 COBOL are described, the book is not a complete reference manual. Instead, it is more a manual of style for COBOL programming in which the emphasis is on the simplification of the language features and not on all the possible ways of coding them.

Two non-ANS COBOL forms are used consistently throughout this book—the THEN keyword in the IF statement and the single quotation mark for enclosing alphanumeric literals. They are illustrated in the following example.

```
IF  A = B

    THEN MOVE 'Y' TO C

    ELSE MOVE 'N' TO C.
```

The THEN keyword is not permitted in ANS COBOL and is optional in System/370 COBOL. It is used in this book for three reasons. First, the IF/THEN/ELSE statement is an important structured programming construct, and it seemed appropriate to code the THEN. Second, it is easier to direct the reader's attention to the THEN clause when the THEN is coded. Finally, the THEN can be aligned with the ELSE to give symmetry to the IF statement and make it easier to follow. Single quotation marks for enclosing alphanumeric literals ('Y') are used rather than the ANS Standard of double quotation marks ("Y") because single quotation marks are usually used in System/370 COBOL. If the reader's COBOL compiler or own inclination prohibit the use of either the THEN or the single quotation marks, the statements can mentally be translated to form the following construct.

```
IF  A = B

    MOVE "Y" TO C

ELSE

    MOVE "N" TO C.
```

There will be objections to using non-ANS COBOL forms because they are not protected by the Standard. However, the 1974 ANS Standard made 42 changes incompatible with the previous standard whereas IBM has shown an intense sensitivity to the problems of compatibility.

II. INTRODUCTION TO COBOL

COBOL differs from most programming languages. It is based on English, which is not unusual, but it is a highly structured language designed especially for business applications, and this is unusual. COBOL programs are highly structured in that they are divided into four divisions. The first division, entitled the Identification Division, names the program and contains optional comments that identify the program's author and describe when it was written and what it does.

The second division, entitled the Environment Division, describes those aspects of the data processing problem that depend on the physical characteristics of a specific computer. It names the source and object computer and describes each file used by the program. In addition, it associates the internal file name with an external Job Control Language statement.

The third division, entitled the Data Division, describes all the data used in the program. Each data item must be described explicitly. COBOL is designed to process files, and the data descriptions take the form of a record structure, which is the best means of describing the contents of an I/O record. For example, the file might contain cards having the format shown in Figure 1.

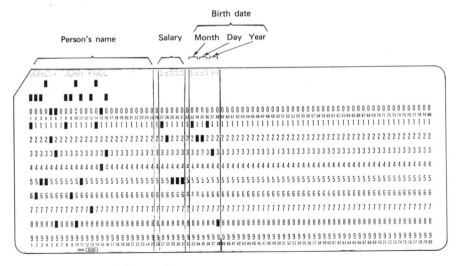

FIGURE 1. Typical data card.

The data description entries to describe this record are written as follows.

```
01  CARD-RECORD.
```

[Names the record.]

```
    05  PERSON-NAME          PIC X(25).
```

[Specifies 25 alphanumeric characters of data.]

```
    05  FILLER               PIC X.
```

[Specifies one alphanumeric character. FILLER indicates that the item is not given a name.]

```
    05  PERSON-SALARY        PIC 999V99.
```

[Specifies a five-digit number with two places to the right of the assumed decimal point. The 12555 on the card is treated as 125.55.]

```
    05  FILLER               PIC X.
```

[Specifies one alphanumeric character. The item is not given a name.]

```
    05  PERSON-BIRTH-DATE.
```

[Names a group item, which is further subdivided.]

```
        10 MONTH            PIC 99.
```

[Specifies two numeric digits.]

```
        10 DAYS             PIC 99.
```

[Specifies two numeric digits.]

```
        10 YEAR             PIC 99.
```

[Specifies two numeric digits.]

```
    05  FILLER               PIC X(42).
```

[Used to pad out the record. Specifies 42 alphanumeric characters, and the item is not given a name.]

The record enables the data to be treated as a unit, and yet one can still refer to each individually named item of data that it contains. Independent elementary items are also described in this same record form, as are tables.

```
77  FLAG-A              PIC X.
```

[Elementary item. It is termed a *noncontiguous elementary item*.]

```
01  CITY.

    05  POPULATION  PIC X(5) OCCURS 100 TIMES.
```

[POPULATION is a table containing 100 elements, and each element contains five characters.]

The several COBOL classes and categories of data are as follows. The value clause assigns initial values to data items as shown.

- NUMERIC CLASS. Arithmetic operations may be performed on this class of data.

```
77  ITEM-A      PIC S999V99 VALUE 1.
```

[Numeric character data.]

```
77  ITEM-B      PIC S999V99 COMP VALUE 1.
```

[Numeric data. Binary data in System/370.]

```
77  ITEM-C      PIC S999V99 COMP-3 VALUE 1.
```

[Numeric packed decimal data in System/370, but not a part of the ANS standard.]

```
77  ITEM-D      COMP-1 VALUE 0.1E+1.
```

[Numeric single-precision floating-point data in System/370, but not a part of the ANS standard.]

```
77  ITEM-E      COMP-2 VALUE 0.1E+1.
```

[Numeric double-precision floating-point data in System/370, but not a part of the ANS standard.]

- ALPHANUMERIC CLASS. Arithmetic operations may not be performed on this class of data.

```
77  ITEM-F      PIC X(3) VALUE 'AB1'.
```

[Alphanumeric data.]

```
77  ITEM-G      PIC $9,999.99.
```

[Numeric edited data. Used to edit numeric data for display.]

```
77  ITEM-H      PIC XX/XX/XX.
```

[Alphanumeric edited data. Used to edit alphanumeric data for display.]

- ALPHABETIC CLASS. Arithmetic operations may not be performed on this class of data.

```
77  ITEM-I     PIC A(3) VALUE 'ABC'.
```

   [Alphabetic data.]

One other form, the *index*, is used only to refer to table elements, and is described along with the table.

```
01  CITY.
    05  POPULATION     PIC X(5)  OCCURS 100 TIMES
                                 INDEXED BY X-POP.
```

   [X-POP can be used to index the POPULATION table.]

The fourth division, termed the Procedure Division, contains the executable program statements. The statements are a rigid subset of English.

`MOVE A TO B.`	[A is stored in B.]
`ADD 1 TO A.`	[1 is added to A.]
`COMPUTE C = D * E / F.`	[The value of D times E divided by F is stored in C.]

COBOL does not check for the beginning of a sentence by context, but by recognizing one of its reserved words. Thus in the previous example it recognizes the ADD as the start of a new statement by the word ADD, not by remembering that it just encountered the end of a previous statement, and that which follows must be the start of a new statement. Because of this, all COBOL language words are reserved. MOVE, ADD, and COMPUTE cannot be used as data items because they are part of COBOL statements. Each COBOL *statement* begins with a reserved-word verb. A COBOL *sentence* contains one or more statements and ends with a period. A sentence composed of several statements is often used in conditional statements, such as the IF, to execute several statements based on the condition. The following IF statement executes just as it reads.

```
IF A = B
    THEN MOVE C TO D        ⎫   [These two statements are executed if A
         MOVE E TO F        ⎬   equals B.]
    ELSE MOVE G TO H        ⎫   [These two statements are executed if A
         MOVE I TO J.       ⎬   does not equal B.]
```

The DISPLAY statement displays the value of alphanumeric literals and numeric and alphanumeric data items on the standard output file.

```
DISPLAY ITEM-A.
```

[The contents of ITEM-A are displayed.]

```
DISPLAY 'THE VALUE IS: ', ITEM-B.
```

[*THE VALUE IS:* is printed, followed by the contents of ITEM-B.]

COBOL files, also termed *data sets* in System/370, must be described explicitly by a series of entries in the Environment and Data Divisions. Files must then be opened before they can be read or written, and closed before the program terminates.

```
OPEN INPUT IN-FILE.          [IN-FILE is opened for input.]

OPEN OUTPUT OUT-FILE.        [OUT-FILE is opened for output.]

CLOSE IN-FILE.               [IN-FILE is closed.]
```

COBOL input/output is record oriented; that is, one logical record is transmitted with each READ or WRITE. (Inside the operating system, several records may be grouped together in a block to be physically transmitted as a unit between the I/O device and the computer's memory.) For example, the CARD-RECORD defined earlier is read and written as shown in the following example. In the example, the AT END phrase in the READ statement contains an imperative statement to be executed if there is no record to be read.

```
READ IN-FILE INTO CARD-RECORD
```

[A record is read into CARD-RECORD.]

```
AT END MOVE SPACES TO CARD-RECORD.
```

[SPACES is a *figurative constant* that assumes the value of literal blank characters equal to the length of the item to which it is moved. Spaces are moved to CARD-RECORD if there is no record to read.]

```
WRITE OUT-REC FROM CARD-RECORD.
```

[A record is written from CARD-RECORD.]

The data is transmitted without conversion. Once read into the computer, the numeric digits may be checked for validity and converted from character to a more efficient numeric form by moving them to a numeric data item.

```
MOVE PERSON-SALARY TO numeric-data-item.
```

COBOL can also label executable statements and branch to the statement with a GO TO statement, but labels in COBOL, termed *procedure names*, are generally used to name a group of statements to be executed as a unit by the PERFORM statement. The PERFORM statement names a procedure and causes all the statements following the procedure name, up to the next procedure name, to be executed. Such a collection of state- ·ments is termed a *paragraph.* COBOL programs are often organized by a series of PERFORM statements that invoke the parts of the program, rather than by the use of GO TOs to thread control through the statements.

```
PERFORM A10-INITIALIZE.
```
[Executes all the statements following A10-INITIALIZE up to the next paragraph name, and then returns control to the next executable statement following the PER-FORM.]

```
PERFORM A20-READ-FILE.
```
[Executes all the statements in the A20-READ-FILE paragraph.]

Execution continues sequentially, and so the paragraphs invoked must not immediately follow the invoking statements, or control will flow through them again.

```
A10-INITIALIZE.
    OPEN INPUT IN-FILE.
    MOVE 0 TO IN-COUNT.
```
Invoked by PERFORM A10-INITIALIZE.

```
A20-READ-FILE.
    READ IN-FILE INTO CARD-RECORD
        AT END MOVE SPACES TO CARD-RECORD.
    IF CARD-RECORD NOT = SPACES
        THEN ADD 1 TO IN-COUNT.
```
Invoked by PERFORM A20-READ-FILE.

This is the essence of COBOL, and should give enough background for the next chapter which develops a set of criteria for developing good programming style. These criteria are then applied throughout the remainder of the book in describing the COBOL statements.

REFERENCES

1. "American National Standard Programming Language COBOL," ANSI X3.23-1974, American National Standards Institute, Inc., New York, 1974.
2. "IBM OS Full American National Standard COBOL," Order No. GC28-6396, IBM Corporation, Kingston, N. Y., 1974.
3. "IBM OS Full American National Standard COBOL Compiler and Library, Version 2, Programmer's Guide," Order No. GC28-6399.
4. "IBM OS Full American National Standard COBOL Compiler and Library, Version 3, Programmer's Guide," Order No. SC28-6437.
5. "IBM OS Full American National Standard COBOL Compiler and Library, Version 4, Programmer's Guide," Order No. SC28-6456.
6. "IBM OS/VS COBOL Compiler and Library Programmer's Guide," Order No. SC28-6483, IBM Corporation, Kingston, N. Y., 1974.
7. "IBM System/360 Operating System: Job Control Language Reference," Order No. GC28-6704, IBM Corporation, Poughkeepsie, N. Y., 1973.

two

CRITERIA

I. RATIONALE FOR RULES AND GUIDELINES

The criteria developed in this chapter are used throughout the book, and lead to several rules and guidelines for style. A *rule* is considered to be that for which there is every reason to observe, and no valid reason not to. Indenting nested IF statements is a rule. A *guideline* has valid reasons for being followed, but exceptional instances for not being followed. Eliminating the GO TO statement is a guideline.

Some rules and guidelines must be ambiguous. We might all agree that IF statements should not be nested to too deep a level, but perhaps not agree how deep. Either there is no precise definition, or it would take so many words to state the rule as to be useless. In these instances, we shall resort to the same test used in a court of law—the rule of the reasonable man. Briefly, this rule states that if a reasonable man would find something wrong, it is wrong.

Frequently we find ourselves objecting to something with feelings like those expressed in the childhood limerick:

> I do not like thee, Doctor Fell;
> The reason why, I cannot tell;
> But this I know and know full well,
> I do not like thee, Doctor Fell.

Rules give us words to express why we feel as we do about something. Rules are often said to detract from creativity, but creativity is hard to suppress. That Shakespeare wrote good English did not detract from his creativity. Good rules are not a panacea, but they help.

At first glance, this chapter may appear to be reinventing the wheel. In fact, it does even less; it simply suggests that we use the wheel. None of the criteria developed in this chapter are new. A selected reading list is given at the end of the chapter, but many of the criteria have been with us since dinosaurs stopped being a menace.

II. THE ENVIRONMENT

The COBOL programming environment is that of production computing for commercial applications. Most computing done today is, or leads to, production computing, and production programs are predominantly COBOL. They have a relatively long life, are perhaps more input/output oriented than computation oriented, and more logical than algorithmic. Communication is vital because there is often a separation of effort in design, programming, running, maintenance, and even documentation, with different people working on different parts. This is the environment for which the programming criteria are derived, and our goal shall be to improve program maintenance, correctness, reliability, and efficiency.

Too often programming techniques are engrossed with the efficiency and implementation of individual language statements. But the life of such knowledge is short, and that avoided in old compilers may be encouraged in new ones. One manufacturer alone provides 20 COBOL compilers, and altogether there are scores of COBOL compilers in existence, making it hard to generalize about the efficiency or correctness of individual language statements. Good programming techniques should not be discouraged because someone wrote a bad compiler. If one were to avoid all COBOL statements that have caused problems, there would be nothing left. Avoiding language features that in the past had errors, but now work correctly brings to mind a wizened old New Englander who says "Tried one of them newfangled automobiles once. Didn't like it."

III. THE RULES AND GUIDELINES

We often fail to appreciate just how hard programming is. Is the following COBOL statement correct?

```
COMPUTE X = Y / Z.
```

Y or Z might not have been assigned values, Z might contain zero, the identifiers might be of improper data types, they might be undefined, the names might be reserved words, precision might be lost, an underflow or overflow might occur, the statement may be in the wrong columns, blanks may not have been properly inserted, the statement might be at the wrong place in the program, or we may have actually wanted Y * Z. These are but the obvious errors from a single statement containing no logic. Programs consist of hundreds of statements with logic and interaction, and systems contain thousands of statements. Each statement is like a moving part in a machine, and if a part fails, the entire system may fail. Additionally, the job control language and the interaction with the operating system can be more complex than the programming language. Programming is a difficult undertaking in which nothing is trivial. This leads to the first and most important rule.

Simplify.

Simplifying programs makes them easier to design, maintain, understand, document, and run. Begin simplifying in the design because if simplicity is lost here, it cannot be regained. Simplicity may not always be possible, but needless complexity can always be eliminated.

We tend to regard complexity highly because it is human nature to hold in awe that which we do not comprehend. But accomplishment comes from making things simple rather than complex. Even in science, the great ideas are simple. Sir Isaac Newton expressed three classic laws of physics with a fraction of the complexity found in the 1040 income tax forms. Were he alive today, surely he too would have an accountant prepare his income tax returns.

The techniques of good expository writing in English also apply to programming, and many of the following rules are borrowed from Strunk and White's *The Elements of Style* and George Orwell's essay on "Politics and the English Language." The essence of good expository writing is to decide what you want to say, and then to say it as simply, concisely, and clearly as possible. This is also the essence of good programming.

Many simple programming techniques appear difficult because they are unfamiliar. A binary search is difficult in COBOL only if one is unfamiliar with the SEARCH statement. A goal of this book is to make all COBOL statements familiar by describing them and giving examples of their use.

Eliminate the unnecessary.

That which is eliminated does not need to be designed, programmed, documented, and maintained, and costs nothing to run. Never use a long word where a short one will do, such as PICTURE for PIC. Omit unused paragraph names because they can distract and confuse. A single discounted cash flow subroutine written to be used by many will save effort, and likely be both more reliable and efficient than separate subroutines written for several individual applications.

Eliminating the unnecessary also simplifies. Notice the apparent difference in complexity in the following two descriptions that produce identical results.

```
77  X PICTURE S999999V99 USAGE IS COMPUTATIONAL VALUE IS ZERO.

77  X PIC S9(6)V99 COMP VALUE ZERO.
```

Neither statement is comprehensible to someone unfamiliar with COBOL, but the first appears more complex. PIC for PICTURE and COMP for COMPUTATIONAL become as familiar to COBOL programmers as are Dr. for doctor, Ms. for Miss./Mrs., and COBOL for common business-oriented language.

Eliminate useless repetition. Useless repetition occurs in many ways. For example, data may be entered into a system and used in several programs. By validating the data only once as it enters the system rather than each place it is used in a program, we save our effort and the computer's resources, and make the system easier to change. Useless repetition often creeps in under the guise of flexibility. Many people feel that it is good to provide a variety of ways in which to do something. They are like the old farmer who is asked for directions back to the main road. He does not realize that by describing several alternatives, he is only making us more lost.

COBOL often gives the appearance of having been designed by the same old farmer. The following statements all add 1 to an identifier.

```
COMPUTE VARIABLE = VARIABLE + 1.

ADD 1 TO VARIABLE.

ADD 1 TO VARIABLE GIVING VARIABLE.

SUBTRACT -1 FROM VARIABLE.

SUBTRACT -1 FROM VARIABLE GIVING VARIABLE.

SET INDEX-ITEM UP BY 1.
```

Each statement has its own options and operates on limited data types. What is essentially simple becomes complex with the many ways in which it can be done. The programmer is forced to make an unnecessary choice and then worry whether it was the correct one.

Clarify. Write to be read by others.

Programs are read more frequently than they are written. Even a program's author writes a program only once, and then reads it many times during debugging. It follows that it is more important that programs be easily read than that they be easily written. Programs are also likely to be read by someone other than the program's author. Often, programs are considered to be readable if someone who understands what the program is to do can understand how the code accomplishes it. This is the absolute minimum in readability. The goal should be to go beyond this to write programs so that someone can understand what the program is to do from reading the code.

Programmers often sacrifice clarity to optimize at the detail level where the results are rarely measurable. Efficiency should come from the design and not during debugging or production. Programs cost little to change during design, but are expensive to change once they have been coded, and it is risky to modify a correct program. Any significant inefficiency is usually localized to a few areas. Avoid cleverness when it is at the expense of clarity.

One way to clarify is to avoid ambiguity. For example, the statement MULTIPLY A BY B is ambiguous because it is not apparent where the result is stored. Surprisingly, it is stored in B. The statement COMPUTE B = B * A avoids the ambiguity. Few people remember the hierarchy of logical and arithmetic operations. In what order will the following operations be performed?

```
IF A = B OR C = D AND E = F ...
```

Use parentheses to show the hierarchy and remove the ambiguity.

```
IF (A = B) OR ((C = D) AND (E = F)) ...
```

Clarify the sequence of execution; things that hide it are bad. This rule is the basis for structured programming. To understand the sequence of instructions at any point in a program, we must know where we came from and where we are going. A good way to clarify the flow of control is to have a single entry and exit in each functional unit of code. This eliminates the threading in and out of statements with a GO TO. For example, if control can reach a paragraph by sequential execution, falling through from the previous paragraph, and by a PERFORM or GO TO, it is difficult to tell where we came from. The following code is typical.

```
A.   IF NOT a-condition THEN GO TO B.

     a-statements.
```

```
B.  IF NOT b-condition THEN GO TO C.

    b-statements.

    GO TO D.

C.  c-statements.

D.  d-statements.
```

The code is intertwined and hard to follow. How do we get to D? Under what conditions do we execute C? Is the above a complete unit, or might C be the target of a PERFORM or GO TO from somewhere else? Now examine the way the above coding reads when we eliminate the unnecessary GO TOs.

```
A.

    IF a-condition

        THEN a-statements.

    IF b-condition

        THEN b-statements

        ELSE c-statements.

    d-statements.
```

Now it is clear that paragraph A is a unit, and that the *d-statements* are always executed. The *c-statements* cannot be the target of a PERFORM or GO TO, and we get to the *c-statements* when *b-condition* is false.

Weinberg, in his book *The Psychology of Computer Programming* points out that a linear sequence is easier to follow than a nonlinear one. A program containing many GO TOs is hard to follow because one must keep track of all the possible paths and also flip back and forth in the listing.

The GO TO is not all bad. It does make it clear where control is going, and it is bad only in that it clouds where control came from and distracts the reader by breaking the linearity of the program. The ALTERed GO TO is totally bad because it is impossible to tell where control might go by reading the statement, and it also clouds where control came from. The ALTERed GO TO is a GO TO statement that appears by itself in a paragraph.

```
A20-SWITCH.

    GO TO A60-START.

A30-CONTINUE.
```

The GO TO will transfer to A60-START if executed. At some other place in the program, the ALTER statement can change the target of the GO TO.

```
ALTER A20-SWITCH TO PROCEED TO B10-DONE.
```

Now the GO TO A60-START acts as if it were a GO TO B10-DONE. Never use the ALTER statement.

Eliminating unnecessary GO TOs is good, but does not ensure that the flow of control is clear. The following example also hides the sequence of execution.

```
IF COST IS EQUAL TO ZERO MOVE ZERO TO PAGE-A, MOVE 1 TO

NEW-LINE, ELSE PERFORM MAX-SIZE, IF COST IS GREATER THAN

ZERO PERFORM ZERO-COST, ELSE PERFORM BIG-COST.
```

It reads well as an English sentence, but it is difficult to read as a sequence of discrete steps. It is better written as follows.

```
IF COST = 0

    THEN MOVE 0 TO PAGE-A

        MOVE 1 TO NEW-LINE

    ELSE PERFORM MAX-SIZE

        IF COST ) 0

            THEN PERFORM ZERO-COST

            ELSE PERFORM BIG-COST.
```

Now the logical sequence is clear. Computer programs are not read for their contribution to the literature of the English language, but to understand the logic and computations within the program. The previous example shows how programs can be made clear by proper indentation. Programs are also more readable and easier to change if a single statement is contained on a line. If a line must be continued, break the statement at a point where it is obvious that it is continued, and indent the continuation. Thus we express the logic and continuation of statements by indentation.

Nested IFs have often been avoided in the past, but they are good if written so that the intent is clear. The following statement is a nested IF, and it is clear.

```
IF A = B

    THEN MOVE C TO D

        MOVE X TO Y

        IF E = F

            THEN PERFORM M

                IF G = H

                    THEN PERFORM Z

                    ELSE PERFORM X.
```

However, COBOL has problems with nested IFs because it lacks a concise statement delimeter. The following statement does not execute as it reads.

```
IF A = B

    THEN MOVE 1 TO X

        IF C = D

            THEN PERFORM U

            ELSE PERFORM V

        PERFORM W.
```

The PERFORM W is a part of the last ELSE clause. (There are several solutions to this problem discussed in Chapter 4.) Avoid nesting to a level at which the indentation forces statements off the right side of the page. THEN clauses can generally be nested to several levels with the meaning remaining clear, but ELSE clauses can cause problems as shown in the following example.

```
IF A = B

    THEN MOVE 1 TO X

        IF C = D

            THEN PERFORM U
```

```
                    IF E = F

                      THEN PERFORM V

                           PERFORM W

                      ELSE PERFORM M

            ELSE PERFORM N

                 MOVE X TO Y

       ELSE PERFORM P .
```

Each ELSE clause has a corresponding THEN clause, and these clauses are hard to pair up if the ELSE does not immediately follow the THEN. A little astigmatism on the part of the reader, and he would be lost. (Perhaps computer paper should have vertical lines.) Nested IFs are good if not nested too deeply, and if the corresponding ELSE clause is kept close to its THEN clause.

Keep the major logic and organization as visible and at as high a level as possible.

This makes programs easier to follow and change. A good way to do this is to use the PERFORM statement:

```
MOVE 'N' TO EOF-MASTER.

PERFORM READ-MASTER UNTIL EOF-MASTER = 'Y'.
```

These statements tell us where we are reading the master file, that it is read within a loop, and that the loop is terminated when EOF-MASTER is set to 'Y', probably by detecting the end of file. It clearly indicates the start of the read loop (the beginning of paragraph READ-MASTER), and the end of the loop (the end of paragraph READ-MASTER).

Make the program *modular* by organizing it into distinct functional parts. Invoke the modules with PERFORMs. This aids in quickly finding one's way into a program by giving the equivalent of a table of contents for program execution. It also divides the program into smaller parts that can be readily digested, and eases maintenance because one can identify the beginning and end of a functionally related part of the program. Additionally, it reduces the interaction, or at least keeps the interacting components together. There is no firm rule on the maximum size of such a functional unit of code or module, but 50 lines of code is often considered a reasonable limit because it is comprehensible and will fit on a single page.

In psychology, breaking up long items into shorter parts is termed chunking. The term may be unfamiliar, but the practice is not; we do it constantly without giving it much thought. The number 12133930911 becomes relatively easy to remember and comprehend as 1-(213) 393-0911. Dividing a complex program into digestible components makes it much more manageable.

Convey as much useful information in the coding as possible.

COBOL is largely self-documenting, and is made more so by selecting meaningful names. For example, the paragraph name READ-LOOP conveys more information than A10, and A10-READ-LOOP conveys even more information because it indicates its location relative to other names, assuming that the names are placed in sequential order within the program. By conveying useful information, we lead the reader through the code. Consider the following two examples that show alternative ways to code a loop.

```
    SET K TO 1.

A20-MAX.

    many-statements.

    SET K UP BY 1.

    IF K NOT ) 20 GO TO A20-MAX.
```

Not until after plowing through many statements to discover a GO TO back to the start, do we discover that it is a loop. The following is a better way to code the loop.

```
    PERFORM A20-MAX

        VARYING K FROM 1 BY 1

        UNTIL K ) 20.

    □ □ □

A20-MAX.

    many-statements.
```

Now it is clear that a loop controlled by K is repeated 20 times. Although the loop is still bad because the statements comprising the loop do not immediately follow the statement controlling them, we can justify something bad if there is no better alternative. Unlike most languages, COBOL does not have DO loops such as the following.

```
DO K = 1 TO 20 BY 1;

    many-statements;

END;
```

Keep the reader in context.

Things are easier to understand when they are in context. The context consists of the surrounding items that, by their presence, tell us something about the item. In the following example, a single word of context is enough to give the word beagle three different meanings, and in one case, enough to indicate a spelling error.

Beagle—dog (a breed of dogs)

Beagle—Darwin (the ship upon which Darwin sailed)

Beagle—lox (a misspelling of bagel)

The first step in making a program understandable is to place the reader in context by a short narrative at the start of the program, telling what the program does, what goes into it, and what comes out of it. Place related items together so that each item contributes to the understanding of the others. Isolating related items also makes them easier to change. Weinberg terms this *locality*, and he also notes that programs are easier to understand if the related items are kept on the same page of the source listing.

Write programs to be changed.

Change is constant for most programs. In theory, programs are written from a complete set of specifications, and when the programs perform according to the specifications, the job is complete. In practice, it rarely works like this. Specifications are written at the time when the least amount is known about the program, and no specifications can be complete enough to account for all contingencies. The program evolves during the implementation. The budget might be cut, requiring a less elaborate program. In a personnel program, new legislation could require the addition of new information and the exclusion of old information. A new personnel director might want a different set of reports. This evolution does not end when the program is placed in production, but continues over its entire life. Information produced by programs acts as a catalyst, generating a desire for more or different information. After the people have worked with the program for a while, they may begin to understand what they really want. Programming is an iterative process.

Often, more is spent on program maintenance than was originally spent in development because a surprising number of items can change. The number of departments and locations within a company can certainly change, but we might forget that the number of states can also change (viva the Virgin Islands!), and that the calendar changes each year. About the only things unlikely to change are the number of months in a year (unless the Aztecs gain power) and physical measurements (until we switch to the metric system).

We can make programs easier to change by making data and data descriptions drive the program wherever possible. If a table may change, read it in from cards or disk rather than building it into the program. Then the change can be made in the external data without disturbing the program. Parameterize all items that are likely to change. The COBOL report writer is good because it parameterizes entire reports.

Be definitive.

Regardless of what a comment says, a program will do as directed by the statements. The statements themselves should serve as the documentation where possible, eliminating a separate documentation effort and the possibility that it will be incorrect or outdated. Experienced maintenance programmers know that program flow charts, while a fine tool for design, are difficult to draw, and are rarely kept up to date.

Comments should be used when the language statements do not make clear what will be done, but never when the statements themselves are clear. Comments are easily confused with language statements in COBOL. Indent or set off the comment so that it does not hide or blend in with the statements. Thus we should use only as many comments as necessary, and not let them obscure the code.

Do not mislead, surprise, or confuse.

Human beings have difficulty in noticing the unexpected. We have all seen examples such as the following.

    PARIS IN THE
    THE SPRING.

Because we do not expect to find the extra THE, we do not see it. Computers lack this tolerance for ambiguity, and this causes problems in our communicating with them. An example of surprising and confusing the reader is to use a variable named DAYS to contain units of months. Exceptions can make programs complex and difficult to follow, and contribute heavily to maintenance problems. Eliminate exceptions where possible. Failing this, comment them as exceptions, giving the reason and explaining how they are handled.

Much of the surprise and confusion in programming comes from inconsistency. Weinberg terms this the principle of *uniformity*. For example, in COBOL, one must READ a *file-name*, but WRITE a *record-name*. This is inconsistent, and as a result it is easy to confuse the two. Rules, standards, and a confidence in one's tools, techniques, and abilities all lead to consistency.

Avoid complex logical expressions such as those combining NOT with OR, or those with double negatives. In the following example, it is not immediately apparent that STOP RUN is always executed.

```
IF (SALARY NOT = 0) OR

    (SALARY NOT = 1)

    THEN STOP RUN.
```

Do not force small incompatibilities for small improvements. It sometimes seems as if a cavalier attitude rather than necessity is the mother of incompatibility. Often it is better to live with bad features than to undergo the slow torture of minor, incompatible improvements.

Check for errors where they can occur on the assumption that things will go wrong.

One of the frustrating aspects of computer programming is that a program may run correctly hundreds of times and then erupt with an error. This inevitably happens, and we should design and program for it. This is done by checking for errors, recovering if possible, and printing error messages. For example, if you read in a table, check for the table exceeding the internal table size. If you divide by a variable, check for zero divide. Validate all raw input data. Do not assume that things have gone correctly. For example, we might think that there is no need to check the sequence of a master file because it is kept in sort order. We forget that the sort key may be updated, an unsorted file may be inadvertently read, or any of a hundred other things may go wrong.

Once an error has been detected, print a clear, concise message describing the error. Error messages should be relevant and directed to the person who will read them. The message 'TABLE OVERFLOW—ABEND' is ambiguous if the program has more than one table. ABEND means "evening" in German, but little else to nonprogrammers. The error message should describe what went wrong, the transaction or data involved, the action taken within the program, and any action that must be taken outside of the program.

Break any of these rules rather than do anything outright barbarous.

IV. SUMMARY

This concludes the set of criteria. Before applying them to the COBOL language features and to structured programming, read them over again carefully.

- Simplify.
- Eliminate the unnecessary.
- Clarify. Write to be read by others.
- Keep the major logic and organization as visible and at as high a level as possible.
- Convey as much useful information in the coding as possible.
- Keep the reader in context.
- Write programs to be changed.
- Be definitive.
- Do not mislead, surprise, or confuse.
- Check for errors where they can occur on the assumption that things will go wrong.
- Break any of these rules rather than do anything outright barbarous.

EXERCISES

1. Critique one of the following computer languages using the criteria developed in this chapter.

ALGOL	COBOL
APL	FORTRAN
Assembler Language	PL/I
BASIC	RPG

2. Write a paper suggesting additions, deletions, or a complete new set of criteria if you disagree with those in this chapter.

3. Write a paper critiquing the computer's operating system or job control language with which you are familiar, using the criteria developed in this chapter.

SELECTED READING

Kernighan, Brian W., and P. J. Plauger, *The Elements of Programming Style*, McGraw-Hill Book Company, New York, 1974.

Ledgard, Henry F., *Programming Proverbs*, Hayden Book Company, Inc., Rochelle Park, N. J., 1975.

Orwell, George, *A Collection of Essays*, Doubleday and Company, Inc., Garden City, N. Y., 1954.

Strunk, William, Jr., and E. B. White, *The Elements of Style*, Revised Edition, The Macmillan Company, New York, 1959.

Weinberg, Gerald M., *The Psychology of Computer Programming*, Von Nostrand Reinhold Company, New York, 1971.

three

GENERAL LANGUAGE RULES

The general language rules in this chapter are explained in light of the criteria developed in the preceding chapter. Several techniques for coding are described, and they will be used throughout the remainder of the book. At the end of the chapter, these techniques are applied to a complete COBOL program to illustrate their use, and also to give the reader a preview of what a complete COBOL program looks like.

I. COBOL CHARACTER SET

The characters A through Z are alphabetic, 0 through 9 are numeric, and b† = + − * / ( ) , . ; $ > < " are special. The single quotation mark (') may be used in place of the double one (") in System/370, and is used in this book. The double quotation mark is the ANS standard, however.

II. STATEMENT FORMAT

The COBOL statement format is oriented toward punched cards. A whole statement, part of a statement, or several statements may be contained on

† The lowercase b is used to represent a blank character.

a line. A period (.) delimits a sentence. A sentence consists of one or more statements, the last of which is terminated by a period.

```
MOVE X TO Y.   MOVE V TO W MOVE M TO N.
```

[Or:]

```
MOVE X TO

    Y.   MOVE V TO W MOVE

        M

    TO N.
```

Code a single statement per line to make the statements easier to read and the program easier to change.

```
MOVE X TO Y.

MOVE V TO W

MOVE M TO N.
```

A series of items may be separated by commas, and the comma is a matter of personal preference.

```
ADD A B C TO D.   [Same as:]   ADD A, B, C TO D.
```

A period is coded only after the last of a series of statements in a sentence, and the statements may be separated by commas. However, commas should not be used here because a comma is easily mistaken for the terminating period, especially if the tail of the comma happens to be printed lightly.

Correct, but prone to errors: Preferred:

```
IF A = B                              IF A = B

    THEN ADD C TO D,                      THEN ADD C TO D

        ADD E TO F.                           ADD E TO F.
```

Columns 1 to 6 contain an optional sequence number, column 7 indicates both the continuation of literals and comments, procedure names begin in columns 8 to 12 (termed the *A area;* column 8 is termed the *A margin*), and statements are coded in columns 12 to 72 (termed the *B area;* column

12 is termed the *B margin*). Columns 73 to 80 are available for deck identification. The sequence numbers in columns 1 to 6 have no effect on the
program and serve only to help put back together a card deck if it is dropped.
Sequence numbers are a bother, but a necessary one. However, many systems have text editors that retain source programs on disk, eliminating
card decks. The text editor then automatically keeps track of the sequence
numbers.

SEQUENCE			CONT.	A	B				...		IDENTIFICATION	
(PAGE)	(SERIAL)											
1	3	4	6	7	8	12	16	20	24	72	76	80

```
010020  START-IT.                           STATETAX
010030      MOVE 10 TO A.          ...      STATETAX
010040      MOVE 10 TO B.                   STATETAX
```

Throughout the remainder of this book, the left margin denotes the A
margin (column 8) and the B margin (column 12) is indented four spaces.

```
LABEL-A.                    [Begins in the A margin.]

    MOVE C TO D.            [Begins in the B margin.]
```

If a statement exceeds one line, continue the statement on the next line
in column 12 or beyond. For readability, break the statement where it is
obvious that it is continued, and indent the continuation.

```
    COMPUTE A = (VAR + 27.6 -

        VAL) / HOMES -

        RENT).
```

To continue an alphanumeric literal, code the literal through column 72,
code a hyphen (–)† in column 7 of the next line, code a quote in column 12
or beyond, and continue the literal.

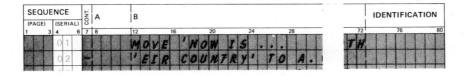

SEQUENCE			CONT.	A	B						IDENTIFICATION	
(PAGE)	(SERIAL)											
1	3	4	6	7	8	12	16	20	24	28	72	76	80

```
        01          MOVE 'NOW IS ...          TH
        02  -       'EIR COUNTRY' TO A.
```

† The hyphen and the minus sign are the same character.

Where possible, avoid continuing alphanumeric literals because it increases the chance for error. The previous statement is better written as follows.

```
MOVE
    'NOW IS ...                              ... THEIR COUNTRY'
    TO A.
```

COBOL has rigid rules on the placement of blanks. Generally, at least one blank must appear wherever one might expect a blank in an English sentence. Several blanks may be coded wherever a single blank may appear.

```
COMPUTE    A = 1.3    + FIVE.
[Or:]
COMPUTE A = 1.3 + FIVE.
```

In System/370, the period (.), comma (,), and semicolon (;) must not be preceded by a blank, but must be followed by a blank. (This restriction is removed in the ANS Standard.)

```
A, B   Correct.              A ,B      Wrong.
A,B    Wrong.                A , B     Wrong.
```

In System/370, the left parenthesis [(] must not be followed by a blank, and the right parenthesis [)] must not be preceded by a blank. (This restriction too is removed in the ANS Standard.)

```
(6)      Correct.
( 6)     Wrong.
(6 )     Wrong.
```

The careful insertion of blank lines and page ejects makes the source listing easier to read. Although not a part of the ANS Standard, System/370 compilers provide an EJECT statement that is not itself listed, but causes a page eject where it appears in the source listing. EJECT has no punctuation and begins in column 12 or beyond.

```
EJECT
```

The ANS Standard provides a page eject by coding a slash (/) in column 7 to denote a comment line that causes a page eject. (This feature is not presently implemented in the System/370 compilers.)

/

    Blank cards may be inserted in a source deck to print blank lines in the source listing. However, a keypunch operator is likely to ignore blank lines. System/370 provides the non-ANS Standard SKIP1, SKIP2, and SKIP3 command to skip one, two, or three lines. They are coded in column 12 or beyond with no punctuation. A better way that works both under the ANS Standard and System/370 is to skip lines with a blank comment line by coding an asterisk in column 7.

*   [Two lines are skipped.]

*

III. NAMES

Paragraph and section names, termed *procedure names*, are 1 to 30 characters composed of 0 to 9, A to Z, or the hyphen (-). The hyphen must not be the first or last character, but all other characters may appear in any position. (-X, and X- are invalid, but X-X is valid.) Section names must be unique, and paragraph names must be unique within a section. Begin the procedure names in columns 8 to 12, and end them with a period.

```
A10-INITIALIZE.
```

    Statements may appear on the same line as the procedure name, provided that they begin in column 12 or beyond and are separated from the name and its period. However, the procedure stands out clearer when the name is on a line by itself.

Correct, but not as clear: Better coded as:

```
A20-END.  MOVE 16 TO RETURN-CODE.    A20-END.

                                             MOVE 16 TO RETURN-CODE.
```

    Make each procedure contain a functionally related unit of code. The procedure name marks the start of such a functional unit, and the name should indicate what the procedure does. Make the procedure easier to locate in the listing by preceding the procedure name with characters or numbers that indicate its position relative to other procedure names.

```
B10-INITIATE.

    PERFORM A10-ZERO.          [A20 should precede B10 in the listing.]

B20-READ-MASTER.               [B20 should follow B10.]

    PERFORM Z10-TERMINATE.     [Z10 would be much further down in the
                                listing.]
```

Often, paragraphs must be established because limitations in COBOL prevent the desired statements from being coded in-line. These paragraphs are functionally a part of the main paragraph, they exist only because of limitations in COBOL, and they should be given names to indicate this.

```
B10-INITIATE.

    IF A = B

        THEN PERFORM B10-PART-A

            MOVE 1 TO A.

    PERFORM B10-PART-B

        VARYING IX FROM 1 BY 1

        UNTIL IX ) 10.


        □ □ □

B10-PART-A.

    IF C = D

        THEN MOVE 0 TO B

        ELSE MOVE 1 TO B.

B10-PART-B.

    MOVE 0 TO TABLE-A (IX).
```

Data names are also 1 to 30 characters (A-Z, 0-9, -), and the hyphen must not be the first or last character. Data names must be unique within a program or subroutine.

```
77  TOTAL-AMOUNT  PIC X.

01  EOF-INPUT     PIC X.
```

Select data names that describe their contents. For example, COUNTER only tells us that something is counted, PAGE-COUNT tells us what is counted, REPORT-6-PAGE-COUNT tells for which report pages are counted, and RPT-6-PAGE-NO conveys the same information by using shorter words and abbreviations.

IV. COMMENTS

Comments are written one per line by coding an asterisk (*) in column 7, and the comments in the remaining columns of the card. In this book, column 7 is indicated by coding the asterisk one space to the left of the left margin.

```
* ASTERISK IN COLUMN 7.

* COMMENTS IN REMAINING COLUMNS OF CARD.
```

Indent the comment or set it off if it might hide or obscure the statements.

```
 A10-INITIALIZE.

*****************************************************************

*      ENCLOSING THE COMMENT IN ASTERISKS SETS IT OFF.

*****************************************************************

     OPEN INPUT FILE-IN.

*                        THIS COMMENT IS INDENTED TO COLUMN 24 TO
*                        SET IT OFF.

     DISPLAY 'FILE OPENED.'.

***** EXIT
```

Write the program to minimize the need for comments. Use comments where necessary, but do not use them to state the obvious or as an expedient to make up for writing obscure code. A NOTE statement is provided on many COBOL compilers for coding comments. However, it is less convenient, is errorprone, and has been dropped from ANS COBOL. Do not use the NOTE statement.

V. SPECIAL WORDS

A. Abbreviations

Several long COBOL reserved words can be abbreviated, such as PIC for
PICTURE. This book generally uses the abbreviation rather than the long
form.

B. Reserved Words

All COBOL defined words are reserved and cannot be used as procedure
names or data names. Appendix A lists COBOL reserved words, although
individual compilers may differ slightly from this list. New reserved words
are constantly added as COBOL is expanded, and a program that compiles properly today may not compile properly tomorrow.

There are over 430 System/370 COBOL reserved words, including such
common words as TIME, DATE, and ADDRESS, and one cannot be
expected to remember them all. Only 85 reserved words contain the hyphen, and so it is common to use a hyphen in names to reduce the chance
of inadvertently selecting a reserved word. However, more of the newer
reserved words contain hyphens. No reserved word currently begins with
a numeric character or the letter X, or contains two consecutive hyphens. Hence 9TOTAL-AMOUNT, XTOTAL-AMOUNT, and TOTAL--
AMOUNT would be relatively safe in never being reserved words, but
this technique results in ugly names. Perhaps the best technique is to select
meaningful names and then, if in doubt, check the name in Appendix A.

C. Optional Words

COBOL has optional words whose sole purpose is to improve readability.

```
    IF A = B GO TO C. [Same as:]          IF A IS = B GO TO C.
```

Optional words make statements more readable, but they also make
programming harder. One must remember the valid optional words, as
not just any word will do, and also remember where the optional words
may be placed. This book gives a single form for coding each statement,
and some optional words are ignored.

D. Figurative Constants

COBOL has several figurative constants that assume the value of an alphanumeric or numeric literal when used. Their advantage is that they assume

the appropriate attributes for the data type depending on the context in which they are used. For example, ZEROS assumes the value of a numeric zero or the characters zero, depending on the context. When used as an alphanumeric literal, ZEROS represents the character literal '000 . . . 0' whose length is that required by the operation. The following figurative constants are provided in COBOL.

* ZEROS (ZERO and ZEROES are also permitted). ZEROS assumes the value of an arithmetic zero or one or more zero characters.
* SPACES (SPACE also permitted). One or more blank characters.
* HIGH-VALUES (HIGH-VALUE also permitted). One or more characters having the highest value in the collating sequence. HIGH-VALUES cannot be used as numeric data, but only as alphanumeric data.
* LOW-VALUES (LOW-VALUE also permitted). One or more characters having the lowest value in the collating sequence. LOW-VALUES cannot be used as numeric data.
* QUOTES (QUOTE also permitted). Represents one or more of the quote character ("). In System/370, QUOTES represents a single quotation mark (') rather than a double one.
* ALL *'characters'*. ALL repeats the *characters* as often as required by the context in which it appears.

```
ALL 'AB'              [Same as:]      'ABABAB...AB'
```

E. Special Registers

COBOL has several built-in registers either used by statements or providing an interface to the operating system.

* LINE-COUNTER. Used by the report writer.
* PAGE-COUNTER. Used by the report writer.

The following special registers are not a part of ANS COBOL, but are provided in System/370 COBOL.

* TALLY. Used in the EXAMINE statement.
* CURRENT-DATE. Yields an 8-character date of the computer run in the form *'mm/dd/yy'*. CURRENT-DATE can appear only in a sending field of the MOVE statement.
```
MOVE CURRENT-DATE TO X.
```

- TIME-OF-DAY. Yields a 6-character field of the current time of the computer run in the form '*hhmmss*'. *hh*-hour (00 to 23), *mm*-minute, *ss*-second. TIME-OF-DAY can appear only in the sending field of the MOVE statement.
  ```
  MOVE TIME-OF-DAY TO X.
  ```
- WHEN-COMPILED. Yields a 20-character field containing the time and compilation date of the form '*hh.mm.ss*MMMbDD,bYYYY'.
  ```
  12.20.00JANb20,b1975
  ```
  WHEN-COMPILED may be displayed to ensure that the current version of the program has been used, and to associate the program with the proper listing.
  ```
  DISPLAY WHEN-COMPILED.
  ```
- RETURN-CODE. Used to return a completion code to the operating system when the run terminates. RETURN-CODE is a PIC S9999 COMP item, and the default value is zero.
  ```
  MOVE 16 TO RETURN-CODE.
  ```

VI. PROGRAM ORGANIZATION

COBOL programs are divided into four divisions. The Identification Division contains comments identifying the program, author, and date written. The Environment Division describes the computer, the I/O devices, and the access methods to be used. The Data Division describes all the data, and all data items must be explicitly described. The Procedure Division contains the executable program statements.

COBOL statements are written in a rigid subset of English. Statements are grouped together into paragraphs, with a paragraph consisting of a paragraph name and all following sentences until the next paragraph name. The Procedure Division is usually composed of paragraphs that are invoked by the PERFORM statement.

COBOL also provides subroutines, which are invoked by the CALL statement. Data is shared between the calling program and the subroutine by including the data as arguments in the CALL statement.

Top-down programming, sometimes termed *stepwise refinement*, is an important part of structured programming. The terms mean that the overall program concept is subdivided into smaller and smaller functionally related parts to give structure to the program. The program is then coded and tested in the same hierarchical order so that the data descriptions and the highest level of logic are coded first. This gives discipline to the design, and ensures that the most important part of the program, its overall design, is coded first. It also serves to organize the program into digestible components consisting of functionally related parts that reflect the original design concept.

Begin the program with comments that summarize the program's purpose. Describe the program in enough detail to give the reader the proper background for reading the program. Generally a few paragraphs will do. Add comments if the program is changed during production so that the reader has a record of the major changes made, the date, and who made them.

Organize the program into paragraphs, and invoke them with PERFORMs. This gives the equivalent of a table of contents to the program as shown in the following example. Notice how the following few statements give the reader a good idea of what the program is to do, and the order in which it is done.

```
PROCEDURE DIVISION.

A10-BEGIN.

    PERFORM B10-INITIALIZATION.

    PERFORM C10-READ-IN-TABLES.

    MOVE LOW-VALUES TO RECORD-KEY.

    PERFORM D10-READ-MASTER-FILE UNTIL RECORD-KEY = HIGH-VALUES.

    PERFORM E10-WRAPUP.

    STOP RUN.
```

Each main paragraph should be a functionally related unit of code, such as initialization or record selection. Make the beginning and end of each such unit stand out. How this is done is a matter of taste; the following example illustrates one method.

```
D10-READ-MASTER-FILE.

*****************************************************************
*   THIS PARAGRAPH READS IN EACH RECORD OF THE MASTER FILE,

*   SELECTING ONLY RECORDS WITH RECORD-TYPE = 'F'.   IT THEN

*   DISPLAYS THE RECORD KEY OF THE SELECTED RECORD.
*****************************************************************

    MOVE LOW-VALUES TO RECORD-KEY.

    PERFORM D20-READ-ALL UNTIL RECORD-KEY = HIGH-VALUES.
```

```
***** EXIT

*

D20-READ-ALL.

      MOVE LOW-VALUES TO RECORD-TYPE.

      PERFORM D30-GET-RECORD

         UNTIL (RECORD-KEY = HIGH-VALUES) OR

                (RECORD-TYPE = 'F').

      IF RECORD-KEY NOT = HIGH-VALUES

          THEN DISPLAY 'RECORD-KEY = ', RECORD-KEY.

***** EXIT

*

D30-GET-RECORD.

      READ IN-FILE INTO IN-RECORD

          AT END MOVE HIGH-VALUES TO RECORD-KEY.

***** EXIT

*****************************************************************

*   END OF D10-READ-MASTER

*****************************************************************
```

Whenever there are several related items in a statement, code each of them on a separate line.

```
      OPEN INPUT FILE-A,

               FILE-B,

               FILE-C.
```

Organize the listing to help the reader. Use blank lines (asterisk in column 7) or lines of asterisks to set off paragraphs. Use a page eject (EJECT coded in column 12 in System/370 or an '/' in column 7 in ANS COBOL) to begin a major part of the program. Place as much related information on a page as possible without crowding or awkward page breaks. It works out nicely if the functional units of code are limited to about 50 lines. Try to save the reader from having to flip pages back and forth to follow the logical flow. This is done by placing the paragraphs of the program in the sequence in which they are executed.

A COBOL program must be in the following order.

* Job card and control statements of the job control language.

```
IDENTIFICATION DIVISION.

PROGRAM-ID.  program-name.

AUTHOR.  name-of-person.

DATE-WRITTEN.  date.

DATE-COMPILED.
```
```
*    comments describing the program.
```
```
ENVIRONMENT DIVISION.

CONFIGURATION SECTION.

SOURCE-COMPUTER.  computer.

OBJECT-COMPUTER.  computer.

INPUT-OUTPUT SECTION.

     SELECT file-name ASSIGN TO ddname.
```

[Associates the file with JCL statements that specify the I/O device.]

```
DATA DIVISION.

FILE SECTION.
```

[All files are described here.]

```
FD   file-name
```

[A FD entry describes each file.]

```
     RECORD CONTAINS integer CHARACTERS

     BLOCK CONTAINS integer RECORDS

     LABEL RECORDS STANDARD.
```
```
01   record-name PIC X(record-length).
```

[This is the *record-area*. The records placed here describe the preceding file's records.]

```
WORKING-STORAGE SECTION.
```

[The data items are described here.]

```
01   J.
```

[J is a record.]

```
     05   K       PIC X(1).
```

[Alphanumeric elementary item.]

```
     05   L.
```

[L is a group item.]

```
          10   M   PIC S9.
```

[Numeric character elementary item.]

```
          10   N   PIC X(4).
```

[Alphanumeric elementary item.]

```
PROCEDURE DIVISION.
```

[Program statements of the main body follow this.]

```
A10-BEGIN.
```

[The Procedure Division is composed of paragraphs or sections.]

```
     OPEN INPUT file-name.

     MOVE 'N' TO K.

     PERFORM A10-READ-FILE UNTIL K = 'Y'.

     CLOSE file-name.

     STOP RUN.
*

A10-READ-FILE.

     READ file-name INTO J

       AT END MOVE 'Y' TO K.

     IF K NOT = 'Y'

         THEN COMPUTE A = B + C - D * E / C ** B

              ADD 1 TO M

         ELSE DISPLAY 'END OF FILE'.
```

```
***** EXIT

***** END OF PROGRAM
```

• Any system control statements and data.

The many required statements give even simple COBOL programs a formidable look, but writing them soon becomes automatic, and they do help in reading programs because you know where to look to find things. A quick look at the INPUT-OUTPUT section tells which files are used, and the Data Division describes all the data used in the program. The next chapter describes each of the basic COBOL statements in detail.

EXERCISES

1.   What problems can the reserved words of COBOL cause?

2.   Tell which of the following COBOL names are incorrect, and why.

```
FORMULA                     Z
2HOT                        NOT-HER
PROGRAM-ID                  7UP
OH*                         UP-OR-DOWN
W-                          EITHER/OR
UP TO                       H24
NOW--OR-LATER               -TO-HERE
TEXT                        MEET-ME@4
F-111                       AVERAGE-AMOUNT-OF-DOLLARS-
HUT_16                         REMAINING
                            HASN'T
```

3.   Explain the syntax errors in the following statements.

```
A1. COMPUTE A = B*C.

MOVE ZERO TO A.

    IF (B=C) THEN GO TO A1.

    MOVE 1 TO X(1,2).

    ****  BEGIN COMPUTATIONS
```

```
START-IT.

     MOVE X

     TO Y, MOVE V

     TO W

     ADD A, B C TO D.

     ADD E,F,G TO H.

NEW-PART

     ADD I ,J TO   K.

     ADD X(1) TO Y.

     COMPUTE A = B+C.

     MOVE STRING TO X.
```

four

BASIC COBOL STATEMENTS

This chapter describes the basic COBOL statements. They are presented here so that they will be familiar to the reader in the next chapter on structured programming. The statements are described in light of the criteria developed in the preceding chapter. The experienced programmer should also read this chapter because, while the statements may be familiar, the style in which they are coded may not be.

I. MOVE STATEMENT

The MOVE statement assigns the value of an item to an identifier. The item is converted to the data type of the identifier if necessary.

```
MOVE item TO identifier.

MOVE 6 TO A.

MOVE 'CHARACTERS' TO B.

MOVE C TO D.
```

The *item* and the *identifier* must not overlap because the results of the MOVE are unpredictable if they do.

```
01  A.

    05  B  PIC X.

    05  C  PIC X(100).

    □ □ □

    MOVE C TO A.                    [Error because C is contained in A.]
```

A single item can be assigned to several identifiers.

```
MOVE 0 TO RECORDS-IN,    [Same as:]      MOVE 0 TO RECORDS-IN.

         RECORDS-SELECTED,              MOVE 0 TO RECORDS-SELECTED.

         RECORDS-IGNORED.              MOVE 0 TO RECORDS-IGNORED.
```

Corresponding elements of records can be moved by appending COR-RESPONDING, usually abbreviated CORR, to the MOVE.

```
01  A.

    05  X  PIC X.

    05  Y  PIC X.

    05  V  PIC X.

01  B.

    05  V  PIC X.

    05  W  PIC X.

    05  X  PIC X.

    □ □ □

    MOVE CORR A TO B.  [Same as:]       MOVE X OF A TO X OF B.

                                        MOVE V OF A TO V OF B.
```

Notice that the data items on the right are *qualified*. When two records have elements with the same names, the element names must be qualified by the record name so that COBOL can know which element is meant. Element X in the previous example must be written as X OF A or X OF B to distinguish the element.

II. ARITHMETIC STATEMENTS

The COMPUTE statement evaluates an arithmetic expression on the right
of an equal sign and assigns it to the identifier on the left. Conversion will
occur if necessary to evaluate the expression or assign its value to the identifier. An *arithmetic expression* is either a single item or several items operated on by the arithmetic operations $(+ - * / **)$. A, A + B, and
A + B * 2 are arithmetic expressions.

```
COMPUTE identifier = arithmetic-expression.

COMPUTE A = B * 2.

COMPUTE A = B + C / D.
```

ANS COBOL, but not System/370 COBOL, permits multiple receiving
fields.

```
COMPUTE A, B = C + D.    [same as:]    COMPUTE A = C + D.

                                       COMPUTE B = C + D.
```

Parentheses specify the order in which the operations are to be performed. Those within inner parentheses are performed first.

```
COMPUTE X = (A + (B - C) * D / E) ** 2.
```

The spaces in the COMPUTE statement are important, and the rules for
placement are as follows.

- One or more spaces before and after the equal sign: A = B but not A = B
- One or more spaces before and after the arithmetic operators + − * /
  and **. A + B but not A+B
- One or more spaces to the left of the left parenthesis: X (but not X(†
- One or more spaces to the right of the right parenthesis:) X but not
)X†
- No space to the right of the left parenthesis: (X but not (X†
- No space to the left of the right parenthesis: X) but not X)†

---

† This restriction applies to System/370 COBOL. The restriction is removed in the ANS
Standard.

Note that the simplest form of the COMPUTE is identical to the MOVE.

```
COMPUTE A = B.          [Same as:]  MOVE B TO A.
```

COBOL also has ADD, SUBTRACT, MULTIPLY, and DIVIDE statements that perform the arithmetic operations implied by their names. They are redundant to COMPUTE, and their advantage is that they are perhaps more readable to someone unfamiliar with algebra. Generally they need not be used, but the ADD statement is convenient for adding an item to an identifier.

```
ADD item TO identifier. [Same as:]  COMPUTE identifier =
                                            identifier + item.

ADD 1 TO A.                          COMPUTE A = A + 1.

ADD B TO C.                          COMPUTE C = C + B.
```

Aside from this, ADD and SUBTRACT are necessary to perform corresponding operations on records with the CORR phrase, as COMPUTE cannot have the CORR phrase and DIVIDE is needed to compute the remainder from a division. The following forms of ADD, SUBTRACT, MULTIPLY, and DIVIDE are permitted. The equivalent COMPUTE statement indicates the operation performed.

```
ADD A TO B.             [Same as:]  COMPUTE B = B + A.

ADD A, B GIVING C.                  COMPUTE C = A + B.

ADD A, B, C TO D.                   COMPUTE D = D + A + B + C.

ADD A, B, C TO D, E.                COMPUTE D = D + A + B + C.

                                    COMPUTE E = E + A + B + C.

ADD A, B, C GIVING D.               COMPUTE D = A + B + C.

ADD A, B, C GIVING D, E.†           COMPUTE D = A + B + C.

                                    COMPUTE E = A + B + C.

SUBTRACT A FROM B.   [Same as:]     COMPUTE B = B − A.

SUBTRACT A FROM B GIVING C.         COMPUTE C = B − A.

SUBTRACT A, B, C FROM D.            COMPUTE D = D − A − B − C.
```

† This form is permitted in the ANS Standard, but not in System/370 COBOL.

SUBTRACT A, B, C FROM D, E.	COMPUTE D = D − A − B − C.
	COMPUTE E = E − A − B − C.
SUBTRACT A, B, C FROM D GIVING E.	COMPUTE E = D − A − B − C.
SUBTRACT A, B, C FROM D GIVING E, F.†	COMPUTE E = D − A − B − C.
	COMPUTE F = D − A − B − C.
DIVIDE A INTO B. [Same as:]	COMPUTE B = B / A.
DIVIDE A INTO B GIVING C.	COMPUTE C = B / A.
DIVIDE A INTO B GIVING C, D.†	COMPUTE C = B / A.
	COMPUTE D = B / A.
DIVIDE A BY B GIVING C.	COMPUTE C = A / B.
DIVIDE A BY B GIVING C, D.†	COMPUTE C = A / B.
	COMPUTE D = A / B.
MULTIPLY A BY B. [Same as:]	COMPUTE B = A * B.
MULTIPLY A BY B GIVING C.	COMPUTE C = A * B.
MULTIPLY A BY B GIVING C, D.†	COMPUTE C = A * B.
	COMPUTE D = A * B.

The CORR phrase option in the ADD and SUBTRACT statements causes the operation to be performed on corresponding elements of records.

```
01  A.
    05  X         PIC 9.
    05  Y         PIC 9.
    05  V         PIC 9.
01  B.
    05  V         PIC 9.
    05  W         PIC 9.
```

† This form is permitted in the ANS Standard, but not in System/370.

```
05  X              PIC 9.

□ □ □

ADD CORR A TO B.          [Same as:]      ADD X OF A TO X OF B.
                                          ADD V OF A TO V OF B.

SUBTRACT CORR B FROM A.[Same as:]      SUBSTRACT X OF B FROM X OF A.
                                       SUBSTRACT V OF B FROM V OF A.
```

COMPUTE is simpler to write and often makes the computation easier to understand than with the other statements. Consider the following two statements.

```
MULTIPLY M BY C GIVING E.

MULTIPLY C BY E.
```

Do the two statements represent a single computation? What is being computed? Now look at the same equation written with the COMPUTE statement.

```
COMPUTE E = M * C ** 2.
```

The COMPUTE makes it easy to see that this is Einstein's famous equation, $e = mc^2$. COMPUTE also keeps track of any intermediate results, and in System/370 compilers gives more accuracy by extending the precision to 30 digits if necessary. However, the intermediate results are more difficult to keep track of in long COMPUTE statements, especially those with divisions. It may be better to break the COMPUTE up and define a data item of the desired precision to control the intermediate results.

```
COMPUTE A = B * (C / D) * E.
```

Perhaps better as:

```
77  TEMP    PIC S9(5)V9(6) COMP-3.

□ □ □

COMPUTE TEMP = C / D.

COMPUTE A = B * TEMP * E.
```

A. Rounding

The final results in arithmetic statements are normally truncated if their precision is greater than that of the identifier to which they are assigned. Thus if a resulting identifier has precision of PIC S999, a result of 22.9 is truncated to 22, and a -6.1 is truncated to -6. The ROUNDED phrase rounds the final results rather than truncating them, and can be used in the COMPUTE, ADD, SUBTRACT, MULTIPLY, and DIVIDE statements. A 22.9 is rounded to 23, and a -6.1 is rounded to -6. COBOL rounds a value whose rightmost digit is 5 up in absolute magnitude so that 1.5 is rounded to 2, and -1.5 is rounded to -2. ROUNDED has no affect on COMP-1 and COMP-2 floating-point numbers. The ROUNDED phrase is coded as follows:

```
COMPUTE A ROUNDED = B + C.

ADD A TO B ROUNDED.
```

Rounding gives more accurate results than does truncation, which is especially important when repetitive operations are performed on numbers. Suppose that in a report dollars and cents are to be summed, but the numbers are to be printed in units of whole dollars. A common error is to sum the rounded or truncated numbers as shown in the following columns that might represent the report.

Full Accuracy	Rounded	Truncated
10.00	10	10
10.50	11	10
10.60	11	10
10.10	10	10
10.60	11	10
51.80	53	50

Summing the rounded or truncated numbers gives a wrong total that appears correct in that the individual numbers do sum to the total, even though this total is wrong. The correct total is 51.80, which is 52 if rounded or 51 if truncated. When many numbers are summed, the results can be off considerably. Always compute the sum with the full precision and then round or truncate this sum as shown in the following columns.

Full Accuracy	Rounded	Truncated
10.00	10	10
10.50	11	10
10.60	11	10
10.10	10	10
10.60	11	10
51.80	52	51

This gives the correct totals. Unfortunately, the totals appear wrong because the individual numbers do not equal the total when summed, and reports lose their credibility when one cannot add a column and obtain the same total printed by the computer. The choice between correct totals that appear wrong and incorrect totals that appear correct is not a happy one, but you should choose the correct totals even at the cost of appearing wrong. This particular problem could be avoided by printing the dollars and cents, even though the cents might not be of interest. Whenever possible, avoid either truncating or rounding.

B. Size Errors

A *size error* results when the magnitude of a result exceeds the size of the identifier into which it is to be stored. The ON SIZE ERROR phrase is appended to an arithmetic statement to execute an imperative statement if a size error occurs. Division by zero always causes a size error.

```
ADD A TO B
   ON SIZE ERROR imperative-statement.
COMPUTE A = B / C
   ON SIZE ERROR imperative-statement.
ADD A TO B
   ON SIZE ERROR MOVE C TO D.
COMPUTE A = B / C
   ON SIZE ERROR MOVE C TO D
                 MOVE E TO F.
```

An *imperative-statement* is one that specifies no conditional actions. An imperative statement may also consist of a sequence of imperative statements. The following list contains the imperative statements.

ADD (without ON SIZE ERROR)
ACCEPT
ALTER
CALL
CANCEL
CLOSE
COMPUTE (without ON SIZE ERROR)
DELETE (without INVALID KEY)
DISABLE
DISPLAY
DIVIDE (without ON SIZE ERROR)
ENABLE
ENTRY
EXAMINE
EXHIBIT (without CHANGED)
EXIT
GENERATE
GO TO (without DEPENDING ON†)
GOBACK
INITIATE
INSPECT
MERGE
MOVE

MULTIPLY (without ON SIZE ERROR)
OPEN
PERFORM (without UNTIL†)
READ (without AT END or INVALID KEY)
RECEIVE (without NO DATA)
RELEASE
RETURN (without AT END)
REWRITE (without INVALID KEY)
SEND
SET
SORT
START (without INVALID KEY)
STOP
STRING (without ON OVER-FLOW)
SUBTRACT (without ON SIZE ERROR)
SUPPRESS
TERMINATE
TRANSFORM
UNSTRING (without ON OVER-FLOW)
WRITE (without INVALID KEY or END-OF-PAGE)

Execution continues if a size error occurs and there is no ON SIZE ERROR phrase, but the results are unpredictable. When ON SIZE ERROR is specified, the result of the operation is not stored in the resultant identifier. When the ROUNDED phrase is specified, the rounding occurs before the check is made for a size error.

```
COMPUTE A ROUNDED = B + C * D

    ON SIZE ERROR MOVE 0 TO A.
```

† An imperative statement without this clause in System/370, but still an imperative statement with this clause in the ANS Standard.

C. Remainder

A remainder is computed in the DIVIDE GIVING statement with the REMAINDER phrase. (REMAINDER cannot be used with COMP-1 or COMP-2 floating-point data.)

```
DIVIDE A INTO B GIVING C REMAINDER D.
```

If A contains 6 and B contains 17, D would contain the remainder 5. REMAINDER must follow ROUNDED if it is present.

```
DIVIDE A INTO B GIVING C ROUNDED REMAINDER D.
```

III. OPERATIONS

A. Arithmetic Operations

The *arithmetic operations* are + for add, − for subtract, * for multiply, / for divide, and ** for exponential. They must be preceded and followed by a space, and usually appear in a COMPUTE or IF statement. The items within the expression are converted to a common base if necessary.

```
COMPUTE X = A + B − C / D ** 2.
IF (A + B) = (C − 1)
    THEN PERFORM B10−ZERO−TABLE.
```

An arithmetic expression may be preceded by a unary plus or minus sign as a prefix. (A unary sign indicates the sign of the item, not a subtraction or addition.) The following statement is interpreted as X plus a minus Y.

```
COMPUTE W = X + − Y.
```

The following conditions, including the relational condition, the sign condition, the class condition, and the condition-name condition, can appear only in the IF, PERFORM, or SEARCH statements.

B. Relational Conditions

⟨	Less than.
NOT ⟨	Not less than, same as greater than or equal to.
⟩	Greater than.
NOT ⟩	Not greater than, same as less than or equal to.
=	Equal.
NOT =	Not equal.

The relational conditions must also be preceded and followed by a space, and may compare identifiers, literals, and arithmetic expressions.

```
IF A = B
    THEN ADD 1 TO C.
IF (X * Y + Z) = 2
    THEN ADD 1 TO D.
```

C. Sign Condition

The *sign condition* tests for positive, negative, or zero values. It is completely redundant to the relational conditions, and need never be used.

```
IF X IS POSITIVE  [Same as:]        IF X ⟩ ZERO
    THEN ADD 1 TO Y.                    THEN ADD 1 TO Y.
```

D. Class Condition

The *class condition* tests whether an identifier contains only numeric or alphabetic data. The NUMERIC condition is true if the identifier contains only the digits 0 to 9. It can only test identifiers declared as alphanumeric (USAGE DISPLAY) or COMP-3 numeric, but not alphabetic characters declared as PIC A. (PIC 999 or PIC XXX, but not PIC AAA.)

```
IF identifier IS NUMERIC ...

IF identifier IS NOT NUMERIC ...
```

```
IF X IS NOT NUMERIC

    THEN MOVE B TO C.
```

For USAGE DISPLAY numeric character data, the data is considered numeric if it is unsigned or has an operational sign carried with the right-most digit, but it is not considered numeric if the characters plus (+) or minus (−) are present unless the SIGN clause, described later, is coded.

The ALPHABETIC test is true if the identifier contains only the characters A to Z or blank. ALPHABETIC can test only alphanumeric or alphabetic identifiers (USAGE DISPLAY) described as PIC A or X. (PIC AAA or PIC XXX, but not PIC 999.)

```
IF identifier IS ALPHABETIC ...

IF identifier IS NOT ALPHABETIC ...

IF X IS ALPHABETIC

    THEN MOVE B TO C.
```

E. Condition-Name Condition

Condition names are another redundant language feature that may make programs harder to read. *Condition-names* are level 88 data items assigned to elementary items and assigned a value. Testing the condition name is the same as testing the data item for the value. The following example illustrates a condition name, and the example on the right is clearer because you can immediately tell that if THING contains 'Y', the condition is true.

```
01  THING            PIC X.

    88  THING-IS-BIG  VALUE 'Y'.

    □ □ □

    IF THING-IS-BIG [Same as:]        IF THING = 'Y'

        THEN MOVE C TO D.                 THEN MOVE C TO D.
```

Each condition name can be assigned to a value, a range of values, several single values, or some combination of these. Within a record, level 88 denotes a condition name and cannot be used for other than this.

```
01   SOMETHING PIC S9(6) COMP-3.

     88   FEW    VALUE 1.

     88   LOTS   VALUE 1 THRU 10.

     88   MANY   VALUE 1, 3.

     88   MYRIAD VALUE 1, 3, 9 THRU 16, 17, 25 THRU 50.


     ▢ ▢ ▢
```

IF FEW [Same as:]	IF SOMETHING = 1
THEN MOVE C TO D.	THEN MOVE C TO D.
IF LOTS	IF (SOMETHING NOT ⟨ 1) AND
THEN MOVE C TO D.	(SOMETHING NOT ⟩ 10)
	THEN MOVE C TO D.

Condition names can also be assigned to group items in a record, but the value must be an alphanumeric literal or a figurative constant. Assigning condition names to group items does not preclude assigning condition names to elementary items. However, the elementary items must all be USAGE DISPLAY.

```
01   DATE-REC.

     88   NEW-YEAR      VALUE '760101'.

     05   YEAR          PIC XX.

          88   THIS-YEAR VALUE '76'.

     05   MONTH         PIC XX.

     05   DAYS          PIC XX.
```

In System/370 COBOL, condition names cannot be assigned to level-66 items (a special level that renames a group of items), a group containing items with JUST (an option to right-justify characters), or SYNC (an option to align binary and floating-point numbers), or indexes. These restrictions are removed in ANS COBOL. Condition names may be assigned to table elements, and the condition name must then be subscripted or indexed when used.

```
05  ARRAY-A OCCURS 10 TIMES PIC X.

    88  YES VALUE 'Y'.


□ □ □


IF YES (3) THEN ...  [Same as:]   IF ARRAY-A (3) = 'Y' THEN ...
```

Condition names make COBOL programs easier to read as English sentences, but harder to read to understand what is happening in the program, and they generally should not be used. However, they are sometimes convenient for testing in which many values must be tested and when the values may change. The change can be made in a single place in the Data Division rather than in several places throughout the program.

F. Logical Operations

The *logical operations*, also termed *boolean operations*, can connect the relational, sign, class, and condition-name conditions. They consist of the AND, OR, and NOT.

1. Logical AND

If X and Y are both true, then X AND Y has the value true. If either X or Y or both are false, then X AND Y has the value false.

```
IF (X = 1) AND (Y = 0)

    THEN PERFORM X10-DONE.
```

[The THEN clause is executed only if X equals 1 and Y equals 0.]

2. Logical OR

If either X or Y or both are true, then X OR Y has the value true. If both X and Y are false, then X OR Y has the value false.

```
IF (X = 1) OR (Y = 0)

    THEN PERFORM X10-DONE.
```

[The THEN clause is executed if X equals 1 or if Y equals 0.]

3. Logical NOT

If X is true, then NOT X has the value false. If X is false, then NOT X has the value true.

```
IF NOT ((X = 1) AND (Y = 2))

    THEN PERFORM X10-DONE.
```

[The THEN clause is executed if X is not equal to 1 or if Y is not equal to 2.]

If the same item is compared to several other items connected by AND, OR, or NOT, the full relational condition need not be written out, but can be implied.

```
A < B OR > C        [Same as:]    (A < B) OR (A > C)

A NOT = B OR > C                  (A NOT = B) OR (A > C)

A = B OR > C AND < D             (A = B) OR ((A > C) AND
                                  (A < D))
```

The relational condition itself can also be implied.

```
A = B OR C          [Same as:]    (A = B) OR (A = C)

A = B AND C AND D                (A = B) and (A = C) AND
                                  (A = D)
```

In these simple forms, the implied relations improve readability, but they quickly become confusing when used to excess. The following is unclear because it is not apparent that the last relational operand (>) applies to D.

```
A = B AND > C OR D  [Same as:]    ((A = B) and (A > C)) OR
                                  (A > D)
```

The NOT is especially troublesome because in System/370 COBOL it is treated as a logical operation rather than a part of the relational condition, unless it is in the first relational condition. In the ANS Standard, NOT is treated as part of the relational condition if it precedes the <, =, or >. Do not write implied conditions containing the NOT.

Complex logical conditions are often a source of error. For example, are the following two logical expressions equivalent?

```
NOT (A = B OR A = C)            (A NOT = B) OR (A NOT = C)
```

It is not obvious that they are different. The first expression is true only if A is not equal to either B or C, and the second expression is true either if A is not equal to B or if A is not equal to C. Try to avoid complex logical expressions, double negatives, and NOT in combination with OR. For example, NOT (A NOT = B) is better written as A = B. Use a decision table to decipher particularly complex logical statement. The following decision table shows that the previous two expressions are not equivalent.

Conditions:				
A = B	Yes	No	Yes	No
A = C	Yes	Yes	No	No
Value of				
NOT (A = B OR A = C)	False	False	False	True
Value of				
(A NOT = B) OR (A NOT = C)	False	True	True	True

If you must write a decision table to decipher a logical expression, the expression is not very readable. Do not write logical expressions that require a decision table to be understood. Recast the logical expression, rewrite it with nested IFs, or even use GO TOs if it will make it clearer.

Unclear: Better as:

```
IF NOT (A = B OR C)

    THEN do something.
```

```
IF A = B OR C

    THEN NEXT SENTENCE

    ELSE do something.
```

[Or:]

```
IF A NOT = B AND A NOT = C

    THEN do something.
```

[Or:]

```
IF A NOT = B

    THEN IF A NOT = C

        THEN do something.
```

[Or:]

```
IF A = B THEN GO TO B10-NEXT.
IF A = C THEN GO TO B10-NEXT.
do something.
B10-NEXT.
```

G. Conditional Expression

A *conditional expression* consists of a relational, sign, class, or condition-name condition, or several relational, sign, class, or condition-name conditions connected by the AND, OR, or NOT logical operations. For example, A = B AND C = 6.

H. Hierarchy of Operations

The hierarchy listed below specifies the order, from highest to lowest, in which operations are performed.

Highest: • Sign as prefix (+B   − C)
           • Exponential (A ** B)
           • Multiply, Divide (A * B / C)
           • Add, Subtract (A + B − C)
           • Relational, sign, class, condition-name conditions (A > B)
           • Logical NOT [NOT (A > B)]
           • Logical AND (A AND B)
Lowest: • Logical OR (A OR B)

Operations having equal hierarchy are evaluated from left to right.

```
A * B * C          [Same as:]        (A * B) * C
A + B − C ** D     [Same as:]        (A + B) − (C ** D)
```

The hierarchy can be overridden by parentheses. Parentheses also specify the hierarchy of operations so that you do not have to remember the previous rules. Since there is no question of the hierarchy of operations when parentheses are used, use them to lessen the chance for error.

Unclear: Better as:

```
IF A + B * D = 2 OR A ⟩ 6        IF ((A + (B * D)) = 2) OR
    THEN ADD 1 TO X.                 (A ⟩ 6)
                                     THEN ADD 1 TO X.
```

IV. GO TO STATEMENT

The GO TO statement transfers control to the first executable statement in the named procedure.

```
A10-START.
    GO TO X10-END-IT-ALL.
X10-END-IT-ALL.
    GO TO A10-START.
```

   Structured programming has given the GO TO some bad press, much of it deserved. However, the GO TO is not all bad, and one need not be fanatical about it. It may be used, but do not transfer backward or inter-twine the code with GO TOs, as this makes the logical flow hard to follow. Intertwining occurs when the path of one GO TO crosses the path of another as shown in the following two examples.

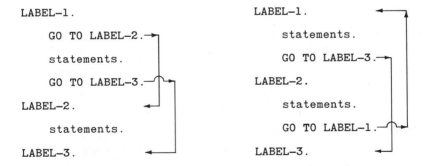

```
LABEL-1.                          LABEL-1.
    GO TO LABEL-2.                     statements.
    statements.                       GO TO LABEL-3.
    GO TO LABEL-3.                 LABEL-2.
LABEL-2.                              statements.
    statements.                       GO TO LABEL-1.
LABEL-3.                          LABEL-3.
```

   GO TOs should not exit from a paragraph to several different points outside the paragraph because this also obscures the logical flow by forcing the reader to follow the various paths. The following example illustrates this.

```
LABEL-1.

    statements.

    GO TO LABEL-3.   Exit
                     here

    statements.

    GO TO LABEL-2.   Exit
                     here

    statements.

***** EXIT

LABEL-2.

    statements.

LABEL-3.

    statements.
```

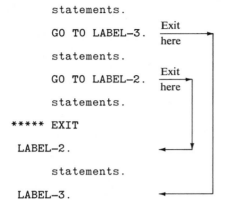

The GO TO DEPENDING ON statement transfers to one of several procedures depending on the contents of an identifier. In System/370, the identifier must be a positive integer of PIC 9 to 9(4), COMP or COMP-3. ANS COBOL allows any integer data item to be used.

```
GO TO procedure, procedure, ..., procedure DEPENDING ON
    identifier.

□ □ □

MOVE 2 TO CASE.

GO TO A10-START,   [Same as:]        GO TO B30-CONTINUE.

    B30-CONTINUE,

    B50-DONE

    DEPENDING ON CASE.
```

If CASE contains a value other than 1, 2, or 3, the GO TO DEPENDING ON is ignored, and execution continues with the next executable statement.

V. PERFORM STATEMENT

A. Execution of Procedures

The PERFORM statement is a brilliant concept that selectively executes groups of statements. It permits a program to be organized into functional

units that are invoked. It is especially useful in invoking functional units
from several points within a program to save having to code the same
function in several places. PERFORM is used in the following chapter on
structured programming to organize and structure a program, and is coded
as follows.

```
PERFORM procedure.
```

PERFORM may invoke either a paragraph or section. A paragraph
consists of a paragraph name and all following statements up to the next
paragraph name. A section is a collection of paragraphs that begins with
a SECTION name and includes all paragraphs up to the next section.

```
A10-A SECTION.

A20-B.                     ⎫
                           ⎬ Paragraph   ⎫
    MOVE A TO B.           ⎭             ⎬ Section
A30-C.                     ⎫             ⎭
                           ⎬ Paragraph
    MOVE D TO E.           ⎭

B10-A SECTION.
```

PERFORM transfers control to the first executable statement in the
procedure. Control is returned to the next executable statement following
the PERFORM when the last statement in the procedure is executed. The
last statement in a procedure is the one preceding the next procedure name.
Since this is a rather passive way of indicating the end of a procedure,
especially if the next procedure is on the following page, use a comment
to highlight the end of a procedure that is invoked by a PERFORM. This
will indicate to the reader that control is expected to return to the invoking
PERFORM rather than continuing on to the next procedure as would
occur if the procedure were the target of a GO TO.

```
PERFORM B10-ONE.

MOVE A TO B.

□ □ □

B10-ONE.

    MOVE 1 TO A.

    COMPUTE B = C + D.
```

```
**** EXIT

B20-TWO.
```

The previous statements are executed in the following sequence.

```
PERFORM B10-ONE.

MOVE 1 TO A.

COMPUTE B = C + D.

MOVE A TO B.
```

PERFORM operates as a GO TO transferring control to the first executable statement in the procedure, with another GO TO implanted at the end of the procedure transferring back to the next executable statement following the PERFORM. PERFORM operates as follows.

```
PERFORM B10-ONE.

    [Operates as GO TO B10-ONE.]

MOVE A TO B.

    □  □  □

B10-ONE.

    MOVE 1 TO A.

    COMPUTE B = C + D.

    [The end of the paragraph operates as a GO TO statement-following-the-
    PERFORM.]

***** EXIT

    [The comment has no effect.]

B20-TWO.
```

[This paragraph name marks the end of the preceding paragraph.]

But how can one exit a procedure from the middle? Suppose the following is desired.

```
paragraph-name.

    statements.
```

```
IF condition

    THEN want-to-exit-paragraph.

statements.
```

***** EXIT

The IF statement can often do this by executing the remaining statements in the procedure as a statement group, but sometimes a GO TO is needed to transfer to the end of the procedure, requiring another procedure name. But the GO TO would transfer out of the first procedure, and control would not return following the PERFORM as shown in the following example.

```
PERFORM B10-ONE.

    □  □  □

B10-ONE.

    READ IN-FILE INTO IN-RECORD

        AT END GO TO B20-TWO.

    MOVE IN-RECORD TO OUT-RECORD.
```

***** EXIT

```
B20-TWO.
```

If the GO TO is executed, control will not return following the PERFORM, but will continue sequentially in paragraph B20-TWO. This problem is solved by the PERFORM THRU, which names a first and last procedure to specify a range of procedures to execute.

```
PERFORM first-procedure THRU last-procedure.
```

Execution begins with the first executable statement in *first-procedure*, and control returns following the PERFORM when the last statement in *last-procedure* is executed. In System/370, *first-procedure* must precede *last-procedure* in the program, but this restriction is removed in the ANS Standard. We can now code the following.

```
PERFORM B10-ONE THRU B10-ONE-EXIT.

    □  □  □
```

```
B10-ONE.

    READ IN-FILE INTO IN-RECORD

    AT END GO TO B10-ONE-EXIT.

    MOVE IN-RECORD TO OUT-RECORD.

B10-ONE-EXIT.    EXIT.

***** END OF B10-ONE.
```

EXIT is a special null statement used to terminate a range of procedures. EXIT is not required, and any sequential range of procedures can be executed. The following example executes the C10-FIRST paragraph and then the C20-SECOND paragraph.

```
    PERFORM C10-FIRST THRU C20-SECOND.


    □ □ □


C10-FIRST.

    MOVE 1 TO A.

    COMPUTE B = C + D.

***** EXIT

C20-SECOND.

    MOVE B TO C.

    COMPUTE D = A - B.

***** EXIT
```

Note that the PERFORM C10-FIRST THRU C20-SECOND is equivalent to:

```
    PERFORM C10-FIRST.

    PERFORM C20-SECOND.
```

The latter is better because the goal is to isolate functionally related code, and invoking different ranges of procedures makes it unclear where the functionally related code begins and ends. Are C10-FIRST and C20-SECOND separate units, or are they part of a single unit? One cannot tell.

The procedure specified in the THRU clause may optionally contain only an EXIT statement. There is less chance for confusion if the THRU clause names an EXIT statement. EXIT is a convenience in terminating PERFORMed procedures, and must be the only statement in a procedure. That is, it must be preceded and followed by a procedure name. If an EXIT statement is executed without being named in a PERFORM, execution continues with the procedure following the EXIT. Always use EXIT to terminate procedures invoked by the PERFORM THRU so that it is apparent that the several procedures constitute a unit. Also include the word *EXIT* in the procedure name to show that it is an EXIT.

```
PERFORM C10-FIRST THRU C20-FIRST-EXIT.

    □  □  □

C10-FIRST.

    READ IN-FILE INTO IN-RECORD

      AT END GO TO C20-FIRST-EXIT.

    MOVE IN-RECORD TO OUT-RECORD.

    MOVE SPACES TO IN-RECORD.

C20-FIRST-EXIT.   EXIT.
```

Any procedures invoked by a PERFORM are executed in sequence if they are encountered during normal execution, but avoid this because it makes the program hard to follow. The following example illustrates this.

```
PERFORM B10-ONE THRU B30-THREE-EXIT.

B10-ONE.          MOVE 1 TO A.

B20-TWO.          MOVE 1 TO B.

B30-THREE-EXIT. EXIT.

B40-FOUR.         MOVE 1 TO C.
```

These statements are executed in the following sequence.

```
PERFORM B10-ONE THRU B30-THREE-EXIT.

B10-ONE.          MOVE 1 TO A.

B20-TWO.          MOVE 1 TO B.
```

```
B30-THREE-EXIT. EXIT.

B10-ONE.       MOVE 1 TO A.

B20-TWO.       MOVE 1 TO B.

B30-THREE-EXIT. EXIT.

B40-FOUR.      MOVE 1 TO C.
```

To reiterate, if a procedure is invoked by a PERFORM, do not also execute it by letting control fall through from the preceding procedure. Although the GO TO can transfer out of the range of statements being invoked by the PERFORM, this leads to confusion and should be avoided. Use the GO TO to transfer out of a procedure only when the flow of control must be broken, such as when the run is terminated because of an error.

B. Execution of Loops

The PERFORM also performs loops. It is awkward to use because it does not directly enclose the statements within the loop, but names remote procedures containing the statements. The simplest loop is to PERFORM a procedure some number of times.

```
PERFORM procedure integer TIMES.

PERFORM first-procedure THRU last-procedure integer TIMES.
```

The *procedure* is executed *integer* times. The *integer* may be a numeric integer literal or identifier. If *integer* is zero or negative, the *procedure* is not performed. Once PERFORM is executed, changes in the value of an identifier *integer* have no effect on the number of times the loop is executed.

```
PERFORM A60-ZERO-TABLE 6 TIMES.
```
   [A60-ZERO-TABLE is executed 6 times.]
```
MOVE 10 TO TABLE-SIZE.

PERFORM A60-ZERO-TABLE TABLE-SIZE TIMES.
```
   [A60-ZERO-TABLE is executed 10 times, even if a new value is assigned to TABLE-SIZE in the A60-ZERO-TABLE paragraph.]

The PERFORM UNTIL executes a procedure until a specified condition is met. If the condition is true when PERFORM is executed, the procedure is not performed.

```
PERFORM procedure UNTIL condition.

PERFORM first-procedure THRU last-procedure UNTIL condition.

PERFORM A10-TEST UNTIL END-FLAG = 'Y'.
```

In the following example, **PERFORM UNTIL** is used to read in a file until a desired record is selected, or until an end-of-file is encountered. Note that the initial conditions are set so that the paragraph is performed at least once. (Assume that IN-RECORD-KEY and IN-RECORD-TYPE are WORKING-STORAGE data items within IN-RECORD.)

```
MOVE LOW-VALUES TO IN-RECORD-KEY,

                   IN-RECORD-TYPE.

PERFORM A10-READ-FILE

   UNTIL (IN-RECORD-KEY = HIGH-VALUES) OR

         (IN-RECORD-TYPE = 'A').


□ □ □

A10-READ-FILE.

   READ IN-FILE INTO IN-RECORD

      AT END MOVE HIGH-VALUES TO IN-RECORD-KEY.

**** EXIT
```

PERFORM can also loop while incrementing a control identifier. This type of loop is often used to manipulate tables. (PERFORM *first-procedure* THRU *last-procedure* may also be coded.)

```
PERFORM procedure

   VARYING subscript FROM start BY increment

   UNTIL identifier ) end.
```

subscript. A numeric identifier that is incremented each time through the loop. It may be an index, but its value then must not exceed the bounds of the table for which it is defined. If *end* is the maximum bounds of the table, *index* > *end* would result in the index exceeding the bounds, resulting in an error.

The terms *start*, *increment*, and *end* may be numeric identifiers or literals. They may also be indexes, but their values must then not exceed the bounds of the table with which they are associated.

- *start.* The first value *subscript* is to assume within the loop.
- *increment.* A value added to *subscript* at the end of each pass through the loop.
- *end.* The last value *subscript* is to assume within the loop.

```
PERFORM A10-LOOP

   VARYING A FROM B BY C

   UNTIL A ) D.
```

In the following example, A10-ZERO-TABLE is executed 10 times with IX assuming values from 1 to 10.

```
PERFORM A10-ZERO-TABLE

   VARYING IX FROM 1 BY 1

   UNTIL IX ) 10.

   □  □  □

A10-ZERO-TABLE.

   MOVE ZEROS TO TABLE1 (IX).

**** EXIT
```

The *increment* may be positive or negative. If negative, *subscript* is decremented, and the UNTIL phrase should be coded as UNTIL *subscript* < *end*. The following statement executes the loop 100 times with IX assuming values from 100 to 1.

```
PERFORM A10-LOOP

   VARYING IX FROM 100 BY -1

   UNTIL IX ( 1.
```

The UNTIL phrase may be any conditional expression. The test is made before PERFORM is executed, and if the UNTIL condition is true, the procedure is not performed. The following loop is not executed if START-IT is greater than 10.

```
PERFORM A10-LOOP

    VARYING IX FROM START-IT BY 1

    UNTIL IX ) 10.
```

At the end of the loop, execution continues with the next executable following the PERFORM. The *subscript* contains the next value greater than *end* (or less than *end* if *increment* is negative.) In the following example, IX will contain 11 at the end of the loop.

```
PERFORM A10-LOOP

    VARYING IX FROM 1 BY 1

    UNTIL IX ) 10.
```

If *increment*, *end*, and *subscript* are identifiers and their values are changed within the loop, it will affect the number of times the loop is performed. Changing the value of *start* within the loop has no effect on the loop. Loops can also be coded in-line. This has the advantage of keeping the statements within the loop in front of the reader rather than in a separate procedure. But generally it should not be used because it requires a GO TO to transfer backwards, and because the beginning and end of the loop are often not apparent. To code an in-line loop, one must set up a control identifier and test it.

```
    MOVE 1 TO IX.

A10-LOOP.

    statements in loop.

    ADD 1 TO IX.

    IF IX NOT ) 10

        THEN GO TO A10-LOOP.
```

PERFORM can be nested to two or three levels. The last AFTER varies most rapidly.

```
PERFORM procedure

    VARYING subscript FROM start BY increment
        UNTIL subscript ) end
```

```
AFTER subscript FROM start BY increment
  UNTIL subscript ⟩ end

AFTER subscript FROM start BY increment
  UNTIL subscript ⟩ end.
```

The *start* values are set for each *subscript*, and then each UNTIL condition is tested to see if the loop should be performed. The loop is performed with the *subscript* in the last AFTER varying the most rapidly as shown in the following example.

```
PERFORM A10-LOOP

  VARYING IX FROM 1 BY 1 UNTIL IX ⟩ 5

    [This varies last.]

    AFTER IY FROM 1 BY 1 UNTIL IY ⟩ 4

      [This varies next.]

      AFTER IZ FROM 1 BY 1 UNTIL IZ ⟩ 8.

        [This varies first.]

  □ □ □

A10-LOOP

  MOVE ZERO TO TABLE-A (IX, IY, IZ).

**** EXIT
```

The loop is performed 160 times with the subscripts varying as shown.

```
IX = 1, IY = 1, IZ = 1 to 8
IX = 1, IY = 2, IZ = 1 to 8
                .
                .
                .
IX = 1, IY = 4, IZ = 1 to 8
IX = 2, IY = 1, IZ = 1 to 8
                .
                .
                .
IX = 5, IY = 4, IZ = 1 to 8
```

Loops can also be nested by including a PERFORM within the loop. This allows loops to be nested to any level, and clarifies the order in which the indexes are varied. The embedded PERFORM must perform statements totally included or totally excluded from the range of statements in the original PERFORM. The following example is identical to the preceding one.

```
PERFORM A10-PART-A

    VARYING IX FROM 1 BY 1

    UNTIL IX ) 5.

□ □ □

A10-PART-A.

    PERFORM A10-PART-B

        VARYING IY FROM 1 BY 1

        UNTIL IY ) 4.

**** EXIT

A10-PART-B.

    PERFORM A10-LOOP

        VARYING IZ FROM 1 BY 1

        UNTIL IZ ) 8.

**** EXIT

A10-LOOP.

    MOVE ZERO TO TABLE-A (IX, IY, IZ).

**** EXIT
```

VI. IF STATEMENT

The IF statement evaluates a conditional expression, and depending on the outcome, executes statements. The general form of the IF statement is as follows.

```
IF conditional-expression

    THEN statement

    ELSE statement.
```

The THEN *statement* is executed if the *conditional-expression* is true, and the ELSE *statement* is executed if it is false.

```
IF  A  ) B

    THEN MOVE 1 TO A

    ELSE MOVE 0 TO A.
```

The THEN keyword is optional in System/370, but is not a part of the ANS Standard. Always indent the IF statement to show the flow of logic. Some people prefer to indent the IF statement as follows.

```
IF  A  ) B

    MOVE 1 TO A

ELSE

    MOVE 0 TO A.
```

Whether you code the THEN or not, align the THEN statements with the ELSE statements to show their relationship. The ELSE portion of the IF statement is optional, and if omitted, the THEN statements are skipped if the condition is false.

```
IF  A = B

    THEN MOVE 0 TO A.
```

The IF statement may be nested to any level. However, do not nest to a level such that statements are forced off the right of the page, and never let an ELSE clause become widely separated from its corresponding THEN clause. Again, always indent to show the logical flow.

```
If A = B
    THEN IF X = Y

            THEN MOVE 0 TO A

            ELSE MOVE 1 TO A

    ELSE IF X ) Y

            THEN MOVE 2 TO A

            ELSE MOVE 3 TO A.
```

The THEN clauses in the IF statement can generally be nested to several levels with the meaning remaining clear as shown in the following example.

```
IF A = B
    THEN ADD 1 TO C
        IF C = D
            THEN PERFORM A10-START
                IF E = F
                    THEN IF G = H
                        THEN MOVE X TO Y
                            IF I = J
                                THEN PERFORM A20-NEXT.
```

Each ELSE is always associated with the innermost unmatched THEN. An ELSE with a NEXT SENTENCE null statement may be required to give the desired results. In the following example, the first ELSE NEXT SENTENCE is required to pair the ELSE IF A = D with the proper THEN. The final ELSE NEXT SENTENCE could have been omitted.

```
IF A = C
    THEN IF B = D
            THEN COMPUTE A = A / B
            ELSE NEXT SENTENCE
    ELSE IF A = D
            THEN COMPUTE A = A * B
            ELSE NEXT SENTENCE.
```

Each THEN or ELSE can execute several statements; simply list the statements, placing a period only after the final ELSE statement, or after the final THEN statement if there is no final ELSE statement. Several statements executed as a group are termed a *statement-group*.

```
IF A = B
    THEN MOVE 100 TO A
        MOVE 200 TO B.
```

```
IF  C = D

    THEN MOVE 100 TO E

         MOVE 200 TO F

    ELSE MOVE 1 TO A

         ADD 2 TO B

         PERFORM A60-READ-FILE.
```

There are limitations in nesting IF statements because the period that terminates a statement group also terminates the IF statement. The following example illustrates this. The PERFORM Z90-HELP is a part of the ELSE.

As coded:

```
IF  A = B

    THEN PERFORM A10-STEP1

         IF  C = D

              THEN PERFORM A20-STEP2

              ELSE PERFORM A30-STEP3

         PERFORM Z90-HELP.
```

As executed:

```
IF  A = B

    THEN PERFORM A10-STEP1

         IF  C = D

              THEN PERFORM A20-STEP2

              ELSE PERFORM A30-STEP3

                   PERFORM Z90-HELP.
```

A period cannot be placed after PERFORM A30-STEP3 as this would terminate the IF statement, and PERFORM Z90-HELP is to be executed only if A = B. There are several ways to solve this in COBOL. First, it might be possible to move the PERFORM Z90-HELP above the IF C = D statement.

```
IF A = B

    THEN PERFORM A10-STEP1

    PERFORM Z90-HELP

    IF C = D

        THEN PERFORM A20-STEP2

        ELSE PERFORM A30-STEP3.
```

However, the PERFORM A30-STEP3 may depend on the results of the IF C = D statement, and cannot precede it. If there are only a few statements, they can be coded in both the THEN and ELSE.

```
IF A = B

    THEN PERFORM A10-STEP1

        IF C = D

            THEN PERFORM A20-STEP2

            PERFORM Z90-HELP

        ELSE PERFORM A30-STEP3

            PERFORM Z90-HELP.
```

If there are many statements, or if the IF statement is nested to several levels, make the IF C = D statement a separate paragraph and perform it. This is unsavory because it breaks the continuity of the code, but it is sometimes necessary in COBOL.

```
IF A = B

    THEN PERFORM A10-STEP1

        PERFORM A00-PART-A

        PERFORM Z90-HELP.
```

□ □ □

```
A00-PART-A.

    IF C = D

        THEN PERFORM A20-STEP2

        ELSE PERFORM A30-STEP3.

**** EXIT
```

An ELSE terminates a statement group, and if the PERFORM Z90-HELP were part of the ELSE, there would be no problem.

```
    IF A = B

        THEN PERFORM A10-STEP1

            IF C = D

                THEN PERFORM A20-STEP2

                ELSE PERFORM A30-STEP3

        ELSE PERFORM Z90-HELP.
```

The NEXT SENTENCE clause causes execution to resume with the next sentence and not the next statement. The following sentence is in error because there is no way for control to reach PERFORM Z90-HELP.

```
    IF A = B

        THEN PERFORM A10-STEP1

            IF C = D

                THEN PERFORM A20-STEP2

                ELSE NEXT SENTENCE

            PERFORM Z90-HELP.
```

A common COBOL error is to misplace a period in a conditional statement. The following examples illustrate the dangers. The examples on the right are indented to show how the statements on the left are actually executed. (The indentation of course has no effect on the way in which the statements are executed.)

As coded: As executed:

```
IF A = B                         IF A = B

    THEN MOVE 100 TO A               THEN MOVE 100 TO A

    ELSE MOVE 1 TO A.                ELSE MOVE 1 TO A.

        ADD 2 TO B.              ADD 2 TO B.
```

As coded: As executed:

```
IF A = B                         IF A = B

    THEN MOVE 100 TO A               THEN MOVE 100 TO A

ADD 2 TO B.                          ADD 2 TO B.
```

The logic within a program is often controlled by flags. Define such flags as PIC X, and use values for the flags that describe their meaning, such as 'Y' for yes and 'N' for no. The following example executes one statement the first time it is encountered, and another statement thereafter.

```
77  FIRST-TIME        PIC X VALUE 'Y'.

    □ □ □

IF FIRST-TIME = 'Y'

    THEN PERFORM A10-INITIALIZE

        MOVE 'N' TO FIRST-TIME

    ELSE PERFORM A10-NORMAL.
```

The language statements described in this chapter are the core of COBOL. The next chapter describes how they are used for structured programming.

EXERCISES

1. What will the identifiers A, B, C, and D contain after each of the following statements has been executed? Assume that each identifier has a precision of S9(4).

```
MOVE 1 TO A, B.

COMPUTE B = A + 1.

ADD B TO A.

MULTIPLY B BY A.

DIVIDE A BY 5 GIVING C REMAINDER D.
```

2. Place parentheses around the following expressions to indicate the hierarchy of operations. Also insert blanks where necessary.

```
1/2*A*T**2

A**B-2/Y-D

A+2*C**2/B+6*4

A+B=ZERO OR NOT A NOT=1 AND B ) A*10-6
```

3. The following table contains paragraph names and associated values of the identifier SWITCH-A. Branch to the proper paragraph name as given by the value of SWITCH-A, using first the IF statement and then a GO TO DEPENDING ON statement.

Value of SWITCH-A	Paragraph Name
1	START-IT
2	FINISH-IT
3	CONTINUE-IT
4	PROCEED-TO

4. Use IF statements to set the identifier ANS to the appropriate value based on the conditions given.

Value of ANS	Condition
0	If X equals zero.
-1	If X is negative and Y is not greater than zero.
-2	If both X and Y+Z are greater than 22.
100	If X equals 1 and Y equals 1 or half of Y+Z equals 1.
200	All other conditions.

5. Rewrite the following IF statement using condition names.

```
IF (X = 1) OR
    ((X NOT < 20) AND (X NOT > 30)) OR
    (X = 50 OR 60 OR 61)
    THEN ...
```

6. Write decision tables to show whether the following IF statements are true or false for all possible conditions.

```
IF (X = 1 AND NOT Y = 1) OR
    NOT (X = OR Y = 1)
    THEN ...
IF (X NOT = 1 OR Y NOT = 1) OR
    NOT (X = Y)
    THEN ...
```

7. What values will X assume within the following loops?

```
PERFORM LOOP1 VARYING X FROM -10 BY 3 UNTIL X > 6.
PERFORM LOOP2 VARYING X FROM 1 BY 1 UNTIL X > 1.

MOVE 4 TO Y.
PERFORM LOOP3 VARYING X FROM 1 BY 1
    UNTIL (X > 10) OR (Y NOT > 0).

    □ □ □

LOOP3.  Y = Y - X.
    PERFORM LOOP4 VARYING X FROM -3 BY -2 UNTIL X < -7.
```

8. Assume that DY, MO, and YR contain the day, month, and year of a start date, and that DUR contains a duration in days. Assuming 30 days per month, use IF and COMPUTE statements to compute the end date from the start date and the duration, and store the results back in DY, MO, and YR.

9. Assume that the day, month, and year of a start date are contained in S-DY, S-MO, and S-YR, and the end date in E-DY, E-MO, and E-YR. Write the statements necessary to store the exact duration in days in DUR, assuming 30 days per month.

10. An equation is given as $Y = (X - 1)/(X^2 + 1)$. Write the statements necessary to evaluate the equation for values of X ranging from -6 to 10 by steps of 0.5.

11. Rewrite the following statements without using the GO TO statement, but using instead the IF or PERFORM statements.

```
        MOVE 1 TO X.
LOOP1.  MOVE ZERO TO A (X).
        ADD 1 TO X.
        IF X ( 10 THEN GO TO LOOP1.
        IF B ) 6 THEN GO TO NEXT1.
        IF B ( 0 THEN GO TO NEXT1.
        IF B ) 3 THEN GO TO NEXT2.
        IF C = 0 THEN GO TO NEXT1.
        MOVE ZERO TO D.
        ADD 1 TO B.
        GO TO NEXT3.
NEXT1.  MOVE ZERO TO E.
        IF X + Y ) 0 THEN GO TO NEXT3.
        ADD 1 TO G.
        GO TO NEXT3.
NEXT2.  ADD 1 TO G.
        GO TO NEXT4.
NEXT3.  ADD 1 TO F.
NEXT4.
```

12. The following IF statement has been coded.

```
IF XX NOT = ZERO AND ZZ = 1 AND XX NOT = 1 OR XX NOT = 2
   THEN GO TO FINI.
```

Tell whether the transfer will be made to FINI based on the following combinations of values of XX and ZZ.

XX	ZZ
0	0
0	1
0	2
0	3
1	0
1	1
1	2
1	3

13. What combinations of values will X, Y, and Z have in the loop?

```
PERFORM LOOP
   VARYING X FROM 1 BY 2 UNTIL X ) 4
   VARYING Y FROM 0 BY -1 UNTIL Y ( -1
   VARYING Z FROM 2 BY 3 UNTIL Z ) 7.
```

14. The following statements each contain an actual or an almost certain potential error. Find each error.

```
MULTIPLY A BY 2.
ADD '125' TO B.
DIVIDE BUDGET-REMAINING BY PERIODS-REMAINING.
MOVE ZERO TO A, B. C.
COMPUTE A = B * C ROUNDED.
IF A = 2 = B
   GO TO START.
ELSE GO TO DONE.
```

five

STRUCTURED PROGRAMMING

A chapter on structured programming should begin with a definition. Alas, there are many definitions of structured programming, but no consensus. Rather than add yet another definition, we shall instead view structured programming as a means of organizing our thoughts and programs to achieve correct and easily modifiable programs. This is done by applying the criteria in Chapter 2 and the structured programming constructs to show the purpose of a program by its form.

The terms top-down design, modular programming, and structured programming are closely related. *Top-down design* consists of identifying the major functions of a program and decomposing these functions into smaller and smaller functional units until the lowest level is specified. The program is then usually written in this same order, with the highest level written first. *Modular programming* consists of organizing the program into functional units. It differs from top-down design in that it does not specify the order that the modules should be designed or written. *Structured programming*, in its most limited definition, consists of a limited number of constructs that specify the flow of control of the program.

Structured programming is sometimes wrongly termed 'GO TO-less programming,' and although the strict adherence to the structured programming rules eliminates the need for the GO TO, sometimes a GO TO is the simplest and most straightforward means of accomplishing something. In practice, structured programming minimizes rather than eliminates the GO TO.

The major advantages of structured programming are that it gives form, order, uniformity, and discipline to programs and simplifies their logical flow. There is controversy over the relative advantage of structured programming, partly because the term is often used to include such things as top-down design,[1,2,3] modular programming,[4] programming teams,[5] structured walk-throughs[6] in which a team goes over the coding, HIPO (Hierarchy plus Input-Process-Output) charts for design and documentation,[7] more readable coding, and generally good programming practices. Another side benefit of structured programming is that it has changed the emphasis from clever to clear programming where it properly belongs.

Structured programming is not a panacea and will not solve all programming problems. However, this says nothing because panaceas do not exist in real life, and not just in computing, but in any field. In fact, such things as top-down design, programming teams, more readable code, good programming practices, and structured walk-throughs may each contribute more to programming than do the structured programming constructs. Structured programming is not a competitor with other means of improving programming, but an ally. The question to ask, then, is not whether structured programming is a panacea, but whether it is an improvement. Based on the experience of those who have used it, structured programming is an improvement. It disciplines programming, enhances clear thinking, and makes programs easier to read, understand, debug, and maintain.

Structured programming consists of three primitive forms or constructs that have been mathematically proved to be the minimum required to code all program logic. Because these three constructs can be proved mathematically to be the minimum required, they enable a program to be mathematically proved to be logically correct. However, proving programs to be mathematically correct is not practical. Also, it does not logically follow that because these three constructs are the minimum required to write a program, they are the only ones that should be used. View them as guidelines and not rules because they are not always the most direct means of programming. Use them only so long as they clarify the sequence of execution.

I. SEQUENTIAL EXECUTION OF STATEMENTS

```
ADD X TO Y.

PERFORM C10-TOTALS.

COMPUTE B = C + D * E.
```

II.   IF/THEN/ELSE CONSTRUCT

The IF/THEN/ELSE construct executes one or the other of two blocks
of code based on the results of a conditional test.

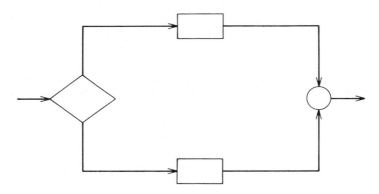

```
IF  A = B

    THEN ADD X TO Y

         MOVE 2 TO Z

    ELSE COMPUTE B = C + D * E

         ADD 1 TO X.
```

Either the THEN or ELSE may be null.

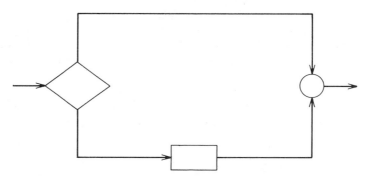

```
IF  A = B

    THEN NEXT SENTENCE

    ELSE COMPUTE B = C + D * E

         ADD 1 TO X.
```

```
IF  A = B

    THEN ADD X TO Y

         MOVE 2 TO Z.
```

A single IF statement nested to great depth is hard to follow, and indenting to show the logical flow can soon force the coding off the right side of the page. Keep each ELSE close to its related THEN. Inner groups can be made separate paragraphs, and the IF statement can PERFORM them to avoid nesting to great depth and to keep an ELSE close to its THEN. The PERFORM statement makes COBOL a convenient language for structured programming.

The IF statement tests a condition, or several conditions connected by AND, OR, or NOT. Try to prevent such logical expressions from becoming too complex. As in English, avoid double negatives. NOT in combination with OR is almost always written incorrectly. Do not confuse AND and OR. Structure the logical expression to show the relationship.

```
IF ((AGE  < 35) OR

   ((WEIGHT  > 110) AND (HEIGHT  > 5)) OR

   (EYES = 'BLUE'))

       AND

   (NAME = 'SMITH')

   THEN PERFORM A30-SELECT-PERSON.
```

Sometimes a logical expression is clearer if it is written as a nested IF. Each nested IF acts as if it were an AND applied to the previous IF.

```
IF (X = 1) AND

   (Y = 1)

   THEN PERFORM B10-LAST.

      [Same as:]

IF X = 1

    THEN IF Y = 1

             THEN PERFORM B10-LAST.
```

Logical expressions are often the hardest part of a computer program to read, even harder than GO TO statements. They can become so complex that one must write a decision table to understand them. Do not eliminate GO TO statements only to end up with logical expressions that are even more difficult to understand. Try to break up long logical expressions into shorter ones that can be more easily understood. Use parentheses, indentation, implied logical operations, and nested IF statements to accomplish this. The following example illustrates an IF statement that is hard to read, and how it can be recast to be more readable.

```
IF SEX = 'F' AND ((AGE > 20 AND AGE < 30) AND (WEIGHT > 90

    AND WEIGHT < 150) AND (HEIGHT > 5 AND HEIGHT < 6)) OR

    WEALTH > 1000000 THEN PERFORM B10-SELECT-PERSON.
```

[Much clearer as:]

```
IF SEX = 'F'

    THEN IF ((AGE > 20 and < 30) AND

            (WEIGHT > 90 AND < 150) AND

            (HEIGHT > 5 AND < 6))

                    OR

            (WEALTH > 1000000)

            THEN PERFORM B10-SELECT-PERSON.
```

III. DOWHILE CONSTRUCT

The DOWHILE construct repeats an operation while a condition is true. The PERFORM UNTIL does this in COBOL.

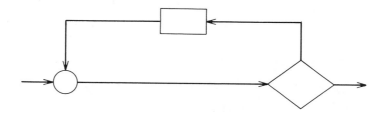

```
PERFORM C10-READ-FILE UNTIL EOF-IN = 'Y'.
```

□ □ □

```
C10-READ-FILE.

    statements.

**** EXIT
```

Any form of the PERFORM is valid.

```
PERFORM D10-ZERO-TABLE

    VARYING I FROM 1 BY 1

    UNTIL IX > 10.
```

Although these three constructs are the minimum required to perform all logical operations, two additional structured programming constructs are provided for convenience.

IV. DOUNTIL CONSTRUCT

The DOUNTIL is identical to the DOWHILE except that the operation is always performed at least once.

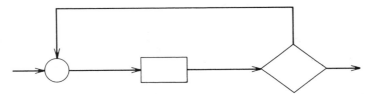

COBOL has no DOUNTIL, as the PERFORM does not execute the statements if the condition is met when PERFORM is executed. The DOUNTIL can be accomplished by performing the operation and then executing a DOWHILE.

```
PERFORM paragraph.

PERFORM paragraph UNTIL condition.
```

The DOUNTIL can also be accomplished with the PERFORM UNTIL by setting a flag at the end of the loop.

```
MOVE 'N' TO flag.

PERFORM paragraph UNTIL flag = 'Y'.
```

        □ □ □

```
paragraph.

     statements.

     IF condition

          THEN MOVE 'Y' TO flag.
```

V. CASE CONSTRUCT

The CASE construct invokes one of several functions, depending on a value.

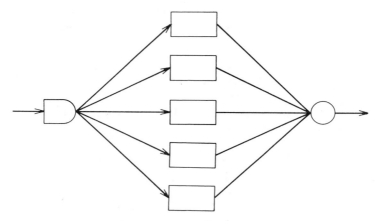

COBOL has no CASE statement. If there are few functions, the CASE can be accomplished by nested IFs. Note how the indentation is used to indicate that it is not really a nested IF, but a CASE.

```
     IF X = 'A'

          THEN PERFORM C10-MAX

     ELSE IF X = 'B'

          THEN PERFORM C20-MIN

     ELSE IF X = 'C'

          THEN PERFORM C20-AVG.
```

If there are many cases, the GO TO DEPENDING ON statement is more convenient. If the conditional value cannot be used directly in the GO TO, set up a table to contain the values for the GO TO DEPENDING

ON. The following example illustrates the CASE construct with the GO
TO DEPENDING ON.

```
77  CASE-VALUE PIC S9(4) COMP.

    □ □ □

    MOVE value TO CASE-VALUE.

    PERFORM B10-CASES THRU B20-CASES-EXIT.

    □ □ □

B10-CASES.

    GO TO B20-CASE1,

        B20-CASE2,

            .
            .
            .

        B20-CASEn

            DEPENDING ON CASE-VALUE.

B20-CASE1.

    statements.

    GO TO B20-CASES-EXIT.

**** EXIT

B20-CASE2.

    statements.

    GO TO B20-CASES-EXIT.

**** EXIT

        .
        .
        .

B20-CASEn.

    statements.

    GO TO B20-CASES-EXIT.
```

```
**** EXIT

B20-CASES-EXIT. EXIT.

**** END OF B10-CASES
```

Note that these statements lie within several paragraphs, and B10-CASES must be invoked by the PERFORM THRU (PERFORM B10-CASES THRU B20-CASES-EXIT.) This concludes the discussion of the structured programming constructs. The following section illustrates how programs are written using these constructs.

VI. WRITING STRUCTURED PROGRAMS

Flags are often required to control the logic in structured programming, although they can be confusing and lead to errors. But generally they contribute less confusion and errors than would the GO TOs that they replace. Use consistent values for each flag such as 'Y' and 'N' for yes and no or 'T' and 'F' for true and false. Define each flag as PIC X to permit such symbolic values to be assigned to it.

Do not reuse a flag for different purposes to conserve storage because the confusion and error potential outweigh the minimal storage savings. When a flag has a single purpose, the cross-reference listing will show wherever that purpose is tested. A common error with flags is to forget to assign to them initial values. Set the flag just prior to its use to ensure that it has a proper initial value. Then the reader need not check elsewhere in the program to find the last place it was assigned a value.

There are several problems associated with loops. First among them is how to get to the top of a big loop, such as one that reads a file and is terminated by the end-of-file. The following example illustrates this with structured programming on the left and GO TOs on the right.

Structured: With GO TOs:

```
77  EOF-IN PIC X.


    □ □ □


    MOVE 'N' TO EOF-IN.

    PERFORM A20-READ                   PERFORM A20-READ
                                         THRU A20-READ-EXIT.
      UNTIL EOF-IN = 'Y'.


    □ □ □
```

```
A20-READ.                              A20-READ.

    READ IN-FILE INTO IN-RECORD            READ IN-FILE INTO IN-RECORD
    AT END MOVE 'Y' TO EOF-IN              AT END TO A20-READ-EXIT.
    IF EOF-IN NOT = 'Y'                    statements-to-process-record.
    THEN PERFORM A30-PART-A.               GO TO A20-READ.
**** EXIT                              A20-READ-EXIT.  EXIT.
A30-PART-A.                            **** END OF A20-READ LOOP

    statements-to-process-record.

**** EXIT

**** END OF A20-READ LOOP
```

The example on the left is simplified if the statements to process the record can be placed in the THEN clause rather than a separate paragraph.

```
    IF EOF-IN NOT = 'Y'

    THEN statements-to-process-record.

**** EXIT
```

If nothing else, this example shows that the advantages of structured programming are not always overwhelming. Even though the example on the left has more statements and requires a flag, it does have the advantage of showing the reader beforehand that a loop is performed. The example on the right has intertwined GO TOs, a bad practice. Generally, structured programming results in fewer statements because the constructs are more direct than shown in the example.

The next problem in a loop is how to terminate it from the middle. There are two ways to do this. First, the loop can be terminated by ending the paragraph, and performing the remainder of the loop. Alternatively, a GO TO can be used to branch to the end of the paragraph. (This requires that the PERFORM THRU to be used to invoke the paragraphs.) The following examples illustrate the two methods.

With PERFORMs: With GO TOs:

```
77  FLAG-A PIC X.                       77  FLAG-A PIC X.


    □ □ □                                    □ □ □
```

```
    MOVE 'N' TO FLAG-A.                        MOVE 'N' TO FLAG-A.

    PERFORM A10-LOOP                           PERFORM A10-LOOP THRU
                                                 A10-LOOP-EXIT

       UNTIL FLAG-A = 'Y'..                       UNTIL FLAG-A = 'Y'.


    □ □ □                                      □ □ □


A10-LOOP.                                   A10-LOOP.

    first-statements..                          first-statements.

    IF A = B                                    IF A = B

       THEN MOVE 'Y' TO FLAG-A                     THEN MOVE 'Y' TO FLAG-A

       ELSE PERFORM A10-PART-A.                       GO TO A10-LOOP-EXIT.

**** EXIT                                       second-statements.

A10-PART-A.                                     IF C = D

    second-statements.                             THEN MOVE 'Y' TO FLAG-A

    IF C = D                                           GO TO A10-LOOP-EXIT.

       THEN MOVE 'Y' TO FLAG-A                  third-statements.

       ELSE PERFORM A10-PART-B.                 IF E = F

**** EXIT                                          THEN MOVE 'Y' TO FLAG-A

A10-PART-B.                                            GO TO A10-LOOP-EXIT.

    third-statements.                           fourth-statements.

    IF E = F                                 A10-LOOP-EXIT.   EXIT.

       THEN MOVE 'Y' TO FLAG-A

       ELSE PERFORM A10-PART-C.

**** EXIT

A10-PART-C.

    fourth-statements.

**** EXIT

**** END OF A10-LOOP
```

Each loop has a single entry and exit. The example on the right is a valid structured program, has no intertwined GO TOs, and results in fewer statements. It also keeps the main line of the loop directly in front of the reader. The example on the left has no GO TOs, but it results in many cascading paragraphs that distract the reader and make the code look more complicated than it is. The example on the right, then, is a valid use of the GO TO, and by all the criteria in Chapter 2 represents a better way to program, even though it contains GO TOs.

Again, if there are only a few simple statements within the paragraph, the example on the left can be coded with nested IFs to simplify it.

```
A10-LOOP.

    first-statements.

    IF A = B

        THEN MOVE 'Y' TO FLAG-A

        ELSE second-statements

            IF C = D

                THEN MOVE 'Y' TO FLAG-A

                ELSE third-statements

                    IF E = F

                        THEN MOVE 'Y' TO FLAG-A

                        ELSE fourth-statements.

**** EXIT
```

The GO TO is also useful for branching to an error exit when a catastrophic error is encountered that breaks the main line of the program. Nested IFs could be used, with the THEN clause as the error routine and the ELSE clause the remainder of the program, but this is needlessly complex and holds the least interesting code, the error termination, in front of the reader, forcing him or her to look elsewhere for the remainder of the program. It is better to terminate a program with a GO TO.

```
    IF error-condition

        THEN GO TO Z10-ERROR-ROUTINE.
```

As has been illustrated in the preceding examples, the benefits of structured programming are not always striking in short examples. The next example is longer, allowing the advantages of structured programming to exhibit themselves. Assume that an input file IN-FILE with a WORKING-STORAGE record IN-REC is to be copied into OUT-FILE with a WORKING-STORAGE record OUT-REC. A transaction file TRANS-FILE with a WORKING-STORAGE record TRANS-REC identical in format to IN-REC is to be read, and if a transaction record matches an input record, the input record is displayed and not written out. Any transaction records not matching an input record are to be displayed.

This sounds simple, but the logic is involved. The limiting cases must also be considered where there may be no input or transaction records. For simplicity, we shall assume that the input and transaction files are in proper sort order, and we shall show only the Procedure Division statements. We shall also omit such niceties as printing the number of records read and written.

We will need flags to indicate an end-of-file for the input and transaction files. Rather than defining a separate flag, we shall use the record item itself and set it to HIGH-VALUES when an end-of-file is encountered. (This requires that the record be defined in the WORKING-STORAGE Section; it cannot be defined in the FILE Section.) Besides eliminating a separate flag, this simplifies the logic because the comparison of the input record against the transaction record works properly when either record has been set to HIGH-VALUES for an end-of-file. The technique of setting a record to HIGH-VALUES to indicate an end-of-file often simplifies the logic of matching files. The nonstructured programming example is shown first, using GO TOs.

```
PROCEDURE DIVISION.

A00-BEGIN.

    OPEN INPUT IN-FILE,

                TRANS-FILE,

        OUTPUT OUT-FILE.

    MOVE LOW-VALUES TO TRANS-REC.

A10-READ-NEXT.

    READ IN-FILE INTO IN-REC

        AT END GO TO A70-PURGE-TRANS.

    IF TRANS-REC = LOW-VALUES GO TO A40-READ-TRANS.
```

```
A20-CHECK-FOR-DELETE.

    IF TRANS-REC < IN REC

        THEN DISPLAY 'TRANSACTION IGNORED: ', TRANS-REC

            GO TO A40-READ-TRANS.

    IF TRANS-REC = IN-REC

        THEN DISPLAY 'RECORD DELETED: ', IN-REC

            MOVE LOW-VALUES TO TRANS-REC

            GO TO A10-READ-NEXT.

A30-WRITE-OUT.

    WRITE OUT-REC FROM IN-REC.

    GO TO A10-READ-NEXT.

A40-READ-TRANS.

    READ TRANS-FILE INTO TRANS-REC

        AT END MOVE HIGH-VALUES TO TRANS-REC

                GO TO A30-WRITE-OUT.

    GO TO A20-CHECK-FOR-DELETE.

A70-PURGE-TRANS.

    IF TRANS-REC = HIGH-VALUES GO TO A90-DONE.

A80-SKIP-TRANS.

    READ TRANS-REC INTO IN-REC

        AT END GO TO A90-DONE.

    DISPLAY 'TRANSACTION IGNORED: ', TRANS-REC.

    GO TO A80-SKIP-TRANS.

A90-DONE.

    CLOSE IN-FILE,

            TRANS-FILE,

            OUT-FILE.

    STOP RUN.

**** END OF PROGRAM
```

Now we shall write the program using structured programming. The first step in writing a structured program is to step back and think about what the program is to do, without getting immersed in the details of programming. Essentially, we want the program to read the IN-FILE until there are no more records. As each IN-FILE record is read, we want to read all TRANS-FILE records that are less than the IN-FILE record and display them because they do not match the IN-FILE record. If a TRANS-FILE record matches the IN-FILE record, we display the IN-FILE record; otherwise we write out the IN-FILE record.

Before starting the code, let us specify the program in more detail. Many programmers use a pseudocode to express the design. We can use English, the structured programming constructs, an idealized COBOL, or whatever helps us to express what the program is to do. The pseudocode is often better for designing a program than a flow chart. Now let us lay out the overall program logic.

Read an IN-FILE record until no more.

So far, so good, but let us take the next step in detail. After each IN-FILE record is read, we want to read all TRANS-FILE records that are less than the IN-FILE record and display them.

Read an IN-FILE record until no more.

  Read a TRANS-FILE record while less than IN-FILE record.

  Display TRANS-FILE record.

  End of read TRANS-FILE loop.

We will fall through the loop when we have a TRANS-FILE record that is equal to or greater than the IN-FILE record. We must compare it to the IN-FILE record, and if equal we display the IN-FILE record; if greater than, we write out the IN-FILE record.

Read an IN-FILE record until no more.

  Read a TRANS-FILE record while less than IN-FILE record.

  Display TRANS-FILE record.

  End of read TRANS-FILE loop.

  If the TRANS-FILE record equals the IN-FILE record

  Then display the IN-FILE record

Else write the IN-FILE record.

End of read IN-FILE loop.

Now let us think about the exceptional cases. When we drop through the read IN-FILE loop, could there still be records left in the TRANS-FILE? There can not be if we move HIGH-VALUES to the IN-FILE records when the IN-FILE end-of-file is detected. What happens if there are no IN-FILE records? If we go through the loop after the end-of-file, and we will if this is a DOUNTIL, then we will read all the TRANS-FILE records. If there are no TRANS-FILE records, we will read all the IN-FILE records and write them out properly. What happens when we reach the end-of-file on both the IN-FILE and the TRANS-FILE? Assuming we set the TRANS-FILE record to HIGH-VALUES too, the TRANS-FILE record will equal the IN-FILE record and we will display the IN-FILE record, which we do not want because there was no IN-FILE record. The IF statement should be changed to the following.

If the IN-FILE record is not HIGH-VALUES

    Then if the TRANS-FILE record equals the IN-FILE record

        Then display the IN-FILE record

        Else write the IN-FILE record.

What happens if the IN-FILE or the TRANS-FILE records are not in the same ascending sort order? The program will not work properly, and so we might think about checking the sort order of these two files. If we wanted to do this, we would add it to our pseudocode as follows.

Read an IN-FILE record until no more.

    If this record not greater than last record

        Then do what must be done.

We would also do this in the two places that the TRANS-FILE is read. What happens if there are duplicate records in either file? Duplicate IN-FILE records are displayed or written properly. Duplicate TRANS-FILE records will be displayed. The specifications did not tell us what to do in the event of duplicates, and we might want to resolve this before writing the program. However, for now the program is probably handling duplicates properly. If we wanted to check for duplicate records, we could add it to the pseudocode as follows.

Read an IN-FILE record until no more.

  If this record is less than the last record

    Then the file is out of sort

    Else if this record equals the last record

      Then this is a duplicate record.

Now we can begin thinking about the code. How do we read the IN-FILE until there are no more records? This is a DOUNTIL because we DO the loop UNTIL there are no more records. COBOL has no DOUNTIL, but we can simulate it by performing the read IN-FILE loop once and then performing it until the IN-FILE end-of-file is encountered. The read TRANS-FILE loop is a DOWHILE because we DO the loop WHILE the TRANS-FILE is less than the IN-FILE, and this is accomplished with a PERFORM. We shall indicate an end-of-file by moving HIGH-VALUES to the record to simplify the programming. The following program is then a COBOL translation of the pseudocode.

```
PROCEDURE DIVISION.
A00-BEGIN.
    OPEN INPUT IN-FILE,
              TRANS-FILE,
         OUTPUT OUT-FILE.
    MOVE LOW-VALUES TO IN-REC,
                      TRANS-REC.
    PERFORM A10-READ-IN-FILE.
    PERFORM A10-READ-IN-FILE UNTIL IN-REC = HIGH-VALUES.
    CLOSE IN-FILE,
          TRANS-FILE,
          OUT-FILE.
    STOP RUN.
*
```

```
A10-READ-IN-FILE.

    READ IN-FILE INTO IN-REC

      AT END MOVE HIGH-VALUES TO IN-REC.

    PERFORM A20-READ-TRANS-FILE UNTIL TRANS-REC NOT < IN-REC.

    IF IN-REC NOT = HIGH-VALUES

      THEN IF TRANS-REC = IN-REC

                THEN DISPLAY 'RECORD DELETED: ', IN-REC

                ELSE WRITE OUT-REC FROM IN-REC.

**** EXIT

*

A20-READ-TRANS-FILE.

    READ TRANS-FILE INTO TRANS-REC

      AT END MOVE HIGH-VALUES TO TRANS-REC.

    IF TRANS-REC < IN-REC

      THEN DISPLAY 'TRANSACTION IGNORED: ', TRANS-REC.

**** EXIT

**** END OF PROGRAM
```

The nonstructured program contains 27 COBOL verbs and 7 paragraph names. The structured program contains only 17 COBOL verbs and 2 paragraph names. Our goal was not to write the program with the fewest statements, but simple, clear programs will generally lead to this. But which is the most efficient? This subject is covered later in this book, but for now let us assume that the efficiency will be about equal unless the compiler generates atrocious code.

If nothing else, there are two things that you should get out of structured programming. First, you should step back and think about what you want to program without getting immersed in the detail. Call this top-down design, stepwise refinement, or simply not worrying about where the trees go until you have planned the forest—it is an essential discipline in programming. Second, you should write the program in the simplest, clearest possible way.

This completes the discussion of structured programming. The next chapters delve into the COBOL data types and data storage.

EXERCISES

1. Develop a set of rules for the use of the GO TO statement with which you would be comfortable.

2. What changes do you believe should be made to COBOL to enhance its use for structured programming?

3. Write a paper on what, if anything, you believe makes structured programming a better way to program.

4. Write a paper discussion and evaluating one of the following:

- Structured walk-throughs.
- Chief programming teams.
- Modular programming.
- HIPO charts.

5. The following is an excerpt from a typical nonstructured program. Rewrite it as a structured program.

```
START-IT.  READ IN-FILE INTO REC-IN AT END GO TO DONE.
     IF REC-TYPE = ' ' GO TO DONE.
     IF REC-TYPE = 'A' GO TO GO-ON.
     IF REC-TYPE = 'B' GO TO START-IT.
     IF REC-TYPE = 'C' GO TO GO-ON.
     GO TO START-IT.
GO-ON.  MOVE 1 TO IX.
     IF REC-NAME (IX) = SPACES GO TO START-IT.
STORE-NAME.  MOVE REC-NAME (IX) TO SAVE-NAME (IX).
     MOVE 1 TO IY.
STORE-POP.  IF REC-POP (IX, IY) = SPACES GO TO MORE-NAMES.
     MOVE REC-POP (IX, IY) TO SAVE-POP (IX, IY).
     ADD 1 TO IY.
     IF IY ⟨ 11 GO TO STORE-POP.
```

```
MORE-NAMES.  ADD 1 TO IX.

    IF IX < 21 GO TO STORE-NAME.

    MOVE REC-NO GO SAVE-NO.

    GO TO START-IT.

DONE.
```

6. Assume that you are attending a symposium on programming techniques, and one speaker claims to have a new composite technique that
has improved programmer productivity as measured by code produced
per day by an order of magnitude. His method is to use structured, top-
down design while regressing stepwise using interactive meditation, aug-
mented with the power of positive thinking, organized into on-line, modular programming teams with frequent work breaks while everyone faces
east, links arms with others, and slowly repeats a mystic Hindu chant.

- Assuming that you have some doubts about the productivity claims,
  what questions would you ask to dispute or verify the claims?
- Assuming that the claim of a tenfold improvement in the ability of programmers to write programs is true, what are some of the possible out-
  comes of each programmer being able to write 10 times the amount of
  code that he or she can produce today?

7. The last two examples in this chapter are a nonstructured and structured program to update a file. Make the following changes to both programs and discuss the difficulty of making the changes.

- Check the IN-FILE and TRANS-FILE for ascending sort order.
- Check the IN-FILE and TRANS-FILE for duplicate records.
- Count the IN-FILE and TRANS-FILE records read, and the number of
  records written.
- If three consecutive TRANS-FILE records do not match an IN-FILE
  record, print an error message and continue.
- If there are no IN-FILE records or if there are no TRANS-FILE records,
  print an error message and continue.

REFERENCES

1. H. D. Mills, "Top Down Programming in Large Systems," *Debugging Techniques in Large Systems*, Prentice-Hall, Inc., Englewood Cliffs, N. J., pp. 41–55.

2. Edward Yourdon, *Techniques of Program Structure and Design*, Prentice-Hall, Inc., Englewood Cliffs, N. J., 1975.

3. Clement L. McGowan and John R. Kelly, *Top-Down Structured Programming Techniques*, Petrocelli/Charter, New York, 1975.

4. Russell M. Armstrong, *Modular Programming in COBOL*, John Wiley & Sons, Inc., New York, 1973.

5. "Chief Programmer Teams Principles and Procedures," Report No. FSC 71-5108, IBM Corporation, Gaithersburg, Md., 1971.

6. "Improved Programming Techniques Management Overview," IBM Corporation, White Plains, N. Y., August 1973.

7. "HIPO-A Design Aid and Documentation Technique," Order No. GC20-1851, IBM Corporation, White Plains, N. Y., 1974.

six

NUMERIC DATA

The internal form of numeric data and the precision of intermediate results are not specified in the ANS standard, but vary from computer to computer. This chapter describes the numeric data types for System/370.

The numeric data types consist of COMP (binary), COMP-1 (single-precision floating-point), COMP-2 (double-precision floating-point), COMP-3 (packed decimal), and DISPLAY (numeric character data). The data types have different characteristics and uses, and are described later in this chapter. COMP-1, COMP-2, and COMP-3 are not included in the ANS Standard, but are widely available. In System/370, COMP-3 is generally the most convenient form of numeric data. COMP-1 and COMP-2 floating-point are rarely used in COBOL, and the following discussion does not apply to them.

Numeric literals are written as decimal numbers with an optional decimal point. The numbers may be signed plus (+) or minus (−) or remain unsigned (assumed positive).

```
23  175.925   −.00973   +16

MOVE 23 TO A.

COMPUTE B = C / 176.925.
```

Numeric literals cannot end with the decimal point because COBOL would confuse it with the period that ends a sentence.

```
2 or 2.0, but not 2.
```

Elementary numeric data items are described with a level number, a name, a PICTURE clause (usually abbreviated PIC), and the data type (COMP, COMP-3, or DISPLAY).

```
01  STATE-POPULATION PIC S999V99 COMP-3.
```

The PIC clause specifies the precision in the form of the number of digits to the left and right of the decimal point. The form is PIC S99...9V99...9, where S indicates a signed number, each 9 represents a decimal digit, and the V specifies the assumed decimal point. Hence S9V999 can contain numbers such as -0.007, 9.265, and 3.000. The V may be omitted, and the decimal point is assumed on the right so that S99 and S99V are equivalent.

If the S is omitted, the number is positive. Always code the S to make the number signed. Negative numbers were heretical during the middle ages, but became accepted at the start of the seventeenth century, and there is no reason for ignoring them today. Perhaps the only valid reason for unsigned numbers is if you wish to treat the number as an absolute value. As an extra bonus, System/370 COMP-3 signed numbers are more efficient than unsigned numbers. Unsigned numbers can give surprising results. The following statements make it appear as if $-1 + 1$ equals 2.

```
77  X  PIC 999 COMP-3.
```

```
    □ □ □
```

`MOVE ZERO TO X.`	[X contains 0.]
`SUBTRACT 1 FROM X.`	[X contains 1 because the minus sign is lost.]
`ADD 1 TO X.`	[X contains 2.]

If there are many 9's, they become tedious to write. Instead, code a single 9 and follow it with the number of 9's enclosed in parentheses. This is preferable because one can tell at a glance the number of digits to the left and right of the decimal point.

`S9(5)`	[Same as:]	`S99999`
`SV9(4)`	[Same as:]	`SV9999`
`S9(6)V9(8)`	[Same as:]	`S999999V99999999`

The maximum number of digits that can be contained in a numeric data item is 18. The decimal point may be specified to lie outside the number to allow very large or small numbers to be represented that occupy only a few digits of storage. Code a P to the left or right of the 9's to specify the position of the decimal point when it lies outside the number. (The V may be omitted.) For example, SP(5)9(4) permits the number .000001234 to be represented with four digits. The following example specifies a data item containing only three digits such as 213, but being treated as if it had the value .0000213.

```
77  A  PIC SP(4)999 COMP-3.
```

Place the P's on the right to specify that the decimal point is to the right of the number. The following example specifies a data item containing only three digits such as 213, but being treated as if it had the value 21300000.

```
77  A  PIC S999P(5) COMP-3.
```

The total number of digits, including those specified by the P's, cannot exceed 18. The P's can be used to conserve file and memory storage, but generally the savings are not worth the extra effort and potential confusion.

Plan the number of digits to carry in data items. Larger numbers require more memory and I/O storage, and one should not be wasteful. But smaller numbers may not allow room for growth, and one way to minimize change is to provide for growth. For example, a company with $50,000 in sales might require a data item of S9(5)V99 today, but what happens if sales grow to over $100,000? Inflation alone could see to this in a depressingly short time. If there is no physical limit on the size of a number, define the item to contain the largest number expected plus at least one digit for safety.

Keep the numeric precisions consistent, even if some numbers are defined to be larger than necessary. In System/370, arithmetic operations are more efficient if all the numbers have the same precision. Generalized subroutines are also easier to write when all the potential applications have the same precision. For example, if the total revenue of a company is $100,000, but the largest revenue of a division is only $10,000, describe all data items used to store revenue as S9(7)V99 for consistency and safety.

Data items containing dollar amounts should provide two digits to the right of the decimal point (V99) to carry the cents, even if only whole dollar amounts are wanted. Carry the cents to prevent rounding errors and to guard against a future requirement of carrying cents.

I. COMP-3 PACKED DECIMAL NUMBERS
(Not in the ANS Standard)

COMP-3 packed decimal numbers are stored in the computer with each group of 4 binary digits representing a single decimal digit. For example, 0000 represents 0, 0001 represents 1, 0100 represents 4, and the number 14 is represented by 0001 0100. Each digit occupies $\frac{1}{2}$ byte, as does the sign. Hence S99V9 occupies $1\frac{1}{2}$ bytes for the digits and $\frac{1}{2}$ byte for the sign, for a total of 2 bytes. To determine the number of bytes of storage required for a number, count the total number of digits, add 1 for the sign, round up to the next even number if necessary, and divide by 2. Hence S9(6)V9(2) and S9(6)V9(3) both occupy 5 bytes.

System/370 deals more efficiently with signed numbers that occupy an integral number of bytes. Specify an odd number of digits so that the number with its sign will occupy an integral number of bytes. S9(4) wastes $\frac{1}{2}$ byte; S9(5) occupies the same 3 bytes and is more efficient.

COMP-3 numbers may contain up to 18 digits, and should be used for most numeric data, except perhaps internal counters and subscripts. They are relatively efficient in both storage and computations, and allow a wide range of numbers with integral precision. COMP-3 numbers are somewhat less efficient for computations than COMP binary numbers, but they are more flexible, and more efficient for input/output because they do not require alignment that results in the messy slack bytes described in Chapter 8.

PIC can be written in its long form as PICTURE, and COMP-3 in its long form as COMPUTATIONAL-3. COMP-3 may also be preceded by the word USAGE. The guideline of never using a long word when a short one will do makes the description on the right preferable.

```
77  A PICTURE S99999 USAGE              77  A  PIC S9(5) COMP-3.
       COMPUTATIONAL-3.
```

The VALUE clause assigns initial values to data items. A data item has no predictable value unless it is assigned an initial value or unless a value is stored into it.

```
77  X  PIC S9(5) COMP-3 VALUE 0.
```

[X is initialized with a value of zero.]

II. COMP BINARY NUMBERS

System/370 COMP binary numbers are stored internally in a computer word, half-word, or double word, as a group of binary digits or bits representing the entire number to the base 2. For example, 5 is represented as 101, and 14 as 1110. Binary numbers are the most efficient numbers for arithmetic computations because computers are binary machines. However, in System/370 they are poor as data in I/O records because their alignment can cause problems as described in Chapter 8. Generally, they are best used for internal counters and subscripts.

```
77  A  PIC S9(4) COMP.
```

COMP may also be written in its long form as COMPUTATIONAL. The following two descriptions are equivalent, but the one on the right is preferable.

```
77  A PIC S9999 USAGE          77  A  PIC S9(4) COMP.
        COMPUTATIONAL.
```

The System/370 word size used to contain the number depends on the number of digits as follows.

- 1 to 4.   Half-word or two bytes.
- 5 to 9.   Full word or four bytes.
- 10 to 18.   Two full words or eight bytes. (Less efficient than half-words or full words.)

The VALUE clause assigns initial values to data items.

```
77  X  PIC S9(4) COMP VALUE 100.
```

[X is initialized with a value of 100.]

III. NUMERIC CHARACTER DATA

Numeric character data is also termed *zoned decimal* numbers, *external decimal* numbers, and *numeric field data* on other computers. It is used for source input and printed output, and consists of character data that contains only numeric digits, one digit per byte in storage. The data can be treated as alphanumeric, and it can be printed without conversion. Arithmetic operations can also be performed on numeric character data; System/370 COBOL first converts the numeric character data to packed decimal and then performs the arithmetic computations. Numeric character data is generally inefficient for computations. Normally, the arithmetic computations are confined to such simple operations as incrementing a page number.

Numeric character data items can contain 1 to 18 numeric digits, and are described as follows.

```
77   A   PIC   S999V99.
```

DISPLAY or USAGE DISPLAY may also be coded. The following three forms are identical, but the first is preferable.

```
77   B   PIC   S9(5).
```

```
77   B   PIC   S9(5) DISPLAY.
```

```
77   B   PIC   S99999 USAGE DISPLAY.
```

The VALUE clause assigns initial values to data items.

```
77   X   PIC   S9(5) VALUE 6.            [X contains the digits '00006'.]
```

Numeric character data must always have leading zeros and not leading blanks. Numeric character data can also be treated as alphanumeric data, and the statements that operate on alphanumeric data such as TRANS-FORM, INSPECT, STRING, and UNSTRING may also operate on it.

If the number is signed, denoted by a leading S, the operational sign in System/370 is carried in the left half of the rightmost digit. Hence the S does not count as a character position; both S999V9 and 999V9 occupy four character positions.

IV. COMP-1, COMP-2 FLOATING-POINT NUMBERS
(Not in the ANS Standard)

Floating-point numbers, normally used in scientific computations, are rarely used in COBOL. Numbers in scientific computations are often derived from physical measurements and are not precise. This contrasts with the integral units common in commercial computations such as dollars and cents. For example, a bicycle might cost exactly $122.98, but the weight might be 21, 21.3, 21.332, or 21.33186, depending on the accuracy of the scale.

Floating-point numbers are stored in a computer word in two parts; one part represents the significant digits of the number, and the other part represents the exponent that determines the magnitude of the number.

This corresponds to scientific notation where for example 0.0000025 is represented as 0.25E-5, and -25000 is represented as $-0.25E5$. This notation allows a wide range of numbers to be used in arithmetic computations without losing significant digits of precision.

To add or subtract numbers expressed in this notation, they must be normalized to the same power of 10 so that 6E4 + 8E2 becomes .06E2 + 8E2 to equal 8.06E2. To multiply numbers, the exponents are added so that 6E4 * 8E2 equals 48E6. To divide two numbers, the exponent of the denominator is subtracted from that of the numerator so that 6E4 / 8E2 equals 0.75E2. Thus to calculate the time in seconds that it takes light traveling at 11,800,000,000 inches per second to pass through a film 0.0001 inches thick, the computation is done as 1.0E-4 / 1.18E10 to equal 0.847E-14. Computers have special floating-point hardware to do such computations efficiently, and one need not worry about normalizing the numbers.

Floating-point numbers are not precise; their precision is limited to some number of significant digits. For example, a computation such as 0.1 + 0.1 may yield a result of 0.19999 when expressed in floating-point binary, rather than exactly 0.2. This is acceptable in scientific computations where answers are given plus or minus some tolerance, but it can be inappropriate for business applications where numbers must balance to the penny. Since 0.1 + 0.1 may result in 0.19999 rather than 0.2, floating-point numbers should never be compared solely for equality. Nor should they be used for counters.

Numeric literals are written as decimal numbers, followed by an E, followed by an exponent. Both the number and the exponent may be signed.

```
2E0 -9E0   18.3E5 2.2E-1
```

COMP-1 single-precision numbers occupy a full word of four bytes. The maximum magnitude is from 10^{-78} to 10^{75}, and the number has at least 6 decimal digits of precision. COMP-2 double-precision numbers occupy a double word of eight bytes. The maximum magnitude is from 10^{-78} to 10^{75}, and the number has at least 16 decimal digits of precision. Data items are declared to be floating-point as COMP-1 (single-precision) or COMP-2 (double-precision). The PIC clause cannot be coded. COMP-1 and COMP-2 may also be coded as COMPUTATIONAL-1 and COMPUTATIONAL-2. The following two descriptions are equivalent.

```
77  A  COMPUTATIONAL-1.   [Same as:]    77  A  COMP-1.

77  B  COMPUTATIONAL-2.                 77  B  COMP-2.
```

Data items can be assigned initial values.

```
77  X  COMP-2 VALUE 1.26E+3.
```

V. DATA CONVERSION AND PRECISION

Conversion occurs automatically when arithmetic operations are performed on numeric data of different types. This can occur both in arithmetic statements such as COMPUTE and ADD, and in relational expressions such as those in the IF statement. The arithmetic statements also result in conversion if the resultant identifier differs from the data type of the data being stored. The data is converted to a common numeric type to perform the operations according to the following hierarchy.

```
Highest:  COMP-2

          COMP-1

          COMP-3

          DISPLAY            [System/370 numeric character data is al-
                             ways converted to COMP-3 for computa-
                             tions.]

Lowest:   COMP
```

In the statement COMPUTE A = B + C + D, if A and B are COMP, C is COMP-3, and D is COMP-1, B and C are converted to COMP-1 to perform the arithmetic operation. This intermediate result is then converted to COMP for the result to be stored in A.

Numeric data is converted to alphanumeric data by moving it to a PIC X data-item. (Numeric data cannot be converted to alphabetic PIC A data.) Only integers can be converted (23 but not 23.1).

```
77  Y  PIC X(3).

    □ □ □

MOVE 22 TO Y.                [Y contains '22b'.]

MOVE 2345 TO Y.             [Y contains '234'.]
```

Alphanumeric data is converted to numeric by moving it to a numeric data item. (Data defined as alphabetic PIC A cannot be converted to numeric.) Data contained in a PIC X item can be converted to numeric only if it contains the characters 0 to 9. (The SIGN clause described in Chapter 14 further allows the item to contain a + or − in a leading or trailing position.) Only integers can be converted to alphanumeric (PIC S99V but not S99V9.)

```
77   Y   PIC S999V.

     □ □ □

     MOVE '023' TO Y.                [Y contains a numeric 23.]
```

Alphanumeric data cannot appear in arithmetic expressions. Conversion also takes computer time, and excessive conversions can make a program run slowly.

Arithmetic precision can be lost during conversion in the low-order digits. In an assignment statement, precision can be lost in both the high- and low-order digits if the data item to which the data is being assigned cannot contain the number being assigned. The loss of high-order digits can be detected by the ON SIZE ERROR phrase, but the loss in low-order digits is not detected. The following example illustrates how high- and low-order digits are lost.

```
77   X   PIC S99V99 COMP-3.

     □ □ □

     MOVE 123.456 TO X.              [X contains 23.45.]
```

In the absence of a ROUNDED phrase in arithmetic operations, low-order digits of precision are lost by truncation, not rounding. For example, if the number 1.999 is stored in a data item of precision S9V99, the number is truncated to 1.99. The ROUNDED phrase in the arithmetic statements rounds a number rather than truncating it. Values whose rightmost digit is less than 5 are rounded down in absolute magnitude, and values whose rightmost digit is 5 or greater are rounded up in absolute magnitude. Thus, 1.995 is rounded to 2.00.

When there is more than one arithmetic operation performed in a single statement, COBOL must carry intermediate results. For example, in COMPUTE X = (A * B) / C, the A * B is first evaluated and held as an intermediate result. This intermediate result is then divided by C, and the intermediate result from this is stored in X.

Loss of precision and overflow in intermediate results are a common source of error. A grade school student would give the correct result of the expression 6 * (2 / 4) as 3, but System/370 COBOL evaluates it as 0. (The ANS Standard leaves the result undefined.) The 2 / 4 yields an intermediate result of precision PIC S9, the 0.5 is truncated to zero to store the intermediate result, and 0 times 6 yields 0. The precision of System/370 intermediate results shown for the arithmetic operations in the following examples is given by iVd. The i signifies the number of decimal digits to the left of the decimal point and d the number of digits to the right.

Add, subtract:

$i_1Vd_1 + i_2Vd_2$ yields $[1 + \max(i_1, i_2)]V[\max(d_1, d_2)]$

$99V9 + 9V999$ yields precision of $9(3)V9(3)$

$99.9 + 9.999$ equals 109.899

Multiply:

$i_1Vd_1 * i_2Vd_2$ yields $(i_1 + i_2)V(d_1 + d_2)$

$99V9 * 9V999$ yields precision of $9(3)V9(4)$

$99.9 * 9.999$ equals 998.9001

Divide:

i_1Vd_1/i_2Vd_2 yields $(i_1 + d_2)V[\max(d)]$
  $\max(d)$ is the maximum of d_1, d_2, or the d of the data item into which the result is stored.

$99V9/9V999$, final result of $99V9$ yields precision of $9(5)V9(3)$

$99.9/0.001$ equals 99900.000

$99V9/9V999$, final result of $99V9(4)$ yields precision of $9(5)V9(4)$

$00.1/3.000$ equals 00000.0333

Exponential: If the exponent is a data item or noninteger literal:

$i_1Vd_1 ** i_2Vd_2$ yields $[(i_1*n) + (n - 1)]V[\max(d)]$
  $\max(d)$ is the maximum of d_1, d_2, or the d of the final result field
  n is the largest integer that i_1 permits

$99V9 ** 9V$, final result of $99V$ yields precision of $9(26)V9$

$99V9 ** 9V$, final result of $99V999$ yields precision of $9(26)V999$

If the exponent is an integer literal n:

i_1Vd_1 ** n yields $[(i_1*n) + (n - 1)]V(d_1*n)$

$99V9$ ** 2 yields precision of $9(5)V99$

25.3 ** 2 equals 00640.09

System/370 COBOL carries up to 30 digits of precision in intermediate results for arithmetic operations except for floating-point numbers. High-order precision is lost only if the intermediate results require more than 30 digits, and the compiler will issue a warning if it is possible for this to occur. COMP numbers are converted to COMP-3 if the intermediate results would require more than 18 digits.

Addition and subtraction generally cause no problems. Multiplication can cause a problem if the result can exceed 30 total digits of precision— unlikely in commercial applications. Division causes the most problems. The result can exceed 30 total digits of precision when a very large number is divided by a very small number. A more likely error is loss in precision caused by a division resulting in a fraction. We have seen how 6 * (2 / 4) yields zero. We could obtain the correct result by any of the following.

- Coding 6 * (2 / 4.0) to force the intermediate result to be carried to one decimal place.
- Defining the final result to have a decimal precision of V9 to force the intermediate result to be carried to one decimal place.
- Coding (6 * 2) / 4 to perform the division last. This method is preferable unless the result of the multiplication could exceed 30 total digits of precision. This works equally well for (6 * 1) / 3 whereas the two previous methods would give a result of 1.8.
- Define a data item to contain the intermediate result and perform the operation in parts.

```
77  TEMP                    PIC S9(4)V9(5) COMP-3.

    □ □ □

COMPUTE TEMP = 6 * 2.

COMPUTE FINAL-RESULT = TEMP / 4.
```

Be careful with division and, whenever possible, perform the division last in a series of computations. An expression such as X * (Y / Z) may lose precision and should be changed to (X * Y) / Z. Except for logical expressions, numeric computations are perhaps the most common source of error. Errors in loss of precision are especially hard to find because a program runs as expected, but the numbers computed may be off slightly. Always hand-calculate critical computations to check the precision.

This concludes the discussion of numeric data. The next chapter describes alphanumeric data, which have entirely different properties, operations, and problems.

EXERCISES

1. Select the data types that would be best for the following uses, and describe why they would be best.

- A count of the input records read from a file.
- The population of states contained within a record.
- Computing rocket trajectories.
- Computing the interest on a house loan.
- Reading numbers in from an input card.

2. The equation for a future amount invested at $i\%$ per year for n years is given by:

$$\text{future amount} = \text{investment} \left(1 + \frac{i}{100}\right)^{n}$$

Write the statements necessary to compute the future amount of 10-year investments ranging from \$100 to \$102 by increments of 5 cents at an interest rate of $7\frac{1}{4}\%$.

3. Assume the following items are declared.

```
77   A          PIC S9(6)V999.

77   B          PIC S9(3)V99 COMP-3.

77   C          PIC S9(4) COMP.

77   D          COMP-1.

77   E          COMP-2.
```

Describe the conversion that will be done in each of the following statements.

```
COMPUTE E = A * D.

COMPUTE A = D * B * C.

ADD 1 TO C.

MOVE B TO A.
```

4. Assume that the following data items are described.

```
77  A           PIC S9(4) COMP.

77  B           PIC S9(6)V9(3) COMP-3.

77  C           PIC S9(3) COMP-3.
```

Show the results of the following statements.

```
COMPUTE A = 3.5.

COMPUTE A ROUNDED = 3.5.

COMPUTE B = 1254.6 * 3.3235 / 6.43229 + 12.1136.

MOVE 12.211 TO B.
COMPUTER B = B / 4.395 * 6.4 + 7.1135.

COMPUTE A = (12 + .1) / 7.

COMPUTE A = (12 / 7) + .1.
```

5. The IRS has called you in to do some programming. It feels that it has not been getting a fair shake from the taxpayers, and so it is going to pay off the national debt by billing each taxpayer his or her share. You are told that the national debt is $627,260,497,937.12. The IRS insists that the national debt be paid off to the penny, and that the share for each person is to be paid in the proportion of his personal income tax to the total income tax. Under these circumstances, is it possible to pay off the national debt to the penny? Assume that there are 107,916,412 taxpayers. Under the worst possible circumstances, assuming that you round, how much over or under might you collect? If you truncate, how much over or under might you collect?

seven

CHARACTER DATA

Character data consists of a string of characters. The names of people, their street addresses, and the words on this page all constitute character data. Character data is not a COBOL term, but is a convenient term for describing data in character form. Character data is also termed *character-string* and *text* data in other languages. In COBOL, data described as USAGE DISPLAY constitutes character data.

COBOL defines three *classes* of character data: alphanumeric (PIC X), numeric (PIC 9), and alphabetic (PIC A). *Alphanumeric* data can consist of any of the characters in the COBOL character set, including alphabetic and numeric characters. Numeric character and alphabetic data are restricted subsets of alphanumeric data. *Numeric character* data was described in Chapter 6, and consists of the digits 0 to 9. Since it contains only numeric digits, it can participate in arithmetic operations. *Alphabetic* data can contain only the characters A to Z and blank. It is rarely required, both because alphanumeric data serves better and because data containing only alphabetic characters are rare. Even people's names, such as O'Reilly, require alphanumeric data items.

The three classes of character data are specified by the PIC and USAGE DISPLAY clauses. Throughout this book, the term USAGE DISPLAY is used to indicate that the data items may be alphanumeric, alphabetic, or numeric character data. However, USAGE DISPLAY is not actually coded in the examples in this book because it defaults in data descriptions if omitted.

COBOL further divides the alphanumeric class of data into three *categories:* numeric edited, alphanumeric edited, and alphanumeric. Numeric edited and alphanumeric edited data consist of data items that have been edited by special characters contained in the PIC clause. They are generally used for printing and are discussed in Chapter 14. Group items may also be operated on as character data, and the group item is treated as if it contained all alphanumeric data. Table 1 summarizes the classes and categories of COBOL character data.

TABLE 1.   COBOL Character Data

Level of Item	Class	Category
Elementary	Alphabetic	Alphabetic
	Numeric character	Numeric character
	Alphanumeric	Numeric edited Alphanumeric edited Alphanumeric
Group	Alphanumeric	Alphabetic Numeric Numeric edited Alphanumeric edited Alphanumeric

Alphanumeric literals are written by enclosing the characters in single quotation marks (') in System/370 and double quotation marks (") in the ANS Standard.

```
'AT'    'FIVE'    'ME TO'
```

The ANS Standard, but not System/370 COBOL, allows the double quotation character (") to be denoted by two consecutive quotation marks.

```
"""WHERE IS IT?"""   [Becomes:]      "WHERE IS IT?"
```

The length of alphanumeric data items is specified in the PIC clause as XX...X or X(*integer*). The *integer* is the number of characters that the data item is to contain, and may be a maximum of 32,767 in System/370.

```
77  data-name  PIC X(integer).
```

[Or:]

```
77  data-name  PIC XXX...X.
```

The data type may also be described explicitly as DISPLAY or USAGE DISPLAY. In the following example, B contains 12 characters and C contains three characters.

```
77  B  PIC X(12) DISPLAY.  [Or:]     77  B  PIC X(12).

77  C  PICTURE XXX USAGE  [Or:]      77  X  PIC X(3).
       DISPLAY.
```

Alphabetic data items are described like alphanumeric items, except that PIC A is used rather than PIC X.

```
77  W  PIC AAAA.           [Or:]     77  W  PIC A(4).
```

The PIC clause may contain A or 9 in combination with X, but the item is treated as if it were all X's.

```
77  Y  PIC XXAA9.     [Same as:]     77  Y  PIC XXXXX.
```

Alphanumeric data items are given initial values by appending the VALUE clause to the description. The following example initializes B with the characters 'ABCD'.

```
77  B  PIC X(4) VALUE 'ABCD'.
```

If too few characters are specified, the string is padded out on the right with blanks. If too many characters are specified, the description is in error.

```
77  B  PIC X(4) VALUE '1'.          [B contains '1bbb'.]

77  C  PIC X(4) VALUE 'VWXYZ'.      [C is in error.]
```

Alphanumeric identifiers and literals are moved to other alphanumeric identifiers with the MOVE statement. In the following example, K is set to '12345'.

```
77  K  PIC X(5).

77  L  PIC X(5) VALUE '12345'.


    □ □ □


    MOVE L TO K.          [Or:]          MOVE '12345' TO K.
```

In the MOVE statement, identifiers are padded on the right with blanks if they are assigned a smaller item; longer items are truncated on the right.

```
77  B  PIC X(4).

    □ □ □

    MOVE 'AB' TO B.              [B contains 'ABbb'.]

    MOVE 'ABCDEF' TO B.         [B contains 'ABCD'.]
```

To repeat a literal to fill an item, precede the literal with ALL.

```
77  Z  PIC X(6) VALUE ALL '1'.    [Z contains '111111'.]

    □ □ □

    MOVE ALL '12' TO Z.          [Z contains '121212'.]
```

Alphanumeric data can be right-justified by appending the JUST RIGHT clause to the description.

```
77  Y  PIC X(4) JUST RIGHT VALUE 'AB'.
```
[Y contains 'bbAB'.]

In the MOVE statement, right-justified identifiers are padded on the left with blanks if a smaller character-string is moved to it; longer strings are truncated on the left.

```
    MOVE 'AB' TO Y.             [Y contains 'bbAB'.]

    MOVE 'ABCDEF' TO Y.        [Y contains 'CDEF'.]
```

Relational conditions, such as those in the IF statement, can compare two character-strings. The two strings are compared character by character from left to right according to the collating sequence of the character set. The collating sequence of the EBCDIC and ASCII character sets are shown in Chapter 16.

In the relational condition, if the strings are of unequal length, the shorter is padded on the right with blanks to equal the length of the longer string for the comparison. In the following example, the characters 'ABCD' are compared with '23bb'.

```
77  X  PIC X(4) VALUE 'ABCD'.

   □  □  □

   IF X = '23'

       THEN MOVE 1 TO B.
```

Alphanumeric (and alphabetic PIC A) items can be tested to determine if they contain only the alphabetic characters A to Z or blank.

IF *identifier* ALPHABETIC THEN . . .

IF *identifier* NOT ALPHABETIC THEN . . .

Alphanumeric (and numeric character data) items can be tested to determine if they contain only the numeric characters 0 to 9.

IF *identifier* NUMERIC THEN . . .

IF *identifier* NOT NUMERIC THEN . . .

Table 2 summarizes the tests that may be made on alphanumeric, alphabetic, and numeric character data.

TABLE 2.   Alphabetic and Numeric Tests

Type of Item	Permissible Tests
PIC A	ALPHABETIC
PIC X	ALPHABETIC NUMERIC
PIC 9	NUMERIC

I. INSPECT, EXAMINE, AND TRANSFORM STATEMENTS

There are three statements that perform much the same function: INSPECT, EXAMINE, and TRANSFORM. INSPECT is the current ANS Standard, although it has not been implemented on System/370 compilers; EXAMINE was the ANS Standard, but has been dropped; and TRANSFORM was never a part of the ANS Standard. INSPECT is the most powerful of the three, and can do all that can the other two. The three statements count specific characters in a character-string, and edit strings by replacing specified characters.

A. INSPECT (Not in System/370 COBOL)

The first form of INSPECT counts characters in an identifier. INSPECT examines the characters in *identifier* from left to right, counting specific characters as specified by the FOR phrase.

```
                                        ALL match-string
                                        LEADING match-string
                                        CHARACTERS
    INSPECT identifier TALLYING count FOR_ _ _ _ _ _ _ _ _ _ _.
```

- *identifier.* A group item or an elementary USAGE DISPLAY item. It is treated as alphanumeric data and any internal sign is ignored for numeric character data.
- *count.* An elementary numeric data item. It must be initialized because INSPECT adds to it.
- ALL. Count all nonoverlapping characters in *identifier* that match the characters in the *match-string*. (A *match-string* of 'AA' counts 2 and not 3 in an *identifier* containing 'AAAABAB'.)
- LEADING. Count one if the *match-string* matches the leftmost characters in *identifier*. (A *match-string* of 'THE' counts one in an *identifier* containing 'THE THE THE'.)
- CHARACTERS. Counts the number of characters in *identifier*. (An *identifier* of PIC X(9) counts nine.)
- *match-string.* A USAGE DISPLAY identifier, alphanumeric literal, or figurative constant. Figurative constants are treated as a single instance of the character. (ZEROS is the same as '0')

In the following example, assume that STRING-A contains 'MISSIS-SIPPI'.

```
    MOVE ZEROS TO COUNT.

    INSPECT STRING-A TALLYING COUNT FOR ALL 'S'.
```

    [Adds 4 to COUNT; COUNT contains 4.]

```
    INSPECT STRING-A TALLYING COUNT FOR CHARACTERS.
```

    [Adds 11 to COUNT; COUNT contains 15.]

```
INSPECT STRING-A TALLYING COUNT FOR LEADING 'M'.
```

[Adds 1 to COUNT: COUNT contains 16.]

```
INSPECT STRING-A TALLYING COUNT FOR ALL 'ISS'.
```

[Adds 2 to COUNT; COUNT contains 18.]

A BEFORE or AFTER phrase may be appended to the FOR phrase to count the characters before or after some other character-string is encountered.

```
    BEFORE stop-string                 AFTER begin-string
```

BEFORE starts the counting with the leftmost character in *identifier* and continues up to but not including the characters matching those in the *stop-string*. If the *stop-string* characters do not appear in *identifier*, the matching terminates with the rightmost characters in *identifier* and BEFORE has no effect. AFTER starts the counting immediately after the *begin-string* characters in *identifier* and continues to the rightmost characters in *identifier*. The FOR phrase is ignored if the *begin-string* characters do not appear in *identifier*. Both *begin-string* and *stop-string* may be USAGE DISPLAY identifiers, alphanumeric literals, or figurative constants. In the following example, again assume that STRING-A contains 'MISSISSIPPI'.

```
INSPECT STRING-A TALLYING COUNT FOR ALL 'S' AFTER 'IS'.
```

[Adds 3 to COUNT.]

```
INSPECT STRING-A TALLYING COUNT FOR CHARACTERS BEFORE 'IP'.
```

[Adds 7 to COUNT.]

```
INSPECT STRING-A TALLYING COUNT FOR LEADING 'I' AFTER 'S'.
```

[Adds 0 to COUNT.]

BEFORE and AFTER cannot be coded together. Thus a phrase such as FOR LEADING 'I' AFTER 'S' BEFORE 'IP' is invalid.

There may be several FOR phrases in the INSPECT statement.

```
INSPECT STRING-A
```

```
        TALLYING COUNT FOR CHARACTERS BEFORE 'SS',

                        LEADING 'I',

                        ALL 'P'.
```

There may also be separate *counts* for the FOR phrase.

```
    INSPECT STRING-A

        TALLYING COUNT-1 FOR CHARACTERS BEFORE 'SS',

                COUNT-2 FOR LEADING 'I',

                        ALL 'PP' AFTER 'M',

                COUNT-3 FOR ALL 'Y'.
```

These forms of INSPECT are complex, and make it possible to write statements that are almost indecipherable. Each FOR phrase is applied as follows.

- Each FOR phrase is applied from left to right in the order written only if any BEFORE or AFTER phrase is satisfied.
- If the FOR phrase is not applied because of the BEFORE or AFTER phrase or if there is no match in the FOR phrase the next FOR phrase is applied.
- If a FOR phrase is satisfied, the appropriate count is incremented, and the FOR phrase that follow are not applied. The next comparison begins with the first FOR phrase at the next character in *identifier* to the right of the rightmost character that participated in the match.
- If no FOR phrases match, the first FOR phrase is applied starting with the character position in *identifier* to the right of where the last comparison began.

The following example illustrates this form of INSPECT.

```
    INSPECT STRING-A

        TALLYING COUNT1 FOR ALL 'AB',

                        ALL 'C',

                COUNT2 FOR ALL 'EFG'.
```

Assume that STRING-A contains 'ABCDEFGH', and that COUNT1 and COUNT2 contain zero. The INSPECT statement then operates as follows:

ABCDEFGH
AB

FOR ALL 'AB' matches the first two characters, and 1 is added to COUNT1. COUNT1 now contains 1, and the matching continues to the right of 'AB' in STRING-A.

ABCDEFGH
AB
C

FOR ALL 'AB' does not match, but ALL 'C' matches, and 1 is added to COUNT1. COUNT1 now contains 2, and the matching continues to the right of 'C' in STRING-A.

ABCDEFGH
AB
C
EFG

Neither 'AB', 'C', nor 'EFG' match. The matching continues to the right of 'D' in STRING-A.

ABCDEFGH
AB
C
EFG

Neither 'AB' nor 'C' match, but FOR ALL 'EFG' matches, and 1 is added to COUNT2. COUNT1 contains 2, COUNT2 contains 1, and the matching continues to the right of 'EFG' in STRING-A.

ABCDEFGH
AB
C
EFG

Neither 'AB', 'C', nor 'EFG' match. COUNT1 contains 2, COUNT2 contains 1, and the INSPECT statement has completed execution.

The second form of INSPECT replaces characters.

```
                        CHARACTERS
                        ALL match-string
                        LEADING match-string
                        FIRST match-string

INSPECT identifier REPLACING _ _ _ _ _ _ _ _ _ _ _
   BY replacement-string.
```

INSPECT examines the characters in *identifier* as specified by the REPLACING phrase and replaces them with the characters in the *replace-*

ment-string. The *identifier*, ALL, LEADING, and CHARACTERS are exactly as in the first form. FIRST *matching-string* searches *identifier* for the first characters that match the characters in *match-spring*. The *replacement-string* may be a USAGE DISPLAY identifier, an alphanumeric literal, or a figurative constant. It must contain the same number of characters as in *match-string*, or one character for CHARACTERS. In the following examples, assume that STRING-A contains 'MISSISSIPPI'.

```
INSPECT STRING-A REPLACING FIRST 'SS' BY 'XX'.
```

  [STRING-A contains 'MIXXISSIPPI'.]

```
INSPECT STRING-A REPLACING ALL 'I' BY 'Z'.
```

  [STRING-A contains 'MZXXZSSZPPZ'.]

```
INSPECT STRING-A REPLACING LEADING 'M' BY 'Y'.
```

  [STRING-A contains 'YZXXZSSZPPZ'.]

```
INSPECT STRING-A REPLACING CHARACTERS BY 'W'.
```

  [STRING-A contains 'WWWWWWWWWWW'. Same as MOVE ALL 'W' TO STRING-A.]

The BEFORE or AFTER phrase may be appended to the REPLACING clause. Again assume STRING-A contains 'MISSISSIPPI'.

```
INSPECT STRING-A REPLACING FIRST 'SS' BY 'XX' AFTER 'SS'.
```

  [STRING-A contains 'MISSIXXIPPI'.]

```
INSPECT STRING-A REPLACING ALL 'I' BY 'Z' BEFORE 'S'.
```

  [STRING-A contains 'MZSSIXXIPPI'.]

There may be several replacing phrases in INSPECT, such as the following.

```
INSPECT STRING-A
    REPLACING CHARACTERS BY 'Z' AFTER 'X',
             ALL 'W' BY 'Y' BEFORE 'T',
                 'M' BY 'N',
             LEADING 'X' BY 'Y'.
```

The REPLACING phrases are applied from left to right in the order they are written. The matching occurs the same as for the first format. Each phrase is applied only if its BEFORE or AFTER phrase is satisfied. If any match occurs, the processing begins again with the first phrase immediately after the rightmost character in *identifier* that was replaced. If no match occurs, the comparison begins with the first FOR phrase, one character to the right of where the previous cycle started.

The TALLYING and REPLACING phrases may appear in the same INSPECT statement. The TALLYING phrase is first applied in its entirety, and then the REPLACING phrase is applied. The effect is exactly the same as if two INSPECT statements had been written.

```
INSPECT STRING-A

   TALLYING COUNT FOR ALL 'X' AFTER 'Y',

   REPLACING ALL 'X' BY 'Z' AFTER 'Y'.

     [Same as:]

INSPECT STRING-A TALLYING COUNT FOR ALL 'X' AFTER 'Y'.

INSPECT STRING-A REPLACING ALL 'X' BY 'Z' AFTER 'Y'.
```

B. EXAMINE (Not in the ANS Standard)

EXAMINE was once a part of the ANS Standard, but was dropped in favor of INSPECT. However, System/370 compilers still support EX-AMINE, and have not implemented INSPECT. EXAMINE looks at a USAGE DISPLAY identifier from left to right, counts the occurrences of a specified character, and then stores this number in the special register TALLY. (TALLY does not need to be set to an initial value, and is automatically defined by COBOL as PIC S9(5) COMP.) The first form of EXAMINE counts characters.

```
                         ALL
                         LEADING
                         UNTIL FIRST

   EXAMINE identifier TALLYING _ _ _ _ _ _ 'character'.
```

- *identifier.* A group item or USAGE DISPLAY elementary data item.
- ALL. Count all occurrences of *character* in *identifier* and store the count in TALLY. TALLY is set to zero if none are found.

- LEADING. Count all occurrences of *character* in *identifier* until another character is encountered, and store the count in TALLY. TALLY is set to zero if none are found.
- UNTIL FIRST. Count the number of characters encountered in *identifier* until the first *character* is encountered, and store the count in TALLY. TALLY is set to zero if *character* is the first character.
- *character*. A single alphanumeric literal character, or a figurative constant treated as a single character.

The following examples illustrate this form of EXAMINE.

```
77  A  PIC X(5) VALUE 'XXYZX'.

    □ □ □

EXAMINE A TALLYING ALL 'X'.
```

    [TALLY set to 3.]

```
EXAMINE A TALLYING LEADING 'X'.
```

    [TALLY set to 2.]

```
EXAMINE A TALLYING UNTIL FIRST 'Z'.
```

    [TALLY set to 3.]

The second form of EXAMINE replaces occurrences of a specified character. Characters in the *identifier* matching the single literal character *char-1* are replaced by the single literal character *char-2* as directed. *char1-* and *char-2* may also be figurative constants.

```
                              ALL
                              LEADING
                              UNTIL FIRST
                              FIRST

    EXAMINE identifier REPLACING _ _ _ _ _ _ 'char-1' BY 'char-2'.
```

- ALL. Replace all occurrences in *identifier* of *char-1* with *char-2*.
- LEADING. Replace *char-1* with *char-2* only if *char-1* is the first character in *identifier*.
- UNTIL FIRST. Replace all characters in *identifier* with *char-2* until a *char-1* character is encountered.
- FIRST. Replace the first *char-1* character in *identifier* with *char-2*.

The following examples illustrate the replacement of characters.

```
77   A     PIC X(5) VALUE 'XXYXY'.

       □  □  □

     EXAMINE A REPLACING ALL 'X' BY 'Z'.
```

   [A contains 'ZZYZY'.]

```
     EXAMINE A REPLACING LEADING 'Z' BY 'X'.
```

   [A contains 'XXYZY'.]

```
     EXAMINE A REPLACING UNTIL FIRST 'Y' BY 'W'.
```

   [A contains 'WWYZY'.]

```
     EXAMINE A REPLACING FIRST 'Y' BY 'T'.
```

   [A contains 'WWTZY'.]

The TALLYING form can also be combined with the REPLACING form.

```
                              ALL
                              LEADING
                              UNTIL FIRST
     EXAMINE identifier TALLYING _ _ _ _ _ _ 'char-1'
       REPLACING BY 'char-2'.

77   A     PIC X(5) VALUE 'XXYXY'.

       □  □  □

     EXAMINE A TALLYING ALL 'Y' REPLACING BY 'Z'.
```

   [A contains 'XXZXZ' and TALLY is set to 2.]

EXAMINE has one serious limitation. The *character* in the first form or the *char-1* and *char-2* in the second must agree with the data type in the PIC clause of the *identifier* being examined. If *identifier* is PIC X, any character may be used; if PIC A, only alphabetic characters are allowed; and if PIC 9, only numeric digits may be used. This limitation, not in

INSPECT or TRANSFORM, is serious because a common use of EX-AMINE is to examine a numeric *identifier* replacing spaces with zeros. The solution is to redefine the numeric *identifier* with a PIC X item.

INSPECT and EXAMINE can be used to edit numeric character data to replace leading blanks with zeros and to accommodate a minus sign. COBOL regards a number such as 'bb-2' in error when moved to a PIC S9(4) DISPLAY item; it must be converted to '0002' as a negative number because COBOL considers neither the blank nor the minus sign to be valid numeric characters. The following example shows how such a data can be edited with the INSPECT and EXAMINE statements.

```
77  A PIC  S9(5) VALUE 'bb-23'.  [Assume A contains this value.]

77  B  REDEFINES A PIC X(5).

    □  □  □

INSPECT:

    MOVE ZERO TO TALLY.

    INSPECT A

       TALLYING TALLY FOR ALL '-',

       REPLACING ALL '-' BY ZEROS,

                      SPACES BY ZEROS.

    IF TALLY ) ZERO

       THEN COMPUTE A = -A.

          [A contains '00023' as a negative number.]

EXAMINE:

    EXAMINE B

      REPLACING ALL SPACES BY ZEROS.

    EXAMINE B

       TALLYING ALL '-'

       REPLACING BY ZEROS.

    IF TALLY ) ZERO

       THEN COMPUTE A = -A.
```

C. TRANSFORM (Not in the ANS Standard)

TRANSFORM is completely redundant to EXAMINE and INSPECT. TRANSFORM is provided on System/370 compilers to take advantage of the hardware, and consequently is slightly more efficient than EXAMINE or INSPECT. TRANSFORM replaces all occurrences of specified characters by other characters.

```
TRANSFORM identifier FROM char-1 TO char-2.
```

* *identifier*. A USAGE DISPLAY identifier that cannot exceed 256 characters in length.
* *char-1*, *char-2*. Alphanumeric literals, identifiers, or figurative constants. Figurative constants are treated as single character literals. All occurrences of any *char-1* characters in *identifier* are replaced by the corresponding character in *char-2*.

In the following example, all blanks in Z are replaced by zeros.

```
77  Z  PIC X(10) VALUE '12bbXUIb9b'.

    □ □ □

    TRANSFORM Z FROM SPACES TO ZEROS.
```

　　[Z contains '1200XUI090'.]

　　　[Same as:]

```
    EXAMINE ALL Z REPLACING SPACES BY ZEROS.

    INSPECT Z REPLACING ALL SPACES BY ZEROS.
```

Note that any character in *char-1* encountered in *identifier* is replaced by the corresponding character in *char-2*.

```
77  Z  PIC X(4) VALUE 'A2B1'.

    □ □ □

    TRANSFORM Z FROM '123' TO 'XYZ'.
```

　　[Z contains 'AYBX'.]

　　　[Same as:]

```
EXAMINE Z REPLACING ALL '1' BY 'X',
                       '2' BY 'Y',
                       '3' BY 'Z'.
INSPECT Z REPLACING ALL '1' BY 'X',
                       '2' BY 'Y',
                       '3' BY 'Z'.
```

char-2 must equal *char-1* in length, or have a length of 1. If its length is 1, all characters in *char-1* found in *identifier* are replaced by *char-2*.

```
77  Z  PIC X(4) VALUE 'A2B1'.
```

□ □ □

```
TRANSFORM Z FROM '123' TO 'X'.
```

   [Z contains 'AXBX'.]

      [Same as:]

```
EXAMINE Z REPLACING ALL '1' BY 'X',
                       '2' BY 'X',
                       '3' BY 'X'.
INSPECT Z REPLACING ALL '1' BY 'X',
                       '2' BY 'X',
                       '3' BY 'X'.
```

II. STRING AND UNSTRING STATEMENTS

The STRING and UNSTRING statements are provided on a few System/370 compilers to manipulate character-strings, and are a part of the ANS Standard.

Character-string manipulation is very different from the operations that have been presented so far, and requires several new concepts. To illustrate character-string operations, consider a string such as 'MARY HAD A LITTLE LAMB.'. One operation we might want to perform is to see if the string contains a given substring such as 'LAMB', and where in the string it is located. The location is indicated by the starting character position, such as 19 for LAMB. Another operation that might be performed is to concatenate two or more strings by appending one to the end of another. Suppose that another string contained 'ITS FLEECE WAS WHITE AS SNOW.'. By concatenating this string to the first, we form a new string containing 'MARY HAD A LITTLE LAMB. ITS FLEECE WAS WHITE AS SNOW.'.

We might also want to break up a string into substrings. This is usually done by specifying the starting character position and the number of characters. By forming a substring of 11 characters, starting at the twelfth character, we form a new string containing 'LITTLE LAMB'. Next, we might want to replace a substring with another substring. This can be done either by specifying a starting character and the number of characters to replace, or by specifying a substring to locate and a string with which to replace it. In our string, we might replace 'LAMB' with 'PORK' so that the string contains 'MARY HAD A LITTLE PORK.'. If the replacement-string is not equal to the length of the substring it is replacing, it is a little more complicated. If we wanted to replace 'LITTLE' with 'BIG' in 'MARY HAD A LITTLE LAMB.', we would search the string to find where 'LITTLE' begins, form a substring of all characters up to this point and a substring of all characters following the 'LITTLE', and concatenate the first substring 'MARY HAD A' with 'BIG' and then with the last substring 'LAMB.' to form 'MARY HAD A BIG LAMB.'.

Substrings are also required when one wants to locate all instances of a substring within a string. If we want to replace all instances of 'MARY' with 'JANE' in the string 'MARY HAD A LAMB. MARY ALSO HAD A HORSE.', we would first replace the first 'MARY' with 'JANE' to form 'JANE HAD A LAMB. MARY ALSO HAD A HORSE.'. Then we would examine the substring beginning just beyond where we replaced and replace 'MARY' with 'JANE' so that 'HAD A LAMB. MARY ALSO HAD A HORSE.' becomes 'HAD A LAMB. JANE ALSO HAD A HORSE.'. This would continue until no more 'MARY' is found to replace.

COBOL is not a good language for text editing. Its statements are directed more toward examining data items to see if they contain valid numeric or alphabetic characters and toward replacing invalid characters with valid ones. The INSPECT, EXAMINE, and TRANSFORM statements already described can locate substrings within a string, and can replace substrings with strings of equal length. The STRING and UNSTRING statements described next can concatenate strings, replace substrings with strings, and form strings.

The STRING statement transmits characters from a send-string into a receiving-string, starting at a specified character position in the receiving-string. Multiple send-strings can be transmitted into a single receiving-

string. The UNSTRING statement transmits characters starting at a specified character position in a send-string into a receiving-string. A single
send-string can be separated and placed in multiple receiving-strings.
STRING and UNSTRING are both complex and difficult statements—perhaps the most difficult statements to be found in any programming language.

As an alternative to STRING and UNSTRING, the REDEFINES
clause can define one substring to overlie another. The following example
stores the characters 'AB' into the first two positions of the identifier A.

```
77   A   PIC X(4) VALUE 'WXYZ'.

77   A-2 REDEFINES A PIC X(2).

     □ □ □

     MOVE 'AB' TO A-2.          [A contains 'ABYZ'.]
```

This method works only if a fixed number of characters are to be moved
to a fixed position in the identifier, but it should be used wherever possible
in place of STRING and UNSTRING because it will not only be more
efficient, but also easier to understand.

A. STRING Statement

The simplest form of the STRING statement transmits the characters in
the *send-string* into the *receiving-string*.

```
STRING send-string DELIMITED SIZE INTO receiving-string.
```

- *send-string*. An alphanumeric literal, figurative constant, or USAGE
  DISPLAY identifier containing the characters to be transmitted. Figurative constants are treated as single characters.
- *receiving-string*. THE USAGE DISPLAY identifier into which the
  characters in *send-string* are transmitted. Characters in *send-string* are
  transmitted from left to right into *receiving-string* until the rightmost
  character in *send-string* is transmitted, or *receiving-string* is filled.

```
77   A   PIC X(4) VALUE 'WXYZ'.

     □ □ □

     STRING 'AB' DELIMITED SIZE INTO A.

         [A contains 'ABYZ'.]
```

The DELIMITED SIZE phrase specifies that all characters in *send-string* are to be transmitted. Alternatively, the transmission can be terminated by *delimiter* characters as follows.

```
STRING send-string DELIMITED delimiter INTO receiving-
     string.
```

* *delimiter.* A figurative constant, alphanumeric literal, or a USAGE DISPLAY identifier containing characters. Transmission terminates if the *delimiter* is encountered in *send-string*. If the *delimiter* contains more than one character, it is treated as a unit. That is, a *delimiter* of 'AB' terminates when 'AB' is encountered, not when an 'A' or 'B' is encountered. The *delimiter* characters themselves are not transmitted.

```
77   A   PIC X(4) VALUE SPACES.
77   B   PIC X(4) VALUE 'ABCD'.

     □  □  □

     STRING B DELIMITED 'C' INTO A.
```

      [A contains 'ABbb'.]

Several *delimiter* characters can be specified, any one of which will terminate transmission if encountered. In the following example, transmission is terminated if the characters 'A', 'ZZ', or 'W' are encountered in SEND-IT.

```
STRING SEND-IT DELIMITED 'A', 'ZZ', 'W' INTO B.
```

The specific *position* in *receiving-string* into which transmission is to begin is specified by the POINTER phrase.

```
                         SIZE
                         delimiter
STRING send-string DELIMITED _ _ _ _ _

     INTO receiving-string

     POINTER position.
```

* *position.* A numeric integer identifier specifying the first character position (the first character is number one) in *receiving-string* into which

the *send-string* characters are to be transmitted. *position* must be set prior to execution of STRING. It is incremented by one as each character is transmitted, and on completion of the statement, it points to one beyond the last character transmitted. The POSITION phrase is optional, and *position* one is assumed if it is omitted.

```
77   A   PIC X(4) VALUE 'WYXZ'.
77   B   PIC S9(4) COMP.

     □ □ □

     MOVE 3 TO B.

     STRING 'AB' DELIMITED SIZE INTO A POINTER B.
```

       [A contains 'WYAB', and B contains 5.]

The STRING statement can also concatenate character-strings by listing several *send-strings*. The strings are concatenated by appending one string to the end of another to form a new string. Hence, 'AB' concatenated with 'CD' yields a new string containing 'ABCD'.

```
                              SIZE
                              delimiter
STRING send-string-1 DELIMITED _ _ _ _ _,

                              SIZE
                              delimiter
       send-string-2 DELIMITED _ _ _ _ _,

       .
       .
       .                      SIZE
                              delimiter
       send-string-n DELIMITED _ _ _ _ _
   INTO receiving-string POINTER position.

STRING 'AB' DELIMITED SIZE,

       'CD' DELIMITED SIZE

   INTO A.                 [A contains 'ABCD'.]
```

Error conditions are detected by appending the ON OVERFLOW phrase to the end of the STRING statement. The error condition occurs when *position* is less than 1 or greater than the size of *receiving-string*. If the ON OVERFLOW phrase is not coded, execution continues with the next executable statement when an error condition occurs.

```
STRING 'AB' DELIMITER SIZE INTO A POINTER B

   ON OVERFLOW PERFORM B30-ERROR.
```

B. UNSTRING STATEMENT

The simplest form of the UNSTRING statement transmits the characters in the *send-string* into the *receiving-string*, and is identical to the simplest form of the STRING statement.

```
UNSTRING send-string INTO receiving-string.
```

   [Same as:]

```
STRING send-string INTO receiving-string.
```

- *send-string*.   An alphanumeric literal, figurative constant, or USAGE DISPLAY identifier containing the characters to be transmitted. Figurative constants are treated as single characters.
- *receiving-string*.   The USAGE DISPLAY identifier into which the characters in *send-string* are transmitted. Characters in *send-string* are transmitted from left to right into *receiving-string* until the rightmost character in *send-string* is transmitted, or *receiving-string* is filled.

```
77   A   PIC X(4) VALUE 'WXYZ'.

   □  □  □

   UNSTRING 'AB' INTO A.          [A contains 'ABYZ'.]
```

Transmission can also be terminated by *delimiter* characters specified in the DELIMITED phrase.

```
UNSTRING send-string DELIMITED delimiter
   INTO receiving-string.
```

- *delimiter*.   A figurative constant, alphanumeric literal, or USAGE DISPLAY identifier containing characters. Transmission is terminated if the *delimiter* is encountered in *send-string*. A *delimiter* containing more than one character is treated as a unit. The *delimiter* characters themselves are not transmitted.

Several *delimiter* characters can be specified, any one of which will terminate transmission if encountered. In the following example, transmission is terminated if the characters 'A', 'ZZ', or 'W' are encountered in SEND-IT.

```
UNSTRING SEND-IT DELIMITED 'A', 'ZZ', 'W' INTO B.
```

The *position* in *send-string* from which to begin transmission is specified by the POINTER phrase.

```
UNSTRING send-string DELIMITED delimiter INTO receiving-string

    POINTER position.
```

• *position.* A numeric integer identifier specifying the first character position (the first character is position 1) in *send-string* from which transmission is to begin. Note that POINTER applies to the *send-string* in UN-STRING, and not the *receiving-string* as in STRING. It is incremented by 1 as each character is transmitted, and on completion of the statement, it points to one beyond the last character transmitted. The POSITION phrase is optional, and *position* 1 is assumed if omitted.

```
77  A  PIC X(4) VALUE 'WXYZ'.

77  B  PIC X(4) VALUE SPACES.

77  C  PIC S9(4) COMP.


    □ □ □


    MOVE 2 TO C.

    UNSTRING A INTO B POINTER C.
```

[B contains 'XYZb', and C contains 5.]

The next form of UNSTRING retrieves the delimiter characters.

```
UNSTRING send-string DELIMITED delimiter INTO receiving-string

    DELIMITER save

    COUNT count

    POINTER position.
```

The DELIMITER phrase (not to be confused with the DELIMITED phrase) specifies a USAGE DISPLAY identifier into which a *delimeter* is to be stored when encountered in *send-string*. The COUNT phrase specifies a numeric integer identifier which is set to the count of characters moved.

- *save*. A USAGE DISPLAY identifier into which the *delimiters* are stored when encountered. Blanks are stored in *save* if a *delimiter* is not encountered in *send-string*.
- *count*. A numeric integer identifier which is set to the number of characters moved into *receiving-string*. (The *delimiter* characters are not counted.)

The *send-string* can be broken up into several substrings by coding several *receiving-strings*. The DELIMITER and COUNT phrases are optional with each *receiving-string*. A TALLYING phrase can specify a numeric integer identifier that is incremented each time a new substring is transmitted.

```
UNSTRING send—string DELIMITED delimiter

   INTO receiving—string—1 DELIMITER save—1 COUNT count—1,

       receiving—string—2 DELIMITER save—2 COUNT count—2,

             .

             .

             .

       receiving—string—n DELIMITER save—n COUNT count—n

   POINTER position

   TALLYING tally.
```

- *tally*. A numeric integer identifier that is incremented as each successive *receiving-string* is filled. *tally* must be set to an initial value, usually zero, before execution of UNSTRING.

Characters are first transmitted from *send-string* beginning at the *position* specified, into *receiving-string-1*. When a *delimiter* is encountered, it is stored in *save-1*, *count-1* is set to the count of characters stored in *receiving-string-1*, and *tally* is incremented by one (assuming that DELIMITER, COUNT, and TALLY phrases are coded). Characters following the *delimiter* are transmitted into *receiving-string-2* until another *delimiter* is encountered. The *delimiter* is stored in *save-2*, *count-2* is set to the count of characters moved, and *tally* is incremented by 1. Transmission continues until all *receiving-strings* are filled, or all characters in *send-string* are transmitted. If a *receiving-string* is filled before a *delimiter* is encountered, blanks are moved to *save*, and transmission continues into the next *receiving-string* with the character following the last character transmitted.

If two *delimiters* are encountered in succession, the next *receiving-string* is filled with blanks, and *count* is set to zero. The *delimiter* may be preceded by ALL to treat successive occurrences of the *delimiter* as a single occurrence. For example, DELIMITED ALL 'A' ALL 'B' would treat the *send-string* 'WAAXBBBY' as if it were 'WAXBY'.

The ON OVERFLOW phrase can be appended to the end of UNSTRING to detect overflow when *position* has a value less than 1 or greater than the size of *send-string* during execution, or if all receiving areas are full, but not all characters in *send-string* have been transmitted. If ON OVERFLOW is not coded, execution continues with the next executable statement.

The following example illustrates the execution of UNSTRING.

```
MOVE 'BALLYbJAZZbTOPAZbA' TO SAVE-IT.

UNSTRING SAVE-IT DELIMITED 'Z', ALL 'L'

    INTO B1 DELIMITER S1 COUNT C1,

         B2 DELIMITER S2 COUNT C2,

         B3 DELIMITER S3 COUNT C3,

         B4 DELIMITER S4 COUNT C4

    TALLYING T

    ON OVERFLOW PERFORM C60-ERROR.
```

Execution proceeds as follows:

- 'BA' is stored in B1, 'L' is stored in S1, and C1 is set to 2.
- 'YbJA' is stored in B2, 'Z' is stored in S2, and C2 is set to 4.
- Blanks are stored in B3, 'Z' is stored in S3, and C3 is set to 0.
- 'bTOPA' is stored in B4, 'Z' is stored in S3, and C4 is set to 5.
- T is set to 4.
- The C60-ERROR procedure is performed.

Such a statement constitutes almost an entire program by itself, and one might have to make a flow chart of it to understand what happens.

STRING and UNSTRING are difficult statements to write and they make programs difficult to read. Use them sparingly, and comment on what they are intended to do.

This completes the discussion of character data. The chapters that follow describe how numeric and character data are formed into record and tables for storing and manipulating groups of related data.

EXERCISES

1. Show what these identifiers will contain when initialized as follows.

```
77  A         PIC X(6) VALUE ZEROS.

77  B         PIC X(6) VALUE 'MARYQUOTES'.

77  C         PIC X(3) VALUE 'ABC'.

77  D         PIC X(6) VALUE ALL '12'.

77  E         PIC X(8) JUST RIGHT VALUE '123'.

77  F         PIC X(6) VALUE 'ABC'.

77  G         PIC X(8) VALUE ALL ZEROS.
```

2. Define a identifier named TEXT-A containing 20 characters and an identifier named STATE containing 4 characters. Write the statements necessary to move the data in STATE to TEXT-A, right-justifying it with leading blanks. Do it once without the JUST RIGHT clause and once with it.

3. Define an identifier named TITLES containing 200 characters. Write the statements necessary to count the occurrences of the character-strings 'ABCD' and 'EFG' in TITLES.

4. Assume that a numeric character identifier named SOME-NUMBER of six numeric digits contains integers such as 34 and 645. The numbers may be signed plus or minus or may be unsigned. Alternatively, the sign may be overpunched over the rightmost character. It may also contain invalid numeric characters. Write the statements necessary to edit this number into valid COBOL form so that it can participate in arithmetic operations.

5. Assume that you have read a card image into an identifier named INPUT-REC. The card image contains integers enclosed between slashes, and the last number in the card is terminated by two slashes. The maximum integer is five digits, and the numbers are unsigned. A typical card would be as follows:

/335/21/4/12562/1986//

Write the statements necessary to retrieve each number from the card and display its value.

6. Assume that you must print numbers of precision S9(5), and you want negative numbers to be enclosed in parentheses. Positive numbers are to appear without parentheses. Define an identifier containing seven characters. Store the number in character positions 2 through 6. Place the parentheses in character positions 1 and 7 if the number is negative. Thus 23 would appear as 'bbbb23b' and −23 as '(bbb23)'.

Repeat this, but let the left parenthesis float so that −23 prints as 'bbb(23)'.

7. Define three identifiers named MONDAY, TUESDAY, and WEDNESDAY containing 10 characters each. Initialize each identifier with the appropriate name of the day. Then define an identifier named WEEK containing 30 characters. Write the statements to concatenate the three identifiers and store them in WEEK.

8. Define an identifier named MAXIMUM containing 7 characters. Assume that the identifier contains characters representing numbers such as −2, +6.9, −43.651, 7, .256426, and 7852390. Write the statements necessary to edit the number into proper COBOL form, and store it in an identifier defined as PIC S9(7)V9(7) COMP-3.

9. Assume that an identifier containing 200 characters contains English text. Change all instances of the abbreviations 'MISS' or MRS.' to 'bMS.'. (Make sure that words such as 'MISSISSIPPI' do not get changed.)

10. Do the same as in the preceding exercise, but change 'MISS' or 'MRS.' to 'MS.'. Pad the shortened string with blanks.

eight

DATA DESCRIPTIONS AND RECORDS

Storage can be allocated for elementary items, for records, and for tables. All data items must be explicitly described, and storage is not automatically set to zero or blanks, but must be initialized or assigned a value before it can be used in computations. Data descriptions are written as follows.

```
level—number   data—name   PIC character—string USAGE clause.
```

- *level-number.* One or two numeric digits specifying the level, such as 01, 02, and 77. Level 01 is the lowest level of a record, and all following levels greater than 01 belong to the record. Level 77 is a special level number for *noncontiguous* elementary data items. They are noncontiguous in that they bear no hierarchical relationship to other items. Level numbers 01 and 77 must begin in columns 8 to 11; all other level numbers may begin in column 8 or beyond.

- *data-name.* A name containing 1 to 30 characters: 0 to 9, A to Z, or the hyphen. The hyphen cannot be the first or last character. FILLER may be coded as the data name to indicate an unnamed item. The name must begin in column 12 or beyond. Level numbers 01 and 77 names must be unique.

- *character-string.* Characters specifying the length or precision of the data item, such as X(10) to specify 10 characters or S999V99 to specify a signed number with three digits to the left and two to the right of the assumed decimal point.

- USAGE clause. Specifies the representation of the data: COMP (binary), COMP-1 (single-precision floating-point), COMP-2 (double-precision floating-point), COMP-3 (packed decimal), or DISPLAY (numeric character, alphanumeric, or alphabetic). PIC must be omitted for COMP-1 and COMP-2. The keyword USAGE is optional. COMP-1, COMP-2, and COMP-3 are not a part of the ANS Standard, but are provided in System/370 COBOL.

Only a single data description entry may be coded on a line, but it may be continued onto other lines. The following level numbers may be used.

- 01. Used for record names. Aligned on a double-word boundary in System/370, and must begin in columns 8 to 11.
- 02 to 49. Used for levels within a record and may begin in column 8 or beyond.
- 66. Used for renaming groups of items within a record and may begin in column 8 or beyond.
- 77. Used for noncontiguous elementary data items not a part of a record. Aligned on a full-word boundary in System/370, and must begin in columns 8 to 11.
- 88. Used for condition names associated with an identifier and may begin in column 8 or beyond.

The data descriptions may appear in any of the five sections within the Data Division. The FILE Section describes I/O records, the WORKING-STORAGE Section describes elementary items, records, and tables, the LINKAGE Section describes subroutine arguments, the COMMUNICATION Section describes messages, and the REPORT Section describes the format of the report generator reports.

```
DATA DIVISION.

FILE SECTION.

FD/SD/CD/RD record-descriptions.

01  record-name.
```

Each File Description (FD), Sort Description (SD), Communication Description (CD), or Report Description (RD) entry is followed by a data description describing the record. This area for describing records is termed the *record-area*. The record descriptions are not allocated storage, and cannot be assigned initial values (except for level 88 condition names). They describe the format of the record within the input or output buffer. They must equal the logical record length.

```
WORKING—STORAGE SECTION.

77   data—name PIC ...

01   data—name.
```

Any level 77 items are allocated storage, and may be assigned initial values. The previous ANS Standard required all level 77 items to appear before any level 01 descriptions, but this restriction is removed in the current ANS Standard.

```
LINKAGE SECTION.

77   data—name PIC ...

01   data—name.
```

All subroutine arguments within a subroutine are described here. They are not allocated storage, and cannot be assigned initial values, except for level 88 condition names. They are associated with the data passed in the arguments of the calling program.

```
COMMUNICATION SECTION.
```

Descriptions placed here may redefine the format of messages in the input or output queues of the communications facility. They are not allocated storage, and cannot be assigned initial values except for level 88 condition names.

```
REPORT SECTION.

01   data—name.
```

The format of all reports to be generated by the report writer are placed here as data descriptions. They are allocated storage, and may be assigned initial values.

I.   DESCRIBING RECORDS

A *record* is a hierarchical collection of related data items, which may be of different data types. I/O records are described as records. For example, a record describing a person might include the person's name and date of birth. Some items might be group items, as for example the date of birth that consists of a month, a day, and a year. The following example shows how such a record is described. The two records are identical to show the hierarchical relationship. Aligning the PIC clauses also makes them easier to read.

```
01   PERSON.

02   NAME PIC X(25).

     02   BIRTH-DATE.

     03   MONTH PIC X(9).

03   DAYS PIC S99 COMP-3.

          03 YEAR PIC S9(4).
```

[Same as:]

```
01   PERSON.

     02   NAME            PIC X(25).

     02   BIRTH-DATE.

          03   MONTH      PIC X(9).

          03   DAYS       PIC S99 COMP-3.

          03   YEAR       PIC S9(4).
```

The record name, PERSON in the previous example, must be level number 01, and all succeeding items within the record must have level numbers greater than 01. The level numbers need not be consecutive, as they serve only to indicate the relative hierarchy of the record. For example, the following record is identical to the previous two.

```
01   PERSON.

     05   NAME        PIC X(25).

     05   BIRTH-DATE.

          10   MONTH  PIC X(9).

          10   DAYS   PIC S99 COMP-3.

          10   YEAR   PIC S9(4).
```

Increment the levels by a number such as 5 to leave room for subdividing items if later required. Level numbers must be consistent. The following example illustrates this requirement.

Incorrect: Correct:

```
01                                  01

    05                                  05

        10                                  10

    06                                  05
```

Items within a record that are not further subdivided are elementary items. They must contain the PIC clause (except for COMP-1 and COMP-2 in System/370). In the previous record, NAME, MONTH, DAYS, and YEAR are elementary items. The group items subdivided into elementary items are referred to by their names. For example, the entire record is referred to by its name, PERSON in the previous example.

The record name must be unique, but the group and elementary names need not be unique as long as they can be qualified to make them unique. The same names may appear in other records or within the same record. For example, the PERSON might also have a college graduation date that has a MONTH, DAYS, and YEAR.

```
    05  GRADUATION.

        10  MONTH       PIC X(9).

        10  DAYS        PIC S99 COMP-3.

        10  YEAR        PIC S9(4).
```

Now the data names must be qualified to make them unique. Data names become qualified by writing them in the hierarchy, from highest level number to lowest, separated by the word OF. MONTH OF GRADU-ATION refers to the month in the birth date. The full hierarchy of data names can also be given. MONTH OF BIRTH-DATE may be written as MONTH OF BIRTH-DATE OF PERSON. Data names need to be quali-fied only enough to make them unique. This is illustrated by the following two structures.

```
01  A.                          01  J.

    05  B.                          05  K.

        10  V  PIC X.                 10  X  PIC X.

        10  W  PIC X.                 10  W  PIC X.
```

The name B is unique and can be written as B or B OF A. The name V is unique and can be written as V, V OF B, V OF A, or V OF B OF A. The name W is not unique, and must be written as W OF B, W OF A, or W OF B OF A to identify the W in the A record. Unfortunately, this can lead to long data names, and so where possible, make the data names unique to avoid long qualifications.

The special data name FILLER describes data items in a record that are never referred to by name, as for example text within a print line. This alleviates having to make up a name that will never be used. FILLER must be an elementary items and contain the PIC clause. It is often used to pad out records to increase their size. FILLER may be assigned an initial value.

```
01  HEADER.

    05  FILLER       PIC X(6) VALUE 'DATE: '.

    10  A-DATE.

        10  MONTH    PIC XX.

        10  FILLER   PIC X VALUE '/'.

        10  DAYS     PIC XX.

        10  FILLER   PIC X VALUE '/'.

        10  YEAR     PIC XX.
```

The USAGE data types COMP, COMP-1, COMP-2, and COMP-3 may be coded at the group item level to apply to all data items within the group. However, this should be avoided because it is easy to mistake the elementary items for numeric character data when in fact they are specified to be another data type at the group level. The example on the right makes it clearer that Y and Z are COMP.

```
05   X   COMP.        [Same as:]        05   X.

   10   Y   PIC S9(5).                  10   Y PIC S9(5) COMP.

   10   Z   PIC S9(5).                  10   Z PIC S9(5) COMP.
```

The VALUE clause may also be coded at the group level if all the group items are alphanumeric data items (USAGE DISPLAY). The VALUE at the group level must be a figurative constant or a nonnumeric literal, and the group area is initialized without regard to the elementary item data types, as if they were all PIC X. The items within the group cannot contain the VALUE, JUST, or SYNC clauses.

```
01   X   VALUE SPACES.   [Same as:] 01   X.

   05   Y   PIC X(3).             05   Y   PIC X(3) VALUE SPACES.

   05   Z   PIC X(2).             05   Z   PIC X(2) VALUE SPACES.
```

II. RECORD ALIGNMENT

In System/370 records, COMP, COMP-1, and COMP-2 are not automatically aligned. If the numbers are not properly aligned, System/370 COBOL moves the numbers to a work area to perform arithmetic operations, which is inefficient. The SYNCHRONIZED clause, abbreviated SYNC, is coded for elementary items to align data on the proper word boundary. Numbers are unaligned if SYNC is omitted. If SYNC is used for a table, each table element is aligned. Use SYNC within records for COMP, COMP-1, and COMP-2 data items. Data types are aligned as follows in System/370.

COMP S9 to S9(4)	Half-word
COMP S9(5) to S9(18)	Full word
COMP-1	Full word
COMP-2	Double word
All else	Byte boundary, no need for SYNC

In System/370, the level number 01 for each record is aligned on a double-word boundary. The first item in the Data Division is also aligned on a double-word boundary. Level number 77 items are aligned on a full-word boundary.

When data items within a record are aligned, some wasted space, termed *slack bytes*, may result. For example, if a System/370 data item aligned on a double word is followed by an item aligned on a full word, and then followed by an item aligned on a double word, a full word of 4 slack bytes will result. These slack bytes must be counted in determining the size of a record. The record in the following example is 32 bytes in length.

```
01   A.

     05   B   COMP-2 SYNC.           [Aligned on a double word.]

     05   C   PIC X(2).

          [Two slack bytes inserted here.]

     05   D   PIC S9(5) COMP SYNC.   [Aligned on a full word.]

     05   E   COMP-1 SYNC.           [Aligned on a full word.]

          [Four slack bytes inserted here.]

     05   F   COMP-2 SYNC.           [Aligned on a double word.]
```

Slack bytes are confusing. They can be avoided in System/370 by placing all the double-word alignment items first in the record, followed by all the full-word alignment items, followed by all the half-word alignment items, followed by all the remaining items. Alternatively, do not use COMP, COMP-1, or COMP-2 items in records.

III. DOCUMENTING RECORDS

Documenting records, especially those describing I/O records, is perhaps the most important of all program documentation. You can read a program and understand the computations done on the data from the statements, but unless you understand the data, the program will have little meaning. Document the records with comments, placing them on the right side of the page so that they do not distract from the data descriptions. The data descriptions describe the form of the data, and the comments describe its meaning. Include the following in the comments.

- A short description of each data item.
- The meaning of values within the item. This applies mainly to flags and codes.

```
      05  FLSA            PIC X.
*                                     EXEMPTION CODE
*                                       E - EXEMPT
*                                       N - NONEXEMPT
      05  STATUS          PIC X.
*                                     MARITIAL STATUS
*                                       M - MARRIED
*                                       S - SINGLE
```

Three other items should also be included for I/O records. Some compilers provide the last two items automatically, saving the programmer this tedious work, and making the record descriptions easier to change because the relative byte locations need not be recomputed if record changes are made.

- A short description of the file.
- The record length in bytes. The reader will want to know this, and here is the best place to document it.
- The relative byte location of each data item. This is needed to specify the sort fields for external sorts, and to locate data items in a file dump. You must do this anyway to compute the record length, and it is little extra effort to document it as the same time. Place the relative byte locations in columns 73 to 80 of the data description. If you must insert a field, all the following relative type locations must be recomputed. Some compilers compute the relative byte locations and print them on the source listing, obviating the need for the relative byte locations.

Give the level 01 item a short name and append this name to all items within the record so that whenever the items are used in the program, it is apparent from which record they come.

```
********   PAY IS THE MASTER PAYROLL FILE.
********   RECORD LENGTH IS 400 BYTES.
   01  PAY.
      05  PAY-NAME        PIC X(25).                          1.
*                                     NAME OF PERSON
```

```
    05  PAY-CODE          PIC X.                              26.
*                                      TYPE OF PAY
*                                      H - HOURLY
*                                      S - SALARIED
    05  PAY-SALARY        PIC S999V99.                        27.
*                                      HOURLY RATE
```

Documentation of this type is easy to maintain because it is right there to change when the record description is changed. Keep all the I/O records in a COPY library as described in Chapter 11 so that all programs using the file will automatically include the file documentation. All the file documentation then exists in one place and is fully descriptive.

IV. RECORD OPERATIONS

Elementary items within a record can be operated on as with any data items, although the data names may have to be qualified to make them unique. Group items named in expressions are treated as elementary alphanumeric data items. Hence group item names can appear only in nonarithmetic expressions such as the IF, MOVE, and INSPECT statements. (They may also appear in arithmetic operations that contain the CORR phrase, but this is a different type of operation explained later.) The following example illustrates the treatment of group items in expressions.

```
01  Y.
    05  B                 PIC S9(7) COMP-3.
    05  C.
        10  D             PIC X(10).
        10  E             PIC S99.

    □  □  □

    MOVE SPACES TO Y.
```

Blanks are moved to the entire record without conversion, just as if Y had been declared as an elementary data item with PIC X(16). Note that this moves blanks into B and E, which are described as numeric items, and an error will occur if they are used in an arithmetic expression because they contain invalid data.

MOVE ZEROS TO Y.	[Sixteen zero characters are moved to Y. This also moves character data into the COMP-3 identifier B, and a data exception will occur if B is used in an arithmetic expression. However, E now contains valid data.]

The IF statement can test group or elementary items. It treats a group item as an elementary alphanumeric data item.

IF Y = SPACES	[Y is considered to be PIC X(16).]
THEN MOVE ZERO TO V.	

The CORRESPONDING phrase, abbreviated CORR, is coded in the MOVE, ADD, and SUBTRACT statements to cause only elements whose qualified names are the same to participate in an operation.

```
MOVE CORR group-name-1 TO group-name-2.

ADD CORR group-name-1 TO group-name-2.

SUBTRACT CORR group-name-1 FROM group-name-2.
```

All elementary items that have the same name and qualification up to but not including the group names, participate in the operation. The elementary items need not be in the same order or be of the same data types. COBOL will convert items of different types.

```
01  DATES.

    05  START-DATE.

        10  MONTH        PIC XX.

        10  DAYS         PIC S999 COMP-3.

        10  YEAR         PIC S99.

        10  CENTURY      PIC S9999.

    05  DAYS-IN-YEAR     PIC S999.
```

```
05  END-DATE.

    10  YEAR        PIC S99.

    10  MONTH       PIC S99.

    10  DAYS        PIC S99.

05  JULIAN-DATE.

    10 DAYS-IN YEAR  PIC S999.
```

□ □ □

```
MOVE CORR START-DATE TO END-DATE.
```

[Same as:]

```
MOVE MONTH OF START-DATE TO MONTH OF END-DATE.

MOVE DAYS OF START-DATE TO DAYS OF END-DATE.

MOVE YEAR OF START-DATE TO YEAR OF END-DATE.
```

Elementary item names must have the same qualification to participaet in the operation. CENTURY does not participate because it is not an elementary item in END-DATE, and DAYS-IN-YEAR does not participate because its fully qualified names do not match. If the group names contain tables, the tables are ignored. Any FILLER is likewise ignored.

```
01  SOMETHING.

    05  B              OCCURS 20 TIMES.

        10  C          PIC X.

        10  D          PIC X.

    05  FILLER         PIC X.

    05  E              PIC X.
```

If SOMETHING were named in a CORR operation, table B and the FILLER would not participate. The group names may be tables, or belong to tables, in which case they must be subscripted or indexed. The following statement would be valid for the previous record.

```
MOVE CORR B (1) TO X.
```

The CORR phrase saves coding effort. With a good compiler, the CORR phrase is neither more nor less efficient than are individual MOVES, ADDS, or SUBTRACTS. The CORR phrase can make programs easier to change, especially when corresponding elements are likely to be added or deleted from records. A single change can be made to the data descriptions rather than the statements scattered throughout the program. However, this also has a negative side. It may not be obvious when a data description is changed that the execution of Procedure Division statements that have a CORR phrase may be changed too.

V. INITIALIZING RECORDS

When a record is used to create an output record, it must first be initialized, generally by moving spaces to the alphanumeric fields and zeros to the numeric fields. Consider the following record to be initialized.

```
01  A.
    05  B           PIC X(10).
    05  C           PIC S9(5) COMP-3.
    05  D           PIC X(3).
    05  E           PIC S9(5) COMP-3.
```

The record can be initialized by assigning initial values to the elementary items. If the record is an I/O record, this initializes only the first record written, and all records should be initialized. The easiest way to initialize a record is to move SPACES to the record as a group item and then move ZEROS to the numeric items.

```
    MOVE SPACES TO A.
    MOVE ZEROS TO C,
              E.
```

If the record is to be initialized from several places within the program, the previous example could be made into a paragraph and then performed. Now consider the following record.

```
01  RECORD-OUT.
    05  SCHOOL        PIC X(25).
```

```
05  CHILDREN          OCCURS 600 TIMES

                      INDEXED BY IX.

    10 AGES           PIC S9(3) COMP-3.
```

The record contains a table of 600 elements. We can initialize the table in a loop, but doing this for each record could be inefficient. A more efficient way to accomplish this, at some cost in storage, is to define a new record that contains the same number of characters as the record to be written. We can initialize the original record only once, and move it to the new record. Then whenever we wish to initialize the original record, we move the new record to it. This also works well when initial values are assigned to the first record, or when the initialization values are computed within the program.

```
01  ZERO-IT           PIC X(1225).
```

[Same size as RECORD-OUT.]

   □ □ □

```
MOVE SPACES TO SCHOOL.

PERFORM A20-PART-A

  VARYING IX FROM 1 BY 1

  UNTIL IX ) 600.
```

[This initializes the record. Rather than doing this each time, we save a copy of the record after it is initialized and simply move the copy to the record hereafter.]

```
MOVE RECORD-OUT TO ZERO-IT.
```

[Save the initialized record.]

   □ □ □

```
A20-PART-A.

  MOVE ZERO TO AGES (IX).
```

Now whenever we wish to initialize RECORD-OUT, we do the following.

```
MOVE ZERO-IT TO RECORD-OUT.
```

[Move the initialized copy to the record.]

VI. REDEFINITION OF STORAGE

The REDEFINES clause assigns different data names to the same storage
by redefining one data item to occupy the same storage as another. In the
following example, A and B occupy the same storage location.

```
77  A     PIC S9(5) COMP-3.

77  B     REDEFINES A PIC X(3).
```

The REDEFINES clause must immediately follow the data name.

Incorrect: Correct:

```
77  B   PIC X(5) REDEFINES A.      77  B     REDFINES A PIC X(5).
```

A redefined item cannot contain the VALUE or, in System/370, the
SYNC clause, but the item which it redefines may. The redefined item may
have a level 88 condition name.

Incorrect:

```
77  A     PIC S9(5) COMP.

77  B     REDEFINES A PIC S9(5) COMP SYNC VALUE 10.
```

Correct:

```
77  A     PIC S9(5) COMP SYNC VALUE 10.

77  B     REDFINES A PIC S9(5) COMP.
```

Records may also be redefined. Except for level number 01 records, the
redefined items must have the same length as the items to which they are
redefined. Level 66 and 88 items cannot be redefined. The redefined item
must have the same level number as the item that it redefines.

Incorrect:

```
    05  A.

        10  B   PIC X(10).

        10  C   PIC X(10).

        10  D   REDEFINES A PIC X(20).
```

Correct:

```
05   A.
     10   B     PIC X(10).
     10   C     PIC X(10).
05   D   REDEFINES A.
     10   E     PIC X(5).
     10   F     PIC X(10).
     10   G     PIC X(5).
```

The redefined item must follow the item that it redefines, with no intervening nonredefined items.

Incorrect: Correct:

```
77  A   PIC X(10).            77  A  PIC X(10).
77  B   PIC X(10).            77  B  REDEFINES A PIC X(10).
77  C   REDEFINES A PIC X(10).  77  C  REDEFINES A PIC X(10).
```

Redefinition can conserve memory storage by allowing the same storage to be reused for different purposes. It must be used for only one purpose at a time, and such usage should be avoided because it leads to confusion and errors. Redefinition is best when used to overlay data of one type with another for files that contain more than one record type. Each record can contain a flag that specifies the record type, and the flag can be interrogated to determine which redefinition item describes the record. (REDEFINES cannot be used for 01 level number items in the record area of the File Section. In this section, 01 level number records are implicitly redefined by placing one after the other.) The following example illustrates a record with a field that may contain two data types.

```
01   REC.
     05   REC-TYPE        PIC X.
     05   REC-CHAR        PIC X(4).
     05   REC-NUM REDEFINES REC-CHAR PIC S9(7) COMP-3.
```

This record might contain alphanumeric data referred to by REC-CHAR, or a packed decimal number referred to by REC-NUM, depending on the value contained in REC-TYPE. Redefinition also allows data of one type to be stored in a data item of another type without conversion.

```
MOVE 'ABCD' TO REC-CHAR.        [REC-NUM also contains 'ABCD'.]
```

Tables can also be redefined to occupy the same storage.

```
01  TABLE-A.

    05  LEVEL-1          OCCURS 100 TIMES.

        10  X            PIC S9(5) COMP-3 OCCURS 50 TIMES.

01  TABLE-B REDEFINES TABLE-A.

    05  LEVEL-1          OCCURS 100 TIMES.

        10  Y            PIC X(3) OCCURS 50 TIMES.
```

The redefined item cannot contain an OCCURS clause. In System/370, the redefined items cannot be subordinate to an item containing an OCCURS clause. The ANS Standard permits the redefined item to be subordinate to an item containing an OCCURS clause, but not an OCCURS DEPENDING ON clause. This means that table elements cannot be redefined. In the previous example, TABLE-A can be redefined, but X cannot.

The REDEFINES clause allows one record to be redefined over another. A special level 66 RENAMES clause allows a single data name to rename a series of data items within a record. There are two forms.

```
66  data-name-1 RENAMES data-name-2.
```

[*data-name*-1 simply renames *data-name*-2.]

```
66  data-name-1 RENAMES data-name-2  THRU data-name-3.
```

[*data-name*-1 renames all items from *data-name*-2 through *data-name*-3.]

The *data-name-1* cannot be used as a qualifier, and it can only be qualified by the record name within which it renames items. The following example illustrates the RENAMES clause.

```
01  A.

    05  B.

        10  C           PIC X(3).

        10  D           PIC X(4).

    05  E               PIC X(5).

    05  F.

        10  G           PIC X(6).

        10  H           PIC X(7).

66  W   RENAMES C.
```

[W is an elementary item containing 3 characters.]

```
66  X   RENAMES B.
```

[X is a group item containing 7 characters.]

```
66  Y   RENAMES B THRU G.
```

[Y is a group item containing 18 characters.]

The level number 66 RENAMES clause must immediately follow the last item in the record description, and several RENAMES clauses can be coded for a single record. Level number 01, 66, 77, and 88 items cannot be renamed, but both elementary items and group items within a record can be renamed. If the RENAMES *data-name-1* THRU *data-name-2* form is used, *data-name-2* must follow *data-name-1* in the record, and it may be subordinate to it. Items that contain an OCCURS clause or are subordinate to an item containing an OCCURS clause cannot be renamed. This means that an element of table cannot be the subject of the RENAMES.

Records are used to contain a single instance of related data. The next chapter describes tables that allow many instances of such data to be contained.

EXERCISES

1. Assume that a record is to contain an employee's name, social security number, age, date of birth, annual salary, and number of dependents. Define and document the record to contain this information. Define the name so that you can retrieve the initials and the last name.

2. Assume that you are being passed a card image transaction generated by the computer. Each 80-character card contains 10 fields of 8 characters each. The first character of each field describes the data contained in the remaining 7 characters of the field. The fields are as follows:

First Character	Remainder of Field
1	7 characters
2	3 characters, left justified
3	4 characters right justified
4	7-digit number
5	2 numbers, one with 3 digits and one with 4 digits
6	5-digit number, left justified, with 2 digits to the right of the assumed decimal point

Define a record to contain this record and allow you to manipulate it. Edit the numeric data to ensure its validity for COBOL.

3. Assume that an old program is run on a new computer, and it terminates with an error. Fortunately, it tells you the statement number at which it terminated. It terminated in the second of the following two statements.

```
MOVE SPACE TO FIRST-BYTE.

MOVE LEFT-PART TO RIGHT-PART.
```

Next you look in the Data Division and find the following record.

```
01  BIG-TABLE.
    05  WHAT-IT-CONTAINS            PIC X(200).
    05  REDEFINE-IT REDEFINES WHAT-IT-CONTAINS.
        10  FIRST-BYTE              PIC X.
        10  RIGHT-PART              PIC X(199).
01  LEFT-PART REDEFINES BIG-TABLE   PIC X(199).
```

What was the programmer attempting to do? Why might it be failing on the new computer? Is this a good programming practice?

4. Two records are defined as follows.

```
01  ONE.
    02  A.
        03  B           PIC X(3).
        03  C           PIC S999 COMP-3.
        03  D.
            04  E       PIC S9(6) COMP-3.
            04  F       PIC X(2).
    02  G               PIC X(6).
    03  H               PIC X(6).
01  TWO.
    02  J.
        03  D           PIC X(3).
        03  C           PIC S9(3) COMP-3.
        03  Q.
            04  E       PIC S9(6) COMP-3.
            04  F       PIC X(2).
    02  R               PIC X(6).
    02  S               PIC X(6).
```

Note the elements that participate in the following statements.

```
MOVE TWO TO ONE.
MOVE CORR TWO TO ONE.
MORE CORR J TO A OF ONE.
MOVE S TO G.
```

nine

TABLES

A *table*, also termed an *array*, is an arrangement of elements in one or more dimensions. Tables, powerful data processing tools, are much more common than one might expect. Our nation can be expressed as a table containing 50 states as elements. The calendar can be represented as a table containing 12 months as table elements. Such a table has one *dimension;* that is a single sequence of elements. The range of elements constitute the *bounds* of the table, and the bounds of the calendar table are 1 to 12.

Tables may have more than one dimension. A table with two dimensions is termed a *matrix*, with the first dimension referred to as the *row*, and the second dimension as the *column*. The seats of an auditorium are elements of a matrix, with rows and columns. COBOL tables may have a maximum of three dimensions. We might make the auditorium table a three-dimensional table with the third dimension representing the auditorium within the city. If we allow for 100 rows, 75 columns, and 10 auditoriums in the city, the table would have $100 \times 75 \times 10$ or 75,000 table elements representing auditorium seats.

To refer to a specific element, the table is *subscripted* or *indexed*. If the three dimensional auditorium table is named SEAT, we can refer to the twelfth seat in the fifth row of the third auditorium as SEAT (5, 12, 3). The subscript may be an integer literal or identifier. An index is a special data item described later in this chapter.

An important property of tables is their ability to hold several records in storage for computations. Suppose that a file contains numbers that are to be printed in a column of a report, with 50 lines per page. Now suppose that the sum of the numbers on each page is to be printed at the top of the page before the numbers themselves are printed. We can read 50 numbers into a table, sum the elements of the table, and print this total at the top of the page. Then the 50 numbers can be printed from the table.

Now suppose that 100 numbers are to be printed in two columns on a page, with the first 50 numbers in the left column and the next 50 numbers on the right. We could define a table of 100 elements to contain the page, but it is easier to define a two-dimensional table with the first dimension representing the line on the page (1 to 50), and the second dimension representing the column (1 or 2).

Furthermore, suppose that the first page of the report is to contain the total of all numbers in the report. We can define a three-dimensional table with the first dimension representing the line on the page, the second dimension the column, and the third dimension the page of the report. By storing the entire report in a table, we can sum the numbers to print the total first, and then print the numbers from the table. A 100-page report would have $100 \times 2 \times 50$ or 10,000 table elements.

The use of tables may also reduce the number of statements required, which in turn may save coding time and internal storage. But more importantly, it is easier to comprehend a few statements than many. As an example illustrating the benefits of a table, first consider a record containing the population of the 50 states described without the use of a table.

```
01  POPULATION-COUNT      PIC S9(11) COMP-3.

01  STATES.

    05  ALABAMA           PIC S9(9) COMP-3.

    05  ARKANSAS          PIC S9(9) COMP-3.

        .
        .
        .


    05  WYOMING           PIC S9(9) COMP-3.
```

To compute the total population of all states, we would code the following.

```
MOVE ZERO TO POPULATION-COUNT.

ADD ALABAMA TO POPULATION-COUNT.
```

```
ADD ARKANSAS TO POPULATION-COUNT.

        .

        .

        .

ADD WYOMING TO POPULATION-COUNT.
```

Now suppose that we wish to determine the largest and smallest populations of the states. This would require the following.

```
77  MIN                PIC S9(9) COMP-3.

77  MAX                PIC S9(9) COMP-3.


    □ □ □

MOVE ZERO TO MAX.

MOVE 999999999 TO MIN.

IF ALABAMA ( MIN

    THEN MOVE ALABAMA TO MIN.

IF ALABAMA ) MAX

    THEN MOVE ALABAMA TO MAX.

        .

        .

        .
```

This would be tedious to code, and if California were to be split into two states or the Virginias were to be reunited, the program would require several changes. We can reduce the amount of coding, make the operations more understandable, and allow for change by making the state populations a table. A table is specified by the OCCURS clause.

```
01  STATES.

    05  NO-STATES      PIC S9(4) COMP VALUE 50.

    05  POPULATION     PIC S9(9) COMP-3

                       OCCURS 50 TIMES.
```

[POPULATION is described as a table with 50 elements.]

The population is then summed and the minimum and maximum are computed as follows.

```
MOVE ZERO TO POPULATION-COUNT,

            MAX.

MOVE 999999999 TO MIN.

PERFORM A10-PART-A

    VARYING IX FROM 1 BY 1
```

[IX is used as a subscript to refer to each individual element of the table.]

```
    UNTIL IX > NO-STATES.

    □ □ □


A10-PART-A.

    ADD POPULATION (IX) TO POPULATION-COUNT.

    IF POPULATION (IX) < MIN

        THEN MOVE POPULATION (IX) TO MIN.

    IF POPULATION (IX) > MAX

        THEN MOVE POPULATION (IX) TO MAX.

**** EXIT
```

Now if a new state is added, the change can be accomplished in the Data Division rather than the Procedure Division.

I. TABLE DESCRIPTIONS

Tables are described by appending the OCCURS *n* TIMES clause to the data description. The *n*, a positive integer literal greater than zero, specifies the table size. The OCCURS clause cannot be coded for 01, 66, 77, or 88 level number data items. In the following example, A-TABLE is described as a single-dimensional table containing 30 elements.

```
01   SOMETHING.

    05   A-TABLE          PIC S9(3) COMP-3

                          OCCURS 30 TIMES.
```

Individual elements of a table cannot be assigned initial values. As an alternative, one can describe a record containing several data items with initial values and then redefine the record as a table.

```
01  A-RECORD.

    05  FILLER          PIC S9(5) COMP-3 VALUE 2.

    05  FILLER          PIC S9(5) COMP-3 VALUE 3.

    05  FILLER          PIC S9(5) COMP-3 VALUE 6.

01  Y REDEDFINES A-RECORD.

    05  A-TABLE         PIC S9(5) COMP-3

                        OCCURS 3 TIMES.
```

COBOL tables may have from one to three dimensions. Multidimensional tables are described as records, with each dimension specified by a lower-level item. In the following example, Y is described as a 2 by 10 by 20 table.

```
01  A-RECORD.

    05  LEVEL-1         OCCURS 2 TIMES.

        10  LEVEL-2     OCCURS 10 TIMES.

            15  Y       PIC S9(3) COMP-3

                        OCCURS 20 TIMES.
```

Y must be subscripted or indexed to refer to a specific element. The subscripts or indexes correspond to the order of the OCCURS clauses. Y (2, 10, 20) refers to the last element in the table. Tables are stored in row-major order, with the rightmost subscript or index increasing most rapidly. Thus the elements of the Y table are stored in the order Y (1, 1, 1), Y (1, 1, 2), . . . , Y (1, 1, 20), Y (1, 2, 1), . . . , Y (2, 10, 20).

Some compilers limit the size of tables. System/370 limits the elements of a table to 131,071 bytes for fixed-length tables. Thus a table whose elements are PIC X(100) could occur 1310 times but not 1311 times. System/370 variable-size tables, those with an OCCURS DEPENDING ON clause, are limited to 32,767 bytes, and for them a PIC X(100) item could occur 327 times but not 328 times.

Group items can also be described as tables. The following record describes 50 states, 5 rivers within each state, 20 counties within each state, and 10 cities within each county.

```
01  NATION.

    05  STATE                      OCCURS 50 TIMES.

        10  STATE-NAME             PIC X(25).

        10  RIVER                  PIC X(25)

                                   OCCURS 5 TIMES.

        10  COUNTY                 OCCURS 20 TIMES.

            15  CITY               OCCURS 10 TIMES.

                20  CITY-NAME      PIC X(25).

                20  CITY-SIZE      PIC S9(7) COMP-3.
```

The subscripts or indexes must be written after the last qualified name of a record.

```
STATE (1) or STATE OF NATION (1)
```

[Refers to the first STATE group item.]

```
COUNTY (2,3)
```

[Refers to the third COUNTY of the second STATE group item.]

```
RIVER OF STATE (2, 3)
```

[Refers to the third RIVER element of the second STATE group item.]

```
CITY-NAME OF CITY OF COUNTY OF STATE OF NATION (4, 3, 2)
```

[Refers to the CITY-NAME element of the second CITY group item of the third COUNTY group item of the fourth STATE group item.]

Subscripts must be positive, nonzero integer literals or identifiers that do not exceed the bounds of the table. In System/370, literals are slightly more efficient than identifiers as subscripts, and the most efficient data type for subscripts in System/370 is PIC S9(4) COMP. The subscript may be qualified but not subscripted. That is, A (J OF K) is valid, but A (I (J)) is not. The form of subscripts is as follows.

```
A (I, J, K)
```

Blanks required as shown for System/370. System/370 also prohibits a blank following the left parenthesis or preceding the right parenthesis. The ANS Standard removes these restrictions.

In addition to being subscripted, table elements can be *indexed*. An *index* is a special data type used to refer to table elements just as are subscripts. Indexes are described by the INDEXED BY phrase of the OCCURS clause. The following example describes BX as an index for table B.

```
01  A.

    05  B               PIC S9(3) COMP-3

                        OCCURS 10 TIMES INDEXED BY BX.
```

In System/370, indexes cannot be used in combination with literals or subscripts. The ANS Standard permits them to be used in combination with literals but not subscripts. Indexes cannot be operated on with the arithmetic statements, such as ADD and COMPUTE. In System/370, an index is a full-word binary item. Several indexes can be defined for each dimension of a table, and only those defined can be used to index that dimension of the table. The general form of the INDEXED phrase is as follows.

```
INDEXED BY index-1, index-2, ..., index-n
```

The *indexes* are any unique, valid COBOL name, and they are defined as indexes for only that dimension of the table. If indexes are defined for one level of a table, they must be defined for all higher levels of the table. The following example shows the specification of two indexes for each level of a three-dimensional table.

```
01  A.

    05  B               OCCURS 4 TIMES INDEXED BY BX1, BX2.

        10  C           OCCURS 6 TIMES INDEXED BY CX1, CX2.

            15  D       PIC S9(3) COMP-3

                        OCCURS 10 TIMES INDEXED BY DX1, DX2.
```

Defining an index does not preclude the use of subscripts, but indexes cannot be used in combination with subscripts (or literals in System/370.) Hence D (BX1, CX1, DX1) and D (SUB1, SUB2, SUB3) are valid, but D (BX1, CX1, SUB3) is invalid. An index, unlike a subscript, can be coded plus or minus an integer literal for relative addressing of table elements.

```
table (index ± integer, ...)
```

The following indexes are then valid for array D.

```
D (BX1 + 2, CX1 - 3, DX1)
```

If BX1 was set to 1, CX1 to 6, and DX1 to 7, the previous item would be the same as D (3, 3, 7).

Index data items may also be described.

```
level-number index-name INDEX.
```

```
01  AN-INDEX  INDEX
```

The *index-name* is any unique, valid COBOL name. Index data items can be used to contain index values, but they cannot themselves be used to index a table.

Indexes and index data items can only be manipulated by the SET, SEARCH, and PERFORM VARYING statements. Index data items also participate in the MOVE statement, but they can only be moved to other index data items. Indexes cannot appear in ACCEPT, DISPLAY, and EXHIBIT statements. The SET statement has the following form.

```
SET index-1, index-2, ..., index-n TO value.
```

One or more *indexes* may be set to the *value*. The *value* may be an integer numeric literal or identifier, another index, or an index data item. Numeric literals must be positive.

```
SET IX1 TO 10.
```

```
SET IX1,
```

```
    IX2 TO IX3.
```

One or more integer numeric identifiers may be set to the current value of an index.

```
SET identifier-1, identifier-2, ..., identifier-n TO index.
```

```
SET A,
```

```
    B TO IX1.
```

```
SET C TO IX2.
```

One or more indexes may be incremented or decremented by a value. The value can be an integer numeric literal or identifier. In System/370, numeric literals must be positive, but the ANS Standard permits them to be negative.

```
SET index-1, index-2, ..., index-n UP BY value.

SET index-1, index-2, ..., index-n DOWN BY value.

SET IX3 UP BY 3.

SET IX3,

   IX4 DOWN BY 5.
```

Indexes can appear in relational conditions, such as those in the IF statement, and they participate in the operation as if they were subscripts. If an index is compared to a nonindex item, the index is automatically converted to a subscript value for the operation. Index data items cannot be converted to subscripts because they are not described for a specific table. Hence they can be compared only to other indexes or index data items.

Functionally, indexes are a redundant language feature. They permit the compiler implementer to make them more efficient than do subscripts. The actual contents of the index are compiler dependent. In System/370, the index contains the relative byte location of the element within the table. A subscript must be converted to the relative byte location each time the table element is referenced, and indexes eliminate this conversion. However, the gain in efficiency is often minimal. Such scientific programming languages as FORTRAN, PL/I, ALGOL, and APL, in which tables are used much more than in COBOL, do not have a special data type for indexes, and there is no complaint about efficiency.

The restrictions on indexes sometimes lead to convoluted programming that negates some of their efficiency. Index values are defined only for the bounds of the table. If a table has 20 elements, the index for that table should contain only the values 1 to 20. Zero is not a valid value for an index, and the following statement is in error.

```
SET IX TO ZERO.
```

The following statements will yield a meaningless result on some compilers.

```
SET IX TO 1.
```

```
    SET DOWN BY 1.                   [A zero value is undefined.]

    SET IX UP BY 1.                  [An undefined value plus 1 is still unde-
                                     fined.]
```

The following statements also illustrate a common error with indexes.

```
01  A-RECORD.

    05  A-TABLE           PIC S9(4) COMP

                          OCCURS 1000 TIMES INDEXED BY AN-INDEX.


    □ □ □


    PERFORM A10-ZERO-A-TABLE

       VARYING AN-INDEX FROM 1 BY 1

    UNTIL AN-INDEX 〉 1000.
```

The PERFORM is in error because it terminates when AN-INDEX is greater than 1000, and a value of AN-INDEX greater than 1000 is undefined. If AN-INDEX were a subscript rather than an index, the problem would disappear. One must be careful in using indexes in the PERFORM VARYING. But how would one zero out the A-TABLE using indexes? Two ways to do it are to use the PERFORM TIMES or to code the loop in-line as shown in the following examples.

With the PERFORM TIMES:

```
    SET AN-INDEX TO 1.

    PERFORM A10-ZERO-A-TABLE 1000 TIMES.


    □ □ □


A10-ZERO-A-TABLE.

    MOVE ZERO TO A-TABLE (AN-INDEX).

    IF AN-INDEX NOT = 1000

       THEN SET AN-INDEX UP BY 1.
```

Coded in-line:

```
    SET AN-INDEX TO 1.

A10-LOOP.

    MOVE ZERO TO A-TABLE (AN-INDEX).

    IF AN-INDEX = 1000

        THEN GO TO A20-LOOP-DONE.

    SET AN-INDEX UP BY 1.

    GO TO A10-LOOP.

A20-LOOP-DONE.
```

In the PERFORM TIMES, it is not clear that much has been gained in efficiency over using subscripts because of the extra IF test that had to be added to ensure that AN-INDEX does not exceed 1000. Whether the PERFORM VARYING using subscripts would be faster depends on the implementation. Coding the loop in-line would probably be more efficient, but it requires intertwined GO TOs with a loss in clarity.

Indexes make debugging harder because they cannot appear in DISPLAY or EXHIBIT statements. If IX is an index, the following two statements are illegal.

```
    DISPLAY IX.           [Or:]        EXHIBIT NAMED IX.
```

One must set a normal numeric data item to the index and then display the data item.

```
    SET SOMETHING TO IX.  [Or:]     SET SOMETHING TO IX.

    DISPLAY SOMETHING.              EXHIBIT NAMED SOMETHING.
```

These examples illustrate some of the problems in the use of indexes. Indexes are required for tables searched by the SEARCH statement, but their use for other purposes should be given careful consideration.

Indexing or subscripting beyond the bounds of a table will cause errors. If an item is moved from a table with an incorrect subscript, its contents are unpredictable, and this may not be discovered until later. If an item is moved to a table with an incorrect subscript, it is moved to another data item or even code within the program, and the error may not manifest itself until later when the other data item is used or the code is executed.

If TABLE-X has 100 elements, the following statement would wipe out parts of the program itself.

```
MOVE 10000 TO X-SIZE.

MOVE ZEROS TO TABLE-X (X-SIZE).
```

[Zeros are moved to somewhere in the program, but not within TABLE-X.]

II. VARIABLE-SIZE TABLES

COBOL can describe tables in which the number of table elements is specified by a data item. For example, a census record for a person might contain a data item specifying the number of children followed by a variable-
size table containing their names. Variable-size tables may be used in
variable-size records for I/O in which the record itself specifies the number
of table elements to be transmitted. Such variable-size records reduce the
record size, and may increase the I/O efficiency. Variable-size tables are
also used when the number of elements in a table may vary. Once the table
size is set, a SEARCH statement referencing the table knows the table
size and will search only the current size of the table.
    Variable-size tables are described by the OCCURS DEPENDING ON
size clause. The *size* is a numeric integer data item that contains the current
table size. Storage for variable-size tables is allocated for the maximum
size that the table can have. Thereafter, the occurrences of the table vary
depending on the contents of the *size* data item. When the table is written,
only the number of table elements specified by the *size* data item are transmitted. The general form for the description of variable-size tables is as
follows.

```
01  record-name.

    05  size            PIC ...

    05  table           OCCURS min TO max TIMES
                        DEPENDING ON size.
```

* *min.*   The minimum size of the table. It must be a numeric integer literal
  of value zero (in System/370) or larger, but less than *max.* The ANS
  Standard requires *min* to be a value of 1 or larger. This is inconvenient
  because zero elements is the null case for an empty table. System/370
  COBOL permits a table to have zero entries, allowing the SEARCH
  statement to work properly for an empty table. The ANS Standard requires some other means to indicate that a table is empty.

- *max.*   The maximum size of the table. It must be a numeric integer literal greater than *min* (but less than 32,768 in System/370).
- *size.*   A numeric integer data item set to values from *min* to *max* to specify the current size of the table. If *size* appears in the same record as the table it controls, it must appear before the table in the record description.

In the following example, TABLE-X is described as a table with a maximum of 100 elements, and the current size of TABLE-X depends on the contents of IX.

```
01  A-RECORD.

    05  IX              PIC S9(4) COMP.

    [Must appear before TABLE-X in the record.]

    05  TABLE-X         PIC S9(5) COMP-3

                        OCCURS 1 TO 100 TIMES DEPENDING ON IX.
```

When IX is assigned a value, the table acts as if it were described to be that size. If IX is set to 75 and the record is written out, only 75 elements of table TABLE-X are written.

```
MOVE 75 TO IX.

WRITE OUT-X FROM A-RECORD.

[A-RECORD consists of IX and 75 occurrences of TABLE-X.]
```

Items containing the DEPENDING ON phrase or items subordinate to them cannot be assigned initial values, except for level 88 condition names. If the table has indexes, the indexes must be reset whenever the value of *size* is changed.

A group item containing a DEPENDING ON phrase may be followed, within that record, only by items subordinate to it. Thus a group item containing a DEPENDING ON phrase must be the last group item of its level in the record, but it may contain subordinate items with DEPENDING ON phrases in their descriptions.

Data base management systems make extensive use of varying-size records. Each related portion of a record is termed a *segment*, and in the form of a varying-size table, the segment may be repeated. This repetition is termed a *repeating segment*. There may be several repeating segments within a record, and the repeating segments may themselves contain repeating segments. For example, the record for a school might have a repeating segment for each administrator and a repeating segment for each teacher. Then for each teacher segment, there may be a repeating segment for each student. COBOL compilers that permit several DEPENDING ON phrases and DEPENDING ON phrases to be described for items subordinate to group items with the DEPENDING ON phrase give some of the facility required for data bases, but data base systems generally require a specialized language. However, COBOL serves as a host language to many generalized data base management systems.

III. SEARCH STATEMENT

The simplest and most efficient means of retrieving elements from a table is to use a subscript or index to address the table directly. However, in many applications this is not possible. Suppose that a table containing 12 elements represents a calendar and contains the number of days per month. Then suppose that we are to read in transactions containing a date and retrieve the number of days in the month. A date containing the month as a number from 1 to 12, such as 12/21/76, would allow us to subscript the table directly. But what if the month is in text form, such as JANUARY or FEBRUARY? Then we must store the month name in the table along with the days, and search the table for the matching month. The two usual means of doing this are with a sequential or a binary search. One further technique, the hash search, is described in the next section, and is used less often.

COBOL provides the SEARCH statement to perform a sequential or binary search to locate elements in a table. It functions like the IF/THEN/ELSE statement: SEARCH searches a table for a specified element; if found, one action is taken; if not found, another action is taken.

A *sequential search* examines each element of a table serially, and may be used regardless of the order of the table elements. A *binary search* requires the elements of the table to be arranged in ascending or descending order. The binary search begins in the middle of the table, and continues to the middle of the lower or upper half of the table, depending on whether the current element was high or low. This continues until the element is found or the table is exhausted.

A binary search is more efficient for large tables than is a sequential search, although it requires the table to be in some sort order. Suppose that we are trying to guess a number from 1 to 100, and that the number is 64. With a sequential search we would guess 1, 2, 3, . . . , 64, requiring a total of 64 tries. With a binary search, our first guess is 50 (too low), but we now know that the number must be in the range from 51 to 100, so that with the first guess we have cut the size of the table we need to search in half. Our next guess is 74 (too high), 62 (too low), 68 (too high), 65 (too high), 63 (too low), 64 (found). Thus the 64 is found with only 7 searches. Notice that with each guess, we cut the size of the table that must be searched in half. The larger the table, the more efficient the binary search becomes. To locate the number 643 in a table of 1000 elements would require 643 sequential searches, but only 9 binary searches.

To locate an element in a table with a sequential search, the number of searches is on the order of $N/2$, where N is the number of entries in the table. For a binary search, the number of searches is on the order of $N \log_2 N$. Note also that this assumes that the entry is in the table to find. If the entry is not in the table to find, the number of sequential searches is on the order of N, whereas the number of binary searches is still on the order of $N \log_2 N$.

A sequential search is slightly faster for small tables than is a binary search. A binary search becomes more efficient than a sequential search when there are roughly 60 elements in the table[1], excluding the time it may take to place the table in sort order for the binary search. In general, use a binary search if the table is in ascending or descending order. If a large, unordered table is searched often, sort it and use a binary search.

A. Sequential Search

The sequential SEARCH statement is written as follows.

```
SET index TO start.

SEARCH table

   AT END imperative-statement

   WHEN condition imperative-statement

      .
      .
      .

   WHEN condition imperative-statement.
```

The *index* of *table* must be set to an initial value, usually 1, prior to execution of the SEARCH statement. If *table* has several indexes, set the first index listed in the OCCURS clause because it is used in the search. The search begins with this element, and the WHEN phrases are applied in the order in which they appear. If any *condition* is true, the search terminates with the *index* pointing to the element satisfying the WHEN phrase, and the *imperative-statement* is executed. If no *condition* is true, the *index* is incremented by 1, and the search continues. If the entire table is searched without a *condition* being met, the AT END phrase is executed, and the *index* has no predictable value.

- *table.* A table that must have the OCCURS clause and INDEXED BY phrase in its description. *table* cannot be subscripted or indexed in SEARCH (SEARCH A (IX) is invalid). If the initial *index* value exceeds the size of *table*, the AT END phrase is immediately executed.

- AT END *imperative-statement.* An optional phrase that causes the *imperative-statement* to be executed if the entire *table* is searched without finding the element. Unless the *imperative-statement* is a GO TO, execution then continues with the next executable statement following the SEARCH statement. Execution also continues there if the AT END phrase is omitted. In either case, the *index* has no predictable value.

- WHEN *condition imperative-statement.* *condition* may be a compound condition connected by the logical operations AND, OR, or NOT. The *imperative-statement* is executed when a condition is true, and unless it is a GO TO, execution then continues with the next executable statement following the SEARCH statement. The *index* points to the table element found. NEXT SENTENCE may be coded as the *imperative-statement*, and execution immediately continues with the next executable statement when an element is found.

The following table is set up to contain the names and ages of people.

```
01  PERSON-RECORD.
    05  PERSON          OCCURS 1000 TIMES INDEXED BY IP.
        10  SURNAME     PIC X(5).
        10  AGE         PIC S9(3) COMP-3.
01  IP-SUB             PIC S9(4) COMP.
    [Subscript for PERSON table.]
```

The following statements search the table for a person named SMITH.

```
SET IP TO 1.

SEARCH PERSON

  AT END DISPLAY 'SMITH NOT FOUND.'

  WHEN SURNAME (IP) = 'SMITH'

      PERFORM A20-FOUND-SMITH.
```

The following statements count the number of occurrences in the table of people less than 21 years old and also counts those who are over 45 years old.

```
MOVE ZERO TO AGE21.

              AGE45.

MOVE 1 TO IP-SUB.                [A subscript is used rather than the index
                                 IP because IP ⟩ 1000 is invalid.]

PERFORM B20-SEARCH

  UNTIL IP-SUB ⟩ 1000.


  ▢ ▢ ▢


B20-SEARCH.

    SET IP TO IP-SUB.

    SEARCH PERSON

      AT END SET IP TO 1000

      WHEN AGE (IP) ⟨ 21

            ADD 1 TO AGE21

      WHEN AGE (IP) ⟩ 45

            ADD 1 TO AGE 45.

    SET IP-SUB TO IP.

    ADD 1 TO IP-SUB.

**** EXIT
```

—

Note that if the search were to count all people under 21 plus those over 45, a single WHEN condition could be written as follows.

```
WHEN (AGE (IP) < 21) OR

     (AGE (IP) > 45)

     ADD 1 TO AGE-21-45.
```

Suppose now that we wish to read in a list of names and add each unique name to the end of the PERSON table. There will be a varying number of elements in the PERSON table. One way to do this is to code the DE-PENDING ON phrase in the PERSON table. Another method is to set the first element of the table to some unique characters, such as HIGH-VALUES. As each name is read, the table is searched for the name. If the name is found in the table, it is not stored because it is already in the table. Another WHEN clause also looks for HIGH-VALUES, and if found, stores the name at that point in the table and sets the next element to HIGH-VALUES. The latter technique is illustrated in the following example.

```
MOVE HIGH-VALUES TO SURNAME (1).
```

Now assume that a record is read in, and the person's surname is contained in THE-NAME. The paragraph to store a new name is performed.

```
PERFORM B20-STORE-NEW-PERSON.

 □ □ □

B20-STORE-NEW-PERSON.

    SET IP TO 1.

    SEARCH PERSON

        AT END DISPLAY 'PERSON TABLE FULL'

        WHEN SURFACE (IP) = HIGH-VALUES

            MOVE THE-NAME TO SURNAME (IP)

            PERFORM B30-CHECK-OVERFLOW

        WHEN SURNAME (IP) = THE-NAME

            NEXT SENTENCE.

**** EXIT
```

```
**** STORE HIGH-VALUES IN THE NEXT ELEMENT UNLESS IT WOULD

**** OVERFLOW THE TABLE.

B30-CHECK-OVERFLOW.

    IF IP < 1000

        THEN MOVE HIGH-VALUES TO SURNAME (IP + 1).

**** EXIT

****END OF B20-STORE-NEW-PERSON
```

If you search a table containing a variable number of entries, you must always limit the search to the number of entries in the table. Otherwise, you would continue the search past the entries stored in the table, and since these entries contain unpredictable values, the results too are unpredictable. The DEPENDING ON phrase limits the search, but if it is not used, limit the search with a WHEN clause by testing when the index exceeds the table size; or if you are using HIGH-VALUES at the end of the table, look for them.

```
    SET IP TO 1.

    SEARCH PERSON

        AT END DISPLAY 'NOT FOUND IN TABLE.'

        WHEN SURNAME (IP) = HIGH-VALUES

            DISPLAY 'NOT FOUND IN TABLE.'

        WHEN ...
```

A sequential search is more efficient if the most frequently retrieved elements can be placed at the front of the table. The sequential search can also search a portion of a table. The following example searches elements 100 to 200 of the PERSON table to see if there is a person named SMITH. The AT END phrase is omitted because the search will stop before it reaches the end of the table.

```
    SET IP TO 100.

    SEARCH PERSON

        WHEN IP > 200

            DISPLAY 'SMITH NOT FOUND'
```

```
WHEN SURNAME (IP) = 'SMITH'

   DISPLAY 'SMITH FOUND'.
```

A VARYING *count* phrase may be appended to SEARCH to increment the *count* as each element is searched. Then *count* must first be set to an initial value, usually zero.

```
MOVE ZERO TO count.

SET index TO start.

SEARCH table VARYING count

   AT END imperative-statement

   WHEN condition imperative-statement.
```

* *count.* An index of this or another table, or an numeric integer identifier. If *count* is an index of this *table*, it and not the first index of the *table* is incremented. If *count* is an index from another table or an identifier, it along with the first index of the *table* is incremented. If SEARCH terminates without finding an element, *count* has no predictable value.

The VARYING phrase allows indexes or subscripts for other tables to be incremented in the SEARCH. This saves having to set them when the element is found.

B. Binary Search

The binary SEARCH statement requires that the table being searched be arranged in ascending or descending order based on selected data items (termed *keys*) of the table. These keys must be specified in the data description as follows.

```
ASCENDING KEY IS key-1, key-2, ...

   [Or:]

DESCENDING KEY IS key-1, key-2, ...
```

Each *key* must be the name of a table element. If more than one *key* is listed, they must be listed in decreasing order of significance. The *keys* cannot be COMP-1 or COMP-2 items. The following table indicates that

PERSON is in ascending order based on SURNAME, and that the child of each PERSON is in descending order based on the contents of CHILD.

```
01   PERSON-RECORD.

     05   PERSON              OCCURS 1000 TIMES INDEXED BY PX

                             ASCENDING KEY IS SURNAME.

          10   SURNAME        PIC X(5).

          10   AGE            PIC S9(5) COMP-3.

          10   CHILDREN       OCCURS 5 TIMES INDEXED BY CX

                             DESCENDING KEY IS CHILD.

               15   CHILD     PIC X(5).

01   PX-SUB                   PIC S9(4) COMP.

     [Subscript of PERSON table.]

01   CX-SUB                   PIC S9(4) COMP.

     [Subscript of CHILDREN table.]
```

There cannot be more than 12 keys per table in System/370, and their combined length cannot be greater than 256 bytes. The binary SEARCH statement is coded as follows.

```
SEARCH ALL table

   AT END imperative-statement

   WHEN key = expression imperative-statement.
```

- *table.* A table that has the OCCURS INDEXED BY clause and KEY phrase in its description. The first index listed in the INDEXED BY phrase of *table* is used for the search if there are several, and if an element is found, the *index* points to that element. If an element is not found, the *index* has no predictable value.
- AT END *imperative-statement.* An optional phrase that causes the *imperative-statement* to be executed if the element is not found in *table.* Unless it is a GO TO, execution then continues with the next executable statement following the SEARCH statement. Execution also continues there if the AT END phrase is omitted. In either case, the *index* has no predictable value.

- WHEN *key* = *expression imperative-statement.* The *key* must be described in the KEY phrase for *table.* The *expression* may be a literal, identifier, or arithmetic expression. Several comparisons may be joined by the logical operation AND. Any *keys* in the KEY clause may be tested, but if several *keys* are described, all preceding *keys* must be tested. The *imperative-statement* is executed when the condition is true, and unless it is a GO TO, execution then continues with the next executable statement following the SEARCH statement. The *index* points to the table element found. NEXT SENTENCE may be coded as the *imperative-statement,* and execution immediately continues with the next executable statement if an element is not found.

The following example searches the PERSON table for the age of a person named SMITH.

```
SEARCH ALL PERSON

    AT END MOVE ZERO TO ANS

    WHEN SURNAME (IX) = 'SMITH'

    MOVE AGE (IX) TO ANS.
```

A table may contain duplicate entries; that is, elements with identical *keys.* This does not affect the search, but which entry it finds of a duplicate entry is unpredictable. It will not necessarily be the first of the duplicate entries in the table. The binary search can also search a variable-size table. It is best to use the DEPENDING ON phrase to specify the current size of the table, and the SEARCH statement will not search beyond this. If you are not using the DEPENDING ON phrase, you must fill the table with HIGH-VALUES, assuming the table is in ascending order, beyond the last entry in the table, so that the binary search can work properly.

Both the sequential and binary forms of the SEARCH statement can also search multidimensional tables; the table may be subordinated to an item containing an OCCURS clause. The *index* of the higher-level OCCURS clause must be set before the lower levels can be searched. For example, if we code SEARCH ALL CHILDREN in the previously described PERSON table, PX must first be set, and all table elements, CHILDREN (PX, 1 to 5), are searched. The following example searches all the CHILDREN of each PERSON and prints the SURNAME if a CHILD named 'BOBBY' is found.

```
      PERFORM A10-SEARCH

        VARYING PX-SUB FROM 1 BY 1

        UNTIL PX-SUB 〉 1000.
```

        [Cannot use PX directly because PX 〉 1000 would be invalid.]

      □ □ □

```
A10-SEARCH.

      SET PX TO PX-SUB.

      SEARCH ALL CHILDREN

        WHEN CHILD (PX, CX) = 'BOBBY'

          DISPLAY SURNAME (PX).

**** EXIT
```

The sequential and binary SEARCH statements can also be used in combination to search a multidimensional table. The following example searches for each PERSON whose AGE is greater than 50, and who also has a CHILD named 'BETTY'.

```
      SET PX-SUB TO 1.

      PERFORM A20-SEARCH UNTIL PX-SUB 〉 1000.
```

      □ □ □

```
A20-SEARCH.

      SET PX TO PX-SUB.

      SEARCH PERSON
```

        [A sequential search is used to find the next person over 50.]

```
        AT END DISPLAY 'ALL DONE'

              SET PX TO 1000

        WHEN AGE (IP) 〉 50

          PERFORM A20-PART-A.

      SET PX-SUB TO PX.

      ADD 1 TO PX-SUB.
```

```
**** EXIT

A20-PART-A.

     SEARCH ALL CHILDREN

     [A binary search is used to find any child named 'BETTY'.]

     WHEN CHILD (PX, CX) = 'BETTY'

        DISPLAY SURNAME (PX, CX).

**** EXIT

**** END OF A20-SEARCH
```

IV. HASH TABLES

Sometimes it is impractical to use a sequential or binary search. Perhaps we must add to the table while it is being searched. We could still use a sequential search by adding new entries to the end of the table, or a binary search by finding where the new entry is to be added and moving all the elements from there on down one slot to make room. However, the sequential search or updating the table for a binary search may be too slow.

An alternative is to use what is termed a *hash table*. Rather than searching the table for a match key, we compute a subscript to the table and use it instead. Suppose that we are using a table to retrieve a person's name given a social security number. Suppose further that there are also transactions to add new employees. Assuming that there are 1000 employees to store, we need a technique that will convert the nine-digit social security numbers into numbers ranging from 1 to 1000.

The simplest method is to divide the social security numbers by 1000, take the remainder as it will then range in value from 0 to 999, and add 1 to the remainder to bring it into the subscript range from 1 to 1000. The remainders are more evenly distributed if we divide by the largest prime number less than 1000. (A *prime number* is a number divisible only by 1 and itself, such as 7 and 11.) The largest prime number less than 1000 is 997. If you do not have access to a prime number table, select the largest odd number less than 1000 that does not end in 5. For our example, we shall use 999.

Now to see how this works in practice. The number 520-44-1461 yields a remainder of 423 when divided by 999, and the number 520-44-1462 yields a remainder of 424. So far so good, but the number 558-56-0304 also yields a remainder of 423, the same as 520-44-1461. This raises the problem of *collisions*—when two numbers yield the same remainder. This means that we cannot use the subscript directly. Instead, we use it as the location at which to begin looking for a place to store the entry. This requires that we initialize the table, probably with zeros, so that we can tell if an element contains an entry. We should also increase the size of the table to provide room for the collisions, perhaps to 1500 elements, and then divide by 1499 to compute the subscripts. The larger the table, the less chance of collisions and the more efficient it becomes. The efficiency begins to drop off when the table becomes more than about 70% full.

There is still a problem at the end of the table. What if several social security numbers yield a subscript of 1500? This is solved by wrapping around to the beginning of the table. To retrieve an entry from the table, we compute the subscript from the social security number, and use this as the location at which to begin looking for the social security number in the table.

To illustrate a hash table, we shall use the social security example to add and retrieve a person's name from a table given his social security number. We shall define the table and write procedures to add new entries to the table and to search it. The table is defined as follows.

```
01   SS-TABLE.

        05   SS-NAME          PIC X(25).
*                                 NAME OF PERSON FOR STORING AND
*                                 RETRIEVAL.
        05   SS-NO            PIC S9(9).
*                                 SOCIAL-SECURITY NUMBER FOR
*                                 STORING AND RETRIEVAL.
        05   SS-DIV           PIC S9(9) COMP-3 VALUE 1499.
*                                 LARGEST ODD NUMBER NOT ENDING IN
*                                 5 LESS THAN SS-MAX-SIZE.
        05   SS-TEMP          PIC S9(9) COMP-3.
*                                 SCRATCH STORAGE TO STORE
*                                 DIVIDEND.
```

```
    05  SS-MAX-SIZE          PIC S9(4) COMP SYNC VALUE 1500.
*                            SIZE OF PERSON ARRAY.
    05  SS-SUBSCRIPT         PIC S9(9) COMP-3.
*                            COMPUTED SUBSCRIPT.
    05  SS-PERSON            OCCURS 1500 TIMES INDEXED BY IP.
        10  SS-PERSON-NO     PIC S9(9).
*                            SOCIAL SECURITY NUMBER.
        10  SS-PERSON-NAME   PIC X(25).
*                            NAME OF PERSON.
```

□ □ □

[First zero out the PERSON array.]

```
PERFORM A20-ZERO-PERSON

    VARYING SS-SUBSCRIPT FROM 1 BY 1

    UNTIL SS-SUBSCRIPT ⟩ SS-MAX-SIZE.
```

□ □ □

```
A20-ZERO-PERSON.

    MOVE ZEROS TO SS-PERSON-NO  (SS-SUBSCRIPT).

**** EXIT
```

Next, we must write a procedure to add entries to the table. The person's name must first be moved to SS-NAME, and the social security number to SS-NO. The procedure is performed as follows:

```
MOVE social-security-number TO SS-NO.

MOVE person's-name to SS-NAME.

PERFORM C10-ADD-NAME.
```

The procedure is written as follows:

```
**** PROCEDURE TO ADD ENTRIES TO PERSON TABLE.
C10-ADD-NAME.
      DIVIDE SS-NO BY SS-DIV GIVING SS-TEMP REMAINDER SS-SUBSCRIPT.
      ADD 1 TO SS-SUBSCRIPT.
      SET IP TO SS-SUBSCRIPT.
      SEARCH SS-PERSON
        AT END PERFORM C10-WRAP-AROUND
        WHEN SS-PERSON-NO (IP) = ZEROS
          MOVE SS-NO TO SS-PERSON-NO (IP)
          MOVE SS-NAME TO SS-PERSON-NAME (IP).
**** EXIT
C10-WRAP-AROUND.
      SET IP TO 1.
      SEARCH SS-PERSON
        WHEN IP = SS-SUBSCRIPT
          DISPLAY 'ERROR - SS-PERSON TABLE FULL, RUN TERMINATED.'
          DISPLAY 'INCREASE SS-PERSON- SS-DIV, SS-MAX-SIZE AND
            RECOMPILE.'
          GO TO Z90-STOP-RUN
        WHEN SS-PERSON-NO (IP) = ZEROS
          MOVE SS-NO TO SS-PERSON-NO (IP)
          MOVE SS-NAME TO SS-PERSON-NAME (IP).
**** EXIT
**** END OF C10-ADD-NAME
```

We also need a procedure to retrieve a person's name given the social security number. The social security number is first moved to SS-NO, and the name is returned in SS-NAME. If the name is not found, SS-NAME contains spaces. The procedure is invoked as follows.

```
      MOVE social-security-number TO SS-NO.

      PERFORM C20-RETRIEVE-NAME.
```

The procedure is written as follows.

```
**** PROCEDURE TO RETRIEVE A PERSONS NAME.

C20-RETRIEVE-NAME.

    DIVIDE SS-NO BY SS-DIV GIVING SS-TEMP

       REMAINDER SS-SUBSCRIPT.

    ADD 1 TO SS-SUBSCRIPT.

    SET IP SS-SUBSCRIPT.

    SEARCH SS-PERSON

       AT END PERFORM A20-WRAP-AROUND

       WHEN SS-PERSON-NO (IP) = ZERO

          MOVE SPACES TO SS-NAME

       WHEN SS-NO = SS-PERSON-NO (IP)

          MOVE SS-PERSON-NAME (IP) TO SS-NAME.

**** EXIT

C20-WRAP-AROUND.

    SET IP TO 1.

    SEARCH SS-PERSON

       WHEN IP = SS-SUBSCRIPT

          MOVE SPACES TO SS-NAME

       WHEN SS-NO = SS-PERSON-NO (IP)

          MOVE SS-PERSON-NAME (IP) TO SS-NAME.

**** EXIT

**** END OF C20-RETRIEVE-NAME
```

There still remains a problem if the key is alphanumeric rather than numeric. This is solved in System/370 by moving the alphanumeric item to a computational data item. (It cannot exceed 18 digits.) When moved to such an item, the zone bits are removed from the alphanumeric characters to yield only numeric digits. For example, A to I becomes 1 to 9, J to R becomes 1 to 9, and S to Z becomes 2 to 9. The following example illustrates this. The person's name and not the social security number is used to compute the subscript.

```
    05   SS—NAME              PIC X(25).

    05   SS—SHORT—NAME REDEFINES SS—NAME PIC X(18).

    05   SS—CONVERT           PIC S9(18) COMP.


    □  □  □

    MOVE SS—SHORT—NAME TO SS—CONVERT.

    DIVIDE SS—CONVERT BY SS—DIV GIVING SS—TEMP
      REMAINDER SS—SUBSCRIPT.
```

Fortunately, hash tables are not often needed. For a table with few entries, a sequential search would be simpler and more efficient. If only a few entries are added to the table but it is searched often, we might use a binary search and move all the entries in the table down to make room for a new entry. The hash table technique is also used for direct-access I/O in which the entries are records stored in a direct file rather than as elements of a table in memory.

VI. READING IN TABLES

Often a table is read in from a file. In the following example a personnel file is read and the employee IDs are stored in a table, perhaps to validate transactions with a binary search. There are several things to note in this example. First, the payroll file has 1000-byte records, but we will need to save only the 10-byte employee ID. The table is a variable-size table because the number of employees will change. If the table overflows, a message is printed telling how to change the program. The payroll file must be sorted in ascending order on the employee ID, and the program checks to ensure that this has been done.

```
WORKING—STORAGE SECTION.

77  OLD—ID               PIC X(10).

*                                       OLD—ID CHECKS THE SORT ORDER OF

*                                       THE INPUT FILE.

**** EMPLOYEE FILE.  RECORD LENGTH = 1000.

01  EMPLOYEE.

    05  EMPLOYEE—ID       PIC X(10).
```

```
    05  FILLER            PIC X(990).

**** TABLE OF EMPLOYEE IDS.

01  ID-RECORD.

    05  ID-MAX            PIC S9(4) COMP VALUE 1000.

*                                        MAXIMUM NUMBER OF IDS IN TABLE.

    05  ID-NO             PIC S9(4) COMP VALUE ZERO.

*                                        CURRENT SIZE OF TABLE.

    05  ID-TABLE          OCCURS 0 TO 1000 TIMES DEPENDING ON ID-NO

                          INDEXED BY IDX

                          ASCENDING KEY IS ID-ID.

    10  ID-ID             PIC X(10).

    □ □ □

    OPEN INPUT PAY-IN.

    MOVE LOW-VALUES TO EMPLOYEE-ID,

                  OLD-ID.
```

[EMPLOYEE-ID is set to HIGH-VALUES at end-of-file, and OLD-ID checks the sequence of the input file.]

```
    PERFORM B20-STORE-IDS

      UNTIL EMPLOYEE-ID = HIGH-VALUES.

    □ □ □

B20-STORES-IDS.

    READ PAY-IN INTO EMPLOYEE

      AT END MOVE HIGH-VALUES TO EMPLOYEE-ID.

    IF EMPLOYEE-ID NOT = HIGH-VALUES

        THEN PERFORM B20-PART-A.
```

```
**** EXIT

B20-PART-A.

    IF EMPLOYEE-ID < OLD-ID

        THEN DISPLAY 'ERROR - PAYROLL FILE NOT IN SORT, RUN TERMINATED.'

            DISPLAY 'OLD ID: ', OLD-ID, ' CURRENT ID: ', EMPLOYEE-ID

            GO TO Z90-STOP-RUN.

    MOVE EMPLOYEE-ID TO OLD-ID.

    ADD 1 TO ID-NO.

    IF ID-NO > ID-MAX

        THEN DISPLAY 'ERROR - ID-TABLE OVERFLOW, RUN TERMINATED.'

            DISPLAY 'PAYROLL RECORD: ', EMPLOYEE-ID

            DISPLAY 'INCREASE ID-MAX, ID-TABLE AND RECOMPILE PROGRAM.'

            GO TO Z90-STOP-RUN.

    MOVE EMPLOYEE-ID TO ID-ID (ID-NO).

**** EXIT

**** END OF B20-STORE-ID
```

Now whenever an ID is to be validated, the following can be coded.

```
SEARCH ALL ID-TABLE

    AT END statement-if-not-found

    WHEN ID-ID (IDX) = id

        statement-if-found.
```

This example works for System/370 COBOL, but it violates the ANS Standard because ID-NO is permitted to contain a value of zero when the table is empty. To comply with the ANS Standard, ID-NO could not have a value of zero, ID-TABLE would have to be described as OCCURS 1 TO 1000 rather than 0 TO 1000, and a separate flag would have to be set up to indicate whether the table was empty. Then this flag would have to be tested to ensure that the table is not empty before the SEARCH statement is executed. This would require several changes to the program, and the SEARCH statement would be coded as follows.

```
IF flag = value-if-table-empty

    THEN statement-if-not-found

    ELSE SEARCH ALL ID-TABLE

        AT END statement-if-not-found

        WHEN ID-ID (IDX) = id

            statement-if-found.
```

VI. TREE STRUCTURES

Tree structures are sometimes required in COBOL to represent hierarchical data. For example, a company may be divided into several divisions, with each division further subdivided. This organization can be represented by a tree structure. Figure 2 shows a company's organization chart, in which each box represents an organizational unit, which is assigned a unique number.

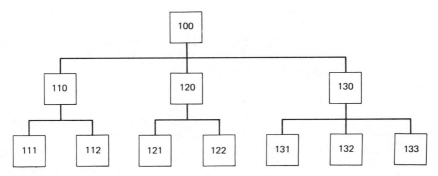

FIGURE 2. Organization chart represented by a tree structure.

One way to represent such a tree structure is to let the department numbers themselves specify the hierarchy. In Figure 2, the first digit represents level 1 of the organization, the second digit level 2, and the third digit level 3. The department table for such a numbering convention would be as follows.

Department Number	Department Name
100	Computer Division
110	Operations Department
111	Computer Operators
112	Bursting and Decollating
120	Programming Department
.	
.	
.	

If the department table is sorted on the department number, it is also placed in hierarchical order. The COBOL statements necessary to contain this department table are as follows.

```
01  DEPARTMENT.

    05  DEPT-SIZE                    PIC S9(4) COMP.

    05  DEPT-TABLE OCCURS 0 TO 100 TIMES DEPENDING ON

            DEPTH-SIZE INDEXED BY X-DEPT.

        10  DEPTH-NO                 PIC X(3).

        10  DEPT-NAME          ·     PIC X(25).
```

The table has a varying size because departments are likely to be added or deleted. If the department table were contained in a file, each record would contain a department, and the records could be read into the DEPT-TABLE.

Tree structures must often be searched, but the search is usually to locate all the entries above or below a specific entry in the hierarchy. For example, if we were adding a new department, we would want to make sure that the departments above it in the hierarchy exist. The number itself contains the hierarchy so that if department 113 is added, we would search for departments 110 and 100. If we delete a department, we may want to delete all departments below it in the hierarchy. To search down in the hierarchy, we must find all records whose high-order digits match this one. For example, if we delete department 110, we could search the table to find all departments that are numbered 11x and delete them too.

The disadvantage of this technique, in which the numbers themselves specify the hierarchy, is that you may run out of numbers or you may want to transfer one number to be under another. For example, we may want to transfer department 111 to be under department 120. For this, we must store the full upward hierarchy for each record. Such a table would look as follows.

Department Number	Level	Upward Hierarchy	Department Name
100	1	100	Computer Division
110	2	100 110	Operations Department
111	3	100 110 111	Computer Operations
112	3	100 110 112	Bursting and Decollating
120	2	100 120	Programming Department
.			
.			
.			

The department numbers are arbitrary and signify nothing. To transfer department 111 under department 120, we change the record for department 111 as follows:

111	3	100 120 111	Computer Operators

Notice that the department number is stored twice in each record. This is redundant data, but it is necessary for sorting the department table on the department numbers into hierarchical order. The COBOL statements to contain the table would be as follows.

```
01   DEPARTMENT.
     05   DEPT-SIZE                PIC S9(4) COMP.
     05   DEPT-TABLE OCCURS 1 TO 100 TIMES
                   DEPENDING ON DEPT-SIZE
                   INDEXED BY X-DEPT.
          10   DEPTH-NO            PIC X(3).
          10   DEPTH-LEVEL         PIC 9.
          10   DEPT-UP-HIER.
               15   DEPT-1         PIC X(3).
               15   DEPT-2         PIC X(3).
               15   DEPT-3         PIC X(3).
          10   DEPT-NAME           PIC X(25).
```

It is easy to find all the departments above any department in the hierarchy because the upward hierarchy is contained in each record. To find all the departments below a given department, search the table for those records whose hierarchy points to this department. For example, to find all departments belonging to department 110, which is a level 2 department, look for all records whose DEPT-2 is '110'.

Tracing down in the tree structure is more complicated if the entire table cannot be contained in memory. We could read the entire department file sequentially to find the records below a given record in the hierarchy, but this may be expensive if the file is large. An alternative is to store for each department all those departments that belong to it in the hierarchy. The record for such a file would look as follows.

Department Number	Level	Upward Hierarchy	Next-Level-Down Hierarchy
100	1	100	120 130
110	2	100 110	111 112
111	3	100 110 111	
112	3	100 110 112	
120	2	100 120	121 122
.			
.			
.			

The COBOL statements to describe the records in the file would be as follows.

```
01   DEPT-RECORD.

     05   DEPT-NO                    PIC X(3).

     05   DEPT-LEVEL                 PIC 9.

     05   DEPT-UP-HIER.

          10   DEPT-1                PIC X(3).

          10   DEPT-2                PIC X(3).

          10   DEPT-3                PIC X(3).

     05   DEPT-DOWN-COUNT            PIC S9(3) COMP-3.
```

```
05  DEPT-DOWN-HIER OCCURS 1 TO 100 TIMES

                 DEPENDING ON DEPT-DOWN-COUNT

                 INDEXED BY X-DOWN.

     10  DEPT-DOWN            PIC X(3).
```

This record would be especially useful for direct or indexed files in which records can be accessed directly. To read all records above a given department, we would use the upward hierarchy as the key and read these records directly. To read all records below a given department, we would use the downward hierarchy and read these records directly. If necessary, we could use the downward hierarchy of the records that are read to go down to the next level in the hierarchy. This could continue until we have read all the records.

An alternative way of tracing down the tree structure is to keep only one downward pointer and then keep a side pointer. (Such a structure is termed a *binary tree* because each element has only two pointers.) Thus one can go down one level in the hierarchy with the down pointer and then look at all items at this level with the side pointers. The table would look as follows:

Department Number	Level	Upward Hierarchy	Down Pointer	Side Pointer
100	1	100	110	—
110	2	100 110	111	120
111	3	100 110 111	—	112
112	3	100 110 112	—	—
120	2	100 120	121	130
.				
.				
.				

To find all the level 2 entries in the table given the department 100, we would use the down pointer to locate 120, and then the side pointer to locate 120, then the side pointer of 120 to locate 130. The advantage of this type of organization over the previous one is that we need not guess the maximum number of entries at each level; only one down pointer and one side pointer are needed. On the other hand, it is slower and more complicated to find all the entries at the next level down if the records reside in a file.

The COBOL statements to describe the records in the file would be as follows:

```
01   DEPT-RECORD.
     05   DEPT-NO          PIC X(3).
     05   DEPT-LEVEL       PIC 9.
     05   DEPT-UP-HIER.
          10   DEPT-1      PIC X(3).
          10   DEPT-2      PIC X(3).
          10   DEPT-3      PIC X(3).
     05   DEPT-DOWN-PTR    PIC X(3).
     05   DEPT-SIDE-PTR    PIC X(3).
```

This completes the discussion of records and tables. There are many other sophisticated record and data structures used in computing, but they generally require dynamic storage allocation and a facility for operating on storage addresses, and COBOL cannot accommodate them. The next chapters go on to describe how the COBOL statements are coded in a program and how the data are stored and transmitted for input/output. But before this, System/370 Job Control Language must be explained because System/370 programs cannot be run nor input/output accomplished without it.

EXERCISES

1. Define a table to contain numbers with a maximum magnitude of 999.99. The table is to contain 100 elements. Write the statements necessary to fill the table with the numbers from 1 to 100.

2. Define two numeric tables named HOURS and SALARY with dimensions 50 by 20. Multiply the corresponding elements of each table together and store the results in a table named WAGES having the same dimensions. All elements are to have precision S9(7)V9(2).

3. Define a numeric table named TABLES containing 200 elements. The largest number the table is to contain is 9.9999. Assume that the table is unordered and write the statements necessary to count the number of times the number 3.6257 appears in the table. Then write the statements to see if the number 0.7963 is in the table. Finally, assume that the table is in ascending numeric order and write the statements necessary to determine if the number 2.1537 is in the table.

4. Define a table named CITY to contain the population of each of 3 cities within each county, 30 counties within each state, and 50 states. What is the size of the table? Write the statements necessary to sum the total population for all states.

5. A single-dimensional table named POPULATION contains 100 numeric elements. Define the table and sort the values of the table into ascending numerical order.

6. Declare and initialize a table named CALENDAR containing 12 elements of nine characters each to contain the names of the months. The first element would contain 'JANUARY', and so on.

7. A table named LOTS has 100 elements, and each element contains four characters. Count the occurrences of the characters 'ABCD' and 'CDBA' in the table.

8. Define a table named TEXT-A containing 50 elements of 9 characters each. Define two character data items named EVEN and ODD containing 225 characters each. Create two character-strings from TEXT-A by concatenating all of the even and all of the odd elements and store them in EVEN and ODD.

9. A table named AMOUNT has 100 elements. Sum the even elements from 2 up to and including element 50, and every third element from 15 to 100, but stop the summation if the total exceeds 1000.

REFERENCE

1. William Gear, *Computer Organization and Programming*, McGraw-Hill Book Company, New York, 1974, pp. 383, 384.

ten

SYSTEM/370
JOB CONTROL LANGUAGE

Job Control Language (JCL) is not a part of COBOL, but nothing can be done in System/370 COBOL without it. JCL is closely entwined with many of the COBOL statements, serving as the link between the operating system, the hardware devices, and the COBOL program. JCL applies only to System/370, and those using COBOL with other computers and operating systems will find the references to JCL less useful. However, most other computers and operating systems have something comparable, although rarely as complex. System/370 is also so widely used that most programmers will come into contact with it some time in their careers. The following brief introduction to JCL gives its form and purpose, but is not exhaustive. Various other JCL features are described throughout the book where they apply.

JCL consists of a set of statements that direct the execution of the computer programs and describe the input/output devices used.

I. JOB STATEMENT

The JOB statement denotes the start of a computer job, which may itself consist of several computer programs to be run in sequence. A typical JOB statement is coded as follows, but each installation will establish its own requirements.

```
//TEST#9   JOB   (5542,30),'PAYROLL JOB',CLASS=A.
```

TEST # 9 is the job name, the (5542,30) is installation-defined accounting information, 'PAYROLL JOB' is any text the programmer wants to use to further identify the job, and the CLASS = A specifies a job class defined by the installation and is used by the operating system to schedule the job. For example, there might be a job class for quick turnaround and one for overnight service.

II. EXEC STATEMENT

Each program within a job is executed in what is termed a *job step*, or simply a *step*. A typical job might consist of a compile step to convert the COBOL statements into machine language, a linkage editor step to combine the compiled program with other subroutines in subroutine libraries, and an execution step to actually run the job. This entails the execution of three separate programs—the compiler and linkage editor, which are systems programs, and the user's program. Each step begins with a single EXEC statement, which specifies the program to execute and may be identified with a step name.

```
//stepname  EXEC  PGM=program
```

[*stepname* and *program* must be 1 to 8 alphanumeric characters with the first character alphabetic. JCL considers the characters A to Z, @ $ # to be alphabetic.]

```
//STEP1  EXEC  PGM=RUN12
```

The JCL statements have had several optional keyword parameters, which can be coded in any order.

```
//STEP1  EXEC  PGM=RUN12,REGION=104K,PARM='XREF'
```

[Same as:]

```
//STEP1  EXEC  PGM=RUN12,PARM='XREF',REGION=104K
```

If the program is in the system library, you need not specify the library containing the program. If the program is not in the system library, but in your own library, specify this library either in a JOBLIB statement immediately following the JOB statement or in a STEPLIB statement following the EXEC statement.

```
//TEST#9   JOB   (5542,30),'PAYROLL JOB',CLASS=A

//JOBLIB   DD   DSN=library,DISP=SHR
```

[The JOBLIB statement applies to all steps within the job. The system will first search this library and then the system library for each program.]

```
//STEP1   EXEC   PGM=RUN12

//STEPLIB   DD   DSN=library,DISP=SHR
```

[A STEPLIB applies only to the step it follows and overrides any JOBLIB statement for that step. The system will search the library specified in the STEPLIB statement, and then the system library to find RUN12.]

III. DD STATEMENT

Each *file* or *data set* (the terms are used interchangeably) is described by a DD statement.

```
//FILEIN   DD   DSN=PAYROLL,DISP=(OLD,KEEP),

//   UNIT=3330,VOL=SER=222222
```

[To continue a statement, break it at a comma, code // in columns 1 and 2, and continue anywhere in columns 4 to 16.]

The DD statement is assigned the name FILEIN, and defines a file named PAYROLL. PAYROLL is an OLD file that we want to KEEP after it is read. It is contained on a 3330 disk unit with a volume serial number 222222. JCL statements are continued as shown in this example by breaking the statement at the comma following a parameter, coding a // in columns 1 and 2 of the next line, leaving a blank, and continuing the statement.

The most-used parameters of the rather complex DD statement are as follows.

```
//ddname   DD   DSN=file-name,

//   DISP=(beginning-disposition,ending-disposition),

//   UNIT=device,VOL=SER=volume,
```

```
//  SPACE=(direct-access-storage-space),

//  DCB=(record-size-and-blocking)
```

- *ddname.* The 1 to 8 alphanumeric character name; first character alphabetic. The file is associated with the *ddname* through the COBOL SELECT statement.
- DSN = *file-name.* Specifies the 1 to 8 character name of the file, first character alphabetic. Names may be *qualified* by separating them by a period such as LAX.UNITED, or LAX.WESTERN. Temporary files that are to exist only for the duration of the job are specified by appending two ampersands (&&*file-name*) to the file name.
- DISP. Specifies the status of the file at the start of the step and the disposition of the file at the end of that step.

- *beginning-disposition:*

  - NEW. Specifies that a new file is to be written. The file is positioned to the starting point, and the UNIT, VOL, and DCB parameters are usually required, as is SPACE for files on direct-access storage.
  - OLD. Specifies an existing file to be read or written. The program is given exclusive use of the file, and the system positions to the start of the file.
  - SHR. Specifies an existing file that is to be read. Other programs may concurrently read the file, and SHR should always be used for reading system libraries. The system positions to the start of the file.
  - MOD. Create the file if it does not exist (same as NEW), or add to the end of the file if it does exist. Positions to the start of the file if it is created, or to the end of the file if it already exists.

- *ending-disposition:*

  - KEEP. Keep the file. Disk files are not scratched, but are retained, and tape files are rewound and dismounted, freeing the tape drive for other jobs.
  - CATLG. Same as KEEP, but in addition *catalogs* the file in the system catalog. The file name, unit, and volume serial number are entered in the catalog so that the file can later be retrieved by name without specifying the UNIT and VOL parameters.
  - UNCATLG. Same as KEEP, except that the file is uncataloged.
  - DELETE. Delete the file. Uncatalogs the file if it was cataloged, and releases direct-access storage space. Tapes are rewound and dismounted.

- PASS.   Pass the file on to subsequent job steps and let them determine the final disposition. Tape files are rewound, but not dismounted.

A disposition of NEW is assumed if no beginning disposition is specified. Thus DISP=(,KEEP) is the same as DISP=(NEW,KEEP). If no ending disposition is specified, the file is left as it was at the start of the job step; NEW files become DELETE, and existing files are KEEP or PASS if the file was passed from a previous step.

- UNIT=*device*.   Specifies the device, either by the device number such as 3330 or by an installation-defined name such as SYSDA.
- VOL=SER=*volume*.   Specifies the tape volume or disk pack.
- DCB.   Specifies the record format (RECFM), record length (LRECL), and blocking (BLKSIZE).
RECFM specifies the record format:
  - RECFM=F.   Fixed-length records.
  - RECFM=FB.   Fixed-length blocked records.
  - RECFM=V.   Variable-length records.
  - RECFM=VB.   Variable-length blocked records.
  - RECFM=U.   Undefined-length records.

LRECL=*length* specifies the record length in bytes. BLKSIZE=*length* specifies the block length in bytes.

The DCB information must be supplied when the file is created. If the information is coded in the program with the BLOCK CONTAINS clause, the DCB parameter may be omitted. However, one should not specify the blocking in the program so that it can be changed in the DCB parameter without recompiling the program. The file name and the DCB information are written into the label of the file. This enables the DCB parameter to be omitted for OLD files, and the information is obtained from the file label.

The DCB information can come from three sources; from the program in either the BLOCK CONTAINS and RECORDING MODE clauses or the record descriptions in the record area, from the DCB parameter on the DD statement, and from the file label, assuming that it is an old file. The DCB information coded in the program overrides that coded in the DCB parameter, and that coded in the DCB parameter overrides that contained in the file label. The DCB information may come from any of the three sources, but it must all be present when the file is opened.

SPACE. Specifies the amount of space to allocate on direct-access storage devices. See Table 3 for the device storage capacities.

```
CYL
TRK
blocks
```

SPACE=(_ _ _ _,(primary,secondary))

- CYL. Allocate space in units of cylinders.
- TRK. Allocate space in units of tracks.
- *blocks*. Allocate space in units of blocks of the length specified. The *blocks* should equal the BLKSIZE parameter. Always allocate in units of blocks where possible because the amount of space allocated with TRK and CYL depends on the hardware device.
- *primary*. The number of units of primary storage to allocate. This space is always allocated.
- *secondary*. The number of units of space for each secondary allocation. This space is allocated only if the primary space is exceeded. The secondary allocation may occur in subsequent runs. The system will allocate the secondary allocation a total of 15 times if required. Beyond this, the program is terminated for lack of space. The total possible allocation is *primary* + 15(*secondary*). (For multiple-volume data sets, 16 secondary allocations may be made on the second and subsequent volumes.) Table 3 shows the track capacity of various direct-access storage devices.

TABLE 3.   Direct-Access Storage Device Capacities

Device Type	Track Capacity (bytes)	Tracks per Cylinder	Number of Cylinders	Total Capacity (bytes)
2305-1 drum	14,136	8	48	5,428,224
2305-2 drum	14,660	8	96	11,258,880
2314/2319 disk	7,294	20	200	29,176,000
3330/3333 disk (Model 1)	13,030	19	404	100,018,280
3330/3333 disk (Model 2)	13,030	19	808	200,036,560
3340 disk	8,368	12	696	69,889,536
			348	34,944,768
3350 disk	19,069	30	555	317,498,850

Reprinted by permission from "OS/VS Data Management Services Guide." © 1975 by International Business Machines Corporation.

The RLSE parameter can also be coded in the SPACE parameter to release unused space.

```
CYL
TRK
blocks
```

```
SPACE=(_ _ _ _,(primary, secondary),RLSE)
```

```
SPACE=(TRK,(100,20),RLSE)
```

RLSE releases the unused space when the file is closed. Space is released in units of cylinders for CYL; otherwise it is released in units of tracks. For example, the space parameter above allocates 100 primary tracks, but if only 30 tracks are used, the excess 70 tracks are released. RLSE should be coded except for temporary files (the entire space will be released anyway) and for files in which more data will be added later such as program libraries.

The following example illustrates the creation of a disk file.

```
//FILEIN   DD   DSN=PAYROLL,DISP=(NEW,CATLG),

//   UNIT=DISK,VOL=SER=222222,

//   DCB=(RECFM=FB,LRECL=80,BLKSIZE=1600),SPACE=(1600,(100,20))
```

The file is retrieved in a subsequent job step or job as follows.

```
//FILEIN   DD   DSN=PAYROLL,DISP=SHR
```

Several files are concatenated for input to act as if they were all one file by coding a DD statement for each file in the order the files are to be read. Only the first file is given a ddname. To the program, it will appear as if only a single file is being read. The files must all reside on the same type of device and have the same record lengths and blocking. The following example concatenates three files for input.

```
//INPUT   DD   DSN=CITY,DISP=SHR

//        DD   DSN=COUNTY,DISP=SHR

//        DD   DSN=STATE,DISP=SHR
```

Dummy files are indicated with the DUMMY parameter coded immediately following the DD. Dummy files give an immediate end-of-file if read, and the output is ignored if they are written. They are often used for testing and to suppress unwanted output. Code the DCB = BLKSIZE = *blocksize* parameter for all dummy files.

```
//SYSOUT   DD   DUMMY,DCB=BLKSIZE=133
```

IV. COMMENT STATEMENT

JCL also has comment statements, denoted by a //* in columns 1 to 3, and they can be interspersed with the JCL statements.

```
//*   COMMENTS IN COLUMNS 4 TO 80
```

Use comment statements as necessary throughout the JCL to describe what the reader needs to know. A solid line of asterisks as comment statements following each EXEC statement makes the steps easier to locate in the listing.

```
//STEP6  EXEC   SORT
//************************************************************
//********   SORT THE PAYROLL MASTER FILE ON ASCENDING
//********   EMPLOYEE NAME
//************************************************************
```

V. EXAMPLE OF JCL

The next example illustrates how the JCL statements are coded to form a complete job. The example is a greatly simplified and hypothetical compile, linkage editor, and execution step. The statements alone are listed first, and then each statement is explained.

```
//TEST#9   JOB   (5542,30),'PAYROLL JOB',CLASS=A
//COB  EXEC   PGM=COBOL
//SYSIN  DD   *
COBOL statements
//SYSLIN  DD   DSN=&&LOADSET,DISP=(NEW,PASS),
```

```
//   UNIT=3330,VOL=SER=222222,

//   DCB=(RECFM=FB,LRECL=80,BLKSIZE=3120),SPACE=(3120,(8,16))

//SYSPRINT   DD   SYSOUT=A

//LKED   EXEC   PGM=LINKEDIT

//SYSPRINT   DD   SYSOUT=A

//SYSLIN   DD   DSN=&&LOADSET,DISP=(OLD,DELETE)

//SYSLMOD   DD   DSN=&&GOSET(GO),DISP=(NEW,PASS),

//   UNIT=3330,VOL=SER=222222,SPACE=(3072,(20,1))

//GO   EXEC   PGM=*.LKED.SYSLMOD

//SYSOUT   DD   SYSOUT=A
```

Now we shall examine each statement in detail.

```
//COB   EXEC   PGM=COBOL
```

> [Assume that the COBOL compiler program name is COBOL. Since it is contained in the system library, no JOBLIB or STEPLIB statement is needed.]

```
//SYSIN   DD   *
```

COBOL statements

> [SYSIN specifies the COBOL program to compile. The DD * tells the system that the file is contained on cards following the DD * statement.]

```
//SYSLIN   DD   DSN=&&LOADSET,DISP=(NEW,PASS),

//   UNIT=3330,VOL=SER=222222,

//   DCB=(RECFM=FB,LRECL=80,BLKSIZE=3120),SPACE=(3120,(8,16))
```

> [SYSLIN specifies the file to contain the compiled program. The two ampersands preceding the file name indicate that it is a temporary file. The DISP is NEW to create the file and PASS to pass it to the next step. The output from the compiler is termed an *object module*, and it must be link edited before it can be executed. The DCB parameter specifies fixed blocked records (RECFM = FB), a record length of 80 bytes (LRECL = 80), and a block size of 3120 bytes (BLKSIZE = 3120). The DCB information is written in the file label and need not be specified in retrieving the file. The SPACE parameter requests space in units of 3120-byte blocks. The primary allocation is 8 blocks, and the secondary allocation is 16 blocks. The secondary allocation is done only as needed, a total of 15 times if necessary.]

```
//SYSPRINT  DD  SYSOUT=A
```

[SYSPRINT specifies the file to print the source listing. The DD SYSOUT = A directs the output to a printer. SYSOUT = B directs the output to the card punch, and other output classes may be defined by the installation for high-volume output or special forms.]

```
//LKED  EXEC  PGM=LINKEDIT
```

[Executes the linkage editor program. The linkage editor combines the compiled program with any subroutines, system I/O routines, and other system routines, to form what is termed a *load module* that can be executed.]

```
//SYSLIN  DD  DSN=&&LOADSET,DISP=(OLD,DELETE)
```

[The input to this step is the output from the previous step. The DISP is OLD because the file already exists, and DELETE to scratch it at the end of the step. For passed or cataloged files, the UNIT and VOL need not be specified.]

```
//SYSLMOD  DD  DSN=&&GOSET(GO),DISP=(NEW,PASS),
//  UNIT=3330,VOL=SER=222222,SPACE=(3072,(20,20,1))
```

[SYSLMOD defines the linkage editor output which is a *load module* capable of being executed. It is placed in a *library* or *partitioned data set* that contains one or more sequential subfiles, termed *members.* New members can be added or old members replaced in permanent libraries. This library is a temporary file named GOSET, and the member name is GO. The DCB parameter is omitted, indicating that all the DCB information is hard-wired in the linkage editor program. If the DCB information is not hard-wired in a program, it can be specified in the DCB parameter. The SPACE parameter requests 20 blocks of primary space, 20 blocks of secondary space, and 1 directory block. *Directory blocks* contain the names of the partitioned data set members, and each block can contain roughly five member names.]

```
//GO  EXEC  PGM=*.LKED.SYSLMOD
```

[The *.LKED.SYSLMOD is termed a *referback*, and it points to the previous step and ddname containing the member to execute.]

```
//SYSOUT  DD  SYSOUT=A
```

[SYSOUT directs the COBOL execution messages to the printer.]

These JCL statements may seem formidable, and they are only a part of the statements actually needed. The JCL may be made into a *cataloged procedure* by placing it in a partitioned data set and then invoking it by its name. If the previous JCL were made into a cataloged procedure named COBUCLG, it could be invoked as follows.

```
//TEST#9  JOB  (5542,30),'PAYROLL RUN',CLASS=A

//  EXEC  COBUCLG

//COB.SYSIN  DD  *
```
COBOL statements

The cataloged procedure has three steps—a compile step named COB, a linkage editor step named LKED, and an execution step named GO. The COB.SYSIN DD statement specifies that SYSIN is to apply to the COB step. The step name must be appended to the ddname so that the system will know which step the DD statement is to apply.

This completes the brief description of JCL, and covers most of what is needed for COBOL programming. Several other features are discussed in the chapters that follow on program organization and input/output. JCL is a difficult language because it violates many of the criteria developed in Chapter 2 and because it deals with a complex subject: the interface between a program and the computer's operating system and hardware. Unlike COBOL, in which many features become easy through constant use, many JCL features are used so seldom that they never become familiar. JCL does simplify many exotic requirements, but it also makes many simple requirements needlessly complex. Consequently, it accounts for a large portion of the programming problems.

REFERENCES

1. "IBM System/360 Operating System: Job Control Language Reference," Order No. GC28-6704, IBM Corporation, Poughkeepsie, N. Y., 1973.
2. "IBM System/360 Operating System: Job Control Language User's Guide," Order No. GC28-6703, IBM Corporation, Poughkeepsie, N. Y., 1970.

eleven

PROGRAM ORGANIZATION

Now we can begin to piece the COBOL statements together to form a complete program. First we examine the ways in which individual statements can be grouped.

I. STATEMENT GROUPINGS

COBOL has three groupings of statements: the statement group, paragraphs, and sections. The *statement group* (not a COBOL term) is one or more statements executed in sequence as if they were a single statement. They are placed in the clauses of conditional statements, such as the IF, SEARCH, and READ statements, to form a unit of code. A *paragraph* consists of all statements following a paragraph name, up to the next paragraph name. It groups statements together, enabling them to be executed by the PERFORM statement. A *section* consists of one or more paragraphs that are to be performed together, and additionally permits portions of the program to be overlaid, sharing the same storage area.

A. Statement Groups

Statement groups consist of several statements that may be placed wherever a single statement may go. The last statement is terminated by a period or another clause or phrase, such as the ELSE or WHEN. The following example shows the use of a statement group in an **IF** and a **SEARCH** statement.

```
IF A = B
    THEN MOVE 1 TO I                    ⎫
            COMPUTE J = K * 2           ⎬  [Statement group terminated by ELSE.]
                                        ⎭
    ELSE MOVE 2 TO I                    ⎫
            MOVE ZERO TO J.            ⎬  [Statement group terminated by period.]
                                        ⎭
SEARCH ALL TABLE-A
    AT END MOVE 1 TO I                  ⎫
            COMPUTE J = K * 2          ⎬  [Statement group terminated by WHEN.]
                                        ⎭
    WHEN A = B
    MOVE 2 TO I                         ⎫
                                        ⎬  [Statement group terminated by period.]
    MOVE ZERO TO J.                    ⎭
```

B. Paragraphs

A paragraph consists of a paragraph name and all the statements that follow, up to the next procedure name. A paragraph collects statements into a unit to be executed by the **PERFORM** statement.

```
PERFORM A10-LABEL-1.

□ □ □

A10-LABEL-1.                  ⎫
    MOVE A TO B.              ⎬                          Paragraph
    MOVE D TO E.             ⎭
A20-LABEL-2.                     [Next procedure delimits the previous
                                 paragraph.]
```

C. Sections

A section begins with a section name, followed by a paragraph name, and contains all paragraphs up to the next section name. Sections may be used to define the range of the PERFORM statement, similar to paragraphs. Sections are redundant to paragraphs, except to segment programs. They are also required for internal sort procedures. The following example illustrates a section.

```
A10-PART-1 SECTION.

A10-PAR-2.

    MOVE A TO B.                                        Section

A10-PAR-2.

    MOVE C TO D.

A30-PART-2 SECTION.        [The next section name delimits the pre-
                           vious section.]
```

COBOL requires paragraph names within a section to be unique, but the same paragraph name may be used in different sections. The paragraph name must then be qualified: *paragraph-name* OF *section-name*. Within the section containing a duplicate paragraph name, the paragraph name need not be qualified. Never use duplicate paragraph names, because confusion may result.

Sections can *segment* programs to divide a large program into smaller segments to reduce the memory requirement. This segmentation is similar to the linkage editor overlays provided in System/370. Sections are assigned literal priority numbers from 0 to 99, with the most frequently used sections assigned lower numbers. Sections having the same priority, termed a *program segment*, are grouped into a single overlay segment by the compiler. Thus sections that frequently communicate with each other should have the same priority. Sections with priority numbers 0 to 49 and sections not assigned a priority constitute a fixed portion, and reside permanently in memory during execution. Sections 50 to 99 constitute the *independent segments*, and are loaded into memory when required. Sections are coded as follows for segmentation.

```
segment-name SECTION priority.


A10-TASK-A SECTION 55.
```

The code in the A10-TASK-A section would not be brought into memory until it or one of the paragraphs it contains is required. When the section is brought into memory, it may overlay some other idle section. This reduces the total memory requirement of the program at some cost in extra I/O and slower execution. Because of the extra cost and complexity, programs should not be segmented unless it is necessary to fit them into the computer. The use of segmentation should disappear with the advent of virtual storage computers.

The SEGMENT-LIMIT clause may be coded in the OBJECT-COMPUTER paragraph to reset the default program segment limit of 0 to 49. It is coded as follows.

```
OBJECT-COMPUTER.   computer, SEGMENT-LIMIT IS integer.
```

The program segment limit is set from 0 to *integer; integer* cannot exceed 99.

II. MAIN PROGRAM

Most COBOL programs consist only of the main program, but larger programs should be divided into a main program and subroutines. (Subroutines are described later in this chapter.) The COBOL statements required to write any program are quite lengthy. Many of the statements serve no purpose other than as comments; however, if you misspell such a COBOL statement or omit the terminating period, it is an error. It is better to use a comment card denoted by an asterisk in column 7 for a comment because the compiler does not check these statements for spelling and punctuation.

A. Main Program Divisions

The main program is divided into four divisions as follows.

- IDENTIFICATION DIVISION. Contains comments identifying the program, author, and date written.
- ENVIRONMENT DIVISION. Names the source and object computer and describes each file used by the program.
- DATA DIVISION. Describes all data items.
- PROCEDURE DIVISION. Contains the executable program statements.

The four divisions are coded as follows, and must appear in the order listed.

```
IDENTIFICATION DIVISION.
```

[Required.]

```
PROGRAM-ID.  name.
```

[Required. Specifies a one to eight character name of the program, first character alphabetic. Must not contain the hyphen (-).]

```
AUTHOR.  comment-entry.
```

[Optional. Names the program's author. Any comments may be coded in columns 12 to 72, and may continue onto several cards, still in columns 12 to 72, but must terminate with a period. The comments may contain periods in addition to the terminating period. (The comments in the following statements also have the same form.)]

```
INSTALLATION.  comment-entry.
```

[Optional. Names the installation.]

```
DATE-WRITTEN.  comment-entry.
```

[Optional. Gives the date the program was written.]

```
DATE-COMPILED.  comment-entry.
```

[Optional. Prints the compilation date.]

```
SECURITY.  comment-entry.
```

[Optional.]

```
REMARKS.  comment-entry.          [Dropped from the ANS Standard, but in
                                   System/370 COBOL.]
```

[Optional. Describes the program. Comment cards containing asterisks in column 7 are a better way to insert remarks as they can be placed anywhere within the program. However, comments should be placed here to describe the program in enough detail to give the reader a good overview. Generally a few paragraphs will do. Do not describe thing that are easily read within the program. For example, do not list the files here as they must be listed in the INPUT-OUTPUT SECTION. The comments are especially important to maintain as the program is modified. Record each change, the date, the person's name making the change, and the version number of the changed program.]

```
ENVIRONMENT DIVISION.
```

[Required.]

```
CONFIGURATION SECTION.
```

[Required.]

```
SOURCE-COMPUTER.   comment-entry.
```

[Required, but treated as comments in System/370. Names the computer that is to do the compilation.]

```
OBJECT-COMPUTER.   comment-entry.
```

[Required, but treated as comments in System/370. Names the computer upon which the compiled statements are to be executed, and is normally the same as the source computer.]

```
SPECIAL-NAMES.
```

[Optional. Specifies a symbol other than the dollar sign ($) to be the currency symbol, and reverses the roles of the comma and period in numbers to enable them to be printed in the European manner. Also specifies mnenonic names used in the DISPLAY, ACCEPT, and WRITE statements.]

```
INPUT-OUTPUT SECTION.
```

[This entire section is optional.]

```
FILE-CONTROL.
```

[Optional. Specifies the files.]

```
I-O-CONTROL.
```

[Optional. Specifies special I/O processing.]

```
DATA DIVISION.
```

[Required.]

```
FILE SECTION.
```

[Optional. Specifies each file and its records.]

```
WORKING-STORAGE SECTION.
```

[Optional. Describes all data items and working-storage records.]

```
LINKAGE SECTION.
```

[Optional. Describes subroutine arguments in a called subroutine.]

```
COMMUNICATION SECTION.
```

[Optional. Specifies communications interface for teleprocessing.]

```
REPORT SECTION.
```

[Optional. Describes the reports for the report writer feature.]

PROCEDURE DIVISION.

  [Required.]

DECLARATIVES.

  [Optional. Provides a group of statements to receive control for error or I/O conditions.]

section—name SECTION.   USE AFTER ERROR PROCEDURE ON file—name.

‚END DECLARATIVES.

procedure—name.

  executable-statements-in-program.

B.   Minimum Required Statements

The minimum required statements are as follows for a normal complete program and are included here for reference. Many programmers keep a deck of these cards already keypunched so that the fixed part of the COBOL program does not need to be rewritten each time.

IDENTIFICATION DIVISION.

PROGRAM—ID.   name.

ENVIRONMENT DIVISION.

CONFIGURATION SECTION.

SOURCE—COMPUTER.   computer.

OBJECT—COMPUTER.   computer.

INPUT—OUTPUT SECTION.

FILE—CONTROL.

DATA DIVISION.

FILE SECTION.

WORKING—STORAGE SECTION.

PROCEDURE DIVISION.

C.   Program Termination

The STOP RUN statement terminates execution, even if executed in a subroutine.

```
PROCEDURE DIVISION.

    paragraphs.

    STOP RUN.

    perhaps more paragraphs.
```

The EXIT PROGRAM statement also terminates execution if executed in the main program, but returns control to the calling program if executed in a subroutine. EXIT PROGRAM must appear by itself in a paragraph.

paragraph-name.

```
    EXIT PROGRAM.
```

System/370 provides a GOBACK statement, not a part of the ANS standard, that is identical to the EXIT PROGRAM statement, except that it need not appear by itself in a paragraph. It may be placed wherever an executable statement may go.

```
    GOBACK.
```

A STOP statement is also provided to print a message to the operator and suspend program execution until the operator responds. Most installations place constraints on the use of this facility, and it should rarely be used.

```
    STOP 'message'.

    STOP 'I AM DONE'.
```

D. System/370 Debugging Aids

System/370 provides several debugging aids that are not a part of the ANS Standard. The trace feature lists each paragraph and section name as it is reached during execution. This allows one to follow the flow of program execution. It can generate a lot of output, however, and should be used with discretion. The READY TRACE statement activates the trace feature (it has no effect if the trace is already on), and the RESET TRACE statement turns it off (it has no effect if the trace is already off.) The trace may be placed anywhere in the Procedure Division, and may be turned on and off at several places in the program.

```
    READY TRACE.              [The trace is turned on.]

    RESET TRACE.              [The trace is turned off.]
```

The ON statement, not a part of the ANS standard, is also useful for debugging. It selectively executes statements based on the number of times it is encountered. In the following statement, the THEN clause is executed the first time the ON statement is encountered, and the ELSE clause is executed every time thereafter.

```
ON 1

    THEN DISPLAY X

    ELSE DISPLAY Y.
```

The ON statement maintains an internal counter that is incremented each time the ON statement is encountered. In the general form of the ON statement, you may specify a *start* time to begin executing the THEN clause, an *increment* to execute the THEN every increment times thereafter, and a *last* time beyond which the THEN clause is not to be executed. In the following forms, *start*, *increment*, and *last* may be positive integer identifiers or literals.

```
ON start AND EVERY increment UNTIL last

    THEN imperative-statement

    ELSE imperative-statement.
```

```
ON 10 AND EVERY 5 UNTIL 20        [The DISPLAY X is executed the 10th,
                                  15th, and 20th time. DISPLAY Y is exe-
    THEN DISPLAY X                cuted all other times.]

    ELSE DISPLAY Y.
```

The UNTIL *last* may be omitted so that the incrementing is not terminated.

```
ON 10 AND EVERY 5                 [DISPLAY X is executed the 10th, 15th,
                                  20th, 25th, . . . time.]
    THEN DISPLAY X.
```

An increment of one is assumed if the AND EVERY *increment* is omitted.

```
ON 10 UNTIL 14                    [DISPLAY X is executed the 10th, 11th
                                  12th, 13th, and 14th time.]
    THEN DISPLAY X.
```

The *start* may also be coded by itself so that the THEN is executed only the *start*th time.

```
ON 10                              [DISPLAY X is executed the 10th time.]

    THEN DISPLAY X.
```

E. ANS COBOL Debugging Module (Not in System/370)

The USE FOR DEBUGGING statement is coded in a DECLARATIVES section to receive control when specified action occurs in files, identifiers, and procedures. Statements may be placed after the USE statement to perform any debugging action or display debugging information. Upon exit from the section, the program execution continues.

Statements throughout the Procedure Division may be marked as debugging statements by coding a 'D' in column 7. The inclusion of these statements for compiling is controlled by the DEBUGGING MODE clause in the SOURCE-COMPUTER paragraph. It is coded as follows.

```
SOURCE-COMPUTER.   computer-name DEBUGGING MODE.
```

The DEBUGGING MODE clause causes any USE FOR DEBUGGING sections to be compiled, along with any statements with a 'D' coded in column 7. If the DEBUGGING MODE clause is omitted, any USE FOR DEBUGGING sections and any statements with a 'D' coded in column 7 are treated as comments for the compilation.

The USE FOR DEBUGGING sections must immediately follow the DECLARATIVES. They are coded as follows:

```
DECLARATIVES.

section-name SECTION.

    USE FOR DEBUGGING ...

    statements.

section-name SECTION.

    USE FOR DEBUGGING ...

    .
    .
    .

END DECLARATIVES.
```

The USE FOR DEBUGGING statement is coded as follows.

```
             cd-name
             All identifier
             ALL PROCEDURES
             procedure-name
             file-name

USE FOR DEBUGGING ON _ _ _ _ _ _ _ _ , ...
```

- *file-name*. Invoked after any OPEN, CLOSE, DELETE, START, or READ (unless the AT END or INVALID KEY phrases are invoked) statements that reference *file-name*.
- *procedure-name*. Invoked just before the execution of the named *procedure*.
- ALL PROCEDURES. Invoked before the execution of each procedure within the program.
- ALL *identifier*. Invoked after the execution in which *identifier* is referenced in the program during execution.
- *cd-name*. Invoked after any ENABLE, DISABLE, SEND, or RECEIVE (unless the NO DATA phrase is executed) statements that reference *cd-name*.

A special register named DEBUG-ITEM is a record into which COBOL inserts information identifying the statement and procedure that caused the USE section to be invoked.

F. Main Program Communication with the Operating System

1. PARM Parameter (Not in the ANS Standard)

System/370 COBOL passes parameters to the main program with the PARM parameter on the EXEC Job Control Language statement. The EXEC statement is coded as follows to pass a character-string containing up to 100 characters to the main program. The PARM.GO indicates that the parameter is for the GO step.

```
// EXEC  COBUCLG,PARM.GO='string'
```

The main program is then coded as follows to receive the *string*. Any valid data names may be used in place of PARM, PARM-LENGTH, and PARM-VALUE.

```
LINKAGE SECTION.

01  PARM.

    05  PARM-LENGTH          PIC S9(4) COMP SYNC.

    05  PARM-VALUE           PIC X(100).
```

The length of *string* is stored in PARM-LENGTH, and the *string* itself is stored in PARM-VALUE. The USING parameter must be coded in the Procedure Division as follows.

PROCEDURE DIVISION USING PARM.

The PARM information is sometimes used in place of data read in from a card, but it is best to reserve it for programming aids, such as debugging flags. The following example illustrates such a use in which the PARM can trigger a debugging trace and also cause an end-of-file after some number of records are read in. If no PARM is coded, the program executes normally. The PARM is coded as follows for load module execution.

```
//  EXEC  PGM=module,PARM='tnnnnn'
```

[*t:* trace flag. Code Y to turn on the trace. *nnnnn:* number of input records to read before causing an end-of-file on the input file. Code 99999 to read all records.]

```
//  EXEC  PGM=RUN12,PARM='Y00020'
```

[The trace is set on, and 20 records will be read.]

```
//  EXEC PGM=RUN12
```

[Normal production run with no debugging.]

The program could then be coded as follows.

```
77  IN-COUNT            PIC S9(4) COMP VALUE 0.
*
                        COUNTS THE IN-FILE RECORDS.


    □ □ □

LINKAGE SECTION.

01  PARM.

    95  PARM-LENGTH          PIC S9(4) COMP SYNC.
```

```
   05   PARM-VALUE.

      10   PARM-TRACE      PIC X.

*                                          'Y' TURNS THE TRACE ON.

      10   PARM-CUTOFF     PIC S9(5).

*                                          CUTOFF COUNT.

   05   FILLER            PIC X(74).
```

PROCEDURE DIVISION USING PARM.

A00-BEGIN.

[First, display any debugging information, or set the flags and cutoff count if there is no PARM.]

```
IF PARM-LENGTH = ZERO

   THEN MOVE 'N' TO PARM-TRACE

      MOVE 99999 TO PARM-CUTOFF

   ELSE DISPLAY 'TRACE FLAG: ', PARM-TRACE

      DISPLAY 'INPUT RECORD CUTOFF: ', PARM-CUTOFF.
```

[Then set the trace on if the flag is set.]

```
IF PARM-TRACE = 'Y'

   THEN READY TRACE.
```

[After an input record is read, force an end-of-file if the specified number of records have been read in.]

```
READ IN-FILE INTO IN-REC.

   AT END MOVE 'Y' TO EOF-IN.

IF EOF-IN NOT = 'Y'

   THEN ADD 1 TO IN-COUNT

      IF (PARM-CUTOFF < 99999) AND

         (IN-COUNT = PARM-CUTOFF)

      THEN MOVE 'Y' TO EOF-IN.
```

2. Return Codes (Not in the ANS Standard)

System/370 allows a program within a job step to return a completion code to the operating system that can be tested in subsequent job steps to determine if those steps should be executed. Thus if a program is writing a file to be read by a program in a subsequent job step, and the file cannot be written for some reason, the return code can be set so that the subsequent job step will not be executed.

Return codes can range in value from 0 to 4095. The convention is for a value of 0 to mean normal completion, 4 a warning, and 16 a catastrophic error. If not set, the return code defaults to zero. The return code is set by moving a value to the special register RETURN-CODE, which is automatically defined as PIC S9(4) COMP.

```
MOVE value TO RETURN-CODE.
```

The following example sets the return code to 16 before program termination.

```
IF ERROR-CODE = 10

    THEN MOVE 16 TO RETURN-CODE

        STOP RUN.
```

A COND parameter is coded on the EXEC statement to test the return codes passed from all previous job steps, and if any code meets the condition, the step is bypassed.

```
//STEP2  EXEC  PGM=RUN2,COND=(9,LT)
```

STEP2 is bypassed if 9 is less than any previous step's return code. This is just an awkward way of telling the system to not execute STEP2 if any return code from a previous step is 10 or greater. The comparisons are LT (less than), LE (less than or equal), GT (greater than), GE (greater than or equal), EQ (equal), or NE (not equal).

```
//STEP3  EXEC  PGM=RUN3,COND=(4095,LT)
```

[STEP3 is executed regardless of the return codes. The return code cannot exceed 4095 so that the condition can never be met.]

```
//STEP4  EXEC  PGM=RUN4,COND=(0,LE)
```

[STEP4 is not executed regardless of the return codes. The return code cannot be less than zero and so the condition is always met.]

Two other options are provided; COND=EVEN to execute the step even if a previous step abnormally terminates, and COND=ONLY to execute the step only if a previous step abnormally terminates. The COND can also be applied to a specific step by coding COND=(*stepname, condition*).

```
//STEP6   EXEC   PGM=RUN6,COND=(STEP2,9,LT)
```

[STEP6 is bypassed if 9 is less than the return code from STEP2.]

Finally, the COND may also be coded on the JOB statement to apply to all steps within the job, overriding the COND coded on the EXEC statements.

```
//TEST#9  JOB   (5542,30),'TEST JOB',COND=(9,LT),CLASS=A
```

[Same as if COND=(9,LT) had been coded for each step.]

G. Writing the Program

There are several ways to make programs easier to update and change and to leave a record of what the program has done. In Chapter 2 it was suggested that a program be organized into paragraphs that are invoked, so that the PERFORMs serve as a table of contents to the program, and the preceding section illustrated how PARM information could be used to turn debugging aids on and off. The next few paragraphs describe some other techniques, and they are all illustrated in the sample program that follows.

It is a good practice to build an audit trail into the program so that in a production run one can tell what processing was done in the program. This is especially important later in the program's life when you are less familiar with the program, or when someone else unfamiliar with the program must assume responsibility for it and an error occurs that must be tracked down. An audit trail is a means of identifying each transaction and tracing its flow through the system; where it came from and where it went.

Print a message when program execution begins and when it terminates. Describe the condition under which the program terminates, either normally or for some error condition. If it is a long-running program that operates in several phases, print a message at the end of each phase. Display any control card or PARM information read. Keep a count of all records read and written for each file, and print these totals at the end of the program. You might also print all input and output transactions themselves, perhaps triggering such detail with a PARM value.

Build the debugging facilities into the program so that production programs can be tested without modification. The most serious bugs occur in production programs, and it is important to be able to quickly track down such errors. Programs are never completely debugged. After thorough testing, they reach a point where bugs are no longer being discovered with the test data, but there will almost always be undiscovered bugs remaining in the program. Devise debugging aids that can be left in a production program at a minimal cost in efficiency. This also eliminates the annoying errors caused by removing debugging aids from a program in preparation for placing it in production.

The following example is a complete program that incorporates these ideas. They are not exhaustive, and the reader will undoubtedly devise better ones for his or her own programs. The A10-INITIALIZE and the A40-TERMINATE paragraphs are so small that they perhaps should be written in-line rather than being made into separate paragraphs as they are here. In such a simple program as this, one might be inclined to take shortcuts, but simple programs often grow into complicated ones.

```
//TEST#9  JOB   (5542,30),'SOURCE.TEST',CLASS=A

//  EXEC COBUCLG,PARM.GO='00500PT'

//COB.SYSIN DD *

        IDENTIFICATION DIVISION.

        PROGRAM-ID.    TEST.

        AUTHOR.        GARY BROWN.

        DATE-WRITTEN.  7/4/1976.

        DATE-COMPILED.

**************************************************************************
********   THIS PROGRAM READS IN A CARD FILE AND SELECTS RECORDS WITH AN
********   'X' IN COLUMN 80.  THE SELECTED RECORDS ARE WRITTEN INTO AN
********   OUTPUT FILE.  THE PROGRAM SERVES NO PURPOSE BUT TO ILLUSTRATE
********   HOW A SIMPLE COBOL PROGRAM MIGHT BE WRITTEN.
**************************************************************************

        ENVIRONMENT DIVISION.

        CONFIGURATION SECTION.

        SOURCE-COMPUTER.  IBM-370.

        OBJECT-COMPUTER.  IBM-370.
```

```
    INPUT-OUTPUT SECTION.

    FILE-CONTROL.

        SELECT CARDIN  ASSIGN TO UT-S-CARDIN.

        SELECT CARDOUT ASSIGN TO UT-S-CARDOUT.

    DATA DIVISION.

    FILE SECTION.

    FD  CARDIN

        RECORD CONTAINS 80 CHARACTERS

        BLOCK CONTAINS 0 RECORDS

        LABEL RECORDS STANDARD.

    01  CARDIN-IMAGE      PIC X(80).

    FD  CARDOUT

        RECORD CONTAINS 80 CHARACTERS

        BLOCK CONTAINS 0 RECORDS

        LABEL RECORDS STANDARD.

    01  CARDOUT-IMAGE     PIC X(80).

    WORKING-STORAGE SECTION.

    77  CARDIN-READ       PIC S9(4) COMP VALUE ZERO.

    77  CARDOUT-WRITTEN   PIC S9(4) COMP VALUE ZERO.

    77  CARDIN-EOF        PIC X.

    01  CARD-IMAGE.

    *                           THIS IS THE CARD READ IN.

        05  FILLER        PIC X(79).

    *                           COLUMNS 1 TO 79 IGNORED.

        05  CC-80         PIC X.

    *                           LOOK FOR 'X' IN COLUMN 80.
    *

    LINKAGE SECTION.
```

```
***********************************************************************
********    THE PARM FIELD IS SET UP TO ALLOW THE PROGRAM TO BE CUT OFF
********    AFTER SOME NUMBER OF RECORDS HAVE BEEN READ.  CODE THE
********    FOLLOWING ON THE EXEC CARD TO CUT OFF EARLY FOR DEBUGGING
********    PURPOSES, WHERE NNNNN IS THE MAXIMUM NUMBER OF RECORDS TO
********    READ.  REMEMBER TO CODE THE LEADING ZEROS.  THE 'P' PRINTS
********    THE INPUT AND OUTPUT RECORDS; CODE 'P' TO PRINT AND 'N' TO
********    NOT PRINT.  THE 'T' CAUSES THE TRACE FEATURE TO BE TURNED ON.
********    CODE 'T' TO TURN ON THE TRACE, AND 'N' FOR NO TRACE.
********
********    // EXEC  COBUCLG,PARM.GO='NNNNNPT'
********
********    // EXEC  COBUCLG,PARM.GO='00100PN'  CUTOFF AFTER 100 RECORDS
********                                        THE INPUT/OUTPUT RECORDS
********                                        WILL BE PRINTED, BUT THE
********                                        TRACE WILL BE TURNED OFF
***********************************************************************
        01  PARM.

            05  PARM-LENGTH    PIC S9(4) COMP SYNC.

            05  PARM-FIELD.

                10 PARM-CUTOFF  PIC S99999.

                10 PARM-PRINT   PIC X.

                10 PARM-TRACE   PIC X.

                10 FILLER       PIC X(93).

        *                           LOOK FOR 'X' IN COLUMN 80.
        PROCEDURE DIVISION USING PARM.

        A00-BEGIN.

            DISPLAY 'PROGRAM TEST EXECUTION BEGINS.'.

            PERFORM A10-INITIALIZE.

            MOVE 'N' TO CARDIN-EOF.

            PERFORM A20-READ-ALL-RECORDS UNTIL CARDIN-EOF = 'Y'.

            PERFORM A40-TERMINATE.

            STOP RUN.
        *

        A10-INITIALIZE.
```

```
**********************************************************************
********  CHECK THE PARM FIELD, SET UP THE DEBUGGING, AND OPEN
********  THE FILES.
**********************************************************************

           IF PARM-LENGTH = ZERO

              THEN MOVE 99999 TO PARM-CUTOFF

                  MOVE 'N' TO PARM-PRINT,

                          PARM-TRACE

              ELSE IF PARM-CUTOFF NOT NUMERIC

                      THEN DISPLAY 'WARNING--INCORRECT PARM IGNORED: ',

                              PARM-FIELD

                          MOVE 4 TO RETURN-CODE

                          MOVE 99999 TO PARM-PRINT,

                                  PARM-TRACE

                      ELSE DISPLAY 'WILL CUTOFF AFTER ', PARM-CUTOFF,

                              'RECORDS READ FOR DEBUGGING'

                          DISPLAY 'PRINT FLAG: ', PARM-PRINT

                          DISPLAY 'TRACE FLAG: ', PARM-TRACE.

           IF PARM-TRACE = 'T'

              THEN READY TRACE.

           OPEN INPUT CARDIN,

              OUTPUT CARDOUT.

      **** EXIT
      *

       A20-READ-ALL-RECORDS.

**********************************************************************
********  READ RECORDS UNTIL EOF OR UNTIL A SELECTED RECORD IS READ.
**********************************************************************

           MOVE SPACE TO CC-80.

           PERFORM A30-SELECT-A-RECORD

              UNTIL (CC-80 = 'X') OR

                      (CARDIN-EOF = 'Y').
```

```
            IF CARDIN-EOF NOT = 'Y'

                THEN WRITE CARDOUT-IMAGE FROM CARD-IMAGE

                    ADD 1 TO CARDOUT-WRITTEN

                    IF PARM-PRINT = 'P'

                        THEN DISPLAY 'OUT: ', CARD-IMAGE.

        **** EXIT
        *

        A30-SELECT-A-RECORD.

**************************************************************************
********   READ A RECORD AND SET EOF FLAG IF END-OF-FILE OR IF
********   MAXIMUM NUMBER OF RECORDS IS READ.
**************************************************************************

            READ CARDIN INTO CARD-IMAGE

              AT END MOVE 'Y' TO CARDIN-EOF.

            IF (CARDIN-EOF NOT = 'Y') AND

                (PARM-PRINT = 'P')

                THEN DISPLAY 'IN: ', CARD-IMAGE.

            IF CARDIN-EOF NOT = 'Y'

                THEN ADD 1 TO CARDIN-READ

                    IF (PARM-CUTOFF ⟨ 99999) AND

                        (CARDIN-READ = PARM-CUTOFF)

                        THEN MOVE 'Y' TO CARDIN-EOF

                            DISPLAY 'CUTOFF FOR DEBUGGING.'.

        **** EXIT
        *

        A40-TERMINATE.

            CLOSE CARDIN,

                CARDOUT.

            DISPLAY 'NORMAL COMPLETION OF PROGRAM TEST.'.

            DISPLAY 'RECORDS READ:   ', CARDIN-READ.
```

```
          DISPLAY 'RECORDS WRITTEN: ', CARDOUT-WRITTEN.

     **** EXIT

********** END OF TEST PROGRAM.

//GO.CARDOUT DD SYSOUT=A,DCB=BLKSIZE=80

//********* PLACE CARD DECK FOLLOWING CARDIN DD CARD.

//GO.CARDIN DD *
```

III. INCLUSION OF STATEMENTS FROM A LIBRARY

The COPY statement is an excellent feature that copies source statements into a program from a library. COPY permits a single file description, record description, or paragraph to be used by several programs. This reduces coding and simplifies maintenance by ensuring that all programs use the same data names for files.

Copy is most useful in copying file and record descriptions. Keep all file and record descriptions used by more than one program in a copy library. (Except for source input and printed output, most files will be used by more than one program.) Paragraphs are harder to share among programs because they may use data that is of a different data type or have different names, and because of the inherent difficulty in publicizing and describing paragraphs so that others will know about them and know how to use them. Code can also be shared with subroutines as described in the next section, and they have a more formal interface that makes them both easier to use and to describe their use.

In System/370, the copy library is a partitioned data set, and the COPY statement specifies a member name. All text contained in the member is copied into the program at the point where COPY appears. A System/370 Job Control Language statement must be included in the compile step to name the partitioned data set containing the library members.

```
//  EXEC  COBUCLG

//COB.SYSLIB  DD DSN=library,DISP=SHR
```

There may be several COPY statements within a program coded as follows.

```
     COPY member.
```

The source statements in the member are copied into the program at the point where COPY appears. The copied statements cannot themselves contain a COPY statement. COPY can appear only in the following forms in System/370. The ANS Standard permits the COPY to be placed wherever a character-string or separator may occur.

```
SOURCE-COMPUTER.   COPY member.

OBJECT-COMPUTER.   COPY member.

SPECIAL-NAMES.   COPY member.

FILE-CONTROL.   COPY member.

I-O-CONTROL.   COPY member.

    SELECT file-name COPY member.

FD   file-name COPY member.

SD   file-name COPY member.

RD   file-name COPY member.

RD   file-name CODE mnemonic-name COPY member.

CD   cd-name COPY member.

01   data-name COPY member.

01   data-name REDEFINES other-data-name COPY member.

77   data-name COPY member.

77   data-name REDEFINES other-data-name COPY member.

section-name SECTION.   COPY member.

paragraph-name.   COPY member.
```

COPY operates differently in the ANS Standard than in System/370 COBOL. In the ANS Standard, the text being copied replaces the keyword COPY. In System/370 COBOL, COPY operates the same except when it appears in a data item. Within a data item, the data name of the copied text replaces the data name of the item containing the COPY. If there is no data name in the copied text, the data name of the item containing the COPY is left intact. The following example illustrates COPY statements in which two members, PAYFD and PAY, are copied into a program.

[Member PAYFD.]

```
    RECORD CONTAINS 80 CHARACTERS

    BLOCK CONTAINS 0 RECORDS

    LABEL RECORDS STANDARDS.

01  PAY-REC              PIC X(80).


      □ □ □
```

[Member PAY.]

```
01  PAY.

    05  PAY-NAME         PIC X(25).

    05  PAY-ADDRESS      PIC X(55).
```

The members may then be copied into a program.

```
FD  PAY-IN COPY PAYFD.
```

[Compiled as:]

```
FD  PAY-IN

    RECORD CONTAINS 80 CHARACTERS

    BLOCK CONTAINS 0 RECORDS

    LABEL RECORDS STANDARD.

01  PAY-REC              PIC X(80).
```

The next example illustrates the difference between System/370 and the ANS Standard when COPY is used within a data item.

```
01  PAY-IN-REC COPY PAY.
```

[In System/370, compiled as:]

```
01  PAY-IN-REC.

    05  PAY-NAME         PIC X(25).

    05  PAY-ADDRESS      PIC X(55).
```

[In the ANS Standard, compiled as:]

```
01  PAY-IN-REC

01  PAY.

    05  PAY-NAME          PIC X(25).

    05  PAY-ADDRESS       PIC X(55).
```

COPY can also edit the text as it is copied into the program. The following example illustrates the need for this. Assume a member named MFILE is contained in a COPY library as follows.

```
01  TEST.

    05  Y               PIC X.

    05  Z REDEFINES Y OF TEST  PIC 9.
```

The library member is copied into the program as follows:

```
01  REAL-THING COPY MFILE.
```

```
    In System/370, it would be compiled as:
```

```
01  REAL-THING.

    05  Y                   PIC X.

    05  Z REDEFINES Y OF TEST  PIC 9.
```

Notice that TEST was renamed REAL-THING at the 01 level, but the Y OF TEST was not changed to Y OF REAL-THING as it should be. This problem can be solved by coding the COPY statement as follows to edit the copied text.

```
    COPY member REPLACING text BY new-text,

                         text BY new-text,

                                .

                                .

                                .

                         text BY new-text.
```

The *text* may be any COBOL word, a literal, identifier, paragraph name, file name, or condition name. The preceding example can now be edited as it is copied.

```
01   REAL-THING COPY MFILE

     REPLACING TEST BY REAL-THING,

           Y BY FIRST-THING.
```

[It is compiled as:]

```
01   REAL-THING.

     05   FIRST-THING      PIC X.

     05   Z REDEFINES FIRST-THING OF REAL-THING   PIC 9.
```

IV. SUBROUTINES

Subroutines are a collection of self-contained statements that may be compiled separately from the main program and other subroutines. They allow code to be shared among different programs. Subroutines can save compilation time because each may be compiled separately and if changes occur, only one subroutine needs to be recompiled, and not the remainder of the program. Subroutines can also break up a large program into smaller, more manageable units which are easier to modify and test. Several people can work on a program composed of separate subroutines at the same time without stumbling over one another as they would if they were all making changes to a single monolithic program.

Subroutines are used less in COBOL than in other languages. (Subroutine is not even a COBOL term.) It is unusual to find a COBOL program with a subroutine, whereas it is unusual to find a FORTRAN or PL/I program without a subroutine. The reason is that the subroutine feature was added rather late in COBOL, it requires more effort to write a COBOL subroutine, and the numeric and character data of COBOL is harder to pass in subroutine calls because all programs calling the subroutine must pass the data in the same precision and character length. The many required COBOL statements by themselves may outnumber the Procedure Divison statements in the subroutine, and programmers find it easier to include the statements as a paragraph than as a subroutine. Nonetheless, subroutines should be used much more in COBOL than they are.

Subroutines are invoked by the CALL statement which gives a list of data names as *arguments*. (Arguments is not a COBOL term.)

```
CALL 'SUBROUTINE' USING A, B, C.
```

The called subroutine describes a corresponding list of *parameters* in the PROCEDURE DIVISION statement. (Parameters is not a COBOL term.) The parameters correspond item for item to the list of arguments in the calling program, although they may have different names, and the arguments are made available to the subroutine through the parameter names.

```
PROCEDURE DIVISION USING A, B. C.
```

Data can be shared only by passing it as arguments in the subroutine call, and literals cannot be passed as arguments. Files cannot be shared between a main program and a subroutine, and so if a subroutine is to retrieve a record from a file with each call, the arguments of the call must tell the subroutine when it is the first call to open the file and when it is the last call to close the file. Since subroutines are separate from the main program extra effort is required to combine them for execution with other subroutines and the main program, and in keeping track and documenting the separate source programs and listings for each subroutine.

Subroutines can call other subroutines, but they cannot call themselves or call subroutines that would result in themselves being called. Often, it is not apparent that a functional unit of code is a candidate for being shared with other programs as a subroutine until after the program is written, and it then requires a modification to lift out the code and make it into a subroutine. Subroutines require careful planning to be successful, both in defining the data that is to be shared and in determining the functional units of code that are candidates for being shared. Any data passed as arguments in a calling program must match the parameter data descriptions in the called subroutine. For example, if a subroutine expects an argument of precision PIC S9(9)V99, but the calling program carries the value with precision S9(5)V99, the item must be moved to an item of precision S9(9)V99 in the calling program before it can be used as an argument in the subroutine call.

Subroutines are coded like a main program. An EXIT PROGRAM statement in the subroutine returns control to the calling program at the next executable statement following the CALL statement. Names described within a subroutine are known only within that subroutine, and these same names may be used in the main program or other subroutines for other purposes. The following example illustrates a CALL statement to a subroutine named TIMER. Note that the subroutine name is enclosed in quotation marks.

```
01  X                     PIC S9(4) COMP.

    □ □ □

    MOVE 1 TO X.

    CALL 'TIMER' USING X.
```

A single argument, X, containing a value of 1, is passed to the subroutine. The subroutine is coded as follows.

```
IDENTIFICATION DIVISION.

PROGRAM-ID.  TIMER.

ENVIRONMENT DIVISION.

CONFIGURATION SECTION.

SOURCE-COMPUTER.  IBM-370.

OBJECT-COMPUTER.  IBM-370.

DATA DIVISION.

LINKAGE SECTION.

01  Y                     PIC S9(4) COMP.
```

[All parameters must be described in the LINKAGE SECTION. The parameters must match the record and data type of the corresponding arguments in the CALL, but the names may be different. The subroutine is entered with Y containing 1, the value of X.]

```
PROCEDURE DIVISION USING Y.

A00-BEGIN.

    MOVE 2 TO Y.                    [Y in the subroutine and X in the calling
                                    program are set to 2.]

A10-EXIT-TIMER.

    EXIT PROGRAM.                   [EXIT PROGRAM returns to the calling
                                    program.]
```

A. CALL Statement

The general form of the CALL statement is as follows.

```
CALL 'name' USING al, a2, ..., an.
```

- *name.* The name of the subroutine, one to eight alphanumeric characters, first character alphabetic.
- *al, a2, . . . , an.* Subroutine *arguments.* They are element or group items that are passed to the subroutine. They may contain data to be passed to the subroutine, and the subroutine may store data into them to return it to the calling program.

```
CALL 'SUBMAX' USING X, Y, Z.
```

The USING phrase is omitted if there are no arguments passed in the call. The ANS Standard and some System/370 compilers permit the subroutine name to be specified by an alphanumeric identifier. In System/370, the leftmost eight characters of the identifier are used.

```
77  SUBNAME  PIC X(8) VALUE 'SUBMAX'.
```

    □ □ □

```
CALL SUBNAME USING X, Y, Z.
```

The ANS Standard and some System/370 compilers also permit subroutines to be loaded into storage dynamically when they are first called. The ANS Standard provides an ON OVERFLOW phrase, not in System/370 COBOL, to specify an imperative statement to execute if there is insufficient storage for the subroutine.

```
CALL 'subroutine' USING arguments

    ON OVERFLOW imperative-statement.
```

The ANS Standard and some System/370 compilers also provide the CANCEL statement to release the storage ocupied by dynamically loaded subroutines after they are no longer needed. CANCEL is a null statement if the subroutine has not been called. If the subroutine has been called, EXIT PROGRAM must have been the last statement executed in the subroutine. CANCEL is coded as follows.

```
CANCEL 'subroutine-l', 'subroutine-2', ..., 'subroutine-n'.

CANCEL 'SUBMAX'.
```

B.   Coding of Subroutines

Subroutines are coded like the main program, with the addition of the LINKAGE SECTION to describe the arguments in the CALL and the USING phrase to list these arguments in the order that they appear in the call.

```
IDENTIFICATION DIVISION.

PROGRAM-ID.  name.
```

[The *name* is the name by which the subroutine is called. It has one to eight characters, first character alphabetic, and must not contain the hyphen (-).]

     □ □ □

```
LINKAGE SECTION.
```

[All arguments in the CALL must be described here. They must match the data descriptions of the arguments in the CALL, but the names of the items may be different. Items declared in this section cannot be assigned initial values because they receive their values from the calling program. However, the VALUE clause may be coded for level 88 condition names.]

```
PROCEDURE DIVISION USING al, a2, ..., an.
```

[Each argument in the CALL must have a *parameter* listed here that is described to be of the same data type in the LINKAGE SECTION. The arguments in the CALL and the subroutine are matched by position, not by name. Execution begins with the first executable statement in the subroutine.]

C.   Return from Subroutine

The EXIT PROGRAM statement returns control from a subroutine. It must be in a paragraph by itself. On return from the subroutine, all data items within the subroutine are left intact, and retain their values if the subroutine is called again (unless a CANCEL statement is executed for the subroutine.)

```
EXIT PROGRAM.
```

System/370 COBOL provides a non-ANS GOBACK statement that also returns control to the calling program. If differs from EXIT PROGRAM only in that it does not need to be in a paragraph by itself, but may appear wherever an executable statement can be placed.

```
IF X = Y

    THEN GOBACK.
```

D. Subroutine Parameters

Subroutines are passed data by arguments in the CALL statement, which lists data names as arguments. These arguments are associated one-to-one from left to right with a corresponding list of parameters in the USING phrase of the Procedure Division. The list of arguments in the call and the parameters in the receiving subroutine must contain the same number of items in the same order, and must be of the same data type. The names may differ because the arguments in the call are associated with the parameters in the subroutine by position and not by name. The subroutine then has access to the values of the arguments on entry, and can store new values to be returned to the calling program. The following example illustrates a CALL statement with four arguments.

```
01   W                          PIC S9(7) COMP-3.

01   X                          PIC S9(4) COMP.

01   Y                          PIC X(10).

01   Z.

     05   U                     PIC X(5).

     05   V                     PIC X(7).


     □ □ □

     MOVE ZERO TO W.

     MOVE 1 TO X.

     CALL 'SUBS' USING W, X, Y, Z.
```

In the following SUBS subroutine, W in the call is associated with A, X with B, Y with C, and Z with D. Thus A has a value of zero, and B a value of one when the subroutine is entered. Since Y and Z have not been initialized, C and D have unpredictable values. The subroutine is coded as follows.

```
IDENTIFICATION DIVISION.

PROGRAM-ID.  SUBS.

DATE-COMPILED.

*   THIS SUBROUTINE IS FOR PURPOSE OF ILLUSTRATION.

ENVIRONMENT DIVISION.

CONFIGURATION SECTION.

SOURCE-COMPUTER.  IBM-370.

OBJECT-COMPUTER.  IBM-370.

DATA DIVISION.

LINKAGE SECTION.

01  A                       PIC S9(7) COMP-3.

01  B                       PIC S9(4) COMP.

01  C                       PIC X(10).

01  D.

    05  E                   PIC X(5).

    05  F                   PIC X(7).

PROCEDURE DIVISION USING A, B, C, D.

A00-BEGIN.

        MOVE B TO A.                [W is set to 1, the value of X.]

        MOVE LOW-VALUES TO C.       [Y is set to LOW-VALUES.]

        MOVE SPACES TO D.           [Z is set to SPACES.]

A10-SUBS-RETURN.

        EXIT PROGRAM.

**** END OF SUBROUTINE
```

On return from the subroutine, W and X will contain 1, Y will contain LOW-VALUES, and Z will contain SPACES. The names of the arguments in the CALL replace the names in the parameter list on entry to the subroutine. Hence the subroutine operates on the actual arguments, not just a copy of the arguments. This is termed *call-by-name*, and is illustrated in the following example.

```
MOVE 3 TO X.

CALL 'THING' USING X, X.

    ▫ ▫ ▫

IDENTIFICATION DIVISION.

PROGRAM-ID.  THING.

    ▫ ▫ ▫

LINKAGE SECTION.

01  A                      PIC S9(7) COMP-3.

01  B                      PIC S9(7) COMP-3.

PROCEDURE DIVISION USING A, B.
```

   [The name of X replaces the names of A and B.]

```
A00-BEGIN.

    MOVE 2 TO A.
```

       [X is set to 2.]

```
    COMPUTE B = B + A.
```

       [X = 2 + 2 = 4.]

```
A10-THING-RETURN.

    EXIT PROGRAM.

**** END OF SUBROUTINE
```

E. Multiple Entry Points (Not in the ANS Standard)

System/370 subroutines can have multiple entry points specified by the ENTRY statement within the subroutine. The ENTRY statement can also list parameters different from those in the PROCEDURE DIVISION USING phrase in number, order, and data type. Surprisingly, control passes through an ENTRY statement, and so it is usually preceded by an

EXIT PROGRAM or GO TO statement. The ENTRY statement is coded as follows.

```
ENTRY 'entry-name'

ENTRY 'entry-name' USING a1, a2, ..., an.
```

- *entry-name*.   The name of the entry point; one to eight alphanumeric characters, first character alphabetic.
- *a1*, *a2*, . . . , *an*.   Subroutine parameters. They must correspond in number and order to the arguments of the call and be defined in the LINKAGE SECTION. Execution begins with the first executable statement following ENTRY.

F.   Tables as Arguments

Tables can also be passed as arguments. The table size and dimensions must match those in the calling program.

```
01   ARRAY-A.
     05   LEVEL-1           OCCURS 10 TIMES.
          10   A            PIC S9(7) COMP-3 OCCURS 2 TIMES.
01   ARRAY-B.
     05   B                 PIC X(10) OCCURS 30 TIMES.

     □ □ □

     CALL 'CHECK' USING ARRAY-A, ARRAY-B.
```

The subroutine is then coded as follows.

```
IDENTIFICATION DIVISION.

PROGRAM-ID.   CHECK.

     □ □ □

LINKAGE SECTION.

01   TABLE-A.
     05   LEVEL-1           OCCURS 10 TIMES.
          10   AA           PIC S9(7) COMP-3 OCCURS 2 TIMES
```

```
01   TABLE-B.

   05   BB                        PIC X(10) OCCURS 30 TIMES.

PROCEDURE DIVISION USING TABLE-A, TABLE-B.
```

G. Compilation of Subroutines

Subroutines may be compiled separately from the main program and other subroutines so that a change in a single subroutine does not require recompilation of the entire program. System/370 needs a special CBL control statement to precede the main program and each subroutine when they are compiled together. BATCH must also be coded as a PARM.

```
//   EXEC COBUCLG,PARM.COB='BATCH'

//COB.SYSIN DD *

CBL                                    [Begins in column 1.]

main program                           [Must come first.]

CBL

subroutine

CBL

subroutine

   .
   .
   .
```

V. COBOL JCL PROCEDURES (NOT IN THE ANS STANDARD)

In System/370, the COBOL compiler is invoked by naming an installation-supplied cataloged procedure that contains the necessary Job Control Language statements. The cataloged procedure name may vary with the installation and with the version of the COBOL compiler. The convention is to append the cataloged procedure name with C to indicate compile, CL to indicate compile and link edit, and CLG to indicate compile, link edit, and go. (GO means to execute the program.)

A. Compile

The compile procedure is used to find compilation errors and to obtain a listing of the program. The program itself is not executed.

```
//TEST#9   JOB  (5543,20),'COMPILE PROGRAM',CLASS=A.

//  EXEC  COBUC,PARM.COB='XREF'
```

[COBUC is the name of the cataloged procedure, but installations may have different names. The PARM.COB = 'XREF' is a compiler option to print a sorted cross-reference listing. There are many compiler options, but this is usually the only one needed. The PARM.COB indicates that the PARM is to apply to the COB step. The convention is for the step names to be COB for the compile step, LKED for the link edit step, and GO for the execution step.]

```
//COB.SYSLIB  DD  DSN=copy-library,DISP=SHR
```

[SYSLIB is needed only if members are being brought in from a copy library.]

```
//COB.SYSIN  DD  *
```

[Place the COBOL program here.]

B. Compile, Link Edit, GO

The compile, link edit, and GO procedure is primarily for test runs. It compiles the program, link edits it to produce an executable load module, and executes this load module. The load module is usually not saved for subsequent runs, although it may be. The next section on the compile and link edit procedure explains how to save the load module.

```
//TEST#9   JOB  (5542,30),'TEST RUN',CLASS=A

//  EXEC COBUCLG,PARM.COB='XREF,STA',REGION.GO=sizeK
```

[The PARM.COB = 'XREF' produces a sorted cross-reference listing, and the PARM.COB = 'STA' prints the statement number of any COBOL statement causing an abnormal termination. This option is extremely handy for debugging, and it should also be used for production jobs because if a program fails, the first thing one wants to know is where the program failed. The REGION.GO = $size$K is required in some systems to specify the amount of memory in units of 1024 (K) bytes required by the GO step. REGION.GO = 104K requests 104K bytes.]

```
//COB.SYSLIB  DD DSN=copy-library,DISP=SHR
```

```
//COB.SYSIN   DD   *
```

[Place the COBOL program here.]

```
//LKED   . . .
```

[If the load module is to be saved, the link edit DD statements described in the following procedure are placed here.]

```
//GO.SYSDBOUT   DD   SYSOUT=A
```

[SYSDBOUT is required when the PARM.COB = 'STA' option is coded. It prints the debugging information.]

```
//GO.ddname   DD   . . .
```

[All DD statements specified in SELECT statements must be included here.]

C. Link Edit

The compilation step creates what is termed an *object module*, which must then be link edited to include all the necessary system routines and create what is termed a *load module*. The load module is executable and can be retained to reexecute the program without the compilation and link edit steps. The following examples illustrate the JCL necessary to link edit a program, save the load module, and later execute it.

1. Creation of a Library to Contain the Load Module

The compile and link edit steps compile the program to produce an object module, link edit it to produce a load module, and save the load module as a member of a partitioned data set.

```
//TEST#9   JOB   (5542,30),'CREATE LIBRARY',CLASS=A
//   EXEC   COBUCL,PARM.COB='XREF,STA'
```

[XREF produces a sorted cross-reference listing, and STA prints the statement number if the program terminates abnormally in execution.]

```
//COB.SYSLIB   DD   DSN=copy-library,DISP=SHR
```

[SYSLIB is needed only if members are being brought in from a copy library.]

```
//COB.SYSIN DD   *
```

[Place the COBOL program here.]

```
//LKED.SYSLMOD   DD   DSN=library-name(module-name),
```

```
//   DISP=(NEW,CATLG),UNIT=device,VOL=SER=pack,
//   SPACE=(3072,(primary,secondary,directory))
```

[The linkage editor writes the load module with the SYSLMOD DD statement. The *primary* space should be roughly 40 blocks of 3072 bytes for each program the library is to contain, and the *secondary* perhaps a fourth of this. The *directory* should be roughly one fifth of the total number of members the library is to contain. For example, a library to contain 10 programs should be coded SPACE=(3072,(400,100,2)).]

```
//LKED.SYSIN  DD  *
     ENTRY program-name
```

[The ENTRY *program-name* statement is required only if there are subroutines. ENTRY tells which program is the main program, where *program-name* is the PROGRAM-ID name of the main program.]

2. Load Module Execution

After the load module is placed in a library, it can be executed repeatedly without further compilation or link editing. This is used for most production jobs because they are run many times without program changes. The JCL statements needed to execute a load module are as follows.

```
//TEST#9  JOB  (5542,30),'PAYROLL RUN',CLASS=A
//EXEC  PGM=module-name,REGION=sizeK
```

[The *module-name* is the name of a load module contained in the program library. REGION = *size*K is needed in some systems to specifiy the amount of storage in units of 1024 bytes required by the program.]

```
//STEPLIB  DD  DSN=library-name,DISP=SHR
```

[STEPLIB names the library containing the module name. Alternatively, a JOBLIB DD statement placed following the JOB statement could have been used. JOBLIB applies to all steps within the job whereas STEPLIB applies only to a single step.]

```
//SYSOUT  DD  SYSOUT=A
```

[SYSOUT is needed by COBOL for printing DISPLAY and EXHIBIT output.]

```
//SYSDBOUT  DD  SYSOUT=A
```

[SYSDBOUT is required if PARM.COB = 'STA' was coded for the compile step that compiled the program. It prints the debugging output.]

```
//ddname  DD  ...
```

[All DD statements specified in SELECT statements in the COBOL program must be included here.]

3. Add a Load Module to an Existing Library

A load module may be added to an existing library, or it may replace a module having the same name in the library.

```
//TEST#9  JOB  (5542,30),'ADD MEMBER',CLASS=A

//  EXEC COBUCL,PARM.COB='XREF,STA'

//COB.SYSLIB  BB  DSN=copy-library,DISP=SHR

//COB.SYSIN  DD  *
```

   [Place the COBOL program here.]

```
//LKED.SYSLMOD  DD  DSN=library-name(module-name),

//  DISP=OLD,SPACE=
```

[The *module-name* is placed in the library, replacing any old module having the same name. The SPACE= parameter requires some explaining. When the library is created, the amount of secondary space to be allocated is writen into the file. However, this can be overridden by coding a SPACE parameter on any DD statement, such as the SYSLMOD, that adds to the library. The LKED.SYSLMOD overrides a SYSLMOD statement in the LKED cataloged procedure that contains a SPACE parameter. This SPACE parameter will override the secondary space allocation specified when the file was created. The SPACE=nullifies the SPACE parameter on the SYSLMOD DD statement in the LKED procedure so that the secondary space is that which you specified when you created the file. This gets deeper into JCL than this book intends to go, and so just code the SPACE= and things will come out as you expect.]

```
//LKED.SYSIN  DD  *

    ENTRY program-name
```

This procedure can be run again and again without making changes. The first time it is run, the module name is added. Thereafter, the old module is replaced by the new module.

4. Replace a Single Subroutine in an Existing Load Module

An advantage of subroutines is that if a single subroutine needs to be changed, it alone needs to be recompiled. Thus if a load module contains a main program and several subroutines, one of the subroutines or the main program can be recompiled by itself, and replace the old subroutine or main program in the load module. This subroutine is compiled and placed in a load module. The linkage editor then copies in the old load module, but if it finds a subroutine name that matches the name of the subroutine just compiled, it ignores the old subroutine. The result is a new load module with all the old subroutines except for the new subroutine just compiled.

```
//TEST#9   JOB   (5542,30),'REPLACE SUBROUTINE',CLASS=A

//   EXEC   COBUCL,PARM.COB='XREF,STA'

//COB.SYSLIB   DD   DSN=copy-library,DISP=SHR

//COB.SYSIN   DD   *
```

[Place subroutine here.]

```
//LKED.SYSLMOD   DD   DSN=library-name(new-module-name),

//   DISP=OLD,SPACE=
```

[The *new-module-name* may be the same as the old module name, and it replaces the old module. If it is a different name, it is added, and the old module is left intact.]

```
//LKED.OLD   DD   DSN=library-name,DISP=SHR
```

[This statement points to the library. Any ddname could be used in place of OLD.]

```
//LKED.SYSIN   DD   *

     INCLUDE OLD(old-module-name)
```

[The INCLUDE tells the linkage editor from where to get the old load module. (The OLD is the ddname of the DD statement pointing to the library.) The compiled subroutine is placed in the load module first, and then the INCLUDE statement copies in the old load module. If a subroutine in the old load module matches the name of the compiled subroutine, it is not copied in.]

```
     ENTRY program-name
```

Remember that if the *new-module-name* is the same as the *old-module-name*, the old load module is replaced. Otherwise, the new module is added and the old load module is left intact. When a member is replaced, the space it occupies is not released. The linkage editor always adds new members to the end of the partitioned data set, and deletes any old members by removing their names from the directory. Hence if members are replaced several times, the file will become full. A special IBM-supplied utility program must then be run to compress the partitioned data set and make available all the space occupied by replaced members. It is executed as follows.

```
//TEST#9   JOB   (5542,30),'COMPRESS LIBRARY',CLASS=A

//STEP1 EXEC   PGM=IEBCOPY
```

```
//SYSPRINT   DD   SYSOUT=A

//SYSUT2   DD   DSN=library-name,DISP=OLD

//SYSUT3   DD   UNIT=device,SPACE=(TRK,(1,1))
```
   [Two scratch files are required.]
```
//SYSUT4   DD   UNIT=device,SPACE=(TRK,(1,1))

//SYSIN   DD   *

     COPY INDD=SYSUT2,OUTDD=SYSUT2
```

Creating program libraries and executing programs in System/370 COBOL requires extensive use of Job Control Language. Now that program organization is out of the way, we can begin the discussion of input/output in the next chapter. Input/output makes equally extensive use of JCL.

EXERCISES

1. The COBOL sentence is terminated by a period. What restrictions does this place on the use of COBOL statement groups?

2. Discuss the advantages and disadvantages of the required statements in COBOL.

3. Discuss the means and limitations of modularizing programs in COBOL. Also discuss the means and limitations of writing general-purpose routines to be used in several programs.

4. Write a subroutine to compute the future value of an amount invested at a given interest rate for a given number of years. The formula for this is: future amount = investment $(1 + i)^n$. The i is the interest rate [PIC SV9(5)] and n is the years [PIC S9(3)]. Define the amounts as PIC S9(11)V99. Verify that the subroutine works properly by checking some results against a table of compound interest.

5. Write a subroutine that is to be called with an argument consisting of a one-dimensional table with a varying size controlled by an OCCURS DEPENDING ON clause. The subroutine is to find the minimum, maximum, and average of the elements in the table. The table is to have a maximum size of 500, and the elements have precision PIC S9(5)V99.

6. Write a subroutine to compute a person's age given his birth date. Use the special register CURRENT-DATE to find the current date.

7. Write a single subroutine to convert distances into meters. The subroutine is to convert units of inches, feet, yards, and miles. (1 inch = 0.0254 meters, 1 mile = 1609.35 meters.) Use a separate entry point within the subroutine for each unit. Test the subroutine and verify that it works properly.

8. List at least 10 candidates to be made into general-purpose built-in subroutines or functions for COBOL. Select functions for business data processing problems similar to the built-in functions provided for FORTRAN or PL/I.

twelve

INPUT/OUTPUT CONCEPTS AND DEVICES

Input/output, the transmission of data between memory and an input/output device, is often the most complex part of programming. It requires a knowledge of the data to be transmitted, the hardware devices, and the language features. The logic is deceptively complex, and the external hardware devices have physical limitations, such as capacity, that can cause problems. Input/output also depends on the specific implementation, and this chapter describes System/370 input/output.

COBOL applications are usually heavily I/O oriented, and one should carefully select the proper I/O device for each file. Specify as little about the I/O device as possible within the program, leaving such details to the job control language. By doing this, a different I/O device can be used or a blocking factor changed without modifying the program. Then if a disk file grows in size requiring it to be moved to tape, or if a tape unit is changed to one of higher density, or if a program is tested with card data and then used to process card images on tape during production, the program does not need to be recompiled.

COBOL input/output is record oriented in that each READ or WRITE statement transmits a single logical record. A *logical record* is a logical unit of data, and may contain several items of differing data types. For example, a personnel record for a company might contain all the personnel data relating to an individual, such as name, age, and length of service. The words *record* and *logical record* are used interchangeably in the context of input/output.

Records are often blocked. A *block*, sometimes termed a *physical record*, consists of one or more records stored as a unit on the I/O device for efficiency. Blocks are described in more detail later in this chapter.

I. SYSTEM/370 RECORD FORMATS AND BLOCKING

System/370 records have three forms: fixed length, variable length, and undefined length. *Fixed-length* records all have the same length. For example, a file containing card images is fixed length because each card contains 80 characters.

FIGURE 3.   Fixed-length records for System/370 (RECFM = F); IBG—interblock gap, used to separate records on the I/O device; LRECL—logical record length; BLKSIZE—block size.

Variable-length records, as their name implies, may have varying lengths. System/370 appends four bytes to the front of the record to specify the record length and four additional bytes to specify the block size. For example, a personnel file containing employee names and the names of their dependents might be variable length because people have a varying number of dependents.

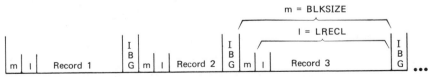

FIGURE 4.   Variable-length records for System/370 (RECFM = V). l—four-byte field containing record length; m—four-byte field containing the block length; LRECL—logical record length of the largest record the file is to contain; BLKSIZE—block size of the largest block record is to contain (LRECL + 4).

System/370 *undefined-length records* also have varying lengths, but the record length is not contained in the record. Records are separated by a physical gap on the storage device called an *interblock gap* (IBG). The computer is able to recognize this gap when transmitting a record, and thus can distinguish between records. Undefined-length records cannot be blocked; each record constitutes a block. Undefined-length records can be used when the record length is not known until after the entire record is written, as for example, data transmitted from a typewriter console. They

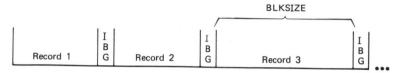

FIGURE 5. Undefined-length records for System/370 RECFM = U). BLKSIZE—block size of the largest record the file is to contain.

can also be used to read files when you do now know the record format or even the record length of the records in a file. The record can be read as undefined, and then displayed to see its length and what it looks like.

Data is transferred between memory and I/O devices in *blocks;* each block is separated by an interblock gap. Several fixed- or variable-length records may be contained in a single block. Blocks of fixed-length records all have the same number of records in each block, except possibly for the last block. Blocks of variable-length records may have a varying number of records in each block. Only one undefined-length record can be contained in a block. A block then consists of one or more records to be transmitted at a time and stored on the I/O device as a physical record. Fixed-length records can be processed slightly faster than variable-length records because they are easier to block and unblock.

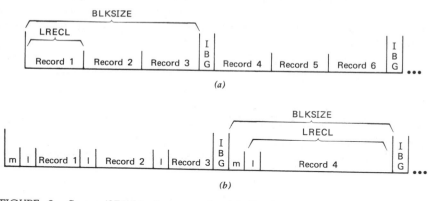

FIGURE 6. System/370 blocked records. (*a*) Fixed-length records (RECFM = FB). LRECL—logical record length; BLKSIZE—block size, a multiple of LRECL. (*b*) Variable-length records (RECFM = VB). l—four-byte field containing record length (includes four-byte l field); m—four-byte field containing block size (includes four-byte m field); LRECL—logical record length of the largest record the file is to contain; BLKSIZE—block size of the largest block the file is to contain.

System/370 records may also be spanned. Spanned records allow the record length to exceed the block length so that the logical record is con-

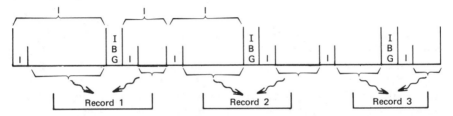

FIGURE 7. Spanned records for System/370 (RECFM = FS, FBS, VS, or VBS). l— four-byte field containing the record segment length.

tained in two or more physical records. Spanned records are not a separate record format, but a special form of either fixed- or variable-length records. (Undefined records cannot be spanned.) Spanned records are specified by appending S to the RECFM parameter: RECFM = FS, FBS, VS, or VBS.

Data can be transmitted very quickly between memory and direct-access devices or magnetic tapes once the transmission of data begins. However, it may take quite long relative to the computer's speed to start the transmission because of mechanical inertia and, for direct-access devices, the time needed to position the access arm over the proper track and the time to rotate the track around to the start of the block. Blocking allows large, efficient groups of data to be transmitted at one time. Many installations charge on the basis of blocks transmitted, and large blocks can significantly reduce the run costs. Blocking also conserves storage space on the I/O device by limiting the number of interblock gaps. For example, if 80-byte records are stored on a 3330 disk, a single track will contain only 61 records when unblocked, but 140 records when blocked 20 records per block.

The number of records per block is termed the *blocking factor*. A block of data is read into an area of memory called a *buffer*. When the last record of a block is processed, the system reads another block. The reverse occurs when data is written. Several internal buffers can be requested so that while data is being processed in one buffer, the system can read the next block of data into another buffer. This results in considerable efficiency because the I/O is overlapped; that is, data can be read or written simultaneously with computations being done in memory. Blocking is done only for hardware efficiency and is unrelated to the way one wants to process the data. The system does all blocking and unblocking in COBOL, and there is no programming effort to block files.

The blocking factor for sequential files is likely to have more impact on the efficiency of the program than any other easily controlled factor. Hence block as high as possible within the constraints of the memory size and the I/O devices. If a record containing 100 characters is blocked at 50 records per block, each block will contain 5000 characters, and for two buffers will require a total of 10,000 bytes for the I/O buffers. In addition to these memory constraints, System/370 limits the block size to a minimum of 18 bytes and a maximum of 32,676 bytes. For disk and drums, select a block size equal to the track size or some even fraction of the track size so that the blocks are stored on a track without wasting space.

II. FILES

Files must be opened before they can be used and closed after processing is completed. When a file is *opened*, the system creates all the internal tables needed to keep track of the I/O, allocates storage for buffers, positions the file to the starting point, and generally readies the file for processing. *Closing* a file releases all buffers and tables associated with the file, frees any tape drives no longer needed, deletes direct-access storage no longer needed, and generally cleans up after processing the file.

Perhaps the most complicated part of System/370 input/output is the terminology. First there are basic two *access methods*, or means by which records in a file are read or written. *Sequential access* transmits the records one after the other in the order in which they are physically stored in the file so that to transmit the last record, all the previous records must be transmitted. *Random access*, often termed *direct access*, permits a single record to be transmitted in a file without disturbing the other records, and irrespective of its position in the file. (The term *random* means that any record can be read regardless of the previous record that was read, not that a record is selected at random when the file is read.) Thus with random access one can read the last record in a file without having to read all the preceding records. Visualize a deck of cards. To locate the ace of hearts with sequential access, one card at a time is dealt off the top of the deck until the card is found. For random access, the entire card deck is spread out, face up, so that each card can be seen, and the ace of hearts selected directly.

A third access method, *dynamic*, is provided in the ANS Standard and some System/370 compilers. Dynamic allows one to switch back and forth between sequential and random. For example, one can use random access to retrieve a specific record, and then switch to sequential to read all the records that follow it.

The *file organization* can be sequential, direct, relative, or indexed. A *sequential file* contains records that are stored consecutively on the I/O device, and can only be retrieved serially in the order that they are stored.

Sequential files are often sorted before processing to arrange the records in the necessary sequence. Direct, relative, and indexed files have a key with each record. For *direct* and *relative* files, the *key* is not a part of the record, but indicates the physical location of the record on the direct-access storage device on which the record resides. For *indexed* files, the *key* is a part of the record, the records are stored in ascending order based on this key, and the system maintains a set of indexes to locate the record on the direct-access storage device.

In System/370, a tape reel or a direct-access storage device unit is termed a *volume*. The volume may have a volume label, and each file stored on the volume may also have a file label. Direct-access storage volumes must have volume labels; volume labels are optional on tape. The *volume label* is written by the installation on each volume to contain the volume serial number. It is matched against the VOL = SER = *volume* parameter in the JCL to ensure that the operator has mounted the proper volume. Files stored on direct-access devices must also have file labels; file labels are optional on tapes. When the file is created, the *file label* is written to contain the file name, the record type, the record length, and the block size. Thereafter, the DSN = *file-name* parameter specified in the JCL is matched with that in the file label to ensure that the proper file is requested, and the DCB information can be obtained from the file label rather than coding it in the JCL.

The hardware devices for I/O include card reader/punches, tape drives, disk and drum direct-access storage devices, and printers. There are other devices such as paper tape readers, typewriter or video screen consoles, plotters, and magnetic card readers, but they are more specialized and less widely used.

III. CARDS

Punched cards are the most universal I/O medium, and most programs and their data originate on cards. Each card contains 80 characters and there is no limit on the number of cards, although beyond 2000 (one box) they get awkward to handle. Cards are read or punched a single card at a time on a relatively slow card reader/punch. Once punched, cards cannot be reused for output, but they can be read many times. They can be interpreted so that one can read the data punched on the card, something not possible with tape or disk.

In multiprogramming systems, cards are rarely read or written directly by the program, but are first queued on disk by the operating system. When the program reads a card, it is actually read from disk. The same thing occurs when cards are punched; they are written onto disk and then punched by the operating system. This process, termed *spooling*, is necessary because several programs running concurrently may be reading or punching cards. It is also faster because the program can run at the speed of the disk and not at the slower rate of the card reader/punch. Also, the card reader/ punch can run at its full speed and not await a single program.

Cards are becoming more of a concept than a physical entity. Card input is often keyed directly onto tape or disk, and the card images are stored on tape or disk.

Cards are slow for I/O, but are easy to use, easy to change, and inexpensive. However, large card decks are bulky, heavy, and slow to read or punch. Card I/O is sequential, and decks can be updated by hand, eliminating complex file update programs for simple applications. Cards are also relatively indestructible. Tapes can be destroyed by a magnet or a crinkle, disks by a speck of dust or by dropping the pack, but a card deck can withstand all kinds of abuse. It is easy to replace a single destroyed card, but it is more difficult to replace a single destroyed tape or disk record. Small card decks are also more portable than tape or disk, and they can be tossed in a drawer for long-term, inexpensive storage.

In System/370, card input is specified by the DD * statement, and punched card output by the DD SYSOUT = B statement.

```
//CARDIN   DD   *                    [Card data immediately follows.]

    card data

*

//CARDOUT   DD   SYSOUT=B
```

IV. MAGNETIC TAPES

Magnetic tapes used for storing computer data are similar to those used in home tape recorders, although the recording method and content are different. A full 2400-foot reel of tape is equivalent in storage to 261,818 cards when blocked at 800 bytes per block and 1600 bits per inch.

A byte of data is stored in a column across the width of the tape; the position of each bit across the width is called a *track*. The *density* is the distance between successive bits along the length of the tape. Densities of 200, 556, 800, 1600, and 6250 bits per inch (*bpi*) are common. If there is a choice, select the highest density because it is the fastest. Older computers had 6-bit bytes, and the data was recorded on seven tracks (1 bit added for parity). Many newer computers have 8-bit bytes, and for them data is recorded on nine tracks (1 bit added for parity.)

A single file can be stored across several tape reels so that an unlimited amount of information can actually be stored. Tapes, like cards, can contain only sequential files. Several files can be stored on a single tape reel by separating them with file marks. This is done with the LABEL=*file-number* parameter in System/370 Job Control Language. The following example writes onto file 2 of the tape. (This would require that file 1 already exist on the tape.)

```
//INFILE  DD  DSN=PAYROLL,LABEL=2,DISP=(NEW,KEEP),UNIT=TAPE,...
```

LABEL = 1 is assumed if the LABEL parameter is not coded. If any file is rewritten, all subsequent files on that tape reel are destroyed and must be rewritten. Thus if a tape contains three files and the second file is rewritten, the first file is unchanged, but the third file is destroyed. Tapes are regenerated by reading the old tape and applying any changes to produce a new tape, and an automatic backup is obtained by keeping the old tape and the changes.

System/370 blocks can range in size from 18 bytes to 32,767 bytes. Blocks written on a tape are separated by an *interblock gap*, which is a length of blank tape about 0.75 inch long. The end-of-file is marked by a 3.6-inch gap followed by a special block written by the hardware called a *file* or *tape mark*. The following formula shows how to compute the length of tape required to store a given number of records:

$$length \ = \ \# \ records \ \frac{(blocksize/density) \ + \ k}{12 \ (records/block)}$$

where *length* = length of tape in feet required to store # *records*
   blocksize = length of the block in bytes
   density = bits/inch: 200, 556, 800, 1600, or 6250
   k = interblock gap in inches: 0.75 for 7-track, 0.6 for 9-track, 0.3 for 6250 bpi tapes

For example, if 400-byte records with 10 records/block are stored on a 9-track, 1600-bip tape, the length required to store 100,000 records is computed as follows:

$$length \ = \ 100,000 \ \frac{(4000/1600) \ + \ 0.6}{12 \ (10)} \ = \ 2583.3 \ feet$$

Since a single tape reel contains 2400 feet, two tape reels would be required to contain this file.

Tapes are read by moving the tape past the read head to transmit the data. If an error is detected, the system attempts to reread the block several times before signaling an I/O error. The user's program is notified that the data is exhausted if the file mark is read. Tapes can also be read backward by moving the tape in the opposite direction. A tape is written by transmitting data from memory onto the tape as it passes the write head. The data is immediately read back as it passes the read head to ensure that it is recorded correctly.

The usable portion of a tape reel is marked by two small aluminum strips; one pasted about 10 feet from the start of the tape to mark the load point and allow a leader for threading; the other about 14 feet from the end of the reel to mark the end-of-volume and allow unfinished blocks to be completely transmitted. In System/370 Job Control Language, multiple-volume tape reels are specified in the DD statement by listing the volumes. The following example requests a file contained on volumes 214 and 125.

```
//INFILE  DD  DSN=PAYROLL,UNIT=TAPE,VOL=SER=(000214,000125),

//  DISP=OLD
```

If the tapes are not to be mounted concurrently, but only as needed, code UNIT = (*device*,,DEFER). Thus the two tapes could be read even if there was only a single tape drive.

Tapes may be rewritten many times, and old data on a tape is erased as the tape is written. As a safety factor, the computer operator must insert a small plastic ring into a circular groove in the tape reel before the tape can be written upon. Removing this ring allows the tape to be read, but protects it against being written upon. The operator must be told whether to write-enable a tape or not as it cannot be specified by System/370 JCL. Installations have various procedures for this, but the safest way is to leave the ring out of all tapes and to have the user note when the tape is to be written on.

Although new tapes are 2400 feet long, only the first few feet of a tape are usually read or written, and, as this portion of the tape becomes worn, the tape is *stripped* by clipping off a few yards. Thus old tape reels may become shorter as they are recycled over their life.

Tape makes excellent long-term storage because a reel of tape is inexpensive and can contain a great deal of information in a small storage space. Tapes are considerably faster to process than cards and may be faster or slower than direct-access storage depending on the particular device. Tapes must be mounted by an operator, and this may increase the turnaround time of the job.

V. DIRECT-ACCESS STORAGE DEVICES

Direct access, the most versatile storage device, can contain sequential, direct, relative, and indexed files. Direct-access storage derives its name from the way data is accessed. Unlike tape or cards, one need not read the first nine records to get to the tenth. Direct-access storage generally consists of disks and drums, with disk devices the most prevalent.

A. Disks

A disk device consists of a stack of rotating recording surfaces similar to a stack of phonograph records. Each disk surface contains many concentric tracks radiating inward toward the center, each containing the same amount of data. A set of electronic read/write heads positioned on top of each disk surface is connected to an access arm. When a specific track is read or written, the access arm is moved to position the read/write head over the track. This arm movement is called a *seek*. The read/write head looks for a special marker on the rotating track to tell it where the track begins. Thus there are two physical delays in accessing a specific track; a *seek delay* which depends on how far the access arm must be moved and a *rotational delay* which averages out to be one-half revolution.

Since there is a read/write head for each disk surface, several tracks can be read without arm movement. The tracks that lie one on top of the other form an imaginary *cylinder* in which all the tracks are accessible without arm movement. Some disk drives have a read/write head for each track. They are called *fixed-head disks*, and since there is a read/write head for each track, the seek is eliminated.

Disks are the most versatile storage device because of their large storage capacity and adequate speed. Many disk devices have removable packs, allowing a disk unit to contain an infinite amount of data, but an installation generally controls the use of private or mountable packs. It requires a few minutes for the operator to change disk packs, and not only are the disk packs relatively heavy, but can be destroyed if dropped. Tape reels are more convenient to mount than are disk packs.

B. Drums

A drum is similar to a disk except that it contains a single cylinder of tracks, each with its own read/write head. The seek delay is thus eliminated, and the rotational delay is minimal because of the drum's high rotational speed. Drums generally contain less data than do disks, but they are considerably faster. They are used for small, frequently used files, usually portions of the operating system.

C. Using Direct-Access Storage Devices

Both disk and drum may be rewritten many times. In System/370, it is possible to delete a disk or drum file, allowing the space to be reallocated and reused. Alternatively, you may specify DISP=OLD on the DD statement to overwrite the data in an existing file. Both disk and drums are relatively expensive storage. They can give immediate access if the pack is already mounted, important in on-line applications; they are generally used for temporary files and frequently used files, and must be used for direct, relative, and indexed files.

In System/370, you must specify the amount of disk space to allocate to each file, and the program will be terminated if the requested space is not available on the disk or if the program needs more space than requested. Space is allocated by the SPACE parameter on the DD statement. With tape, the entire tape reel is always available, and you need not code the SPACE parameter. Estimating the disk space is a difficult task, particularly when a file tends to grow over time. In multiprogramming systems where many users share the same disk packs, there is also no easy way to tell if enough space will be available on the pack to run the program.

Blocks on disk are separated by interblock gaps. Set the block size for disk to a fraction of the track length, allowing some room for the interblock gaps. For example, an IBM 3330 disk contains 13,030 bytes per track. If 700-byte records are blocked at 10, only one 7000-byte block would fit on a track. By blocking at 9, two of the 6300-byte blocks would fit on a track, reducing the amount of disk space required by almost half.

Take special care in production jobs to set up the JCL to reduce the risk of terminating because disk storage is not available, and to be able to restart the job in the event that it does terminate. If a job creates temporary files in one step and terminates in a subsequent step, the temporary files are deleted, and the job must be restarted from the step that created them. This can be expensive. Catalog all such temporary files and delete them in the last step to use them.

To ensure that there is enough space for all steps within a job, allocate all the space in the first step. A special IEFBR14 null program is provided to allocate space as follows.

```
//stepname  EXEC  PGM=IEFBR14

//any-ddname  DD  all-parameters-to-create-the-file
```

Include a DD statement for each file for which space is to be allocated. The following example allocates space for the PAYROLL file.

```
//TEST#9   JOB   (5542,30),'PAYROLL RUN',CLASS=A

//STEP1   EXEC   PGM=IEFBR14

//A   DD   DSN=PAYROLL,DISP=(NEW,CATLG),UNIT=DISK,VOL=SER=222222,

//   DCB=(RECFM=FB,LRECL=80,BLKSIZE=1600),SPACE=(1600,(200,50))
```

Subsequent steps can now write the PAYROLL file by coding the DD statement as follows.

```
//ddname   DD   DSN=PAYROLL,DISP=OLD
```

Delete all nonpermanent disk files in the last step in which they are used to free up space for subsequent steps and for other jobs. If a production job has difficulty obtaining disk space, you might permanently allocate space for all the files, even temporary ones. Although this reduces the disk space available to the installation, it guarantees that this job will not be terminated for lack of disk space.

This completes the discussion of I/O devices and concepts, except for the printer. The printer and printed output are described in a separate chapter. But before we get to this, the next chapter tells how files are defined in COBOL, and how the OPEN, CLOSE, READ, and WRITE statements are used to program the I/O.

thirteen

SEQUENTIAL INPUT/OUTPUT

Sequential input/output in which records are read and written in sequence is the simplest and most common form of I/O. It may be performed on all I/O devices, including tapes, disks, card readers/punches, and printers. Input/output tends to be compiler and computer dependent, and System/370 is assumed in these instances.

I. FILE DEFINITION

All files must be specifically defined. COBOL permits several I/O options to be coded in the program that can also be specified in the job control language. COBOL also has several anachronisms in the language remaining from the past when there was no JCL to specify the I/O devices and their attributes. These anachronisms are omitted from this book unless they are required by the compiler.

Each file is given a COBOL name, termed a *file-name*, in a separate SELECT clause in the Environment Division. The SELECT statement associates the file with an external name. In System/370, the external name is a ddname, and a DD statement must give the operating system information about the file and assign it to an I/O device.

```
INPUT-OUTPUT SECTION.
```

```
FILE-CONTROL.

    SELECT file-name ASSIGN TO UT-S-ddname.

    □  □  □

//GO.ddname  DD  ...
```

Each file is then further described in the program with a File Description (FD) entry in the File Section of the Data Division, and the FD entry is followed immediately by the file's record description.

```
DATA DIVISION.

FILE SECTION.

FD  file-name

    RECORD CONTAINS integer CHARACTERS
```

[Specifies the record length. The literal *integer* should match the length of the following *record* description. It is ignored if it does not.]

```
    BLOCK CONTAINS integer RECORDS
```

[Specifies the blocking. Code a zero to allow the block size to be specified in the BLKSIZE DCB parameter in System/370 JCL.]

```
                    OMITTED
                    STANDARD

    LABEL RECORDS _ _ _ _ _ .
```

[Specifies the file label. OMITTED indicates that the file is unlabeled, and must be coded for on-line unit record devices such as the printer and card reader/punch. In System/370, file labels are STANDARD in most other instances.]

```
01  record.
```

[The *record* descriptions following the FD entry describes the record and defines its length. This record description area is termed the *record area*. Records become available here when they are read, and data is moved to this area before the records are written. There may be several *record* description entries placed one after the other to describe the same input/output record. This is often required for variable-length records and for records that may have different formats. Each level 01 *record* following the FD entry implicitly redefines the previous *record*. If more than one file has the same *record* name, these *record* names must be qualified within the program: *record* OF *file-name*. Avoid this problem by making the *record* names unique.]

A DATA RECORDS clause may be coded to name the records. However, it serves only as documentation and may be omitted. It is coded as
follows:

```
FD  file-name

    RECORD CONTAINS integer CHARACTERS

    BLOCK CONTAINS integer RECORDS

    LABEL RECORDS STANDARD

    DATA RECORDS ARE record-1, record-2, ..., record-n.
01  record-1.

01  record-2.

       .
       .
       .

01  record-n.
```

The file and record names should be selected to convey information to
the reader. Choose names that make it apparent that the file name, record
name, and ddname all relate to the same file. Specify whether the file is
input or output, perhaps by appending -I or -O to the file name. Precede each record item with the file name. If a file needs further documentation, place the comments immediately following the SELECT clause defining the file. The following example illustrates these suggestions.

```
FILE-CONTROL.

    SELECT PAY-I ASSIGN TO UT-S-PAY.

*                                   PAY IS THE CURRENT PAYROLL
*                                       FILE.

    SELECT RPT-O ASSIGN TO UT-S-RPT.

*                                   RPT PRINTS THE PAYROLL
*                                       LISTING.

DATA DIVISION.

FILE SECTION.
```

```
FD  PAY-I

    RECORD CONTAINS 80 CHARACTERS

    BLOCK CONTAINS 0 RECORDS

    LABEL RECORDS STANDARD.

01  PAY-I-REC.

    05  PAY-NAME                PIC X(20).
*                               NAME OF PERSON.

    05  PAY-ADDRESS             PIC X(60).
*                               PERSON'S MAILING ADDRESS.

       □ □ □

//GO.PAY DD ...
```

Records are normally fixed length, which is the default. Different record formats must be specified either explicitly or implicitly. The record format is not a part of the ANS Standard, and System/370 COBOL provides the non-ANS Standard RECORDING MODE clause to specify the record format explicitly. The RECORDING MODE clause can specify fixed-length, variable-length, or undefined-length records. It can also specify spanned records, which may in turn be fixed or variable length.

```
    FD  file-name

                          F    [Fixed.]

                          V    [Variable.]

        RECORDING MODE IS U    [Undefined.]

                          S    [Spanned.]
```

A. Fixed-Length Records

Fixed-length records are explicitly specified by coding RECORDING MODE IS F. If the RECORDING MODE clause is omitted, the record type will default to fixed length unless the record descriptions implicitly defines a variable-length record with an OCCURS DEPENDING ON clause, or a RECORD CONTAINS *min* TO *max* clause, or if there are several level 01 record descriptions for the same file, each having different lengths. RECORDING MODE IS F overrides any implicit specification.

```
FD  IN-FILE

    RECORD CONTAINS 100 RECORDS

    BLOCK CONTAINS 0 RECORDS

    LABEL RECORDS STANDARD.

01  IN-REC    PIC X(100).
```

B. Variable-Length Records

Variable-length records are specified either explicitly by coding RECORD-ING MODE IS V, or implicitly by coding RECORD CONTAINS *min* TO *max* CHARACTERS, or by coding a record description containing an OCCURS DEPENDING ON clause, or by coding several 01-level record descriptions for the same record, each having different lengths. To specify the length of each record and block, the operating system appends a four-byte field containing the record length to each record and a four-byte field containing the block size to each block. Exclude these fields in the count for the RECORD and BLOCK CONTAINS clauses, and do not provide space for them in the record descriptions; this is done automatically by the operating system. However, you must count these fields in coding the LRECL and BLKSIZE DCB parameters in System/370 Job Control Language. A typical variable-length record might be described as follows.

```
FD  IN-FILE

    RECORDING MODE IS V

    RECORD CONTAINS 1 TO 400 CHARACTERS
```

> [The smallest and largest record sizes are specified in the form *min* TO *max*. The *min* cannot be less than one nor greater than *max*.]

```
    BLOCK CONTAINS 0 RECORDS
```

> [You may also code BLOCK CONTAINS *min* TO *max* RECORDS to specify the blocking in the program.]

```
    LABEL RECORDS STANDARD.

01  IN-REC.

    05  IN-INFO      PIC X(98).

    05  IN-SIZE      PIC S999 COMP-3.
```

```
05  IN-TABLE       OCCURS 0 TO 100 TIMES
                   DEPENDING ON IN-SIZE.

10  IN-ENTRY  PIC X(3).
```

C. Undefined-Length Records

Undefined-length records can only be explicitly specified by coding RE-CORDING MODE IS U. The record description may contain the OC-CURS DEPENDING ON clause, or there may be several level 01 record descriptions having different lengths. Omit the BLOCK CONTAINS clause because undefined records cannot be blocked. A typical undefined-length record might be described as follows.

```
FD  IN-FILE

    RECORDING MODE IS U

    RECORD CONTAINS 100 TO 200 CHARACTERS

    LABEL RECORDS STANDARD.

01  IN-REC1    PIC X(100).
```

[The record would probably need to contain a code to indicate which record description is applicable.]

```
01  IN-REC2    PIC X(200).
```

D. Spanned Records

Spanned records are records in which the logical record length exceeds the block size, and the record must be spanned across more than one block. Spanned records are specified by coding RECORDING MODE IS S. They may be fixed or variable length. They are variable length if RECORD CONTAINS *min* TO *max* is coded, if there are several level 01 record descriptions of different lengths for this file, or if a record description contains the OCCURS DEPENDING ON clause. In all other cases the records are fixed length. A typical spanned record might be described as follows:

```
FD  IN-FILE

    RECORDING MODE IS S

    RECORD CONTAINS 0 TO 200 CHARACTERS
```

[This will be a variable-length record.]

```
BLOCK CONTAINS 0 CHARACTERS
```

[Note that you must code CHARACTERS rather than RECORDS for spanned records.]

```
LABEL RECORDS STANDARD.

01   IN-REC1              PIC X(100).

01   IN-REC2              PIC X(200).
```

II. OPENING AND CLOSING FILES

Opening a file allocates the buffers, may load the access routines into memory, creates or checks the file labels, and positions the I/O device to the start of the file. Closing a file writes out any remaining records in the output buffers, writes an end-of-file on output files, and rewinds any tape reels.

In System/370, each job step is allocated a fixed amount of storage termed a *region* or *partition*. The program is loaded into such a region. Then as each file is opened during execution, the operating system suballocates storage for the buffers from the pool of available storage within the region. This process of suballocating storage during program execution is termed *dynamic storage allocation*. When a file is closed, the operating system releases any dynamically allocated storage obtained by the open. Thus it is possible for a program to be loaded into memory, run for some time, and then open a file and be terminated because there is insufficient storage to allocate to the buffers.

Files must be opened by the OPEN statement before being used and closed by the CLOSE statement before program termination. Files can be opened more than once as long as they are closed before the second and subsequent opens. That is, open-close-open is valid, but open-open is not. (Do not open-close-open unit record card input files because the results are unpredictable.) The OPEN and CLOSE statements are written as follows.

```
 OPEN INPUT file-name,

             file-name,

      OUTPUT file-name,

             file-name.

 CLOSE file-name,

       file-name.
```

The following are examples of the OPEN and CLOSE statements.

```
OPEN INPUT FILE-A.

OPEN OUTPUT FILE-B.

OPEN INPUT FILE-C,

        FILE-D,

    OUTPUT FILE-E.

CLOSE FILE-A.

CLOSE FILE-B,

    FILE-C.
```

It may or may not be more efficient to open and close several files with a single statement, depending on the operating system. However, buffers are allocated to each file, and the memory requirement is greater if all files are open concurrently. If the processing permits, each file may be opened, processed, and closed before opening the next file to reduce the memory requirements. This also permits the same file to be read several times by closing it and then opening it again, or a file to be written, closed, opened, and then read in the same program.

```
OPEN INPUT FILE-A.

□  □  □

CLOSE FILE-A.

OPEN INPUT FILE-A.
```

An end-of-file marker is automatically written on the file when the file is closed. If the file is contained on a tape reel, the tape is automatically rewound. To close a tape file without rewinding it, append the NO RE-WIND phrase to the close. This speeds processing when another file is to be read or written beyond the end of the first file.

```
CLOSE file-name NO REWIND.
```

Files may also be closed with LOCK to prevent the file from being opened again by the program during the run.

```
CLOSE file-name LOCK.
```

The EXTEND phrase may be coded instead of OUTPUT. EXTEND differs from OUTPUT in that it positions the file to its current end to write new records beyond the last record in the file. For new files, the I/O device is positioned to the beginning of the file. EXTEND can also be accomplished by coding DISP=(MOD, . . .) in the System/370 Job Control Language. EXTEND or MOD provide a convenient means of adding records to a sequential file. However, if the program terminates before the file is closed, as can occur if the program terminates abnormally, the entire file is lost.

```
OPEN EXTEND file-name.

OPEN EXTEND FILE-A,

           FILE-B.

   [Or:]

//GO.ddname  DD  DISP=(MOD,KEEP),...
```

Tape files containing fixed-length records can also be opened reversed. The tape is positioned to the end of the file, and then the tape is read backward so that the records are read in reverse order. This feature is rarely needed, but you might use it to read a tape containing a file sorted into ascending order as if it were in descending order. The OPEN is coded as follows.

```
OPEN INPUT file-name REVERSED.
```

III. READ AND WRITE STATEMENTS

Each READ statement reads a single logical record, and each WRITE statement writes a single logical record. There are two ways of reading or writing records. First, you can READ INTO or WRITE FROM an identifier, or you can omit the INTO or FROM phrases and process the records directly in the record area or buffers. The READ INTO and WRITE FROM are less efficient, but perhaps easier to understand and are described first.

A. READ INTO, WRITE FROM Forms

```
READ file-name INTO identifier

   AT END imperative-statement.

WRITE record FROM identifier.
```

- *file-name.* A file name described in a FD entry.
- *identifier.* A record described in the Data Division whose length equals the record length. The ANS Standard does not permit the READ INTO for variable-length records; System/370 COBOL does.
- *record.* A record described in the record area following the FD entry.
- AT END *imperative-statement.* An imperative statement that is executed when an attempt is made to read a record after the last record has been read.

Remember that you must READ a file and WRITE a record. Also remember that the file must be open for either a read or write. The following example illustrates a single file that is first written and then read. This is an unusual application, but it illustrates both the READ and WRITE statements.

```
DATA DIVISION.

FILE SECTION.

FD  PAY-FILE

    RECORD CONTAINS 80 CHARACTERS

    BLOCK CONTAINS 0 RECORDS

    LABEL RECORDS STANDARD.

01  PAY-REC          PIC X(80).

WORKING-STORAGE SECTION.

01  DATA-REC         PIC X(80).

    □ □ □

PROCEDURE DIVISION.

A00-BEGIN.

    OPEN OUTPUT PAY-FILE.
```

[First the file is opened for output.]

```
    WRITE PAY-REC FROM DATA-REC.
```

[Then a record is written.]

```
    CLOSE PAY-FILE.
```

[The file is closed.]

```
OPEN INPUT PAY-FILE.
```

[Now the file is opened for input.]

```
READ PAY-FILE INTO DATA-REC

    AT END DISPLAY 'END OF FILE'.
```

[This AT END will not be executed because there is a record in the file.]

```
READ PAY-FILE INTO DATA-REC

    AT END DISPLAY 'END OF FILE'.
```

[An attempt is made to read another record, but the AT END will be executed because there are no more records in the file.]

```
CLOSE PAY-FILE.
```

When the end-of-file is detected in a READ and the AT END phrase is executed, no record is read and the contents of *identifier* are unchanged. Once the end-of-file is detected, a subsequent READ to that file will abnormally terminate the program. (However, you may close the file, open it again, and then read it.) The AT END phrase may be omitted if the USE AFTER ERROR PROCEDURE is coded in the Declaratives Section, which is described at the end of this chapter.

In a READ, if the *identifier* is shorter than the length of the record being read, the record is truncated on the right; if longer, the *identifier* is padded on the right with blanks. For a WRITE, if the *identifier* is shorter than the file's record length, it is padded on the right with blanks; if longer, the *identifier* is truncated on the right.

B.   READ, WRITE in the Record Area

Records can also be processed directly in the record area (the I/O buffers in System/370) by omitting the INTO or FROM phrase and the records can be referred to by the record names in the record area. (For the READ, the record is also available in the record area when the INTO phrase is coded.) The following example illustrates this with the previous PAY-FILE.

```
READ PAY-FILE
```

[The record is available in PAY-REC.]

```
    AT END DISPLAY 'END-OF-FILE'.

MOVE PAY-REC TO DATA-REC.
```

[The record is moved to DATA-REC.]

The WRITE works in the reverse. You must move the data to the record.

```
MOVE DATA-REC TO PAY-REC.        [The data is moved to PAY-REC.]

WRITE PAY-REC.                   [The data in PAY-REC is written.]
```

The concept of processing data in the buffers is confusing. Figure 8 illustrates what occurs inside the computer when a READ statement is executed. The buffer is equal in length to the block size, and Figure 8 illustrates a block containing three records. The OPEN, READ, and CLOSE do the following.

- Prior to the OPEN. PAY-REC has no predictable value.
- OPEN. Allocates storage for the buffer, and reads in the first block from the file. The contents of PAY-REC are undefined.
- 1st READ. No data is transmitted, but PAY-REC is made to point to record 1 in the buffer. An INTO phrase would move record 1 to DATA-REC.

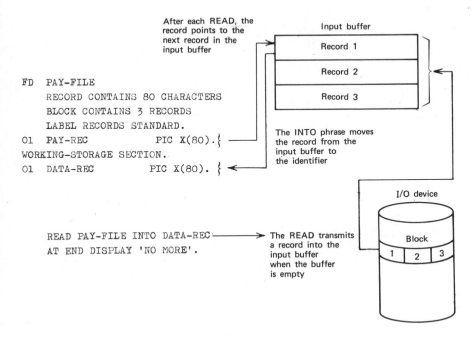

FIGURE 8. READ statement.

- 2nd READ.   No data is transmitted, but PAY-REC is made to point to record 2 in the buffer. Record 2 is moved to DATA-REC if the INTO phrase is coded.
- 3rd READ.   Same as 2nd READ, but PAY-REC points to record 3 in the buffer.
- 4th READ.   The next block is transmitted into the buffer, PAY-REC is made to point to record 1 in the buffer, and an INTO phrase moves record 1 to DATA-REC.
- CLOSE.   Releases storage for the buffer. PAY-REC has no predictable value.

Figure 9 illustrates this process for the WRITE. The OPEN, WRITE, and CLOSE do the following.

- Prior to the OPEN.   PAY-REC has no predictable value.
- OPEN.   Allocates storage for the buffer, and PAY-REC is made to point to record 1 in the output buffer.
- 1st WRITE.   Any FROM phrase moves DATA-REC to record 1. No data is transmitted, but PAY-REC is made to point to record 2 in the buffer.

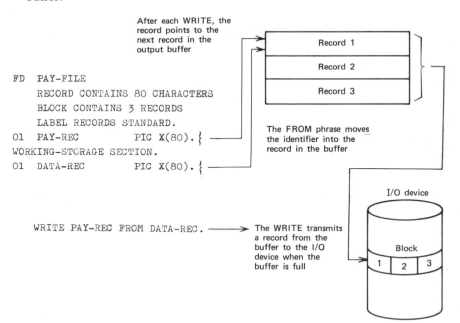

FIGURE 9.   WRITE statement.

- 2nd WRITE. Same as the first WRITE, but PAY-REC is made to point to record 3 in the buffer.
- 3rd WRITE. Any FROM phrase moves DATA-REC to record 3. The buffer is transmitted to the I/O device as a block, and PAY-REC is made to point to record 1 in the buffer.
- CLOSE. Transmits any partially filled buffer, and releases storage for the buffer. PAY-REC has no predictable value.

Processing records in the record area is more efficient because COBOL does not move the data to another area. However, the READ or WRITE is harder to follow because one must look back to the FD and locate the record to find out what is read or written. One must also remember the circumstances under which the record becomes unavailable. It is not hard to write programs with this in mind, but someone can easily forget the restrictions when the program is modified. Records become unavailable under the following circumstances.

For a READ:

- Opening the file does not make the record area available.
- A READ makes a new record available and the old record unavailable.
- An end-of-file makes the current record unavailable.
- Closing the file makes the current record unavailable.

For a WRITE:

- Opening the file makes the current value of the record unpredictable.
- A WRITE makes the current record unavailable.
- Closing the file makes the current record unavailable.

Processing records in the buffers introduces potential problems that are better avoided. The following examples illustrate some common errors.

```
WRITE PAY-REC.

MOVE PAY-REC TO SOMETHING.

    [Error, PAY-REC contains unpredictable values.]

MOVE FIRST-RECORD TO PAY-REC.

OPEN INPUT PAY-FILE.

    [Error, PAY-REC no longer contains FIRST-RECORD.]

WRITE PAY-REC.
```

```
READ PAY-FILE

    AT END MOVE PAY-REC TO LAST-RECORD
```

[Error, PAY-REC contains unpredictable values.]

```
        PERFORM A10-LOOK-AT-LAST-RECORD.

READ PAY-FILE

    AT END GO TO B10-NO-MORE.

CLOSE PAY-FILE

MOVE PAY-REC TO LAST-RECORD.
```

[Error, PAY-REC contains unpredictable values.]

To summarize, the READ INTO combines reading a file and moving the record into the *identifier* and the WRITE FROM moves the *identifier* to the record and writes out the record. The following statements are logically equivalent.

```
READ PAY-FILE INTO DATA-REC

    AT END GO TO Z10-DONE.
```

[Same as:]

```
READ PAY-FILE

    AT END GO TO Z10-DONE.

MOVE PAY-REC TO DATA-REC.


WRITE PAY-REC FROM DATA-REC.
```

[Same as:]

```
MOVE DATA-REC TO PAY-REC.

WRITE PAY-REC.
```

Keep the number of READ and WRITE statements for each file to a minimum. If a file must be read or written from several places in the program, place the READ or WRITE in a paragraph and PERFORM it. This simplifies program maintenance because there is only a single place where each file is read or written.

IV. I/O ERRORS

A section may be written to receive control if an I/O error occurs. The section is placed in a Declaratives Section immediately following the Procedure Division, and the section is automatically invoked when an I/O error occurs.

```
PROCEDURE DIVISION.

DECLARATIVES.

section-name SECTION.
                                    INPUT
                                    OUTPUT
                                    I-O
                                    EXTEND
                                    file-name

    USE AFTER ERROR PROCEDURE ON _ _ _ _ _,  ...
paragraphs.

section-name SECTION.

    USE AFTER ...

        .

        .

        .


END DECLARATIVES.
```

The section is executed in an I/O error occurs on any of the named files. Coding INPUT, for example, would detect an I/O error on any input file. Coding *file-name* would detect only the errors on the specified file. The paragraphs within the sections cannot contain any statements that refer to nondeclarative procedures. Control is returned to the statement causing the error when the exit is made from the section.

```
PROCEDURE DIVISION.

DECLARATIVES.

FILE-I-ERROR SECTION.

    USE AFTER ERROR PROCEDURE ON FILE-I.
```

```
A10-START.

    MOVE 'ERROR' TO ERROR-MESSAGE.

    ADD 1 TO ERROR-COUNT.

END DECLARATIVES.


    □  □  □


    READ FILE-I INTO X

    AT END MOVE 'Y' TO EOF-FILE-I.
```

The ANS Standard permits a two-character data item to be declared into which status codes for the file are stored at the completion of each I/O statement. These status codes can then be tested after completion of the I/O statement, either in a USE AFTER ERROR PROCEDURE or in the main line code. In System/370, the file status is available only with the Virtual Sequential Access Method (VSAM), and the ASSIGN clause must specify AS-*ddname*. (VSAM is a new System/370 access method generally used only for indexed files, and is described in Chapter 17.)

```
    SELECT file-name ASSIGN TO AS-ddname STATUS IS status.

    □  □  □

WORKING-STORAGE SECTION.

01  status.

    05  key-1     PIC X.

    05  key-2     PIC X.
```

The status codes are shown in Table 4.

A USE AFTER ERROR PROCEDURE is invoked for the following conditions.

- An end-of-file condition (*key-1* = 1) and the AT END clause is omitted in the READ statement.
- An invalid key error (*key-1* = 2) and the INVALID KEY is omitted in the READ or WRITE statement.
- A permanent I/O error (*key-1* = 3) or other error (*key-1* = 9).

TABLE 4.   Input/Output Status Codes

key-1	key-2	Cause
0	0	Successful completion
1	0	End-of-file
2	1	Invalid key: Sequence error
	2	Duplicate key
	3	No record found
	4	Boundary violation
3	0	Permanent I/O error: No further information
	4	Boundary violation
9	1	Other error: Password failure
	2	Logic error
	3	Resource not available
	4	Sequential record not available
	5	Invalid or incomplete file information
	6	No DD statement

Programs terminate if an open is unsuccessful unless a USE AFTER ERROR PROCEDURE is coded. The USE AFTER ERROR PROCEDURE can take action when an unsuccessful open occurs.

The AT END phrase coded in the READ statement contains an imperative statement to execute when no record remains to be read. Unless the AT END phrase contains a GO TO, control continues with the next executable statement following the READ.

```
READ FILE-I INTO X

    AT END MOVE 'Y' TO EOF-FILE-I.
```

The USE AFTER ERROR PROCEDURE in the ANS Standard, but not in System/370, may be coded to receive control when an end-of-file condition occurs by omitting the AT END phrase in the READ statement.

```
DECLARATIVES.

A10-END-FILE-I SECTION.

    USE AFTER ERROR PROCEDURE ON FILE-I.

A20-CHECK-EOF.

    IF KEY-1 = '1'

        THEN MOVE 'Y' TO EOF-FILE-I.
```

```
END DECLARATIVES.

    □ □ □

    READ FILE-I INTO X.
```

The preceding statements are equivalent to the following statement. The following statement is better because it is simpler, and makes it much easier to tell what happens on an end-of-file.

```
    READ FILE-I INTO X

        AT END MOVE 'Y' TO EOF-FILE-I.
```

Files written on direct-access storage devices may exceed the amount of space allocated to the file, terminating the job. However, some System/370 compilers permit you to detect this by appending the INVALID KEY phrase to the WRITE statement. (The ANS Standard does not allow this, but one can accomplish the same thing by the USE AFTER ERROR PROCEDURE.) An imperative statement is executed if the storage space is insufficient to contain the next record being written.

```
    WRITE record FROM identifier

        INVALID KEY imperative-statement.

    WRITE PAY-REC FROM DATA-REC

        INVALID KEY PERFORM D30-OUT-OF-SPACE.
```

V. SPECIAL I/O FEATURES

The special I/O features in this section are all optional and seldom required. Some of them are compiler dependent.

A. Checkpoints

Checkpoints consist of a snapshot of a program's status at selected points during execution so that if the program terminates for some reason, the run can be restarted from the last checkpoint rather than the beginning of the run. Checkpoints are only done because of the potential cost or time limitations of restarting a large program. The checkpoints themselves are expensive and complex, and you may not always be able to successfully restart the run anyway. The problem may be caused by something that occurred prior to the checkpoint and introduced bad data into the system. Checkpoints are used more as a protection against hardware and operating system errors than against application program errors.

The COBOL checkpoint facility copies the contents of storage and notes the position of all files. The checkpoint is taken after some number of records have been read or written for a specified file or when the end of a tape or disk volume is reached. Use checkpoints with discretion. They should only be used for long-running job steps in which it would be too costly to rerun the job, as for example a 10-volume tape file. A job that ran only 10 or 15 minutes would not merit a checkpoint.

Checkpoints are not infallible. In System/370, it is relatively easy to create a checkpoint; the hard part is to restart the job from the checkpoint. The system notes the position of all files, but does not save them; you must do this. If disk files are released, as occurs for temporary files, if there are card input files, or if there are files created within the step, the step cannot be restarted. Checkpoints can lead to a false sense of security.

Checkpoints are specified as follows in the Environment Division.

```
INPUT-OUTPUT SECTION.

FILE-CONTROL.   ...

I-O-CONTROL.

                          END REEL
                          END UNIT
                          number RECORDS

      RERUN ON ddname EVERY _ _ _ _ _ _ _ _ OF file-name.
```

- *ddname.* The name of a DD statement defining the file on which the checkpoint is to be written. A SELECT clause is not required and must not be coded for the checkpoint file.
- *file-name.* The name of the file controlling the frequency with which the checkpoint is taken. It may be any file in the program.
- *number* RECORDS. Take a checkpoint each time the number of records are read or written from or to *file-name*. The *number* is a integer literal.
- END REEL. For tape reels, checkpoint when a tape volume switch is made.
- END UNIT. For disk files, checkpoint when a disk volume switch is made.

The following example takes a checkpoint each time 10,000 records are read from PAY-I.

```
I-O-CONTROL.

    RERUN ON CHECKPT EVERY 10000 RECORDS OF PAY-I.


    □  □  □


//GO.CHECKPT  DD   ...
```

B. SAME AREA Clause

The SAME AREA and SAME RECORD clauses in the I-O-CONTROL paragraph illustrate how the desire to squeeze the last bit of efficiency from the system can result in making simple things complex. The clauses are coded as follows:

```
I-O-CONTROL.

    SAME AREA file-name, file-name, ...

    [Or:]

    SAME RECORD AREA file-name, file-name, ...
```

The SAME AREA clause causes the listed files to share the same storage for their access routines and buffers. The files cannot be opened concurrently or contain the BLOCK CONTAINS 0 RECORDS clause. In the following example, FILE-A and FILE-B could not be open at the same time because they share the same storage. In System/370, storage is obtained dynamically with the open and released with the close, and any savings are minimal.

```
I-O-CONTROL.

    SAME AREA FILE-A, FILE-B.
```

The SAME RECORD AREA clause allows several files to share the same record area. The files may be open at the same time. In essence, the records following the FD entry are implicitly redefined to each other for all the files listed. This allows a record to be read from one file and written by another without moving the data. The following example illustrates this.

```
I-O-CONTROL
     SAME RECORD AREA FOR FILE-A, FILE-B.
DATA DIVISION.
FILE SECTION.
FD FILE-A ...
01  FILE-A-REC              PIC X(80).
FD  FILE-B ...
01  FILE-B-REC             PIC X(80).
     □ □ □
     OPEN INPUT FILE-A,
               FILE-B.
     READ FILE-A
```

       [Record is read into FILE-A-REC.]

```
         AT END PERFORM Z90-END.
     WRITE FILE-B-REC.
```

[The record in FILE-A-REC is also the FILE-B-REC record, and is written onto FILE-B.]

C. Password (Not a part of the ANS Standard)

Some System/370 compilers permit a password to be specified to limit access to VSAM files. The password is eight characters, and is written into the file when it is created. The password must be specified thereafter to match the password of the file when the file is opened. The password is a PIC X(8) item, and can be specified only for VSAM files in which the ASSIGN clause specifies AS-*ddname*.

```
FILE-CONTROL.
     SELECT file-name ASSIGN TO AS-ddname
         PASSWORD is password.
     □ □ □
77  password              PIC X(8) VALUE '33496273'.
```

D. Allocating Buffers

Buffers provide an area in which to block and unblock records. This allows the operating system to be reading or writing one buffer while the program is processing records in the other buffer, overlapping the I/O with the computations. The System/370 default allocation is usually two buffers, and this is adequate in most instances. The RESERVE clause in the SELECT clause changes the number of buffers allocated to a file. (The number of buffers can also be specified by the BUFNO DCB parameter on the DD statement.)

```
SELECT file-name ASSIGN TO UT-S-ddname

    RESERVE integer AREAS.

    [Or:]

//ddname  DD  DCB=(BUFNO=total,...
```

The *integer* in the RESERVE clause is a literal integer number specifying the buffers to allocate. In the ANS Standard, *integer* buffers are allocated. In System/370 COBOL, *integer* + 1 buffers are allocated. The *total* in the BUFNO subparameter is the total number of buffers to allocate.

E. MULTIPLE FILE Clause

The MULTIPLE FILE clause may be coded when there is a reference to files on a tape that contains multiple files. This is accomplished through the JCL in System/370 with the LABEL subparameter, and the clause is treated as comments. It is coded as follows in the ANS Standard.

```
I-O-CONTROL paragraph.

I-O-CONTROL.

    MULTIPLE FILE file-name-n POSITION integer-n, ...
```

The POSITION clause specifies the file's position on the tape reel. It may be omitted if the files on the tape are in the same sequence as they are listed in the MULTIPLE FILE clause.

VI. ACCEPT STATEMENT

The ACCEPT statement accepts input from the operator's console or from a file. No file definition needs to be coded; simply code the ACCEPT statement. ACCEPT requests an operator response from the console keyboard when coded as follows.

```
ACCEPT identifier FROM CONSOLE.
```

An AWAITING REPLY message is typed on the operator's console, and program execution is suspended until the operator responds. The operator's response is stored in *identifier* truncated on the right if it exceeds the length of *identifier*. A DISPLAY statement should always precede the ACCEPT to tell the operator what he is supposed to enter, and the installation will generally control such communications. The DISPLAY is coded as follows to display messages on the operator's console.

```
DISPLAY item, item, ..., item UPON CONSOLE.
```

- *item.* A literal or any data item except an index.

In the following example, a message is displayed to the operator, and program execution is suspended until the operator responds with a message typed in on the console keyboard. This message is stored in ANSWER.

```
77  ANSWER            PIC X(80).

    □ □ □

DISPLAY 'WHAT IS YOUR NAME?' UPON CONSOLE.

ACCEPT ANSWER FROM CONSOLE.
```

ACCEPT can also read a single record into an identifier when coded as ACCEPT *identifier*. In System/370, input consists of an 80-character card image read in from the standard SYSIN file, and the file is automatically opened and closed. The characters in the card image are transmitted into the *identifier*, truncated on the right if the *identifier* is less than 80 characters. If the *identifier* contains more than 80 characters, additional card images are read to fill the *identifier*. In the following example, assume the standard input file SYSIN contains the following card.

```
//GO.SYSIN  DD  *

24MCONTINUE
```

A program might be written with ACCEPT statement to read the card.

```
01  RUN—CONTROL.

    05  RUN—NO          PIC S999.

    05  RUN—TYPE        PIC X(5).


    □ □ □


ACCEPT RUN—CONTROL.
```

[The card is read, and RUN-NO contains -244, and RUN-TYPE contains 'CONTI'.]

The ANS Standard permits the date and time to be retrieved by the ACCEPT statement. (System/370 provides the TIME-OF-DAY and CUR-RENT-DATE special registers for these functions.) The ANS Standard ACCEPT statement is coded as follows.

```
                          DATE
                          DAY
                          TIME

       ACCEPT identifier FROM _ _ _.
```

- DATE. Returns six-digit date in the form '*yymmdd*'. *yy*-year, *mm*-month, *dd*-day.
- DAY. Returns five-digit date in the form '*yyddd*'. *yy*-year, *ddd*-day of the year, 001 to 366.
- TIME. Returns eight-digit time in the form '*hhmmsstt*'. *hh*-hour (00 to 23), *mm*-minute, *ss*-second, *tt*-hundredths of a second.

VII. MULTIPLE-FORMAT RECORDS

Sometimes a file may contain several record formats. For example, suppose that a variable-length record contains a 200-byte record if the first byte contains an '1', and a 100-byte record if the first byte contains a '2'. The following example shows how such a file could be processed.

```
FD  PAY—FILE

    RECORDING MODE IS V

    RECORD CONTAINS 100 TO 200 CHARACTERS
```

```
      BLOCK CONTAINS 0 RECORDS

      LABEL RECORDS STANDARD.

01    PAY-REC-1.

      05   PAY-TYPE-1    PIC X.

      05   PAY-1         PIC X(199).

01    PAY-REC-2.
```

      [PAY-REC-2 implicitly redefines PAY-REC-1.]

```
     05   PAY-TYPE-2     PIC X.

     05   PAY-2          PIC X(99).


     □ □ □


     OPEN INPUT PAY-FILE.

     READ PAY-FILE

        AT END GO TO Z10-DONE.

     IF PAY-TYPE-1 = '1'

             THEN MOVE PAY-REC-1 TO BIG-RECORD

                  PERFORM A10-PROCESS-BIG-RECORD

     ELSE OF PAY-TYPE-2 = '2'

             THEN MOVE PAY-REC-2 TO SMALL-RECORD

                  PERFORM B10-PROCESS-SMALL-RECORD

     ELSE DISPLAY 'ERROR-RECORD TYPE NOT 1 OR 2.'.
```

VIII.   UPDATING FILES

A sequential file is updated by reading it sequentially and applying the transactions to it from another sequential file. The file being updated is termed the *old master file*, the file containing the transactions is termed the *transaction file*, and the updated file is termed the *updated master file*. The old master file is read, and if there is no transaction to update it, it is simply written out; otherwise the transaction is applied and then it is written out. The records in the old master file and the transactions must be in ordered on a record key, and this record key is used to match a transaction to the old master file. A *record key* is a portion of the record that uniquely identifies it, such as the person's social security number in a personnel file. The keys may be composed of several noncontiguous fields within the record.

The following example illustrates a sequential file update in which a MASTER-IN file is updated by a TRANS file to produce a MASTER-OUT file. For simplicity, the entire record is considered to be the key.

```
WORKING-STORAGE SECTION.

01  MASTER-REC.

    05  MASTER-KEY    PIC X(10).

01  TRANS-REC.

    05  TRANS-KEY    PIC X(10).


    □ □ □


    OPEN INPUT MASTER-IN,

             TRANS-IN,

         OUTPUT MASTER-OUT.

    MOVE LOW-VALUES TO MASTER-KEY,

             TRANS-KEY.
```

[The record keys will be set to high values to denote an end-of-file. This is convenient and does not disturb the sort order.]

```
    PERFORM A10-READ-MASTER UNTIL MASTER-KEY = HIGH-VALUES.
```

[All the master file records are read, along with any matching transactions.]

```
    □ □ □


A10-READ-MASTER.

    READ MASTER-IN INTO MASTER-REC

      AT END MOVE HIGH-VALUES TO MASTER-KEY.

    PERFORM A20-READ-TRANS UNTIL TRANS-KEY NOT ⟨ MASTER-KEY.
```

```
IF MASTER-KEY NOT = HIGH-VALUES

    THEN IF TRANS-KEY = MASTER-KEY

            THEN ...
```

[The transaction matches the master file record, update the master
file record with the transaction.]

```
            WRITE MASTER-OUT-REC FROM MASTER-REC

        ELSE ...
```

[No transaction for this record.]

```
**** EXIT

A20-READ-TRANS.

    IF TRANS-KEY < MASTER-KEY AND NOT = LOW-VALUES

        THEN ...
```

[The transaction does not match a record in the master file.]

```
    READ TRANS-IN INTO TRANS-REC

        AT END MOVE HIGH-VALUES TO TRANS-KEY.

**** EXIT
```

The preceding files can only be matched if they are in the same order
based on their keys, and often there is a need to check that the files are in
the proper order and that there are no duplicate records. The following
example shows how the previous MASTER-IN file would be checked for
this.

```
77  OLD-MASTER-KEY          PIC X(10).

    □ □ □

    MOVE LOW-VALUES TO OLD-MASTER-KEY.

    □ □ □

A10-READ-MASTER.

    READ-MASTER-IN INTO MASTER-REC

        AT END MOVE HIGH-VALUES TO MASTER-KEY.
```

```
IF MASTER-KEY = OLD-MASTER-KEY

    THEN ...

        [Duplicate record.]

ELSE IF MASTER-KEY ⟨ OLD-MASTER-KEY

    THEN ...

        [File not in sort order.]

MOVE MASTER-KEY TO OLD-MASTER-KEY.
```

Usually if a single record is changed in a sequential file, the entire file must be rewritten. However, it is possible to rewrite individual records in files that reside on direct-access storage devices. COBOL permits files to be opened for I-O (input-output), and they can then be both read and written. The REWRITE statement, coded similar to the WRITE, can rewrite a record that has just been read.

```
OPEN I-O file-name.

    [The file is opened for input/output.]

READ file-name INTO identifier

    AT END imperative-statement.

        [A record must first be read.]

REWRITE record FROM identifier.

    [The last record read is rewritten.]
```

The following example illustrates the REWRITE statement. The first record in a file is rewritten with blanks in PAY-REST.

```
FD  PAYROLL-IO

    RECORD CONTAINS 80 CHARACTERS

    BLOCK CONTAINS 0 RECORDS

    LABEL RECORDS STANDARD.

01  PAYROLL-RECORD        PIC X(80).

WORKING-STORAGE SECTION.
```

```
01  PAY-REC.

    05  PAY-KEY          PIC X(10).

    05  PAY-REST         PIC X(70).


    □  □  □


    OPEN PAYROLL-IO I-O.

    READ PAYROLL-IO INTO PAY-REC

      AT END MOVE-VALUES TO PAY-KEY.

    IF PAY-KEY NOT = HIGH-VALUES

      THEN MOVE SPACES TO PAY-REST

          REWRITE PAYROLL-RECORD FROM PAY-REC.
```

REWRITE can also rewrite from the record area by omitting the FROM phrase.

```
    REWRITE record.
```

Transactions are usually applied to an old master file by allowing records to be deleted, added, or changed. There may also be a replace, which is equivalent to a delete and an add. The operation, whether a delete, add, or change, should be specified within the transaction. The advantage of specifying the operation within the transaction is that one can detect errors. With the alternative of adding the transaction if it does not match a record in the old master file or of changing or replacing it if it does match, the following errors could not be detected.

- Add.   Error if the record already exists in the old master file.
- Delete.   Error if the record does not exist in the old master file.
- Change.   Error if the record does not exist in the old master file.

If there can be more than one operation on the same old master file record, the order should be delete, add, and then change. This may seem unnecessary. Why add a record and then change it in the same update run? However transactions are often batched for a periodic update, and it may be perfectly logical for one clerk to add a transaction on Monday, another clerk enter a change on Tuesday, and then process all the transactions on a Friday update run.

The delete and add are straightforward because you either write or do not write a record, but the change operation is more difficult. With a change, you do not want to update all the fields (that would be a replace), but only certain fields. The usual way of changing a record is to establish a different transaction type for each field to be changed. In critical applications, a change transaction can be made to contain two values. One value can be the current contents of the field being changed to ensure that the proper field is changed, and the second field can contain the change.

Another way to update individual fields within the old master file records is to use the same transaction format as in the add transaction, but change only the fields that are nonblank in the transaction. The advantage of this is that the same input form used for the add can be used for the update. One simply fills in the record key and the fields to change and leaves all the other fields blank. (An alphanumeric data item can be redefined over numeric fields to determine if they are blank.) The disadvantage of this technique is that if you wish to replace a field with blanks, you must indicate this by some means such as asterisks in the field.

A common error in updating records is to update the record key and forget that this affects the sort order. In sequential updating, the master file is written out in the same order in which it is read, but if the record key is updated, the record may no longer be in the proper sort order. Keep in mind that if you update the record key, the file should be resorted.

IX. FILE INTEGRITY

In crucial applications, such as an accounting or payroll system, there may be many safeguards built in. One may need to protect the integrity of the files by ensuring that the proper files are used and that the data they contain is correct.

One way to ensure that the proper files are used and to protect their integrity is to write a header and trailer record in addition to the header and trailer labels written by the operating system. The header record might contain a date so that the program can read the first record and check to see that the current file is supplied by comparing the data in the header record against a transaction date. The trailer record can contain any hash totals and record counts. (Hash totals are described later.) It also gives positive proof that the file contains the last record it was intended to contain.

An additional safeguard of the file's integrity is to check the sequence of the records as they are read in. If a transaction is made up of multiple records, one can ensure that all the parts are present and that they too are in the proper order.

Source data entering a system should always be validated to ensure that it is correct, or at least as correct as one can logically ensure it to be. The validation might include batch totals, hash totals, and field validation.

All of the validation should be done in a single place. This makes the data consistent so that a transaction will not be accepted in one part of the system and rejected in another as can occur when validation is done in several places. If the validation is changed, all the validation is in one place to change. Also if you want to know what validation is done, it is all in one place to see.

Do not stop with the first error discovered in a transaction. Check for all possible errors before rejecting the transaction. This may result in some redundant error messages, but each pass through an editor should catch all possible errors.

A. Batch Totals

Batch totals are frequently used to ensure that the input is entered correctly. With each group of transactions, generally all those on a single input form, critical numeric fields are totaled by hand. This batch total and perhaps a transaction count are entered with the transactions so that if a transaction is lost or keypunched improperly, the error can be detected. You can also add all the individual batch totals to obtain a grand total and a batch count. This gives an additional safeguard against losing an entire batch.

B. Hash Totals

The batch total is not so much a check against the computer doing something wrong as it is to ensure that transactions are not lost or entered improperly through human error. The usual internal safeguard against the computer making an error or dropping a record or transaction is the hash total. A *hash total* is created as the file is written by summing a numeric field within the record, and this total is written as the last record in the file. (Nonnumeric fields in System/370 can also be summed by moving them to a PIC 999 . . . 9 field to strip off the zone bits and leave only numeric characters which can be summed.) Then, whenever the file is read, the fields are again summed and checked against the total in the last record. If the totals do not match, either a record was lost or a field was changed.

C. Field Validation

Batch and hash totals do not ensure that the data is correct, only that it is present. To ensure that the data is correct, individual fields must be validated. The secret of validating is to make few assumptions about the data. If a field is to contain numeric data, do not assume that it is numeric; it may contain invalid characters. The following validation checks may be made on individual fields and combinations of fields.

- Character checking.   One can ensure that fields that are to contain blanks do contain blanks and that nonblank fields are in fact nonblank. Numeric fields can be validated to ensure that they contain only numeric data, and alphabetic fields only alphabetic data.
- Field checking.   A range check may be applied to numeric or alphanumeric fields to ensure that the data is within an acceptable range. Note that there may be two ranges, a range that is reasonable and a range that is valid. The field may be tested to see that it contains only specific values by looking them up in a table or file. Fields can also be checked for consistency. For example, if a person's age is less than 21 and he shows as a registered voter, there is likely to be an error.

Alphanumeric fields are more difficult to validate. You may be able to look them up in a table if there are relatively few possible values, but when there can be many combinations of characters, as in names and text, it is almost impossible to validate the data with the computer. You can sometimes use the ALPHABETIC test, but character data such as a name often contains nonalphabetic characters. You can also check the presence or absence of alphanumeric data, its length, and that it is left justified. But humans are much better at validating text, and so to validate text, print it so that it can be proofread.

D. File Backup

In designing a system with files, give careful thought to recovering each file in the event that it is destroyed. Disk files can be deleted, tape files can be overwritten, and card decks can be lost. The usual method of backing up files is to make a copy or keep the old master file and the transactions. Copying a file takes extra effort and expense whereas keeping the old master file and transactions requires no extra effort or expense. In the grandfather, father, son (generation data set) technique, the master file and transactions are retained for three or more cycles so that one can go back one, two, or more previous cycles to recreate the new master file. Tapes are generally the most convenient medium for this technique, but System/370 provides generation data groups for disk storage to accomplish the same thing.

Commercial applications generally differ from scientific applications in file recovery. In scientific applications, there may be no means of regenerating a file. Telemetry data transmitted from a satellite cannot be recreated if it is lost. Hence in scientific applications, programmers often must recover as many records from a bad file as possible, and in many instances, such as with the telemetry data, it is not critical if some of the data are missing. In commercial applications, you would rarely try to recover records from a bad file; rather you would recreate it because it is critical that none of the data be missing; the accounting books must balance, and all the employees must get paid.

X. READING NUMERIC DATA IN COBOL

Reading numeric data presents a special challenge in COBOL. It requires numbers to have leading zeros and any minus sign overpunched over the rightmost digit, such as 0025, 013N, and 0001. COBOL cannot directly accept the numbers to which we are accustomed such as 2.5, −13.5, and 0.1.

This generally presents no problem when trained keypunch personnel enter the data. However, in on-line systems the computer is often made available to a wide range of individuals. Suppose that you tell the marketing manager to punch leading zeros and overpunch any minus sign when he inquires about sales information from his on-line terminal. The manager is never going to accept the fact that a multimillion dollar computer can use only 013N rather than −13.5. Besides, his on-line terminal probably lacks the hardware features that make punching leading zeros and overpunching minus signs easy on a keypunch.

Numbers entered in human-readable form rather than in computer-readable form are much easier to validate. Suppose that someone at an on-line terminal just entered a transaction containing a person's weight, age, height, and net assets. Now he or she wants to list the transaction on the terminal to ensure that he entered it correctly. The following two lines show how the transaction might look, first if entered with leading zeros and overpunches and, second, as it might look if entered in human-readable form. Errors would be much easier to spot in the second line than in the first.

```
0143501606630160236N

143.5 16 6.63 −16023.65
```

The SIGN clause does permit a sign to be coded in a fixed position in the field. However, a sign must be present; COBOL does not assume an unsigned number to be plus when the SIGN clause is coded. The sign (+ or −) is carried as a separate leading or trailing character in numeric character data. The PIC clause must contain an S denoting a signed number, and the S occupies a character position. Arithmetic operations may be performed on such a number even though it contains the nonnumeric characters + or − .

```
77   X          PIC S999 SIGN IS LEADING SEPARATE.
```

[X occupies four character positions.]

```
    MOVE -14 TO X.
```

[X contains ' −014'.]

```
    MOVE 14 TO X.
```

[X contains '+014'.]

```
77   Y          PIC S999 SIGN IS TRAILING SEPARATE.
```

[Y occupies four character positions.]

```
    MOVE 23 TO Y.
```

[Y contains '023+'.]

```
    MOVE -23 TO Y.
```

[Y contains '023−'.]

If data is moved to an item with the SIGN clause and conversion is necessary, COBOL inserts the sign in the proper position. If data is moved to an item with the SIGN clause without conversion, the sign is not set and COBOL will terminate the job if it tries to do an arithmetic operation on the number. This can occur when data is read into the item or by a group move. With the SIGN clause, the preceding card could be coded as follows.

```
+1435+16+663-1602365
```

This is better, but suppose we want to read in signed or unsigned numbers with a floating sign, and with a decimal point in a fixed position in the field. Suppose that a card file contains numbers in columns 1 to 7, such as the following.

```
bbb2.53
```

```
B-13.56
```

bb+7.24

bbb0.17

To read such numbers, first define an area into which the cards are to be read.

```
01   CARD-IN.
     05   CARD-NUM-PART      PIC 9(4).
     [Leading digits.]
     05   FILLER            PIC X.
     [Decimal point.]
     05   CARD-DEC-PART      PIC XX.
     [Decimal digits.]
     05   FILLER            PIC X(73).
     [Pad out to 80 characters.]
```

Then define an area to contain the number in character form.

```
01   EDIT-CHAR.
     05   EDIT-LEFT-HALF     PIC X(4).
     [Leading digits.]
     05   EDIT-RIGHT-HALF    PIC XX.
     [Decimal digits.]
01   EDIT-NUM REDEFINES EDIT-CHAR PIC S9(4)V99.

        □  □  □

     READ FILE-I INTO CARD-IN
     [Read in a card.]
        AT END GO TO B20-END-FILE.
     MOVE CARD-NUM-PART TO EDIT-LEFT-HALF.
     [Move the numeric digits to get rid of the decimal point.]
     MOVE CARD-DEC-PART TO EDIT-RIGHT-HALF.
```

```
      EXAMINE EDIT-CHAR
```

[Replace all blanks with zeros.]

```
      REPLACING ALL SPACES BY ZEROS.

      EXAMINE EDIT-CHAR
```

[Replace any plus sign with zeros and ignore it.]

```
      REPLACING ALL '+' BY ZEROS.

      EXAMINE EDIT-CHAR
```

[Replace any minus sign with zero and count its presence in TALLY.]

```
      TALLYING ALL '-'

      REPLACING BY ZERO.

   IF TALLY > ZERO
```

[If the number had a minus sign, make it negative.]

```
      THEN COMPUTE EDIT-NUM = - EDIT-NUM.
```

EDIT-NUM now contains the number, and arithmetic operations can be performed on it.

```
      COMPUTE X = EDIT-NUM * 2.
```

It is more complex if the decimal point is not in a fixed position or if it might not appear, as in the numbers 0.0002, 25, -3.1, and 22.6645. The STRING and UNSTRING statements must then be used to dissect the characters to construct the number. Such numbers might be uncommon in a computer production environment, but they are common when noncomputing people enter the numbers, such as in an on-line environment.

This concludes the discussion of sequential input/output, except for the next chapter on printed output. Printed output is discussed in a separate chapter because of the additional considerations in producing output for the printed page.

EXERCISES

1. An input file consists of 80-column cards divided into six fields, each alternating seven and nine characters in length. The last 32 columns of the cards are blank. The first two fields contain integer numbers, the next two fields contain numbers with two digits to the right of the assumed decimal point, and the final two fields contain character data. The numbers may be signed with a minus sign to the left of the leftmost digit, or they may be unsigned. The numbers also have leading blanks. Write a program to read in this file and store each column in a table. Store the numeric data as COMP-3. Assume that there can be a maximum of 100 records in the file, but print an error message and terminate the job if this number is exceeded. Print out the records as they are read in.

2. Copy a file containing 80 characters per record, and an unknown number of records. Exclude all records that contain the character 'I' in the sixty-third character position of the record. Print out the number of records read, number excluded, and the number of records written.

3. Define a record that contains a four-digit project number, a 25-character name, and an overhead percentage of precision PIC S(5)V99 COMP-3. Read in a file of such records and print the number of duplicate project numbers. Check the sort sequence of the records to ensure that they are in order on the project number.

4. Read in a deck of cards containing eight integer numbers per card, 10 columns per number. The numbers are right-justified with leading blanks. Store the numbers in a two-dimensional table with the card number as one dimension and the numbers within the card as the other. Store the data as PIC S9(9) COMP-3. Allow for a maximum of 100 cards, and print an error message and terminate the run if this number is exceeded. Print the number of records read, and then write out the entire table as a single record. Then read this single record back into an identical table and verify that the data was transmitted properly by comparing the first table with the second.

5. A card deck must be read that is set up as follows. Column 1 of the first card describes the format of the data contained in the cards that follow. If column 1 contains a 1, the cards following contain integer numbers in columns 1 to 5. If column 1 contains a 2, the cards following contain a decimal number in columns 1 to 10 with two digits to the right of the assumed decimal point. If column 1 contains a 3, the cards following contain integer numbers in columns 1 to 4. Read in the file, edit the data to ensure that it is numeric, and print an error message if any invalid data is found. The numbers may or may not be signed, and there may be leading blanks. Print out the number on each card as it is read.

6. Two files each have records containing 100 characters. Each file is in ascending sort order on the first 10 characters of the records. There may be duplicate records in each file. Read in the two files and merge them to write out a new file containing only records with unique keys.

7. A file contains 80-character card images. The first 10 characters of the record constitute the record key. We want to write a file containing only unique record keys. The input file is unsorted. Read the records in and store each unique key in a table. Allow for 1000 unique keys, and print an error message if there are more than this. Write the output file from the table.

8. The program listed below was extracted from an actual program, and a very poor one at that. The program reads an old master file and a transactions file and writes out master file records for which there is a matching transaction. The program has been running for some time, but suddenly you are told that the last run did not write out enough records in the output file. The MASTER-IN file is read, and only records that match records in the TRANS-IN file are written out in the MASTER-OUT file. Any record in TRANS-IN is supposed to match a record in MASTER-IN, but the transactions are prepared by hand. Both MASTER-IN and TRANS-IN are in ascending sort order, and they are sorted just prior to being read, and so their sort order is likely to be correct, although the program does not check for the sort order.

Find the error in the program. Since the program has been running for some time, you might suspect that the error is caused by the data's not living up to the program's assumptions. Rewrite the program following the rules of structured programming, and check for any data errors and print clear error messages.

```
77  ISKIP           PIC 9.


    □  □  □


    MOVE ZERO TO ISKIP.

A10.  READ MASTER-IN INTO IN-REC AT END GO TO A60.

    IF ISKIP NOT = ZEROS GO TO A20.

    READ TRANS-IN INTO TRANS-REC AT END GO TO A50.

    GO TO A30.

A20.  IF ISKIP = 2 GO TO A10.

    MOVE ZERO TO ISKIP.

A30.  IF TRANS-REC NOT = IN-RED GO TO A40.

    WRITE OUT-REC FROM IN-REC.
```

```
      MOVE ZERO TO ISKIP.

      GO TO A10.
A40.  MOVE TO ISKIP.

      GO TO A10.
A50.  MOVE 2 TO ISKIP.

      GO TO A10.
A60.  ...
```

fourteen

PRINTED OUTPUT

Printed output is the most common form of output, and can become very complicated. It is read by humans rather than by a computer, and is two dimensional, consisting of characters within a line (a line corresponds to a record) and lines on a page. It also requires an aesthetic sense that is not always inherent in the cool logic generally required of programmers. But the most difficult part of printing output is the reaction of the end user to the printed page. Somehow printed output evokes a response from the reader much like that of newlyweds to a roomful of new furniture. They have definite ideas where each piece should go, but after they see it there, they are apt to change their minds. The same occurs when the reader first sees a report. This is especially true of management reports which are less standardized and are used for making decisions. It is not necessarily capriciousness on the reader's part to want to make changes to the report. Only by seeing actual numbers and working with them can the reader know what further information is needed. It is hard for the programmer to second-guess the reader, and although the reader should be pressed to think about his or her needs, the needs may not be apparent until the information begins to be used.

The first thing to come to terms with in designing reports is that they are likely to change. Make them easy to change. This chapter describes how to use the WRITE statement to produce a report, but you should also consider the report writer feature described in the next chapter because it makes reports easier to write and easier to change.

I. PRINTERS

Line printers print a line at a time on continuous form paper. The paper stacks at roughly 2700 pages per foot. The paper is normally 14 × 11 with 66 lines per page (6 lines per inch), and 132 characters per line (10 characters per inch.) Some printers can print 8 lines per inch for 88 lines per page. Line widths of 100, 120, and 160 characters are also found. Paper also comes in an $8\frac{1}{2}$ × 11 size with 66 or 88 lines per page, depending on the lines per inch, and 85 characters per line. Other paper sizes are also available, but these are the most common.

Although the normal $8\frac{1}{2}$ by 11 paper can contain 66 lines per page, most installations set the printer carriage control to print fewer lines, usually 60. The result is a few blank lines at the top and bottom of the page. This is done not only for aesthetics, but also to make it less necessary for the operators to be careful in aligning the print line to the paper's perforation.

There are two ways of printing; by *impact* (striking a character through a carbon like a typewriter) or *nonimpact* (photocopying like an office copier.) Impact printers are generally a drum, or a chain or train. The *drum* has a spinning cylinder for each character position in a line, and each cylinder contains all the characters in the character set. As each cylinder spins into the appropriate character position, it is hammered onto the paper through a carbon ribbon. Drum printers generally give the lowest quality printing because if the hammer hits a little early or late, the character will appear slightly above or below the line. This is noticeable on a printed line, giving it a wavy appearance.

In *train* or *chain* printers, the characters move laterally across the page, and as the proper character moves into position, it is hammered onto the paper through a carbon ribbon. If the hammer hits a little early or late, the character will appear slightly to the right or left of its proper position, but variations in horizontal spacing are not as noticeable to humans. (This phenomenon allows the columns in newspapers to be both right and left justified by varying the character spacing.)

There are several types of nonimpact printers. The usual method is to chemically treat the paper and expose the characters onto it by some means such as a laser. The characters are then fused onto the paper by heating it. These newer devices are much faster and allow any character set to be used, in addition to drawing lines and shading. Light can be flashed through a translucent slide to expose a drawing onto the paper. The IBM 3800 printer can print 10, 12, or 15 characters per inch for 136, 163, or 204 characters per line.

Slow impact printers print at rates from 100 to 600 lines per minute, and fast impact printers print at rates from 1100 to 3000 lines per minute.

Very fast nonimpact printers are capable of rates of up to 13,360 lines per minute.

Microfilm is often used as an alternative to the printer. The output is "printed" on microfilm rather than paper, which, besides being faster, also condenses large stacks of paper down into small amounts of microfilm with no special programming. The drawback of computer output microfilm (COM) is that it takes a special device to print the microfile and a special viewer to read it.

Multiple copies can be made either by printing the report several times or by using multipart paper. (Nonimpact printers cannot use multipart paper.) One can request a print file to be printed several times through the System/370 VS Job Control Language in the DD statement as follows.

```
//GO.ddname  DD  SYSOUT=A,COPIES=copies
```

However, for long reports in which several copies are required, this can tie up a printer for a long time. Alternatively, one can use multiple-part paper to print several copies at one time. Multiple-part paper comes with interleaved carbons, and up to eight copies can be made with the last copy retaining legibility. Multiple-part paper has several drawbacks. The paper costs more than the same number of copies of regular paper, each successive copy is less clear, the ink in the copies smears and comes off on your hands, the forms must be mounted and dismounted from the printer, and the carbons must be removed from the paper. A deleaving machine is available to remove the carbons, as it is a messy job to do by hand. Even with the deleaving machine, the paper may jam and tear a few pages.

Another way of making copies is with a continuous forms copying machine. It is like an office copier, but it accepts the continuous form computer paper after it comes off the printer. (Some copiers can accept tape input.) The 14×11 paper is reduced to a more convenient $8\frac{1}{2}$ by 11 size, and several copies may be made. As with the nonimpact printer, one may mount a translucent slide to project drawings onto the paper.

Special forms can also be made up into many sizes, and are most widely used to print checks. The special forms can have anything preprinted on them, and may come in colors and multiple-part paper. Never use special forms unless you must because they are more expensive and the forms must be mounted and dismounted on the printer. They also make reports inflexible because a report change may require designing a new form, with a lead time to have it made up and delivered.

II. SIMPLE I/O

COBOL provides the DISPLAY statement, and System/370 compilers also provide the EXHIBIT statement, to print a line of information. These statements are suited for printing run statistics and error messages and for debugging information rather than formal reports. DISPLAY and EX-HIBIT are simple to use and do not require the files to be described, opened, or closed.

A. DISPLAY Statement

DISPLAY prints both alphanumeric literals and the value of data items on the standard output file, SYSPRINT in System/370. The file is auto-matically opened and closed. The general form is as follows:

```
DISPLAY item, item, ..., item.
```

The *item* must not be an index, but it may be any other type of item or a literal. If you display a group item, it is printed as alphanumeric. Each DISPLAY statement starts on a new line, and if more than 120 characters are displayed, they continue onto the next line.

```
DISPLAY 'THIS IS A MESSAGE'.
```

THIS IS A MESSAGE is printed on the next line. Identifiers are printed according to their descriptions in the PIC clause. An item of PIC X(10) would print 10 characters, and PIC S9(5)V99 would print 7 characters (regardless of whether described as DISPLAY, COMP, or COMP-3) with leading zeros and no decimal point. The sign in negative numbers is indi-cated in the rightmost digit as shown in the following table.

Digit	Printed As	Digit	Printed As
0	&†	5	N
1	J	6	O
2	K	7	P
3	L	8	Q
4	M	9	R

† The minus zero is a zero overpunched with a minus sign in System/370, and there is no print character defined for this combination. It usually prints as an ampersand, but it also prints as a percent on some printers and does not print at all on others.

If VALUE-A is declared S9(5)V99 and contains 23 and VALUE-B is declared S9(3)V9999 and contains −23.2345, they would be printed as follows.

DISPLAY VALUE-A.   [Prints as: 0002300.]

DISPLAY VALUE-B   [Prints as: 023234N.]

Blanks are not inserted between printed items as shown in the following example.

DISPLAY VALUE-A, VALUE-B.   [Prints as: 0002300023234N.]

So, to ensure that the numbers can be read, separate numeric values with literal blanks. Since only the values of items are printed, include some text to describe what they signify.

DISPLAY 'VALUE-A = ', VALUE-A, ' VALUE-B = ', VALUE-B.

[Prints as: VALUE-A = 0002300 VALUE-B = 023234N.]

B. EXHIBIT Statement (Not in the ANS Standard)

EXHIBIT is provided in System/370 as a convenience for printing the value of literals and the name and value of identifiers. This is especially useful for debugging. The output is printed on the standard SYSPRINT output file, and the file is automatically opened and closed. EXHIBIT is coded as follows:

EXHIBIT NAMED item, item, ..., item.

The *item* must not be an index, but it may be any other type of data item, or an alphanumeric literal. For identifiers, the name is printed preceding its value. Each EXHIBIT statement starts a new line, and it will continue onto the following line if necessary.

EXHIBIT NAMED 'HERE IT IS: ', VALUE-A, VALUE-B.

[Prints as: HERE IT IS: VALUE-A 0002300 VALUE-B 023234N.]

For debugging, EXHIBIT can also display the data name and its value only if the value has changed since the last EXHIBIT statement was executed. This form is as follows.

```
                    CHANGED
                    CHANGED NAME

        EXHIBIT _ _ _ _ _ _ _ item, item, ..., item.
```

- CHANGED NAMED.   Display the names and values of all *items* the
  first time the statement is executed. Thereafter, display the names and
  values only if the value of the *item* has changed since the last execution
  of the statement. Any literals are printed each time the statement is
  executed.
- CHANGED.   Identical to CHANGED NAMED except that only the
  value and not the name of the identifier is displayed. (Similar to DIS-
  PLAY.)

```
        EXHIBIT CHANGED X, Y, Z.
```

   [Prints as: 0123 0015 05.]

```
        EXHIBIT CHANGED NAMED A, B.
```

   [Prints as: A 00443 B 03040.]

III.   PRINT FILES

A.   FD Entry

Print files are defined as normal files with the record length set to the number of print positions plus one for the carriage control. If the printer is
on-line, LABEL RECORDS OMITTED must be coded; otherwise either
STANDARD or OMITTED may be coded.

```
FD  file-name

    RECORD CONTAINS 133 CHARACTERS

    BLOCK CONTAINS 0 RECORDS

    LABEL RECORDS STANDARD.

01  record               PIC X(133).
```

   The print lines are defined as records, and values may be moved to data
items within the record. In System/370, the first character position of the
print line controls the printer and is not itself printed. The remaining characters, 132 on most printers, are printed. The WRITE statement moves a

carriage control character to the first character position of the print line. Print files must be opened and closed as with all other files.

B. WRITE ADVANCING

The ADVANCING phrase is appended to the WRITE statement to print lines, and COBOL inserts the proper carriage control character in the first character position of the printed line. System/370 COBOL requires the ADVANCING phrase to be used for all WRITEs for a file if it is used for any WRITE.

```
                                      AFTER
                                      BEFORE

     WRITE record FROM identifier _ _ _ _ ADVANCING integer LINES.
```

The AFTER prints the line after advancing the *integer* lines, and BEFORE prints the line before advancing the *integer* lines. The *integer* is an integer numeric identifier or unsigned literal with a value from 0 to 99. Although not in System/370 COBOL, the ANS Standard provides the keyword PAGE to be coded in place of *integer* LINES to eject to a new page. (The only way to eject to a new page in System/370 is to use the mnemonic names described next.)

```
FD  RPT-O

    RECORD CONTAINS 133 CHARACTERS

    BLOCK CONTAINS O RECORDS

    LABEL RECORDS STANDARD.

01  RPT-RECORD     PIC X(133).

      □ □ □


WORKING-STORAGE SECTION.

01  RPT-LINE.

    05  FILLER     PIC X.

    05  FILLER     PIC X(6) VALUE 'NAME: '.

    05  RPT-NAME   PIC X(5).

    05  FILLER     PIC X(3) VALUE SPACES.
```

```
05  RPT-AGE    PIC 999.

□  □  □

MOVE 'SMITH' TO RPT-NAME.

MOVE 21 TO RPT-AGE.

WRITE RPT-RECORD FROM RPT-LINE

    AFTER ADVANCING 1 LINE.
```

The following line is printed with single spacing.

```
NAME:bSMITHbbb021
```

The FROM phrase may be omitted to write directly from the record area. ADVANCING may also specify a mnemonic name that is defined in the SPECIAL-NAMES section and is associated with a carriage control character. The mnemonic names shown are for System/370.

```
OBJECT-COMPUTER.  computer.

SPECIAL-NAMES.

    CSP IS name-0              [Suppress spacing.]

    C01 IS name-1              [Eject to a new page.]

    C02 IS name-2              [Skip to channel 2, action is installation
                               defined.]

        .
        .
        .

    C12 IS name-12.           [Skip to channel 12, action is installation
                               defined.]
```

The following example uses mnemonic names for suppressing spacing and ejecting to a new page.

```
SPECIAL-NAMES.

    CSP IS OVER-PRINT

    C01 IS NEW-PAGE.

    □  □  □
```

```
WRITE RPT-RECORD FROM RPT-LINE

    AFTER ADVANCING NEW-PAGE.

WRITE RPT-RECORD FROM RPT-LINE

    AFTER ADVANCING OVER-PRINT.

WRITE RPT-RECORD FROM RPT-LINE
```

[The use of mnemonic names does not preclude the use of *integer* LINES.]

```
AFTER ADVANCING 1 LINE.
```

An EOP (end-of-page) phrase can be appended to the ADVANCING phrase to specify an imperative statement to execute when an end-of-page is encountered. In System/370, the EOP phrase can only detect an end-of-page when the printer is on-line; however, most large installations do not have on-line printers, but spool the output onto disk before printing so that the EOP does not work.

```
WRITE record FROM identifier

    AFTER
    BEFORE

    _ _ _ _ ADVANCING integer LINES

    AT EOP imperative-statement.

WRITE RPT-RECORD FROM RPT-LINE

    AFTER ADVANCING 1 LINES

    AT EOP PERFORM C20-NEW-PAGE.
```

C. WRITE POSITIONING (Not in the ANS Standard)

The WRITE POSITIONING statement is also available on System/370 compilers to control the printer. It is similar to the WRITE AFTER ADVANCING, and if used in any WRITE, must be used for all WRITES for that file. It is coded as follows:

```
WRITE record FROM identifier

                integer
                carriage-control

AFTER POSITIONING _ _ _ _ _ _ _ _ _
```

```
AT EOP imperative-statement.
```

The AT EOP phrase is optional and is identical to that in the WRITE ADVANCING. The *carriage-control* is a single-character PIC X data item that contains one of the carriage control characters.

Character	Action
1 (one)	Skip to the first line on the next page before printing.
+ (plus)	Suppress spacing; carriage return without line spacing before printing.
b (blank)	Single-space before printing.
0 (zero)	Double-space before printing.
− (minus)	Triple-space before printing.
2 thru 9	Skip to channels 2 through 9 respectively. Action depends on the printer carriage tape.
A thru C	Skip to channels 10 through 12, respectively. Action depends on the printer carriage tape.

The *integer* is an unsigned integer constant having values from 0 to 3 as follows.

Integer	Action
0	Eject to a new page before printing.
1	Single-space before printing.
2	Double-space before printing.
3	Triple-space before printing.

```
WRITE RPT-RECORD FROM RPT-LINE

   AFTER POSITIONING 0.

   [Same as:]

WRITE RPT-RECORD FROM RPT-LINE

   AFTER POSITIONING '1'.
```

D. WRITE

The normal WRITE statement can also print, and it writes each line single spaced. System/370 COBOL appends a blank to the print line so that the line is single spaced.

E.   LINAGE Clause (Not in System/370)

The ANS Standard provides the LINAGE clause in the FD entry for
setting the logical page size in terms of lines. One can specify the number
of lines of top margin, the number of lines on the page within which to
print, and the number of lines of bottom margin. The line number of a
footing line can also be specified. The LINAGE clause is coded as follows:

```
FD   file-name

     LINAGE IS lines-on-page

        FOOTING AT footing-line

        TOP top-margin

        BOTTOM bottom-margin.
```

The *lines-on-page, footing-line, top-margin,* and *bottom-margin* may be
integer literals or elementary unsigned numeric integer data items. The
values are set for the first page with the OPEN statement. These values
stay in effect unless new values are moved to the data items. The values of
data items are reset after the ADVANCING PAGE phrase is executed in
a WRITE statement.

- *lines-on-page.*   The number of lines within which to print. Must be
greater than zero.
- *footing-line.*   The line number upon which to print a footing line. The
WRITE ADVANCING PAGE will write on this line before advancing
to a new page. The *footing-line* must lie within the *lines-on-page.*
- *top-margin.*   Number of lines preceding the *lines-on-page.* May be zero.
- *bottom-margin.*   Number of lines following the *lines-on-page.* May be
zero.

The FOOTING, TOP, and BOTTOM phrases are optional. The *top-
margin* and *bottom-margin* are assumed to be zero if omitted, and *footing-
line* is assumed equal to *lines-on-page* if omitted.

A special register LINAGE-COUNTER is automatically described for
each file with the LINAGE clause. If there are more than one, they must
be qualified as LINAGE-COUNTER of *file-name.* COBOL stores the current line number in LINAGE-COUNTER. It may be referenced, but values
cannot be moved into it.

IV. PRINTING NUMERIC DATA

Numeric data is usually edited for printing to suppress leading zeros and insert commas and decimal points. The numbers are edited by defining an item in the print line that specifies the editing and then moving the number to the item to convert and edit it. The editing is specified by special edit characters in the PIC clause. There cannot be more than 30 edit characters in a PIC clause. The maximum length of the edited data item is 127 characters in System/370.

The 9, S, V, and P edit characters are those for numeric data and do not preclude arithmetic operations from being performed on the item. These edit characters were described in Chapter 6, but they are included here again for review.

A. Edit Characters for Numeric Character Data

1. 9 (Decimal Digit)

The 9 edit character in a PIC clause represents a decimal digit (0 to 9) within the number and occupies a character position. The 9 does not imply a signed number; the S, $+$, $-$, DB, or CR edit characters do this.

```
77  X  PIC 9999.              [X occupies 4 character positions.]

    MOVE 2 TO X.              [X contains '0002'.]

    MOVE -2 TO X.             [X contains '0002'.]
```

2. S (Sign)

The S edit character specifies that the number is signed, but it does not cause the sign to be printed nor to occupy a character position. In System/370, the sign is carried in the left half of the rightmost byte. A plus sign is a hexadecimal F, and a minus sign is a hexadecimal D. The S must be the leftmost edit character if included.

```
77  X  PIC S999.              [X occupies 3 character positions.]

    MOVE 2 TO X.              [X contains '002' as a positive number.]

    MOVE -2 TO X.             [X contains '002' as a negative number.
                              In System/370, this would be '00K'.]
```

3. V (Decimal Alignment)

A single V edit character coded in a PIC clause indicates the position of the internal decimal point. If V is not coded, the decimal point is assumed to be to the right of the number. V is not stored as a character and does not occupy a character position.

```
77   X   PIC S999V99.
```
[X occupies 5 character positions.]

```
     MOVE 2.3 TO X.
```
[X contains '00230'.]

```
     MOVE -2.3 TO X.
```
[X contains '00230' as a negative number.]

  High- or low-order digits will be truncated if the value is too large to be contained in the identifier.

```
     MOVE 1234.123 TO X.
```
[X contains '23412'.]

4. P (Scaling Factor)

The P edit character specifies a decimal point outside the range of the number. The P's can be coded to the left or right of the 9's, and the number of P's indicate the number of places to the left or right of the number to which the decimal point lies. (The number is limited to 18 total digits, including the positions specified by the P.)

```
77   X   PIC SP(3)999.
```
[X occupies 3 character positions.]

```
     MOVE .000476 TO X.
```
[X contains '476', but is treated as .000476 in arithmetic computations.]

```
77   Y   PIC S999P(3).
```
[Y occupies 3 character positions.]

```
     MOVE 476000 TO Y.
```
[Y contains '476', but is treated as 476000 in arithmetic computations.]

  The V edit character may be coded, but it is not needed because the P specifies the assumed decimal point. The X and Y could also be coded as follows:

```
77   X   PIC SVP(3)999.
```

```
77   Y   PIC S999P(3)V.
```

The next group of edit characters insert such nonnumeric characters as the comma, decimal point, and blanks for printing numbers. If the data item also contains numeric edit characters, the item is termed a *numeric edited* data item; otherwise it is termed an *alphanumeric* edited data item. Arithmetic operations cannot be performed on numeric or alphanumeric edited data items.

B. Edit Characters for Numeric Edited Data

Although the following edit characters are usually used for numeric edited data, alphabetic data items may contain the B edit character. Alphanumeric edited data items may contain the 0, B, and / edit characters. Numeric edited items may contain any of the following edit characters, subject to their rules of construction, in addition to the edit characters already discussed.

1. Z (Leading Zero Suppression)

The Z edit character, like the 9 edit character, represents a decimal digit (0 to 9) within the number. However, the Z causes leading zeros to be replaced with blanks. Each Z occupies a character position and cannot appear to the right of a 9 edit character.

```
77  X  PIC ZZ9V99.          [X occupies 5 character positions.]

    MOVE 2.31 TO X.         [X contains 'bb231'.]

    MOVE 26.3 TO X.         [X contains 'b2630'.]

    MOVE .94 TO X.          [X contains 'bb094'.]
```

If the item contains all Z's and no 9 edit characters, the entire item is set to blanks if it is assigned a value of zero. This includes any decimal points, commas, etc. inserted by other edit characters. Coding all Z's is equivalent to coding the BLANK WHEN ZERO clause described later in this chapter.

```
77  Y    PIC ZZZVZZ.

    MOVE ZERO TO Y.         [Y contains 'bbbbb'.]
```

2. * (Leading Asterisks)

The * edit character is identical to the Z edit character, except that it replaces leading zeros with asterisks rather than blanks. It cannot appear in the same PIC clause as the Z; nor can it appear to the right of a 9 edit character.

```
77   X   PIC **9V99.            [X occupies 5 character positions.]

     MOVE 26.31 TO X.           [X contains '*2631'.]
```

If the item contains all *'s and no 9 edit characters, the entire item is set to blanks, except for any decimal point, if the item is assigned a value of zero. The BLANK WHEN ZERO cannot be coded if the * edit character is coded.

```
77   Y   PIC **.**.

     MOVE ZERO TO Y.            [Y contains 'bb.bb'.]
```

The next group of edit characters, the +, −, DB, and CR, are for signed numbers. The S edit character must not be coded in combination with any of these. If the +, −, DB, or CR are not coded, minus numbers print with the minus sign indicated in the rightmost digit as described earlier in this chapter for the DISPLAY statement. Since no one would like to see a −23 print as 2L, the following edit characters should be used when printing numbers. A series of minus or plus edit characters also suppress zeros similar to the Z edit character.

3.   − (Minus Sign)

The − edit character indicates a signed number and inserts the minus sign where it appears in the PIC clause if the number is negative; a blank is inserted if the number is positive. A series of −'s represent numeric digits and suppress leading zeros in the same manner as the Z edit character. The minus is inserted to the left of the first nonzero digit if the number is negative; a blank is inserted if the number is positive. Each minus sign counts as a character position. The minus sign must be to the left or right of all 9 or V edit characters. The + and − edit characters cannot appear in the same PIC clause.

```
77   X   PIC ---9.             [X occupies four character positions.]

     MOVE -2 TO X.             [X contains 'bb-2'.]

     MOVE 2 TO X.              [X contains 'bbb2'.]

     MOVE 1234 TO X.           [X contains 'b234'; remember that a
                                blank is inserted, not a digit. Also notice
                                that the leading digit is truncated.]
```

```
77  Y  PIC 999-.                [Y occupies four character positions.]

    MOVE -2 TO Y.               [Y contains '002-'.]

    MOVE 2 TO Y.                [Y contains '002b'.]

77  Z   PIC -999.

    MOVE 2 TO Z.                [Z contains 'b002'.]

    MOVE -2 TO Z.              [Z contains '-002'.]
```

4. + (Plus Sign)

The + edit character specifies a signed number and inserts the sign (+ or −) where it appears in the PIC clause. A series of +'s represent numeric digits and suppress leading zeros in the same manner as the Z edit character, and the sign is inserted to the left of the first nonzero digit. Each plus sign counts as a character position. The + must be to the left or right of all 9 or V edit characters.

```
77  X  PIC +999.               [X occupies 4 character positions.]

    MOVE 2 TO X.               [X contains '+002'.]

    MOVE -2 TO X.              [X contains '-002'.]
```

5. CR (Credit Symbol)

A single CR edit character can only be coded in the rightmost position of the PIC clause. If the number is negative, CR is inserted; otherwise two blanks are inserted. CR counts as two character positions.

```
77  X  PIC 999CR.              [X occupies five character positions.]

    MOVE -27 TO X.            [X contains '027CR'.]

    MOVE 27 TO X.             [X contains '027bb'.]
```

6. DB (Debit Symbol)

The DB edit character is identical to the CR edit character, except that the DB is inserted if the number is negative.

```
77  X  PIC 99DB.               [X occupies five character positions.]

    MOVE -1 TO X.             [X contains '01DB'.]

    MOVE 1 TO X.              [X contains '01bb'.]
```

7. . (Decimal Point)

The decimal point edit character is inserted where it appears in the PIC clause and occupies a character position. Only one decimal point can be coded; it specifies the decimal alignment, and so the V edit character must not be used. The decimal point cannot be the rightmost character in a PIC clause.

```
77  X  PIC ZZ9.99.                [X occupies six character positions.]

    MOVE 22.31 TO X.              [X contains 'b22.31.]
```

8. , (Comma)

The comma edit character is inserted where it appears in the PIC clause and counts as a character position. If leading zeros are suppressed, the comma is replaced by a blank if the characters to the left of the comma are all zero. The comma cannot be the rightmost character in the PIC clause.

```
77  X  PIC 9,999.                 [X occupies five character positions.]

    MOVE 4 TO X.                  [X contains '0,004'.]

    MOVE 4000 TO X.              [X contains '4,000'.]

77  Y  PIC Z,ZZ9.                 [Y occupies five character positions.]

    MOVE 4 TO Y.                  [Y contains 'bbbb4'.]

    MOVE 4000 TO Y.              [Y contains '4,000'.]

77  W  PIC *,**9.                 [Y occupies five character positions.]

    MOVE 4 TO W.                 [W contains '****4'.]

77  Z  PIC --,--9.                [Z occupies six character positions.]

    MOVE -4 TO Z.                [Z contains 'bbbb-4'.]

    MOVE -4000 TO Z.            [Z contains '-4,000'.]
```

9. $ (Dollar Sign)

A single $ edit character is inserted where it appears in the PIC clause and counts as a character position. A series of $'s represent numeric digits, suppressing leading zeros in the same manner as the Z edit character, and a single $ is inserted to the left of the first nonzero digit. The $ must be to the left of all 9 or V edit characters.

```
77  X  PIC $999.          [X occupies four character positions.]

    MOVE 4 TO X.          [X contains '$004'.]

77  Y  PIC $$$9.          [Y occupies four character positions.]

    MOVE 4 TO Y.          [Y contains 'bb$4'.]
```

The edit characters $+$, $-$, $*$, Z, and $, when used as floating edit characters, cannot appear in the same PIC clause. That is, they are mutually exclusive unless there is a single instance of the characters.

10. B (Blank)

The B edit character causes a blank to be inserted wherever it appears in a PIC clause and counts as a character position.

```
77  X  PIC B9B9B.         [X occupies five character positions.]

    MOVE 21 TO X.         [X contains 'b2b1b'.]

    MOVE 123 TO X.        [X contains 'b2b3b'.]
```

11. 0 (Zero)

The 0 edit character causes a zero to be inserted wherever it appears in a PIC clause and counts as a character position.

```
77  X  PIC 0990.          [X occupies four character positions.]

    MOVE 21 TO X.         [X contains '0210'.]

    MOVE 123 TO X.        [X contains '0230'.]
```

12. E (Floating Point) (Not a Part of the ANS Standard)

System/370 compilers permit the E edit character for COMP-1 and COMP-2 numbers. Floating-point numbers are specified by an E separating the number from its exponent. The E occupies a character position. Either a $+$ or $-$ sign may be used for both the number and its exponent. A $+$ causes either a plus or minus sign to be inserted, and a $-$ causes only minus signs to be inserted.

```
77  X  PIC +9(3)V99E+99.   [X occupies 10 character positions.]

    MOVE 2.33E6 TO X.      [X contains '+00233E+06'.]
```

13.   X (Alphanumeric Character)

The X edit characters represent any alphanumeric character and occupy character positions.

```
77  Y  PIC X999X.
```

      `MOVE ' ⟨234⟩' TO Y.`   [Y contains ' ⟨234⟩'.]

14.   A (Alphabetic Character)

The A edit characters represent any alphabetic characters or blanks and occupy character positions.

```
77  Y  PIC A999A.
```

      `MOVE 'Z234Z' TO Y.`   [Y contains 'Z234Z'.]

15.   / (Stroke Edit Character) (Not in System/370 COBOL)

The / edit character causes a stroke character to be inserted wherever it appears in a PIC clause and occupies a character position.

```
77  X  PIC 99/99/99.
```

      `MOVE '122577' TO X.`   [X contains '12/25/77'.]

16.   BLANK WHEN ZERO

The BLANK WHEN ZERO clause is not an edit character, but is a clause added to the data description entry to set the entire data item to blanks if a value of zero is stored in it.   The * edit character cannot be coded in the PIC character-string if BLANK WHEN ZERO is coded.

```
77  X  PIC ZZ9.9 BLANK WHEN ZERO.
```

    [X contains five character positions.]

      `MOVE 1 TO X.`

        [X contains 'bb1.0'.]

      `MOVE 0 TO X.`

        [X contains 'bbbbb'.]

17.   SPECIAL-NAMES SECTION.

The SPECIAL-NAMES SECTION may specify a symbol other than the $ to be the currency symbol. It may also specify that the roles of the comma and period are to be reversed as edit characters (9,999.99 becomes 9.999,99) to print numbers in the European manner.

```
OBJECT-COMPUTER. computer.

SPECIAL-NAMES.

    CURRENCY SIGN IS 'character'

    DECIMAL POINT IS COMMA.
```

Either CURRENCY SIGN or DECIMAL POINT or both may be coded. The character may be any character except 0 to 9, A to D, P, R, S, V, X, Z, blank, or the special characters [* − , . ; ( ) + ']. (L / and = are also prohibited in the ANS Standard.)

Only alphanumeric literal initial values can be assigned to numeric or alphanumeric edited data items, and no editing is performed on the value.

```
77  X    PIC ZZ9 VALUE '006'.    [X contains '006'.]
```

There are two additional techniques used in printing numbers, although they are not a part of the editing. Often a column of numbers must be underlined to denote a total, and the total is double underlined to highlight it.

```
1432
3216
5648
====
```

A single underline is accomplished by printing the underscore character (_) and suppressing line spacing. This overprints the underscore over the previous line, underlining the item: 3216. The double underline is accomplished by printing a line of equal signs (=) on the next line.

```
5648
====
```

V. PRINTING REPORTS

A report should contain a title describing what it is and some unique identification in the heading, perhaps the program name, to tie it back to the program generating it. Paginate reports, and date them with either the date of the computer run, the date of the period covered in the report, or both. Print clear column and row titles to make the report self-descriptive.

The column headings and at least a portion of the page heading should be repeated on the second and subsequent pages. Indent row titles if they have a hierarchical relationship.

```
STATE

    COUNTY

       CITY
```

Print totals at each level in the hierarchy for columns of numbers unless the numbers would have no meaning, as for example the ages of people in a personnel listing.

Perhaps the most common problem in printing reports is to exceed the columns on a page. What can you do if you need 150 columns and the print page is limited to 132 columns? There are several alternatives.

- Squeeze any blanks from between columns. Columns should not be run together, but often several blanks can be squeezed down to one.

```
   23    15    64.7    [Squeezed down to:]   23 15 64.7
```

- Eliminate the nonessential. The 132 characters in a print line is a considerable amount of information, and there is likely to be something printed that is nonessential. For example, if three columns contain a starting date, an ending date, and a duration, all of the information is contained in any two of the columns. The third column may be convenient, but it is also redundant.
- Print two or more lines, staggering the columns.

```
              START DATE    FIRST 6-MO

                 END DATE       SECOND 6-MO
DEPARTMENT 115

    JOE DOE   01/01/76     100,000.00

                 12/31/77       250,000.00
```

- Print two reports, where the second report is a logical continuation of the columns of the first so that the two reports placed side by side form a complete report. Print all the page and column headings of the second report too so that it can stand by itself. In practice, people will not lay the reports side by side because it is awkward. The second report can be printed on the following page by storing it in a table and printing it from the table after printing the first page, or it can be printed as a separate file so that it forms a completely separate report.

Unnecessary lines should be eliminated from reports. A line containing all zeros might not be printed, and a total line might be eliminated if only one item goes into the totals.

```
           HOURS    [Better as:]                          HOURS

ENG DEPT                                       ENG DEPT

   JOHN DOE      0                                MARY ROE 10

   MARY ROE     10

   DEPT TOTAL   10
```

Give careful thought to the credibility of reports. Column totals can be correct but appear wrong through rounding, and they also can be wrong but appear right through truncation. The former diminishes a report's credibility, but the latter shatters it if it is discovered. The first thing many people do when they receive a new report is to add up the columns by hand to check the totals. If a person cannot understand how the numbers in a report are derived, he is quite justified in placing little faith in it.

Reports are made more credible by printing numbers and totals in a logical sequence so that a person can see how the totals are derived. This is not difficult with most reports, but it can be a problem in management reports because the reader often does not want to see the full detail, but only a condensation of it. For example, it is logical to print totals at the bottom of a column of numbers, and this is also easier to program, but to a manager the total may be the most important item, hence should appear at the top of the page.

If a report must print totals at the top of the page before the detail lines, there are three normal solutions. First, you can store the lines of data in a table, total the table, and then print the lines from the table. This does not work when the report becomes large, however, because of the size of the table that would be required. If this happens, you can pass through the file twice—the first time to compute the totals and the second time to print the report. However, this has limitations if there are many subtotals to compute.

The third alternative is to write the lines into a file with a sort key appended containing the report, page, and line number. When the last line is written and the total line is formed, it is given a page and line number to cause it to be sorted in front of the detail lines. After the report is completed, the lines can be sorted, the file read and the sort key dropped, and the actual report printed.

In generating a report from a file, the file must usually be sorted so that the lines will come out in the proper order. If only certain records are selected to go into the report, the sequence for this should be select, sort, and then report because sorts are expensive, and doing the selection before the sorting reduces the number of records that need to be sorted.

The COBOL READ and WRITE statements are a primitive way in which to write reports. Before you write a report using them, you should consider using the COBOL report writer described in the following chapter. It makes it easier to write, understand, and change reports.

EXERCISES

1. Show what the following numbers will look like in the following statements.

```
77   W   PIC $$,$$$,$$9.99CR.

     MOVE 23658.97 TO W.

     MOVE -2 TO W.

     MOVE .01 TO W.


77   X   PIC Z,ZZZ,ZZ9.

     MOVE 26531 TO X.

     MOVE -4 TO X.


77   Y   PIC -****9.

     MOVE -16 TO Y.

     MOVE 327 TO Y.

     MOVE -823945 TO Y.


77   Z   PIC $--,---,--9.99 BLANK WHEN ZERO.

     MOVE 35278.6 TO Z.
```

```
MOVE -247.96 TO Z.

MOVE ZERO TO Z.
```

2. Print a table containing the square roots of the integers from 1 to 1000. Print 50 values per page in the following format.

```
SQUARE OF NUMBERS              PAGE xxx

NUMBER      SQUARE

   1            1

   2            4

   .            .

   .            .

   .            .

1000      1,000,000
```

3. Print a table containing the square roots of the integers from 1 to 1000. Print the square roots with five significant digits of accuracy to the right of the decimal point. Print 50 lines per page with each line containing two columns of values as shown. Print the page heading at the top of each new page.

```
                    TABLE OF SQUARE ROOTS              PAGE xxx

NUMBER   SQUARE ROOT              NUMBER   SQUARE ROOT

   1        1.00000                 51        7.14143

   2        1.41421                 52        7.21110

   .           .                     .           .

   .           .                     .           .

   .           .                     .           .

  50        7.07107                100       10.00000
```

4. Print a table showing the future value of an amount invested at 8% per annum in increments of 1 year for 30 years. The equation for the future value is: amount $(1.08)^n$, where n is the year. Print the table in the format shown. Print the table for amounts ranging from $100 to $1000 in increments of $200.

```
        FUTURE VALUE TABLE                     PAGE xxx

AMOUNT:  $100.00       INTEREST RATE:  8.00%

Year                     FUTURE VALUE

    1                      $103.00

    2                      $116.64

    .                         .
    .                         .
    .                         .

   30                     $1,006.27
```

5. Write a program to read in a card containing an initial investment, an interest rate, a number of years, and a starting date. The card has the following format. Given this information, you are to produce the following report.

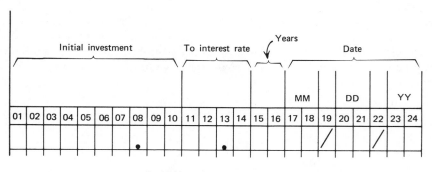

```
                    INVESTMENT ANALYSIS                    PAGE xxx

PREPARED ESPECIALLY FOR:   your name

INITIAL INVESTMENT: $xxx,xxx.xx     INTEREST: xx.x%     YEARS: xx

   DATE     CURRENT BALANCE   INTEREST EARNED   NEW BALANCE   YEAR

xx/xx/xx   $xxx,xxx.xx       $xx,xxx.xx        $xx,xxx.xx     xx
```

Allow 30 lines per page. The interest earned is computed as the current balance times the interest divided by 100. The new balance is the current balance plus the interest earned.

fifteen

REPORT WRITER

Many examples have been presented throughout this book to illustrate the advantages of structured programming over conventional programming. The examples show the structured programming techniques to be better, but often the difference between structured programming and conventional programming is not dramatic. The COBOL report writer is not a part of structured programming, but its advantages over the conventional programming of reports are often dramatic. The report writer greatly simplifies the writing of reports and should be used whenever possible.

The report writer generates reports with much less Procedure Division coding than printing each individual line, although the Data Division becomes more complex because it specifies the report format, source of the data, and the totals to print. The entire report is parameterized, making it easier to change. Once the report format has been specified, the report writer automatically takes care of page breaks, page headings and footings, moving data to the print line, and column and row subtotaling and totaling.

Part of the reason the report writer is easier for writing reports than the conventional manner with WRITE statements is that it knows that it is printing output on a printer, and is adapted especially for this. For example, if WEEKLY STATUS is to print in column 60, it is coded as:

```
05  COLUMN 60 PIC X(13) VALUE 'WEEKLY STATUS'.
```

With the conventional method of printing reports with the WRITE statement, FILLER must be inserted and set to SPACES, making it more complicated, harder to understand, and harder to change.

```
05  FILLER PIC X(59) VALUE SPACES.

05  FILLER PIC X(13) VALUE 'WEEKLY STATUS'.
```

The main reason for using the report writer is to make reports easier to write and maintain. It will probably be less efficient than writing the report in the conventional manner because of the report writer overhead, but the loss in efficiency is likely to be negligible. Report writer programs are easy to maintain, but in practice few programmers have become familiar with the report writer, which complicates maintenance. However, the report writer is not difficult to follow because it lays the entire report out in the Data Division, specifying the format, contents, and control breaks.

The report writer simplifies the deceptively complex logic required to compute totals and subtotals and roll them forward. The report writer performs these operations automatically, but if the report does not come out as expected, it may be difficult to discover the cause of the error. The logical flow and intermediate results cannot be printed with debugging statements as would be possible if the report were programmed in the conventional way. The report is specified in the Data Division, and if there is an error, the programmer has only his or her intellect to aid in debugging the problem. Mitigating this, though, the report writer produces an output that usually gives enough information for debugging.

Do not use the report writer for reports with complex formats such as those in which different data require different page headings. Nor should it be used where there are significant exceptions to be handled in the report, such as printing totals first, followed by the detail lines. The report writer is best for reports that have the same page heading format on each page of the report and are composed of rows and columns. The columns can be crossfooted, and the detail lines can be summed to several levels with appropriate totals printed according to some specified hierarchy. Each level in the hierarchy can also have a heading line printed.

I. SAMPLE REPORT

The following simple example illustrates the report writer. A file containing the population of cities is read, and the report writer prints a report in the following format.

```
                                    CITY LISTING

                                              PAGE xx


CITY:   name of city          population

CITY:   name of city          population

            .
            .
            .
```

The report writer writes a normal print file that must be opened before being used and closed when the report is completed. The WRITE statement cannot write on the same file. The FD entry specifies a report name, and this report name is then defined in the REPORT SECTION.

```
INPUT-OUTPUT SECTION.

FILE-CONTROL.

     SELECT RPT-FILE ASSIGN TO UT-S-FILEO.
```

　　　[RPT-FILE is the print file upon which the report is written.]

```
     SELECT IN-FILE ASSIGN TO UT-S-MFILE.
```

　　　[IN-FILE is the input file containing the cities.]

```
DATA DIVISION.

FILE SECTION.

FD   RPT-FILE

     RECORD CONTAINS 133 CHARACTERS

     BLOCK CONTAINS 0 RECORDS

     LABEL RECORDS STANDARD

     REPORT IS CITIES.
```

　　　[The FD entry describes the print file. The REPORT clause names the report, CITIES, to be written on the file.]

```
FD   IN-FILE

     RECORD CONTAINS 65 CHARACTERS

     BLOCK CONTAINS 0 RECORDS

     LABEL RECORDS STANDARD.

01   FILE-REC   PIC X(65).
```

[A FD is required for the input file.]

```
WORKING-STORAGE SECTION.

01   NEXT-CITY.

     05   STATE        PIC X(20).

     05   COUNTY       PIC X(20).

     05   CITY         PIC X(20).

     05   POPULATION   PIC S9(9) COMP-3.
```

[The input file will be read into NEXT-CITY.]

```
REPORT SECTION.
```

[The REPORT SECTION describes the reports.]

```
RD   CITIES
```

[A RD entry describes each individual report, CITIES in our example.]

```
     PAGE 60 LINES
```

[The report size is 60 lines per page.]

```
     HEADING 1
```

[The first item printed, the page heading in this example, begins on line 1.]

```
     FIRST DETAIL 5.
```

[The body of the report begins on line 5.]

```
01   TYPE PAGE HEADING.
```

[The data items that follow describe the page heading report group. It is termed a
report group because it may consist of several lines. The page heading is automatically
printed at the top of each page. A report may consist of a report heading printed once
at the start of the report, a page heading printed at the top of each page, control headings
printed before a group of detail lines to title them, detail lines constituting the main

body of the report, control footings for totaling detail lines, page footings to print something at the bottom of each page, and a report footing to print something once at the end of the report such as a grand total. Each item is optional, and this report has only a page heading and detail lines.]

```
05  LINE 1 COLUMN 40 PIC X(12) VALUE 'CITY LISTING'.
```

[CITY LISTING is printed in columns 40 to 51 of line 1. The LINE clause defines the start of a new line and tells where the line is printed on the page. COLUMN specifies the starting column in which to print the data, and the PIC clause specifies its format. Data to be printed can be literals specified in a VALUE clause, identifiers named in a SOURCE clause, or subtotals generated by the report writer specified in a SUM clause.]

```
05  LINE PLUS 2.
```

[The next line is spaced two lines beyond the last line.]

```
10 COLUMN 80 PIC X(4) VALUE 'PAGE'.
```

[PAGE prints in columns 80 to 83.]

```
10  COLUMN 85 PIC ZZ9 SOURCE PAGE-COUNTER.
```

[The value of PAGE-COUNTER is printed in columns 85 to 87 of the same line. The SOURCE clause names the item to be printed and moves it to the print line according to the PIC clause. PAGE-COUNTER, automatically maintained by the report writer, is a special register described in System/370 as PIC S9(5) COMP-3 containing the current page number.]

```
01  DTL-LINE TYPE DETAIL LINE PLUS 2.
```

[This line is a detail report group. It must be assigned a name, DTL-LINE here, and it is printed with the execution of each GENERATE statement that names it. Each line is printed two lines beyond the previous line.]

```
05  COLUMN 1 PIC X(5) VALUE 'CITY: '.
```

[*CITY.* will print in columns 1 to 5.]

```
05  COLUMN 8 PIC X(20) SOURCE CITY.
```

[The value of the identifier CITY from the input file is printed in columns 8 to 27.]

```
05  COLUMN 29 PIC Z(8)9V SOURCE POPULATION.
```

[The value of the identifier POPULATION from the input file is printed in columns 29 to 37.]

```
PROCEDURE DIVISION.

A00-BEGIN.

    OPEN INPUT IN-FILE,

            OUTPUT RPT-FILE.
```

[The report file must be opened as with all files.]

```
    INITIATE CITIES.
```

[The INITIATE statement names the report and does all the housekeeping required to begin the report.]

```
    MOVE LOW-VALUES TO CITY.
```

[The paragraph that reads the file is performed until an end-of-file terminates the loop.]

```
    PERFORM PRINT-IT UNTIL CITY = HIGH-VALUES.

    TERMINATE CITIES.
```

[The TERMINATE statement names the report and does all the housekeeping required to terminate the report.]

```
    CLOSE IN-FILE,

            RPT-FILE.
```

[The report file must be closed as with all files.]

```
    STOP RUN.
```

[The program is terminated.]

```
PRINT-IT.

    READ IN-FILE INTO NEXT-CITY

        AT END MOVE HIGH-VALUES TO CITY.

    IF CITY NOT = HIGH-VALUES

        THEN GENERATE DTL-LINE.
```

[The GENERATE statement prints the detail lines by naming the detail report group. The page heading is automatically printed at the top of each page.]

```
**** END OF PROGRAM
```

II. CONTROL BREAKS

Most reports need control breaks to print headings and totals. In the previous example, the file might be sorted on state, county, and city. A detail
line is generated for each city. We might want to make the county a control
break to print the total population for all cities in the county, and also
make the state a control break to print the total population for each state
by summing all the counties in the state. This is accomplished by CON-
TROL FOOTINGs. In addition to the CONTROL FOOTINGs, we might
want to print a heading with each new state, and for each new county within
a state. This is accomplished by CONTROL HEADINGs. When a control
break occurs, the CONTROL FOOTINGs print first to total the previous
lines, then the CONTROL HEADINGs print to title the new detail lines,
and then the detail lines print. The report is to appear as follows:

```
                          CITY LISTING

                                                  PAGE xx

STATE                                        )
                                             }   Control headings
    county                                   )

        CITY: name of city       population  )
                                             }   Detail lines
        CITY: name of city       population  )

          .
          .
          .

    COUNTY TOTAL                 population   )
                                             |
          .                                  |
          .                                  }   control footings
          .                                  |
                                             |
STATE TOTAL                      population   )
```

To accomplish this, the report is coded as follows.

```
REPORT SECTION.

RD   CITIES

     PAGE 60 LINES
```

```
    HEADING 1

    FIRST DETAIL 5

    CONTROLS ARE STATE,

                COUNTY.
```

The CONTROLS clause names the items that are to cause the control breaks. The items are listed in order from major to minor, and the input file must be sorted in the same order.

```
01  TYPE PAGE HEADING.

    05  LINE 1 COLUMN 40 PIC X(12) VALUE 'CITY LISTING'.

    05  LINES PLUS 2.

        10  COLUMN 80 PIC X(4) VALUE 'PAGE'.

        10  COLUMN 85 ZZ9 SOURCE PAGE-COUNTER.

01  TYPE CONTROL HEADING STATE LINE PLUS 2.
```

[The CONTROL HEADING, spaced two lines beyond the previous line, is printed as each new STATE is encountered.]

```
    05  COLUMN 1 PIC X(20) SOURCE STATE.

01  TYPE CONTROL HEADING COUNTY LINE PLUS 1.

    05  COLUMN 3 PIC X(20) SOURCE COUNTY.
```

[This CONTROL HEADING prints when a new COUNTY is encountered.]

```
01  DTL-LINE TYPE DETAIL LINE PLUS 1.

    05  COLUMN 5 PIC X(5) VALUE 'CITY:'.

    05  COLUMN 12 PIC X(20) SOURCE CITY.

    05  COLUMN 33 PIC Z(8)9 SOURCE POPULATION.

01  TYPE CONTROL FOOTING COUNTY LINE PLUS 2.
```

[This CONTROL FOOTING prints the total of the previous county.]

```
    05  COLUMN 3 PIC X(12) VALUE 'COUNTY TOTAL'.

    05  S1 COLUMN 33 PIC Z(8)9 SUM POPULATION.
```

[The SUM clause sums the POPULATION as each detail line is printed and resets it to zero after the footing is printed. The line is given a name, S1, because it is referred to in a subsequent line.]

```
01  TYPE CONTROL FOOTING STATE LINE PLUS 2.
```

[This CONTROL FOOTING prints the total for each state.]

```
    05  COLUMN 1 PIC X(11) VALUE 'STATE TOTAL'.

    05  COLUMN 33 PIC Z(8)9 SUM S1.
```

[This SUM counter sums the previous S1 SUM counter to give the county population.]

This completes the report changes; the Procedure Division need not be changed at all. The example illustrates a major advantage of the report writer—that substantial changes can be made to reports solely within the Data Division where the changes are relatively easy. Had the report been written conventionally with WRITE statements, this change might have required scores of Procedure Division statements and taken days to debug.

When a control break occurs, it first causes a control break for all lower levels. The first GENERATE statement prints any REPORT HEADING report group, then any PAGE HEADING report group, and then causes a control break for all CONTROL HEADINGS so that they print before the first detail line. The TERMINATE statement causes a control break for all CONTROL FOOTINGS so that the final totals are printed at the end of the report. The control breaks occur in the following order:

- Minor to major for the control footings.
- Major to minor for the control headings.
- The detail lines are printed.

Thus when a GENERATE statement is executed and a new state is encountered, the following occurs.

- Control footing for the old county prints the total for the previous cities in the county, adds its sum to the state SUM counter, and resets the county SUM counter to zero.
- Control footing for the old state prints the total for the previous counties in the state and resets the state SUM counter to zero.
- Control heading for the state to print the new state.
- Control heading for the county to print the new county.
- Print the detail line for the city and sum its population into the county SUM counter.

A FINAL control heading can be specified to print once when the first GENERATE statement is executed, perhaps to print something that is to go only on the first page of the report. A FINAL control footing can also be specified to print once when the TERMINATE statement is executed, perhaps to print the total for all the states. The CONTROLS clause is coded in the RD statement as follows. The *data-names* must be listed in order from major to minor. (The ANS Standard prohibits control *data-names* from being subscripted or indexed, or from having a subordinate item containing the OCCURS DEPENDING ON clause. These restrictions are not in System/370 COBOL.)

```
RD   report-name

                    FINAL
                    data-name, data-name, ...
                    FINAL, data-name, data-name, ...

     CONTROLS ARE _ _ _ _ _ _ _ _ _ _ _ _ _ _ _ _ _ _
```

There can be only a single nonoverlapping item used for each control break. To define a control break to occur when any one of several items change values, place them in a record and then name the group item in the CONTROLS clause. For example, if you want a control break to occur when either AGE or WEIGHT changes value, define them within the same group item.

```
05   AGE-WEIGHT.

     10   AGE             PIC S9(3) COMP-3.

     10   WEIGHT          PIC S9(3) COMP-3.

     □ □ □

RD   report-name

     CONTROLS ARE AGE-WEIGHT.
```

The same control break will occur if either AGE or WEIGHT changes value. If the report is printed from a file, the record may not contain the proper record to produce the report. For this, define the record you want in WORKING-STORAGE and move the I/O record items to the record as each I/O record is read.

III. REPORT GROUPS

The report groups have already been illustrated, but they provide several additional facilities. A *report group* is one or more lines printed together as a group, such as a page heading. A report group may also be a null group that is not printed, but is used for control breaks or for summing items to be printed. A report must contain at least one DETAIL report group, and all other report groups are optional. The seven report groups are as follows.

- REPORT HEADING. Optional. Printed automatically once at the start of the report when the first GENERATE statement is executed. A single REPORT HEADING group may be specified per report to print a cover sheet, distribution list, or any other information that pertains to the entire report. The REPORT HEADING starts on a new page.
- PAGE HEADING. Optional. Printed automatically at the top of each new page. A single PAGE HEADING group may be specified per report to print the page heading, page number, and column headings. A PAGE HEADING is automatically printed when a page overflows, and can also be programmed to occur either before an individual line is printed with the LINE NEXT PAGE clause or after a report group is printed with the NEXT GROUP NEXT PAGE clause. The first GENERATE statement prints the first PAGE HEADING following any REPORT HEADING. For this reason, page breaks should usually be caused by the NEXT GROUP NEXT PAGE clause in a CONTROL FOOTING. If they are caused by a CONTROL HEADING, the report will begin with two page headings; one for the first GENERATE statement, and one from the first CONTROL HEADING break caused by the same GENERATE.
- CONTROL HEADING. Optional. A heading printed automatically above a DETAIL line group when a control break occurs. Control items are named in the CONTROLS clause, and a control break occurs when an item is presented with a changed value. A FINAL control heading break occurs only once when the first GENERATE statement is executed, to print a control heading at the start of the report. For each report, there may be a single CONTROL HEADING group for each control item and for FINAL.
- DETAIL. Required. Prints the main body of the report. The GENERATE statement prints each group of detail lines. There may also be

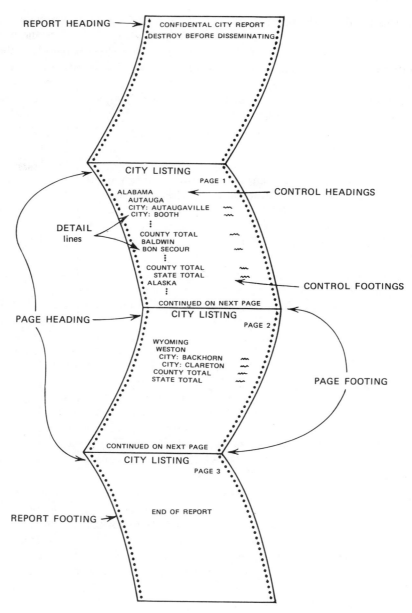

FIGURE 10. Report groups.

several DETAIL report groups in each report, useful if some detail lines are to be formatted differently than others.

- CONTROL FOOTING. Optional. Printed automatically following a DETAIL report group to print totals when a control break occurs. The controls are identifiers named in the CONTROLS clause or FINAL. The FINAL control footing break occurs at the end of the report when the TERMINATE statement is executed. For each report, there may be a single CONTROL FOOTING group for each control item and for FINAL.

- PAGE FOOTING. Optional. Printed automatically at the bottom of each page when a page break occurs. Only one PAGE FOOTING group may be specified per report, to print totals or remarks.

- REPORT FOOTING. Optional. Printed automatically at the end of the report by the TERMINATE statement, perhaps to print a trailer sheet for the report. Only one REPORT FOOTING group may be specified per report. The REPORT FOOTING group does not automatically start on a new page.

The report groups are printed in the order shown in Figure 10. The PAGE HEADING automatically begins on a new page; the NEXT GROUP clause described later can specify the line spacing or eject to a new page following each report group.

IV. RD STATEMENT

Each report is assigned a name in the REPORT clause of the FD entry and then described by a RD entry in the REPORT SECTION. The RD entry specifies the lines on the page within which the report groups are printed and the data items to be used for control breaks. The RD entry is followed by the description of each of the report groups in the report.

```
DATA DIVISION.

FILE SECTION.

FD  file-name

    RECORD CONTAINS 133 CHARACTERS

    BLOCK CONTAINS 0 RECORDS

    LABEL RECORDS STANDARD
```

```
REPORT IS report-name.
```

[Several reports can be written consecutively on the same file by coding **REPORTS ARE** *report-name, report-name, ...*]

```
WORKING-STORAGE SECTION.
```

```
LINKAGE SECTION.
```

```
REPORT SECTION.
```

```
RD   report-name
```

`PAGE 60 LINES`	[Number of lines per page. Maximum of 66 on most printers. If omitted, HEADING, FIRST DETAIL, LAST DETAIL and FOOTING must also be omitted, and the report is printed single spaced with no page breaks.]
`HEADING 1`	[Line number of first item on each page. If omitted, one is assumed.]
`FIRST DETAIL 5`	[First line number of report body on page. If omitted, HEADING line is assumed.]
`LAST DETAIL 40`	[Last line number of report body on page. If omitted, FOOTING line is assumed.]
`FOOTING 50`	[Last line number of control footing. Page footing begins on next line. If omitted, LAST DETAIL line is assumed, unless it too is omitted, then the PAGE line number is assumed.]
`CONTROLS clause.`	[Specifies items used for control breaks, and is described later.]

The integer literal line numbers must be in ascending order and cannot exceed the PAGE size specified. Figure 11 illustrates the positioning of the report groups on the page as specified by the previous RD statement.

V. REPORT FORMAT

The report format is specified as a record following the RD entry. The report is composed of one or more report groups, each in turn composed

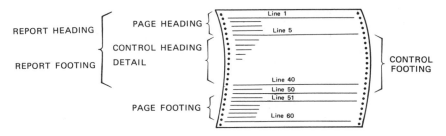

FIGURE 11.   Line positioning of report groups.

of one or more lines. Lines within a report group cannot be selectively printed; either all the lines are printed or none. (The report writer cannot write lines longer than the line size of the printer.) The 01 level defines a report group with the TYPE clause. The LINE clause starts a new line, and it may be coded at the group level in which the several subordinate items are printed on the same line, or at the detail level if the line consists of only a single detail item. The record may have levels from 01 to 48. Elementary items specifying data to be printed must have the COLUMN clause indicating the starting column in which to print the data, a PIC clause specifying the format of the data, and a VALUE, SOURCE, or SUM clause to specify the source of the data. The following examples illustrate the composition of lines in a report.

```
01  TYPE clause LINE clause COLUMN clause PIC clause VALUE clause.
```

[This report group contains a single line with a single value. The ANS Standard prohibits the 01 level from being an elementary item.]

```
01  TYPE clause.
```

[This report group contains the following two lines.]

```
    05  LINE clause.
```

[The first line of the report group contains the following two items.]

```
        10  COLUMN clause PIC clause SOURCE clause.

        10 COLUMN clause PIC clause VALUE clause.

    05  LINE clause COLUMN clause PIC clause VALUE clause.
```

[The second line of the report group contains a single item.]

The following two DETAIL lines are equivalent.

```
01   DTL-LINE TYPE DETAIL LINE PLUS 1.

     05   COLUMN 10 PIC X(20) SOURCE STATE.

     [Or:]

01   DTL-LINE TYPE DETAIL LINE PLUS 1 COLUMN 10 PIC X(20)
     SOURCE STATE.
```

Each record may be assigned a unique name. Detail lines must be named, and names are also required for subtotaling and in the USE BEFORE REPORTING statement described later in this chapter.

```
01   group-name TYPE ...

     05   line-name LINE ...
```

The report format is specified by the following clauses.

A. TYPE Clause

The TYPE clause can only be coded at the 01 level where it is required. It is coded as follows.

```
01   TYPE REPORT HEADING
```

[REPORT HEADING may be abbreviated as RH.]

```
01   TYPE PAGE HEADING
```

[PAGE HEADING may be abbreviated as PH.]

```
                              FINAL
                              identifier

01   TYPE CONTROL HEADING _ _ _ _ _
```

[CONTROL HEADING may be abbreviated as CH. The CONTROLS clause in the RD entry must name the *identifier* or FINAL that is to trigger the control heading.]

```
01   group-name TYPE DETAIL
```

[DETAIL may be abbreviated as DE, and must be assigned a name.]

```
                              FINAL
                              identifier
01   TYPE CONTROL FOOTING _ _ _ _ _
```

[CONTROL FOOTING may be abbreviated as CF. The CONTROLS clause in the RD entry must name the *identifier* or FINAL that is to trigger the control footing.]

01   TYPE PAGE FOOTING

[PAGE FOOTING may be abbreviated as PF.]

01   TYPE REPORT FOOTING.

[REPORT FOOTING may be abbreviated as RF.]

B. LINE Clause

Specifies the start of the print line and where it is to print on the page.

```
        line
        PLUS lines
        NEXT PAGE

   LINE _ _ _ _ _ _
```

- *line.*   A positive integer literal specifying the absolute line number.
- PLUS *lines.*   A positive integer literal specifying the relative line number.
- NEXT PAGE.   Ejects to a new page, causing any PAGE HEADING to be printed. The item begins on the next page in the FIRST DETAIL *line* specified in the RD entry. NEXT PAGE can be coded for CONTROL HEADING, DETAIL, CONTROL FOOTING, and REPORT FOOTING types only, and only on the first line of the report group.

Within the report group, line numbers must be in ascending order. A relative line number cannot precede an absolute line number.

Incorrect: Correct:

```
   LINE PLUS 2               LINE 30

   LINE 30                   LINE PLUS 2

   LINE NEXT PAGE            LINE NEXT PAGE
```

The line spacing is not difficult except when a page eject occurs. LINE NEXT PAGE causes a page eject, and the line is printed on the FIRST DETAIL *line.* An absolute line number less than the current line number also causes a page eject, and the line is printed on the LINE *line* of the RD statement. A LINE PLUS *line* will also cause a page eject if the line will not fit on the page, and the line is then printed on the FIRST DETAIL *line*. If LINE PLUS 2 is coded and the PLUS 2 would put the line off the page, the line is printed on the FIRST DETAIL *line* of the next page, not the FIRST DETAIL *line* plus 2.

C. COLUMN Clause

COLUMN specifies the starting column in which to print the elementary data item. The column number is a positive integer literal with values from 1 to the maximum print positions on the printer.

```
COLUMN column

COLUMN 64

COLUMN 112
```

Items are not printed if COLUMN is omitted. This enables items to be totaled for control footings without printing the values in detail lines. To suppress an entire detail line so that all items are totaled without a line being printed, see the GENERATE statement further on in this chapter.

D. PIC Clause

Specifies the format of the data item. Only USAGE DISPLAY is permitted, and PIC may contain any edit characters. Data items are moved to the print line and converted according to the PIC clause when they are printed. The JUST and BLANK WHEN ZERO clauses may also be included in the PIC clause.

```
PIC X(10).

PIC ZZZ9.99 BLANK WHEN ZERO.

PIC X(15) JUST.
```

The data to be printed is specified by either a VALUE, a SOURCE, or a SUM clause.

E. VALUE Clause

Assigns a literal value to the print line.

```
05   COLUMN 30 PIC X(3) VALUE 'ABC'.
```

```
05  COLUMN 40 PIC ZZ9 VALUE 10.
```

[The 10 prints as '010' in column 40 to 42. Remember that items coded in the VALUE clause are not edited. Hence the VALUE used with PIC clauses that contain edit characters must specify alphanumeric data.]

F. SOURCE Clause

Names an identifier to be moved to the print line and converted according to the PIC clause.

```
05  COLUMN 20 PIC ZZ9 SOURCE POPULATION.
```

The identifier may be qualified, subscripted, or indexed.

```
05  COLUMN 30 PIC X(10) SOURCE STATE (INDX1).

05  COLUMN 40 PIC X(20) SOURCE CITY OF STATE (10).
```

SOURCE may also name an identifier that a CONTROL FOOTING is to sum, but which itself is not to print. Printing is suppressed by omitting the COLUMN clause.

```
05  PIC ZZ9 SOURCE POPULATION.
```

The report writer gives the detail lines and control headings and footings access to data with the SOURCE clause. When a control break occurs, data in the SOURCE items is as follows.

- REPORT HEADING. SOURCE value when the first GENERATE is executed.
- PAGE HEADING. SOURCE value when the page break occurs.
- CONTROL HEADING. SOURCE value when the GENERATE is executed. For a FINAL CONTROL HEADING, SOURCE value when the first GENERATE is executed.
- DETAIL. SOURCE value when the GENERATE is executed.
- CONTROL FOOTING. SOURCE value when the GENERATE is executed unless the SOURCE item is named in the CONTROLS clause. If it is named in the CONTROLS clause, the SOURCE value is the value from the previous detail line. This is handy because the CONTROL FOOTING caused by a detail line prints totals related to the previous detail lines. For a FINAL CONTROL FOOTING, SOURCE value when the TERMINATE is executed.

- PAGE FOOTING.   SOURCE value when the page break occurs.
- REPORT FOOTING.   SOURCE value when TERMINATE is executed.

The data presented to the report writer usually comes from a record read from a file, and the record often contains data that is to be printed in PAGE HEADINGS, CONTROL HEADINGS, and CONTROL FOOTINGS, in addition to the DETAIL lines. CONTROL FOOTINGS usually print the totals for the previous detail lines, and the SOURCE items should come from the previous record. For example, if the populations for states are printed and the previous DETAIL line was for Alabama and the current detail line is for Arkansas, the control footing first prints the total for Alabama, and the SOURCE items must come from the previous record which contained the name Alabama. This is done automatically if the SOURCE item is listed in the CONTROLS clause.

Items listed in the CONTROLS clause retain their old values from the previous DETAIL line until after the CONTROL FOOTINGS are printed. After the CONTROL FOOTINGS are printed, the new values from the current record are moved in and then the CONTROL HEADINGS and DETAIL lines are printed. Data in the PAGE HEADING that come from the records should also appear in the CONTROLS clause because the page break may occur prior to printing the CONTROL FOOTINGS.

G. SUM Clause

Defines a SUM counter and names an identifier or another SUM counter to be automatically summed. SUM may appear only in CONTROL FOOTING report groups. The PIC clause specifies the size of the internal SUM counter and how it is to be edited when it is printed, and it must specify an item large enough to contain the totals. PIC may contain edit characters as the sum is kept internally as numeric data, and it is not converted according to the PIC clause until it is printed. SUM is coded as follows.

```
SUM item, item, ...

05   COLUMN 10 PIC ZZ,ZZ9.99 SUM POPULATION.

05   COLUMN 30 PIC ZZ9 SUM THIS, THAT, THINGS.
```

   [Three items are summed.]

```
05   PIC ZZ9 SUM AGE.
```

   [The item is summed but not printed because the COLUMN clause is omitted.]

SUM names either identifiers, or other SUM counters that are in the same or lower control hierarchy as specified in the CONTROLS clause. If SUM lists several items, each item is added to the SUM counter. All SUM identifiers must appear in the SOURCE clause in the DETAIL report group (this restriction is removed in the ANS Standard), and they must be qualified, subscripted, or indexed exactly as they are in the SOURCE clause.

The SUM counter is added to any higher-level SUMS, printed unless COLUMN is omitted, and reset to zero with each CONTROL FOOTING break within which it appears, unless the RESET clause described later is coded. Items are added once from a detail line, even if they happen to appear more than once in the detail line. Items summed to a higher level must be assigned names.

```
05   item-name COLUMN 10 PIC ZZ9 SOURCE POPULATION.
```

Columns are totaled by naming the column item in the SUM clause. SUM can also total across the line to produce cross-footings by naming other SUM counters in the same line. This requires that the report items be assigned names as illustrated in the following example.

```
01   TYPE DETAIL LINE PLUS 1.

     05   COLUMN 10 PIC 999.9 SOURCE JAN-JUNE.

     05   COLUMN 30 PIC 999.9 SOURCE JULY-DEC.

01   TYPE CONTROL FOOTING YEARLY LINE PLUS 2.

     05   FIRST-HALF COLUMN 10 PIC 999.9 SUM JAN-JUNE.

     05   SECOND HALF COLUMN 30 PIC 999.9 SUM JULY-DEC.

     05   FULL-YEAR COLUMNS 50 PIC 999.9 SUM FIRST-HALF,

                                        SECOND-HALF.
```

The FIRST-HALF sum contains the total of the JAN-JUNE column and the SECOND-HALF sum the total of the JULY-DEC column. FULL-YEAR contains the sum of FIRST-HALF and SECOND-HALF.

SUM and SOURCE are easily confused. SUM can name another SUM counter or an identifier that appears in a DETAIL report group whereas SOURCE can name only identifiers. (The ANS Standard permits SOURCE to name a SUM counter.) The following is incorrect.

```
01  DTL—LINE TYPE DETAIL LINE PLUS 1.

    05  S1 COLUMN 1 PIC S9(9) SOURCE POPULATION.

01  TYPE CONTROL FOOTING COUNTY LINE PLUS 1.

    05  COLUMN 1 PIC S9(9) SOURCE POPULATION.
```

The last line prints the POPULATION from the next detail line rather than the sum of the previous detail lines. If coded as follows, it is still incorrect.

```
    05  COLUMN 1 PIC S9(9) SUM S1.
```

The SUM can only name an identifier or a SUM counter. S1 is not a SUM counter because it does not contain the SUM clause. The following is the correct way to sum the POPULATION in the CONTROL FOOTING.

```
    05  COLUMN 1 PIC S9(9) SUM POPULATION.
```

The DETAIL line must name an identifier with the SOURCE clause, the lowest-level CONTROL FOOTING must name the same identifier in a SUM clause, and each higher-level CONTROL FOOTING must name the preceding CONTROL FOOTING in a SUM clause. The following example illustrates this.

```
01  DTL—LINE TYPE DETAIL LINE PLUS 1 COLUMN 1 PIC S999
                SOURCE POPULATION.

01  CF1 TYPE CONTROL FOOTING COUNTY LINE PLUS 1 PIC S999
                SUM POPULATION.

01  CF2 TYPE CONTROL FOOTING STATE LINE PLUS 1 PIC S999 SUM CF1.
```

The CF2 CONTROL FOOTING could also SUM POPULATION, giving the same results.

```
    01  CF2 TYPE CONTROL FOOTING STATE LINE PLUS 1 PIC S999
                SUM POPULATION.
```

The SUM POPULATION is less efficient because COBOL must sum POPULATION as each DETAIL line is printed; SUM CF1 needs to sum only when the CF1 CONTROL FOOTING is printed.

The internal precision of the SUM counter is defined by the PIC clause. This can cause problems if the full precision is not printed. The following example illustrates this with a dollar amount whose sum is to be printed in whole dollars.

```
05   COST PIC S9(5)V99.

     □  □  □

01   TYPE DETAIL-LINE LINE PLUS 1.

     05   COLUMN 10 PIC -(4)9.99 SOURCE COST.

01   TYPE CONTROL FOOTING MONTH LINE PLUS 1.

     05   COLUMN 10 PIC -(4)9 SUM COST.
```

COST is printed in dollars and cents in the detail line, but is truncated to whole dollars when summed in the CONTROL FOOTING. This can lead to significant errors. If two costs each equaling 1.99 are truncated and summed, the sum is 2 whereas the correct total is 3.98—a significant difference considering that only two numbers were summed. An unacceptable solution is to print the COST line as PIC —(4)9 so that the 1.99 amounts print as 1. This makes the report appear correct as the column does sum to 2, but the answer is still wrong. A better solution is to print both the detail and footings at the full precision of PIC —(4)9.99. If there is not enough room on the report or if only dollar amounts are wanted, set up separate SUM counters that do not print. The following example omits the COLUMN from the S1 line so that it does not print, but only sums. This correct sum is then truncated and printed.

```
01   TYPE CONTROL FOOTING MONTH LINE PLUS 1.

     05   S1 PIC S9(5).99 SUM COST.

     05   COLUMN 10 PIC -(4)9 SUM S1.
```

If a SOURCE item appears in more than one DETAIL report group, it is summed whenever any of the DETAIL lines are printed. If the SOURCE item is to be summed only when one of the DETAIL lines is printed, the UPON phrase must be appended to the SUM clause to name the DETAIL line from which to obtain the sum.

```
01   LINE-A TYPE DETAIL ... SOURCE POPULATION.
```

```
01  LINE-B TYPE DETAIL ... SOURCE POPULATION.

01  TYPE CONTROL FOOTING ... SUM POPULATION UPON LINE-B.
```

H. RESET Phrase

RESET, used for computing running totals, specifies when a SUM counter is to be reset to zero if the automatic reset to zero is not wanted after the CONTROL FOOTING in which the item is printed. RESET can appear only with a SUM clause and specifies another item in a higher-level CONTROL FOOTING that is to cause the SUM counter to be reset to zero.

```
            FINAL
            identifier

    RESET _ _ _ _ _
```

The *identifier* or FINAL must be specified in the CONTROLS clause and be of higher hierarchy. The following example sums POPULATION, resetting it to zero when a new state is encountered. This prevents the sum from being reset to zero when a county causes a control break, giving a running total of the counties within the state.

```
01  S1 TYPE CONTROL FOOTING COUNTY PIC S9(6) SUM POPULATION
        RESET STATE.
```

Remember that if a higher-level SUM counter names a SUM counter controlled by a RESET phrase, the summation is done only when the lower-level SUM counter is reset to zero. In the following example, the S2 SUM counter is intended to print a running total of the states population. However, the S2 SUM counter is summed only once at the end of the report, yielding incorrect results.

```
01  S1 TYPE CONTROL FOOTING COUNTY PIC S9(6) SUM POPULATION
        RESET FINAL.

01  S2 TYPE CONTROL FOOTING STATE PIC S9(6) SUM S1 RESET FINAL.
```

This problem is corrected by coding the SUM counter as follows.

```
01  S2 TYPE CONTROL FOOTING STATE PIC S9(6) SUM POPULATION
        RESET FINAL.
```

I. GROUP Clause

GROUP specifies that an elementary item is to be printed only the first time after a control or page break. It can be coded only in DETAIL report groups, and prints titles at the start of each new page or control break for the detail lines.

```
01  DTL-LINE TYPE DETAIL LINE PLUS 1.

    05  COLUMN 1 GROUP PIC X(7) VALUE 'CITIES:'.
```

[Prints only the first time after a control or page break.]

```
    05  COLUMN 9 PIC X(20) SOURCE CITY.
```

[Prints each time.]

These statements would produce the following report lines:

```
CITIES:   ABBEVILLE

          ALABASTER

          ALBERTVILLE
```

J. NEXT GROUP Clause

NEXT GROUP specifies the starting line spacing following the last line of the report group. NEXT GROUP can be coded only for REPORT HEADING, DETAIL, and CONTROL FOOTING report groups with the TYPE clause at the 01 level.

```
                    line
                    PLUS lines
                    NEXT PAGE

    NEXT GROUP _ _ _ _ _ _
```

* *line.*   A positive integer literal specifying the absolute line number.
* PLUS *lines.*   A positive integer literal specifying the relative line number.
* NEXT PAGE.   Eject to a new page.

NEXT GROUP is often used in a CONTROL FOOTING to skip lines or cause a page eject when the next item is printed. It generally works better to do such spacing and page breaks in CONTROL FOOTINGS with the NEXT GROUP than in CONTROL HEADINGS. The following example would cause any following items to begin on a new page.

```
01   TYPE CONTROL FOOTING COUNTY NEXT GROUP NEXT PAGE.
```

The NEXT GROUP spacing is done only when the next line is printed. This prevents a needless page heading to be printed if nothing more is to be printed. NEXT GROUP NEXT PAGE causes a page eject and the next line prints in the FIRST DETAIL *line*. NEXT GROUP PLUS *line* also causes a page eject if the next line would not fit on the page, and the line is again printed in the FIRST DETAIL *line*. NEXT GROUP *line* causes a page eject if *line* is less than the current line. If the next line to be printed contains a LINE PLUS clause, it prints in the NEXT GROUP *line* plus 1. If the next line contains a LINE *line* clause, the line is printed on this line unless the LINE *line* is less than the NEXT GROUP *line;* then another page eject occurs, and the line is printed on the LINE *line* on the next page.

VI.   PROCEDURE DIVISION STATEMENTS

A.   INITIATE Statement

The INITIATE statement must be executed prior to any GENERATE or TERMINATE statements. It sets the PAGE-COUNTER to 1, the LINE-COUNTER to zero, and all SUM counters to zero. INITIATE is coded as follows.

```
INITIATE report-name, report-name, ...

INITIATE CITIES.
```

B.   GENERATE Statement

The GENERATE statement prints the report. It names either a DETAIL line report group to print detail lines or a report name to do summary reporting. The first GENERATE statement prints any REPORT HEADING, and then any PAGE HEADING. It is coded as follows:

```
GENERATE detail-line.

GENERATE report-name.

GENERATE DTL-LINE.
```

For summary reporting, the report writer performs the equivalent of a GENERATE detail line for each DETAIL report group in the report so that the summation includes all the detail lines. (The ANS Standard allows only one DETAIL report-group for summary reporting.) However, the detail lines themselves are not printed. The summation is done in the order that the report groups are defined in the program. The CONTROL FOOTINGS and CONTROL HEADINGS do print so that the report contains summary lines with no detail lines. A GENERATE CITIES could be executed for a city that is not to be printed, but is to be included in the totals. The following statement causes cities with a population less than 1000 not to print, but to be included in the totals.

```
IF POPULATION < 1000
    THEN GENERATE CITIES
    ELSE GENERATE DTL-LINE.
```

C. TERMINATE Statement

The TERMINATE statement must be executed for the report after all GENERATE statements have been executed. It generates a FINAL CONTROL FOOTING break, which causes a control break for all lower-level CONTROL FOOTINGS, and produces any REPORT FOOTING. It is coded as follows.

```
TERMINATE report-name.

TERMINATE CITIES.
```

D. USE BEFORE REPORTING Statement

The USE BEFORE REPORTING statement is coded in the DECLARATIVES section to gain control just prior to a report group being printed. Control is received after any summation is done. There may be only one USE BEFORE REPORTING statement for each individual report group, and it can be used for all but DETAIL report groups. (The ANS Standard permits DETAIL report groups.) DETAIL report groups are printed by the GENERATE statement, and can be preceded by whatever statements are required. The USE BEFORE REPORTING statement is coded as follows.

```
PROCEDURE DIVISION.
```

```
DECLARATIVES.

section-name SECTION.

    USE BEFORE REPORTING group-name.
```

    [Must immediately follow a SECTION.]

```
paragraph-name.

    statements.

        .

        .

        .


END DECLARATIVES.
```

The USE BEFORE REPORTING statement cannot contain INITI-ATE, GENERATE, or TERMINATE statements, and it cannot reference nondeclarative sections of the program. USE BEFORE REPORTING may be used to perform computations on values before they are printed, perhaps to compute an average column from a row of sums. The SUP-PRESS statement is available in the ANS Standard to suppress printing the report group. It can suppress unnecessary totals such as a line of zeros, or a total formed from a single detail line. The report group is not printed, the LINE-COUNTER is not incremented, and the function of any NEXT GROUP is nullified. The suppression applies only to this instance of the report group; the report group will print the next time unless SUPPRESS is again executed.

```
    SURPRESS.
```

System/370 compilers provide a PRINT-SWITCH special register to suppress the report group instead of the SUPPRESS. Moving a value of 1 to PRINT-SWITCH gives the same result as executing SUPPRESS.

```
    MOVE 1 TO PRINT-SWITCH.
```

Suppose that we wish to suppress the county total if there is but a single city in the county. Such a total is redundant to the detail line, and the report could be shortened by omitting such needless lines as the following.

```
77  NO-CITIES PIC S9(4) COMP VALUE 0.
```

    □ □ □

```
01  COUNTY-LINE TYPE CONTROL FOOTING COUNTY LINE PLUS 2.
```

        □ □ □

```
PROCEDURE DIVISION.

DECLARATIVES.

A10-NO-COUNTY SECTION.

    USE BEFORE REPORTING COUNTY-LINE.

A20-PARAGRAPH.

    IF NO-CITIES ( 2

      THEN MOVE 1 TO PRINT-SWITCH.

        [Or]

      THEN SUPPRESS.

    MOVE O TO NO-CITIES.

END DECLARATIVES.
```

        □ □ □

```
    IF CITY NOT = HIGH-VALUES

      THEN GENERATE DTL-LINE

          ADD 1 TO NO-CITIES.
```

E. LINE-COUNTER

LINE-COUNTER is a special register automatically described in System/
370 as PIC S9(5) COMP-3, and contains the line number of the last line
printed or skipped. The INITIATE statement sets it to zero, and it is automatically incremented by the report writer as lines are printed. Values cannot be moved to it. If there is more than one report, qualify LINE-
COUNTER with the report name, such as LINE-COUNTER OF CITIES.

F. PAGE-COUNTER

PAGE-COUNTER is a special register automatically described in System/
370 as PIC S9(5) COMP-3 and contains the current page number. It is
set to 1 by the INITIATE statement, but other values can be moved to it

thereafter. The report writer increments it by 1 as each new page is printed. If there is more than one report, qualify PAGE-COUNTER by the report name, such as PAGE-COUNTER OF CITIES.

VII. PAGE HEADINGS

Page breaks cause several problems. The first GENERATE statement prints any REPORT HEADING on a new page, immediately followed by the PAGE HEADING on the same page. The NEXT GROUP NEXT PAGE clause must be coded in the REPORT HEADING to cause the first page heading to print on a new page. If the page break is caused by a LINE NEXT PAGE clause in a CONTROL HEADING, the report will begin with two page headings. The first GENERATE statement prints a page heading, and then prints the CONTROL HEADING, which will cause a second page break if it contains LINE NEXT PAGE. To solve this problem, cause the page breaks in the CONTROL FOOTING with the NEXT GROUP NEXT PAGE clause so that the page break comes after a group of items.

The next item after a page break is printed on the NEXT DETAIL *line*. The only exception to this is if the preceding item contains a NEXT GROUP *line* clause and the current item contains a LINE PLUS or a LINE *line* clause. A LINE PLUS clause prints the item in the NEXT GROUP *line* plus 1. LINE *line* prints the item on this line—unless it is less than the NEXT GROUP *line;* then another page eject occurs, and the line is printed on the LINE *line* on the next page.

Data in the page heading that comes from records should also appear in the CONTROLS clause because the page break may occur prior to printing the CONTROL FOOTINGS. Neglecting this can cause the wrong information to be printed in a page heading. In the CITIES report illustrated earlier in this chapter, suppose we wish to start each new state on a new page and to print the information from the NEXT-CITY record in the page heading. To cause such a page break, we would simply code NEXT GROUP NEXT PAGE in the COUNTY CONTROL FOOTING.

```
01  TYPE CONTROL FOOTING COUNTY LINE PLUS 2 NEXT GROUP NEXT PAGE.
```

Suppose that the NEXT-CITY record contains the following data.

```
01  NEXT-CITY.

    05  STATE            PIC X(20).

    05  COUNTY           PIC X(20).
```

```
05  CITY            PIC X(20).

05  POPULATION      PIC S9(9) COMP-3.

05  CAPITAL         PIC X(20).
```

We may wish to print both the STATE and the CAPITAL in the page heading as follows.

```
01  TYPE PAGE HEADING LINE 1.

    05  COLUMN 1 PIC X(20) SOURCE STATE.

    05  COLUMN 30 PIC X(20) SOURCE CAPITAL.
```

Now suppose that we have just printed the last city in Wisconsin and the next record is for the first city in Wyoming. This new detail line causes a control footing to print for Wisconsin, but if it will not fit on the page, a page break occurs and the page heading prints the proper value for STATE (Wisconsin) because it is in the CONTROLS clause and the new value from the record, Wyoming, has not been moved in yet. However, CAPITAL is not in the CONTROLS clause, and the current value from the record, Cheyenne, prints rather than the previous value, Madison. There is no way to solve this incorrect page heading except to place all the page heading SOURCE items from the record in the CONTROLS clause. If the items do not appear within a group item in the record, describe a record in WORKING-STORAGE to contain them.

```
01  PAGE-BREAK.

    05  PAGE-STATE      PIC X(20).

    05  PAGE-CAPITAL    PIC X(20).
```

The CONTROLS clause must then name PAGE-BREAK rather than STATE.

```
RD  CITIES

    PAGE 60 LINES

    HEADING 1

    FIRST DETAIL 5

    CONTROLS ARE PAGE-BREAK,

                 COUNTY.
```

The page heading must also be changed to print the new items.

```
01  TYPE PAGE HEADING LINE 1.

    04  COLUMN 1 PIC X(20) SOURCE PAGE-STATE.

    05  COLUMN 30 PIC X(20) SOURCE PAGE-CAPITAL.
```

As each record is read, store the information in **PAGE-BREAK**.

```
READ IN-FILE INTO NEXT-CITY

  AT END MOVE HIGH-VALUES TO CITY.

IF CITY NOT = HIGH-VALUES

  THEN MOVE STATE TO PAGE-STATE

       MOVE CAPITAL TO PAGE-CAPITAL

       GENERATE DTL-LINE.
```

Since all the items in the page heading are named in the CONTROLS clause, the values from the previous record will be printed in any page break until all the control footings are printed. Then the values from the current record will be moved in so that the proper page heading will print for the control headings and detail line.

VIII. MULTIPLE REPORTS

Several reports can be generated concurrently on separate files. Simply define each file and report separately. The only difference is that the special registers PAGE-COUNTER, LINE-COUNTER, and PRINT-SWITCH must be qualified by the report name; for example, PAGE-COUNTER OF *report-name*.

Several reports can be written consecutively on the same file by specifying the report names in the FD entry. Then the INITIATE, GENERATE, and TERMINATE statements can be coded for each successive report.

```
FD  file-name

    REPORTS ARE report, report, ..., report.
```

A single report may also be written on two files at the same time, although this would rarely be needed. (The ANS Standard prohibits this.)

To automatically write the same report on two files, code the same report name in each FD entry. No more than two files can be written.

```
FD   file-name-1

     REPORT IS report-name.

FD   file-name-2

     REPORT IS report-name.
```

The CODE clause permits a character to be appended to each print line preceding the carriage control character, perhaps to distinguish the report. Such a report could not be printed directly, but must be processed to remove the first character before it can be printed. This option too is seldom needed. It is coded as follows.

```
RD   report-name

       .
       .
       .

     CODE mnemonic-name.
```

The *mnemonic-name* must be a name assigned a character value in the SPECIAL-NAMES section. (The ANS Standard requires a two-character literal to be coded in place of the *mnemonic-name*. It further requires that CODE be specified for all files if it is specified for any.)

```
SPECIAL-NAMES.

     'character' IS mnemonic-name.
```

This completes the discussion of the report writer. It makes report writing much simpler, and should be used for most reports. Reports are usually produced from a file that has been sorted into the required order, and the next chapter describes sorting.

EXERCISES

1. For the CITIES report described earlier in this chapter, make the following modifications.

• Print the total population for all states.

- Print the cumulative population for each city within a county, each county within a state, and the cumulative populations of the states.
- Suppress the line if any population is zero. Do this for each city, county, and state.
- Do not print any totals if only one item is summed in the totals.
- Do not print any city whose population is less than 10,000, but include the population in the totals.
- Print a control heading before each group of cities in a county. Start each new state on a new page.

2. Sketch out three separate reports for which it would not be appropriate to use the COBOL report writer.

3. What changes would you make to the COBOL report writer to enhance it.

4. Use the report writer to print a table containing the square roots of the integers from 1 to 1000. The square roots are to be printed with five significant digits of accuracy to the right of the decimal point. Print 50 lines per page with each line containing two columns of values as shown. Print the page heading at the top of each new page.

```
                    TABLE OF SQUARE ROOTS                    PAGE xxx

NUMBER   SQUARE ROOT              NUMBER   SQUARE ROOT

   1       1.00000                  51       7.14143

   3       1.41421                  52       7.21110

   .          .                      .          .
   .          .                      .          .
   .          .                      .          .

  50       7.07107                 100      10.00000
```

5. Write a program to read in a card containing an initial investment [PIC 9(7)V99], an interest rate [PIC 99V9], a number of years (PIC 99), and a starting date (mm/dd/yy). Given this information, produce the following report using the report writer. For the date, assume 30 days per month. Allow 30 lines per page. The interest earned is computed as the current balance times the interest divided by 100. The new balance is the current balance plus the interest earned.

```
                    INVESTMENT ANALYSIS                    PAGE xxx

PREPARED ESPECIALLY FOR:  your name

INITIAL INVESTMENT: $xxxxxxx.xx    INTEREST: xx.x%    YEARS: xx

   DATE     CURRENT BALANCE   INTEREST EARNED   NEW BALANCE   YEAR

xx/xx/xx  $xxxxxxx.xx        $xxxxxx.xx        $xxxxxxx.xx   xx
```

sixteen

SORTING

Sorting consists of arranging items in ascending or descending order. The usual case is a sequential file that must be sorted into some order for updating or reporting. For example, a personnel file may be sorted in descending order on age, then in descending order on salary within age, and then in ascending order on name within salary. The sort is performed on three items, termed *sort keys*, within each record: age, salary, and name. The following shows how records in such a file would be sorted.

Before sorting:

Name	Salary	Age
ABLE	19000	65
BAKER	19000	65
JONES	20000	65
NOBEL	25000	50
SMITH	30000	50
WATTS	21000	50

After sorting:

Name	Salary	Age
JONES	20000	65
ABLE	19000	65
BAKER	19000	65
SMITH	30000	50
NOBEL	25000	50
WATTS	21000	50

Sorting can be deceptively complex. For example, it should not be hard to sort names in a personnel file into alphabetic order—as long as you remember to sort on the last names first and then on the first name or initials. Then, it is customary to sort names such as O'BRIAN as if they were spelled OBRIAN. Also, names that begin with Mc, such as McDonald, should sort after the Ma's. Thus something as simple as sorting names into alphabetic order does present problems. The usual solution is to carry the name twice in the file, once as it is (O'BRIAN), and once as it is to act in a sort (OBRIAN).

Perhaps the most common error in sorting is to confuse the sort order. For example, if a file is sorted on state and city, one may try to use it to produce a report by cities. After all, the file was sorted on cities. But this is in error because the file is in sort by cities within state, not by cities. Thus all the cities for Alabama will come first, then all the cities for Arkansas. So to produce a report by cities, the file must be sorted again on just cities.

There are three methods of sorting for COBOL programs: the COBOL SORT verb, an external sort, and writing one's own sort. Writing one's own sort, usually a last resort when the COBOL or external sorts cannot be used, is described at the end of this chapter. The external sort, invoked as a separate job step in System/370, is not a part of COBOL, but is a part of most operating systems. It is simpler than the COBOL sort because one need not write a COBOL program to invoke it. An external sort can also be changed without recompiling the program, and the sort program does not reside in memory with the COBOL program, reducing the maximum storage requirement. It may also make it easier to isolate errors when the sort is a separate job step. External sorts for System/370 are described later in this chapter. The COBOL sort, invoked by the SORT statement, is most useful in sorting an internal table or in sorting a file generated within a program. It is also useful when the records to be sorted must be selected or manipulated before being sorted, or if only a single program is to read the sorted file.

In System/370 COBOL, several Job Control Language statements are required in a step containing a sort. Check your installation's operating system requirements to obtain the exact coding of the Job Control Language statements. The required JCL statements are as follows for a System/370 COBOL sort.

```
//GO.SYSOUT   DD   SYSOUT=A

//GO.SORTLIB   D   DSN=SYS1.SORTLIB,DISP=SHR

//GO.SORTWKO1  DD   ...

//GO.SORTWKO2  DD   ...

//GO.SORTWKO3  DD   ...

//GO.SORTWKnn  DD   ...          [A minimum of three SORTWK DD
                                  statements are required.]
```

COBOL sorts should be simple, but they depend on the operating system, and there can be surprises. If you are using the IBM Sort Program Product,[1,2] the sort messages overwrite any DISPLAY and EXHIBIT output on the SYSOUT file, resulting in lost output. To prevent this, specify a special ddname for the sort as follows when using the IBM Sort Program Product. The IBM Sort Program Product may also require a STEPLIB DD statement, depending on the particular installation.

```
    MOVE 'ddname' TO SORT-MESSAGE.


    □  □  □

//GO.STEPLIB  D   DSN=SYS1.SORT,DISP=SHR

//GO.ddname   DD  SYSOUT=A

//GO.SYSOUT   DD  SYSOUT=A

//GO.SORTLIB  DD  DSN=SYS1.SORTLIB,DISP=SHR

//GO.SORTWKnn DD   ...
```

I. SIMPLE SORT

A simple sort consists of sorting an input file to produce a sorted output file. The input and output files must be sequential files specified by the SELECT and FD entries. In addition, a SELECT clause must specify the name of a *sort-file*, and a Sort Definition (SD) entry is required to describe the records to be sorted and establish their sort keys. The SELECT and SD entries describing the sort file do not define a physical file, but provide a means of describing the fields within the record of the file that is to be sorted. There may be several sort files within a program.

```
FILE-CONTROL.
    SELECT sort-file ASSIGN TO UT-S-SORTWK.
    SELECT sort-in ASSIGN TO UT-S-ddin.
    SELECT sort-out ASSIGN TO UT-S-ddout.
DATA DIVISION.
FILE SECTION.
SD  sort-file.
```

```
01   record.

     05   data-item ...
```

[The *record* describes the records being sorted. The SORT statement names *data-items* in the *record* upon which to sort.]

```
FD   sort-in ...

FD   sort-out ...


     □ □ □

//GO.STEPLIB  DD  DSN=SYS1.SORT,DISP=SHR

//GO.ddin  DD  ...

//GO.ddout  DD  ...

//GO.ddname  DD  SYSOUT=A

//GO.SYSOUT  DD  SYSOUT=A

//GO.SORTLIB  DD  DSN=SYS1.SORTLIB,DISP=SHR

//GO.SORTWKnn  DD  ...
```

The sort is invoked in the Procedure Division by the SORT statement. There may be several SORT statements within a program, coded as follows.

```
SORT sort-file

     ASCENDING
     DESCENDING

ON _ _ _ _ _ KEY key, key, ..., key

     ASCENDING
     DESCENDING

ON _ _ _ _ _ KEY, key, key, ..., key

     .
     .
     .

     USING sort-in
     GIVING sort-out.
```

- *sort-file.* The name in a SD entry describing the records to be sorted.

- ON. Specifies an ASCENDING or DESCENDING order of the sort *keys*. The *keys* must be listed from left to right in decreasing order of significance, and the ON phrases must also be listed in decreasing order of significance in the sort. Records in the input file with duplicate keys will be sorted together, but not necessarily in the same order in which they are read.

- *key*. One or more data items in the *record* of the *sort-file* on which the file is to be sorted, listed from left to right in decreasing order of significance. For variable-length records, the keys must be in the fixed portion of the record. In System/370, up to 12 keys with a total length of 256 bytes can be specified, but all keys must be in the first 4092 bytes of the record.

- USING. Specifies the input file to sort. In System/370, the JCL can concatenate several input files for the sort, and the concatenated files can reside on different device types. The blocking may also be different, as may the record length for variable-length files, as long as the largest BLKSIZE and LRECL are specified in the first DD statement of the concatenated files. In the ANS Standard, but not in System/370, several *sort-in* file names can be listed: USING *sort-file-1*, *sort-file-2*, . . .

- GIVING. Specifies the output file into which the sorted output is to be written. Neither *sort-in* nor *sort-out* may be open when the sort is invoked; SORT automatically opens and closes them. The *sort-in* and *sort-out* must be sequential files; they cannot be direct or indexed.

The following example sorts the FILE-I input file on ascending order on PART-X and SIZE-X, and on descending order on NAME-X, and on ascending order on COST-X. The sorted records are written into FILE-O.

```
SORT SORT-A

    ON ASCENDING KEY PART-X, SIZE-X

    ON DESCENDING KEY NAME-X

    ON ASCENDING KEY COST-X

    USING FILE-I

    GIVING FILE-O.
```

In System/370, the entire *sort-in* file is read before the sorting begins, and only after the sorting is completed is the output written onto the *sort-out* file. This enables the *sort-in* and *sort-out* files to be the same physical file. Remember, though, that if you write the *sort-out* file over the top of the *sort-in* file and the sort is unsuccessful, both your *sort-in* and *sort-out* files will contain unpredictable data. In sorting files on tape, you can also sort one file and write the output onto the same or a following file on the same tape reel. For example, you might sort file 1 of a tape and write the output onto file 2. This is often done to minimize tape mounts, but it should not be done for important files because the tape ring must be present to write enable the tape. This increases the element of risk.

Although not in the ANS Standard, the System/370 COBOL sort stores a return code in a special register named SORT-RETURN upon completion of the sort. A value of zero is successful, and a value of 16 means an unsuccessful sort. A value in units of bytes can be stored in the special register SORT-CORE-SIZE to change the amount of memory allocated to the sort. (The sort operates more efficiently with large amounts of memory because it reduces the I/O.) In the following example, an input file is sorted on SORT-AGE in descending order, and SORT-NAME in ascending order.

```
      SELECT SORT-IT ASSIGN TO UT-S-SORTWK.

      SELECT FILE-I ASSIGN TO UT-S-SORTIN.

      SELECT FILE-O ASSIGN TO UT-S-SORTOUT.

FILE SECTION.

SD  SORT-IT.

01  SORT-REC.

      05  SORT-NAME         PIC X(25).

      05  SORT-AGE          PIC S9(3)V99 COMP-3.

      05  FILLER            PIC X(30).

FD  FILE-I ...

FD  FILE-O ...


      □  □  □


PROCEDURE DIVISION.

A00-BEGIN.

      MOVE 'SORTMSG' TO SORT-MESSAGE.
```

[Must prevent DISPLAY and EXHIBIT meessages from being overwritten.]

```
      MOVE 44000 TO SORT-CORE-SIZE.
```

[The sort is given 44K bytes of memory.]

```
SORT SORT-IT

   ON DESCENDING KEY SORT-AGE

   ON ASCENDING KEY SORT-NAME

   USING FILE-I

   GIVING FILE-O.

IF SORT-RETURN = 16

   THEN DISPLAY 'UNSUCCESSFUL SORT.'.
```

II. SORT INPUT PROCEDURE

An input procedure can be written to supply records to the sort by coding an INPUT PROCEDURE phrase in place of the USING phrase in the SORT statement. The records may be read from a file, allowing specific records to be selected or modified prior to the sort, or they may be from an internal table or from data generated within the program. The input procedure is a normal procedure, such as one written for a PERFORM statement, although it must be one or more sections rather than a paragraph. The input procedure can only be invoked by the SORT statement, and cannot refer to procedure names outside of itself.

```
SORT sort-file

   ON ...

   INPUT PROCEDURE IS section-name
```
   [Can also specify *section-name-1* THRU *section-name-2*.]
```
   GIVING sort-out.
```

□ □ □

```
section-name SECTION.

paragraph-name.

   statements to create each record.

   RELEASE record FROM variable.
```
   [RELEASE passes each record to the sort.]
```
   perhaps more statements.

paragraph-name.   EXIT.
```

The sort will invoke the section once to receive all the records. Each record is passed to the sort by executing the RELEASE statement. After the last record has been passed, one must exit from the procedure to allow the sort to proceed. The RELEASE statement is coded as follows.

```
RELEASE record FROM identifier.
```

- *record.* A record in the record area specified for the *sort-file* in the SD entry.
- *identifier.* A record or data item containing the data to be passed to the sort. (The FROM phrase can be omitted if the data is moved directly to the *record* in the record area of the *sort-file.*)

The following example sorts an internal table.

```
SD  SORT-A.

01  SORT-REC.
    05  SORT-AGE    PIC S9(3)V99 COMP-3.
    05  SORT-NAME   PIC X(25).

DATA DIVISION.

01  TABLE-DEF.
    05  TABLE-X     PIC S9(4) COMP.
    05  TABLE-A OCCURS 100 TIMES.
        10  TABLE-AGE   PIC S9(3)V99 COMP-3.
        10  TABLE-NAME  PIC X(25).

    □ □ □

    SORT SORT-A
        ON ASCENDING KEY SORT-NAME
        INPUT PROCEDURE IS P20-SORT-INPUT
        GIVING FILE-O.

    □ □ □

P20-SORT-INPUT SECTION.
```

```
P30-SORT-START.

      PERFORM P40-GET-ITEM

         VARYING TABLE-X FROM 1 BY 1

         UNTIL TABLE-X  > 100.

      GO TO P50-EXIT.

P40-GET-ITEM.

      RELEASE SORT-REC FROM TABLE-A (TABLE-X).

**** EXIT

P50-EXIT.   EXIT.
```

III. SORT OUTPUT PROCEDURE

COBOL also permits a procedure to be written to receive the sorted records from the sort rather than having the sort write them out into a file. This permits the sorted records to be modified or selected before they are written, or to be stored in an internal table. The output procedure is specified in the SORT statement by coding an OUTPUT PROCEDURE phrase in place of the GIVING phrase.

```
      SORT sort-name

         ON ...

         USING sort-in

         OUTPUT PROCEDURE IS section-name.
```

   [Can also specify *section-name-1* THRU *section-name-2*.]

   □ □ □

```
section-name SECTION.

paragraph-name.

      statements to prepare to receive sorted records.

      RETURN sort-file INTO identifier
```

   [The RETURN statement retrieves each sorted record.]

```
     AT END imperative-statement.

   statements to process retrieved record.

paragraph-name.  EXIT.
```

The output procedure is invoked only once when the sorting is completed. The RETURN statement, executed to receive each record, is coded as follows.

```
   RETURN sort-file INTO identifier

     AT END imperative-statement.
```

- *sort-file.* The sort file specified in the record area for a SD entry.
- *identifier.* A record or data item into which the sorted record is to be moved. The INTO phrase can be omitted so that the data is available only in the *record* in the record area of the *sort-file.*
- *imperative-statement.* An imperative statement executed when no more records remain to be passed. (Procedures outside of the output procedure cannot be referenced.)

The output procedure is terminated by exiting the section, and control is returned to the next executable statement following the SORT. To stop passing records even if more remain to be passed, simply exit the procedure. The following example stores sorted output into the TABLE-A used in the previous example.

```
   SORT SORT-A

     ON ASCENDING KEY SORT-NAME

     USING FILE-I

     OUTPUT PROCEDURE IS P60-GET-RECORD.

   □ □ □

P60-GET-RECORD SECTION.

P70-START.

   PERFORM P80-NEXT

     VARYING TABLE-X FROM 1 BY 1

     UNTIL TABLE-X > 100.

   GO TO P90-EXIT.
```

```
P80-NEXT.

    RETURN SORT-A INTO TABLE-A (TABLE-X)

        AT END DISPLAY 'ERROR--NOT 100 RECORDS SORTED.'

            GO TO P90-EXIT.

**** EXIT

P90-EXIT.  EXIT.
```

IV. SORT INPUT AND OUTPUT PROCEDURES

Both an input and output procedure can be supplied for the sort by coding both the INPUT and OUTPUT PROCEDURE phrase.

```
SORT sort-file

    ON ...

    INPUT PROCEDURE IS input-section-name

    OUTPUT PROCEDURE IS output-section-name.
```

To illustrate the use of sort input and output procedures, along with some other sorting techniques, consider the following sort problems.

- A file contains more than one record type, and each type must be sorted on a key that appears in a different place in each record type.
- A file contains more than one record type, and each record type is to be sorted on different sort keys into the same output file for later processing.
- A variable-length record is to be sorted on a key that is in the variable portion of the record.

All of the items above can be accomplished by appending a sort key to the front or end of the record. The sort keys must have the same length, and the sort order is controlled by placing the appropriate items in the appropriate fields of the sort key. The following example illustrates the sort key technique in which two record types are sorted into ascending order on state and town. Notice that state and town appear in different places in each record type.

```
01  REC-A.
    05  REC-A-TYPE              PIC X.
*                                          'A' FOR REC-A.
    05  REC-A-STATE            PIC X(20).
    05  REC-A-TOWN             PIC X(10).
    05  REC-A-REMAINDER        PIC X(100).
01  REC-B REDEFINES REC-A.
    05  REC-B-TYPE             PIC X.
*                                          'B' FOR REC-B.
    05  REC-B-TOWN            PIC X(10).
    05  REC-B-STATE           PIC X(20).
    05  REC-B-REMAINDER       PIC X(100).
```

To sort such a file, a sort record is defined as follows, with a sort key appended.

```
SD  SORT-FILE.
01  SORT-RECORD.
    05  SORT-ORIGINAL     PIC X(131).
    05  SORT-KEY.
        10  SORT-STATE     PIC X(20).
        10  SORT-TOWN      PIC X(10).
```

The SORT statement is then written with a sort input procedure to move the record to the sort record and build the sort key, and an output procedure to strip off the sort key and write the record.

```
    SORT SORT-FILE
    ON ASCENDING KEY SORT-STATE,
                SORT-TOWN
      INPUT PROCEDURE IS B10-GET-RECORDS
      OUTPUT PROCEDURE IS C10-WRITE-RECORDS.

    □ □ □
```

```
B10-GET-RECORDS SECTION.

B20-FIRST.

    MOVE LOW-VALUES TO REC-A-TYPE.

    PERFORM B30-READ UNTIL REC-A-TYPE = HIGH-VALUES.

    GO TO B50-EXIT.

B30-READ.

    READ FILE-I INTO REC-A

      AT END MOVE HIGH-VALUES TO REC-A-TYPE.

    IF REC-A-TYPE NOT = HIGH VALUES

      THEN PERFORM B40-RELEASE-RECORD.

**** EXIT

 B40-RELEASE-RECORD.

    MOVE REC-A TO SORT-ORIGINAL.

    IF REC-A-TYPE = 'A'

      THEN MOVE REC-A-STATE TO SORT-STATE

            MOVE REC-A-TOWN TO SORT-TOWN

      ELSE MOVE REC-B-STATE TO SORT-STATE

            MOVE REC-B-TOWN TO SORT-TOWN.

    RELEASE SORT-FILE.

**** EXIT

 B50-EXIT.  EXIT.

C10-WRITE-RECORDS SECTION.

C20-FIRST.

    MOVE LOW-VALUES TO SORT-KEY.

    PERFORM C30-WRITE UNTIL SORT-KEY = HIGH-VALUES.

    GO TO C40-EXIT.

C30-WRITE.

    RETURN SORT-FILE
```

```
      AT END MOVE HIGH-VALUES TO SORT-KEY.

  IF SORT-KEY NOT = HIGH VALUES

      THEN WRITE FILE-O-REC FROM SORT-ORIGINAL.

**** EXIT

C40-EXIT.  EXIT.
```

V. SORT SEQUENCE

The SORT statement specifies the sort keys left to right in decreasing order of significance, and each ON phrase in decreasing order of significance.

```
SORT SORT-FILE

    ON ASCENDING KEY STATE,

                    COUNTY

    ON DESCENDING KEY CITY

    ON ASCENDING KEY PRECINCT

    USING FILE-I

    GIVING FILE-O.
```

This statement sorts states into ascending order, the counties within a state into ascending order, each city in a county into descending order, and each precinct within a city into ascending order. Numeric fields are sorted in order of their algebraic values, taking into consideration the sign. Alphanumeric fields sort from left to right, with each character compared according to the collating sequence of the character set. The EBCDIC character set has the following collating sequence.

Low to high: blank
             . < (+ $ *) ; - / , > ' = "
             A through Z
             0 through 9

The ASCII character set has the following collating sequence.
Low to high: blank
             " $ ' ( ) * + , - . /
             0 through 9
             ; < = >
             A through Z

The ANS Standard, but not System/370, provides a facility for specifying the collating sequence. System/370 allows the ASCII character set to be specified for tape files in the JCL, or by coding the ASSIGN clause as ASSIGN TO UT-C-*ddname*. In the ANS Standard, the collating sequence is specified as follows.

```
OBJECT-COMPUTER.  computer-name,

                  COLLATING SEQUENCE IS alphabet-name.

SPECIAL-NAMES.

                  STANDARD-1
                  NATIVE
                  implementor-name

       alphabet-name IS _ _ _ _ _ _ _ _ _,  ...
```

- STANDARD-1.   Specifies the ASCII collating sequence.
- NATIVE.   Specifies the collating sequence native to the computer.
- *implementor-name*.   Specifies a collating sequence defined by the implementor.

This collating sequence is applicable throughout the entire program, and would affect alphanumeric comparisons in the IF statement and the sequence of the keys of random-access files. A particular collating sequence can also be specified in the SORT or MERGE statements in the ANS Standard as follows:

```
SORT file-name

    ON ...

    COLLATING SEQUENCE IS alphabet-name

    INPUT PROCEDURE ...

MERGE file-name.

    ON ...

    COLLATING SEQUENCE IS alphabet-name

    USING ...
```

VI. SORT EFFICIENCY

Sorts are relatively expensive and can account for a large portion of the running cost of a system. Sorting and merging may consume 25% of today's computing capacity.[3] In searching for ways to reduce a system's running costs, look carefully at the sorts. Are all the sorts necessary? Sorts are heavily I/O bound, and so one should block the sort input and output as high as possible. The manufacturer may provide ways to optimize a sort's performance. The cost of a sort increases exponentially with the number of records sorted; it costs more than twice as much to sort 1000 records as 500 records. The cost of a sort also increases proportionally to the record length and number of sort keys; it costs more to sort a 1000-byte record than a 400-byte record.

Often the number of records and the record length can be reduced for a sort. Suppose that a file containing 10,000 fixed-length records of 1000 bytes must be sorted to produce a report, but that only 5000 records are selected for the report, with 100 bytes of each record going into the report. Such a file would be relatively expensive to sort. It would require reading 10,000 records into the sort, sorting 10,000 records, writing out the 10,000 records, and reading the 10,000 records back into the report program. Each record contains 1000 bytes, resulting in a total of 30 million bytes transmitted, and 10,000 records of 1000 bytes sorted. To reduce this, read in the 10,000 records in a sort input procedure, select only the 5000 records needed, move the 100 bytes that go into the report to the sort record, sort the 5000 records with an internal sort, and write the report in a sort output procedure. The result is 10 million bytes read and 5000 records of 100 bytes sorted.

The System/370 sort is also sensitive to the amount of memory allocated to it. The default memory size is set by the installation, and the sort will operate more efficiently if more memory is allocated by moving the memory size in bytes to the SORT-CORE-SIZE special register. The larger amount of memory reduces the I/O, but the effect of the cost will depend on the installation's charging algorithm. Generally, one should give the sort a relatively large amount of memory.

VII. MERGE STATEMENT

MERGE allows several input files having identical record formats and arranged in the same sort order to be merged into a single output file in this same sort order. Merging yields the same results as if the several files were concatenated as input to a normal sort, but merging is more efficient because it knows that the input files are already in the proper sort order.

The MERGE statement is similar to the SORT statement. All input and output files must be defined as normal files with SELECT and FD entries. Like the sort file, the merge file is defined by a SD entry, and the MERGE statement is written as follows.

```
MERGE merge-file

    ASCENDING
    DESCENDING

ON _ _ _ _ _ _ KEY key, key, ...
    .
    .
    .

USING merge-in-1, merge-in-2, ...

GIVING merge-out.
```

- *merge-file*. The merge file described in a SD entry.
- *merge-in*. Two or more file names to be merged based on the order specified in the ON phrases. Records with identical keys in several files are merged in the order the files are listed in the USING phrase. In System/370, the records must be of the same record type, and except for variable-length records, must have the same record length. Both the device type and blocking can differ, but the largest block size and record length must be in the first *merge-in* DD card.
- *merge-out*. An output file name to contain the merged files. Neither the *merge-in* nor *merge-out* files may be open when MERGE is executed. MERGE automatically opens and closes the files. The *merge-in* and *merge-out* must all be sequential files; they cannot be direct or indexed.

The *merge-in* files and the single *merge-out* file are normal files and must be specified by SELECT and FD entries. The GIVING phrase may be replaced by the OUTPUT PROCEDURE phrase to permit a procedure to be written to receive the merged records. (No input procedure is permitted.)

```
MERGE SORT-A

    ON ASCENDING KEY PART-X, SIZE-X
```

```
      USING FILE-1, FILE-2, FILE-3

      OUTPUT PROCEDURE C30-STORE-MERGE.
```

VIII.   EXTERNAL SORT

External sorts are not a part of COBOL, but they are used in combination with many COBOL programs. An external sort is often simpler and more convenient than a COBOL sort. The sort order can be changed by a control card whereas a COBOL sort requires the COBOL program to be recompiled. However, if you change the sort order of a file, the program reading it must often be recompiled anyway. External sorts are invoked as a separate job step in System/370. The JCL is a cataloged procedure like the one following, but check with your installation as there may be differences.

```
//SORT1  EXEC   SORTD

//SORTIN   DD   DSN=sort-input-file,DISP=SHR,...
```

[SORTIN specifies the input file to sort.]

```
//SORTOUT   DD   DSN=sort-out-file,DISP=(NEW,...
```

[SORTOUT specifies the output file to contain the sorted records.]

```
//SYSIN   DD   *
      SORT FIELDS=(1,4,CH,A,20,10,CH,D),FILSZ=E1000
```

The SORT statement specifies the sort order. The FILSZ = E1000 is an estimate of the number of records in the file, 1000 in this example, and the sort order is as follows.

`1,4,CH,A`	[Starting in character position 1, sort 4 CHaracters in Ascending order.]
`20,10,CH,D`	[Starting in character position 20, sort 10 CHaracters in Descending order.]

The general form of the sort control card is as follows:

```
SORT FIELDS=(sort-key,sort-key,...,sort-key),FILSZ=Enumber
```

- FILSZ = E*number*.   An estimate of the number of records to be sorted, and enables the sort to be more efficient. It may be omitted and the sort will proceed with a slight performance degradation.

- *sort-key*. Specifies the fields within the record upon which to sort, their data type, and whether they are to be sorted in ascending or descending order. The keys are listed from left to right in major to minor order in which they are to be applied in the sort. Each *sort-key* has four parts as follows:

      start,length,format,order

- *start*. The starting byte position in the record. The first byte is number 1. For binary fields, one can specify *start* in the form *byte.bit*, where *byte* is the byte number and *bit* is the bit number within the byte. (The first bit is number 1.) Hence 3.2 indicates that the key begins in the second bit of the third byte.
- *length*. The length of the field in bytes. For binary fields, one can specify the length in the form *bytes.bits*, where *bytes* is the number of bytes and *bits* is the number of bits. Hence 0.3 indicates that the key is three bits long.
- *format*. The format of the sort field. It must be one of the following.
  - CH. Character (PIC X).
  - ZD. Zoned decimal (numeric character data, PIC 9).
  - PD. Packed decimal (COMP-3).
  - FI. Fixed-point (COMP).
  - BI. Binary (treated as a string of bits without a sign).
  - FL. Floating-point (COMP-1 or COMP-2).
- *order*. The sort order.
  - A. Ascending.
  - D. Descending.

The following example sorts records into ascending order with two sort keys.

      SORT FIELDS=(4,6,ZD,A,12,3,PD,D)

The sort order is:

4,6,ZD,A	[Bytes 4 to 9 as zoned decimal in ascending order.]
12,3,CH,D	[Bytes 12 to 14 as packed decimal in descending order.]

To continue the SORT statement, break it after a comma and continue it columns 2 to 16 of the following card.

```
SORT FIELDS=(4,6,CH,A,

     12,3,CH,D)
```

The MERGE statement, coded similar to the SORT statement, is used to merge files. Additionally, there may be up to 16 SORTIN*nn* statements, with the *nn* ranging in consecutive values from 01 up to 16.

```
//TEST#9  JOB  (5542,30),'MERGE',CLASS=A

//  EXEC  SORTD

//SORTIN01  DD  ...

//SORTIN02  DD  ...

//SORTOUT  DD  ...

//SYSIN DD  *

     MERGE FIELDS=(1,4,CH,A,20,10,10,CH,D),FILSZ=E1000
```

IX. PROGRAMMING A SORT

The SORT verb or the external sort is likely to be more efficient and simpler than writing your own sort. However, there may be situations where you must write your own sort, perhaps to sort a table in which memory is severely limited. There are many techniques for internal sorts, but the *bubble sort* is the simplest and is reasonably efficient. In the bubble sort, the first table element is compared to each successive element. For an ascending sort, the two elements are switched if the first element is greater than the second. This bubbles the largest value to the top of the table. This is repeated for the second through the next-to-last element until the entire table is in the desired order. The following example illustrates a bubble sort in which the 1000 elements of table AMOUNT are sorted into ascending order.

```
77  SWAP            PIC S9(7)V99 COMP-3.
```

  [SWAP is a data item used to swap table elements.]

```
01  A-TABLE.

    05  X-AMT       PIC S9(4) COMP.
```

```
05  Y-AMT              PIC S9(4) COMP.

05  AMOUNT            PIC S9(7)V99 COMP-3

                      OCCURS 1000 TIMES.
```

[AMOUNT is the table to sort. Two subscripts are needed for the sort.]

□ □ □

```
B-10-BUBBLE-SORT.

**** BUBBLE SORT TO PLACE ARRAY AMOUNT INTO ASCENDING ORDER.
     PERFORM B10-PART-A

        VARYING X-AMT FROM 1 BY 1

        UNTIL X-AMT > 999.

**** EXIT

        □ □ □

B10-PART-A.

     PERFORM B10-PART-B

        VARYING Y-AMT FROM X-AMT BY 1

        UNTIL Y-AMT > 1000.

**** EXIT

B10-PART-B.

     IF AMOUNT (X-AMT) > AMOUNT (Y-AMT)

        THEN MOVE AMOUNT (Y-AMT) TO SWAP

             MOVE AMOUNT (X-AMT) TO AMOUNT (Y-AMT)

             MOVE SWAP TO AMOUNT (X-AMT).

**** EXIT

**** END OF B10-BUBBLE-SORT
```

This concludes the chapter on sorting. External sorts are the simplest. COBOL sorts are often convenient, especially when records are selected before sorting. Rarely would one need to program his or her own sort. The next chapter describes direct and indexed files.

EXERCISES

1. Assume that a file contains 80-character records. Sort the file in ascending order on the first 8 characters and in descending order on the next 12 characters. Write the sorted output into a file.

2. Assume the same file as in Exercise 1. Write a sort input procedure to read the file and select for the sort, only records with an X in column 40. Write the sorted output into a file.

3. Assume the same file as in Exercise 1. Write a sort output procedure to print the keys of the sorted records, but do not write the sorted output into a file; store it in an internal table.

4. Assume the same file as in Exercise 1. Write a sort input procedure to read the file and select for the sort only records with an X in column 40. Write a sort output procedure to print the keys of the sorted records. Also, since only the sort keys are used for output, shorten the record for the sort to a 20-character record containing just the sort keys.

5. Assume that a file contains 80-character records. Sort the file on the first 3 characters so that the records come out in the order shown.

991

992

999

981

982

989

891

899

6. Assume that you are called upon to develop a set of standards for the use of the sort. Give guidelines for the use of an external sort, an internal sort, and hand-coded sorts.

REFERENCES

1. "OS Sort/Merge Programmer's Guide," Program Number 5734-SM1, IBM Corporation, Kingston, N. Y., 1975.
2. "IBM System/360 Operating System Sort/Merge," Program Number 360S-SM-023, IBM Corporation, Kingston, N. Y., 1968.
3. Donald E. Knuth, *The Art of Computer Programming*, Volume 3, *Sorting and Searching*, Addison-Wesley Publishing Company, Reading, Mass., 1973.

seventeen

RELATIVE, DIRECT, AND INDEXED FILES

Relative, direct, and indexed files (termed *random-access files*) depend heavily on the facilities provided by the computer's operating system. Although they are included in the ANS Standard, their implementation varies among compilers and operating systems. Direct files are not a part of the ANS Standard. The facilities described in this chapter are for the System/370 implementation.[1-4]

The advantage of indexed, direct, and indexed files is their ability to access records randomly. To see how random access might be used, suppose that payroll transactions contain an employee's social security number and department. Suppose further that another file contains all the valid social security numbers, and yet another file contains all the valid department numbers. How could the social security and department numbers in each payroll transaction be validated against the social security file and the department file?

First, we might consider reading the social security file and the department file into a table to use the SEARCH statement. This is perhaps the best solution if the table will fit in memory, but the files may be too large for this. Next, we might sort both the payroll transactions and the social security file on the social security numbers and then write a program to match the two sequential files to see if all social security numbers in the payroll transactions match a social security number in the social security file. Then a similar program must be written to do the same for the department numbers. This is unduly complicated, and if there are only a few payroll transactions and the social security or department files are large, the method is inefficient. The problem is compounded if there are additional items to validate in the payroll transactions against other files.

Random access solves the problem. Each record can be read irrespective of the previous record read. If we make the social security file and the department file random-access files, each payroll transaction can be read and the social security number and the department number can be used as the key to read a record from the social security file and the department file. If a record is found, the payroll transaction field is valid. If not found, the payroll transaction field is invalid.

This example illustrates the advantage of random access in simplifying the logic where records in a file must be accessed in an unpredictable order. Another advantage of random access is that it is faster to update a few records in a large file than with sequential access. On-line applications usually require random access because they process relatively few transactions against large files that require fast retrieval or updating. An on-line reservation system could not exist with sequential access because it would be too slow to update the files sequentially as each reservation is received. Nor can one batch the reservations to run a large group of them together because any reservation must immediately update the file to avoid over-booking. Random access allows each reservation to update the file as it is received. Thus random access is required when only a few transactions in a large file are updated, when a single transaction must update multiple files, or when a file must be immediately accessed or updated.

Random-access files can exist only on direct-access storage devices (termed *mass storage* in the ANS Standard), but they can be accessed either sequentially or randomly. The records in random-access files can be read sequentially and written into a sequential file, and records can be read from a sequential file and written sequentially into a random-access file. Sequential access is often used to backup and restore the random-access files onto a sequential I/O device such as tape. The file is backed up by reading it sequentially and writing it as a sequential file. It is restored by reading the sequentially copy and writing it sequentially as a relative, direct, or indexed file.

The three types of random-access files are relative, direct, and indexed. For *relative files*, the key is a sequential number that specifies the record's relative position within the file, analogous to the subscript of a table. For System/370 *direct files*, the key has two components. The first part specifies the relative track number on which the record is stored, and the second part identifies the record on the track. To retrieve records randomly, the system locates the track containing the record, and then searches the records on the track for one with a matching key. For System/370 *indexed files*, a portion of the file is set aside to contain a directory that tells on which track the records are stored. To retrieve a record randomly, the system first searches the directory, termed the *index area*, to find on which track the record is stored. It then goes to that track to search it for a record with a matching key.

Relative and direct files, because they go to the track immediately without having to search an index, are faster for random access. Indexed files, because the system maintains an index of where the records are stored rather than requiring the user to tell where they are stored, are easier to use. Also, the separate index for indexed files makes it easier to expand the file when records are added.

Relative and direct files must be written in their entirety when they are created, and records cannot be added thereafter unless space is reserved with dummy records. The user supplies the operating system with the key when each record is written, and to later retrieve a record, the user must supply the same key. For example, suppose that a personnel record for SMITH is written as the 100th record and ends up on the 10th track of the file. For a relative file, the user would specify the key of 100 to retrieve the record. For a direct file, the track key of 10 and the name SMITH would be specified for retrieval of the record. Relative and direct files are inconvenient because to access a given record one must somehow derive the key. Relative and direct files are relatively inefficient for sequential processing because the records cannot be blocked and the records might not be in a useful order.

With indexed files, no special effort is required to derive the track key for random retrieval of the record for SMITH; the system searches the index to find the track on which the record is stored. Indexed files need not be written in their entirety when they are created. New records can be added later.

Relative, direct, and indexed files can be updated in place, permitting records to be added, deleted, or changed without copying the entire file. Updating records in place simplifies the updating logic, but leads to a serious backup problem. When a file is updated in place, the original version of the file is changed, and if the job must be rerun, the file must first be restored from a backup copy, presuming that a backup copy of the file has been made. Sequential files do not have this problem because the original version of the file is not changed when it is updated, and it can be used to rerun the job if necessary. Hence, while it is easy to update direct and indexed files, one must give more thought to backing up the files. The usual technique is to back up the entire file at some point and save all subsequent transactions.

Random-access files are less efficient than sequential files for sequential access, and should not be used unless random retrieval of records is required. As an alternative to direct or indexed files, a small sequential file can be read into an internal table so that the records can be retrieved using the SEARCH statement. (Records in a relative file could be subscripted directly in an internal table.)

The same statements used for sequential files are also used for relative, direct, and indexed files with the following additions.

- SELECT. Contains several additional clauses described later in this chapter.
- OPEN. In addition to INPUT and OUTPUT, files may be opened for I-O (input/output). This permits records to be updated in place.

```
OPEN I-O file-name.
```

The READ and WRITE statements for random access have an INVALID KEY phrase appended to them to specify an imperative statement to be executed if a record with the specified key cannot be found in the READ, or if the key is invalid for a WRITE. (The INVALID KEY phrase may be omitted if the USE AFTER STANDARD ERROR statement is coded in the DECLARATIVES section.)

```
READ file-name INTO identifier

    INVALID KEY imperative-statement.
```

[The INVALID KEY phrase is executed if the record is not found in the file.]

```
WRITE record FROM identifier

    INVALID KEY imperative-statement.
```

[For relative and direct files, the INVALID KEY phrase is executed if the key for the record being written is outside the limits of the file. For indexed files, the INVALID KEY phrase is executed if the record being written already exists in the file. If a record already exists in the file for a direct file, the record is added anyway.]

```
REWRITE record FROM identifier

    INVALID KEY imperative-statement.
```

[REWRITE locates a specified record in the file and replaces it with the contents of *identifier*. The INVALID KEY phrase is executed if the specified record is not found in the file.]

The INTO and FROM phrases may be omitted if the data is moved directly to the record area in the FILE section.

```
WRITE record

INVALID KEY imperative-statement.
```

I. RELATIVE FILES

Relative files are primarily used when records must be accessed in random order, and the records can easily be associated with a sequential number. When a System/370 relative file is created, the disk space allocated to the file is formatted and additional space cannot be added thereafter. However, records can be replaced, and so dummy records can be inserted to be replaced later with real records, giving the effect of adding records. After a relative file is created, it can be updated by replacing or deleting records. Records are replaced by writing the new record over the top of the old one.

Relative files contain fixed-length records that are assigned numeric keys ranging in value from 0 to n indicating their relative position in the file. The first record has a key of 0 in System/370 and a key of 1 in the ANS Standard. Thus a file containing 500 records would be assigned keys 0 to 499 in System/370. The system stores as many records on each track as will fit, and since each record has the same length, the system can easily compute the track and location of the record on the track from the key. The keys are not a part of the record, but are supplied by the user to read or write records.

Relative files are used like tables. Their advantage over tables is that their size is limited by the amount of direct-access storage rather than the more limited memory. However, it takes much more time to retrieve an element from a relative file than from a table. Relative files are best for records that are easily associated with ascending, consecutive numbers, such as years (the years 1960 to 1980 could be stored with keys 0 to 20), months (keys 0 to 11), or the 50 states (keys 0 to 49).

If the records being stored cannot be easily associated with the keys, as in a personnel file, some unique part of the record such as the social security number can be stored in a table along with the key. Records are then retrieved by searching the table for the social security number to pick up the key. The table could be written as a sequential file, and then be read back in when records are to be retrieved from the relative file. This increases the effort required to access the file, and one might instead consider using a direct or indexed file.

Relative files can contain only unblocked, fixed-length records (RECFM = F), and the files can only be created sequentially. Once created, records can be accessed either sequentially or directly. In System/370, dummy records are denoted by setting the first byte of the record to HIGH-VALUES. Always reserve the first byte for this purpose. The ANS Standard allows variable-length records and does not provide for dummy records. However, setting the first byte to HIGH-VALUES in System/370 has no effect on the processing whatsoever for relative files. Since there is no effect on the processing, dummy records are just a convention, and as such are equally adaptable to the ANS Standard. The ANS Standard also provides a DELETE statement to delete records. DELETE is not permitted in System/370 for relative files.

A. Specifying Relative Files

The following statements are required to specify relative files.

```
FILE-CONTROL.

     SELECT file-name ASSIGN TO DA-R-ddname

               RANDOM
               SEQUENTIAL

     ACCESS IS _ _ _ _ _
```

[The ANS Standard permits ACCESS IS DYNAMIC.]

```
NOMINAL KEY IS key.
```

[The ANS Standard is for RELATIVE KEY rather than NOMINAL KEY. The STATUS clause described later in this chapter for indexed files is also permitted in the ANS Standard.]

□ □ □

```
FILE SECTION.

FD   file-name

     RECORD CONTAINS number CHARACTERS
```

[The BLOCK CONTAINS clause is not needed.]

```
     LABEL RECORDS STANDARD.
```

```
01   record.

     05   delete-byte          PIC X.

     05   rest-of-record       PIC ...

     □  □  □
```

WORKING-STORAGE SECTION.

```
77   key                       PIC S9(8) COMP.
```

[The *key* must be defined in WORKING-STORAGE.]

B. Creating Relative Files

Relative files are created sequentially, and either COBOL or the user can supply the key. COBOL writes the records with keys 0 to *n* if the NOMINAL KEY clause is omitted, and dummy records are inserted by writing records with the delete-byte set to HIGH-VALUES. One can supply the key by coding the NOMINAL KEY clause and moving a value to the *key* as follows.

- Setting the *key* greater than the next available key causes COBOL to insert dummy records. Thus, if records are written in increments of 10 with values 10, 20, 30, . . . , dummy records are inserted for keys 0 to 9, 11 to 19, 21 to 29, . . . , allowing records to be inserted later between the records written.
- Setting the *key* less than the next available key causes it to be ignored and the record is written in the next available key position. Hence, if keys 0 to 3 have been written and the key is set to 1, the record is written as key 4.

When the NOMINAL KEY clause is coded, COBOL stores the key of the last record written into the *key* data item after each WRITE and after the CLOSE. When the file is closed, the system fills the remainder of the last track written upon with dummy records and any following tracks are unusable. (Code RLSE in the SPACE parameter of the JCL DD statement to release such space and prevent waste.) The following example writes 10 records with COBOL assigning keys 0 to 9.

```
SELECT file-name ASSIGN TO DA-R-ddname

  ACCESS IS SEQUENTIAL.

□  □  □
```

```
OPEN OUTPUT file-name.

PERFORM A10-WRITE 10 TIMES.

   □ □ □
```

```
A10-WRITE.

   WRITE record FROM identifier

      INVALID KEY imperative-statement.
```

   [The INVALID KEY phrase is executed if there is insufficient space to store
   the record.]

```
**** EXIT
```

The following example shows how the user supplies the keys in writing
relative files.

```
SELECT file-name ASSIGN TO DA-R-ddname

   ACCESS IS SEQUENTIAL

   NOMINAL KEY IS key.

   □ □ □

OPEN OUTPUT file-name.

PERFORM A10-WRITE

   VARYING key FROM 1 TO 9 BY 2.
```

   [Ten records are written: 1, 3, 5, 7, and 9 are the written records, and 0, 2, 4, 6,
   and 8 are dummy records.]

```
MOVE 0 TO key.

PERFORM A10-WRITE.
```

   [The 11th record is written with key 10. The value 0 is less than the next available
   position and is ignored.]

```
   □ □ □

A10-WRITE.

   WRITE record FROM identifier

      INVALID KEY imperative-statement.

**** EXIT
```

The following System/370 JCL statement is required to create a relative file. There are other forms, but the following is typical.

```
//GO.ddname  DD  DSN=file-name,DISP=(NEW,CATLG),
//  UNIT=device,VOL=SER=pack,DCB=DSORG=DA,
//  SPACE=(TRK,(primary,secondary),RLSE)
```

C. Sequential Reading of Relative Files

The records in relative files are read sequentially in the order that they are stored; that is, in the order of ascending keys. Dummy records are read, and one must test for HIGH-VALUES in the delete-byte to detect them.

```
SELECT file-name ASSIGN TO DA-R-ddname
    ACCESS IS SEQUENTIAL.

□ □ □

OPEN INPUT file-name.
READ file-name INTO identifier
    AT END imperative-statement.
```

The following System/370 JCL statement is required to read a relative file sequentially. There are other forms, but the following is typical.

```
//GO.ddname  DD  DSN=file-name,DISP=SHR
```

D. Random Reading of Relative Files

```
SELECT file-name ASSIGN TO DA-R-ddname
    ACCESS IS RANDOM
    NOMINAL KEY IS key.

□ □ □

OPEN INPUT file-name.
MOVE relative-record-number TO key.
```

```
READ file-name INTO identifier

  INVALID KEY imperative-statement.
```

The INVALID KEY phrase is executed if the *key* is outside the range of the file. Dummy records are read, and one must test for HIGH-VALUES to detect them. The same DD statement is required as for sequential reading.

E. Random Updating of Relative Files

The file must be opened for I-O, and the record must be read and then rewritten to update the records.

```
SELECT file-name ASSIGN TO DA-R-ddname

  ACCESS IS RANDOM

  NOMINAL KEY IS key.
```

□ □ □

```
OPEN I-O file-name.

MOVE relative-record-number TO key.

READ file-name INTO identifier

  INVALID KEY imperative-statement.

    [The record to be updated must first be read.]

MOVE value TO identifier.

REWRITE record FROM identifier

  INVALID KEY imperative-statement.
```

The record is rewritten from *identifier*. The INVALID KEY phrase is executed if the *key* is outside the range of the file. The same DD statement is required as for sequential reading. Records are flagged as deleted by moving HIGH-VALUES to the *delete-byte* and rewriting the record. (The records are not physically deleted, but remain in the file and can be read.)

```
MOVE HIGH-VALUES TO delete-byte.

REWRITE record FROM identifier

  INVALID KEY imperative-statement.
```

The ANS Standard provides a DELETE statement to delete records. Once deleted, the record is logically removed from the file and cannot be read. However, it may be written again to be added to the file. DELETE, not in System/370 COBOL for relative files, is coded as follows:

```
MOVE relative-record-number TO key.

DELETE file-name

INVALID KEY imperative-statement.
```

II. DIRECT FILES (NOT IN THE ANS STANDARD)

Direct files are primarily used when records must be accessed in random order and new records are seldom added. When a direct file is created, the disk space allocated to the file is formatted and additional space cannot be added thereafter. However, records can be replaced, and so dummy records can be inserted to be replaced later with real records, giving the effect of adding records. After a direct file is created, it can be updated by replacing or deleting records. Records are replaced by writing the new record over the top of the old one.

Direct files have keys composed of two parts, a track key and a record key. The *track-key* contains values from 0 to n indicating the relative track in the file. The *record-key* contains data to identify the record on the track.

The key for direct files consists of a track key specifying the relative track number (0 to n) on which the record is written, and a record key that uniquely identifies the record on the track. Several records may be stored on a track, and the system writes the record key preceding the record on the track. To retrieve a record randomly, one must supply both the track key and record key. The system goes to the specified track and searches it for a record with the specified record key.

Records in direct files are unblocked, and may be fixed length (F), variable length (V), undefined length (U), or spanned (S). For fixed-length records, the same number of records will fit on each track, and space can be reserved with dummy records by placing HIGH-VALUES in the first byte of the record key (not the first byte of the record itself). This method does not work for V, U, and S records because COBOL cannot know how long the records might be. Instead, it maintains a count on each track of the available space. Thus one can add a record to a track as long as there is space available. The records on a track are not stored in the order of their record keys, but in the order that they are written; thus if the file is read sequentially, they will be retrieved in the order in which they were written.

The difficult part of direct files is in deriving the track key. The record key often comes from the record itself, and for a personnel file it might be a social security number. There are two usual ways of deriving the track key. First, one can let COBOL supply the track key as the records are written, and then save this track key, along with the record key, in a separate table or file. Then to retrieve a record, one can use the record key to search the table or file to obtain the track key. This is both complicated and inefficient. A better way is to compute the track key from the record key and supply it to COBOL when the record is written.

The efficiency of the direct access for direct files depends primarily on the method used to translate the record key into a track key. There are many techniques,[5] and for some applications, it may pay to study the various techniques to determine which might be the most efficient for your particular application. In most instances, the remaindering method used for hash tables works well and is simple. Divide the record key by the largest prime number less than the number of tracks allocated, and use the remainder for the relative track number. If a prime number table is not available, use the largest odd number not ending in 5 that is less than the number of allocated tracks.

Consider a personnel file containing 8000 employees in which 10 records will fit on a single track. Such a file would require 800 tracks, but we might want to allocate 1000 tracks to allow for growth. Also, the efficiency begins to drop off when the file becomes more than about 70% full. To compute the relative track number, divide the social security number by 999, the largest odd number not ending in 5 that is less than 1000. A social security number of 520-44-1461 divided by 999 yields a remainder of 423, which becomes the relative track number.

In System/370, if the key is alphanumeric rather than numeric, move it to a COMPUTATIONAL item (it cannot exceed 18 digits). When moved to such an item, the zone bits are removed from the alphanumeric characters to make them numeric. The following example illustrates this.

```
01  REC-A.

    05  STATE           PIC X(15).

    □ □ □

77  CONVERT-IT          PIC S9(15) COMP.

    □ □ □

    MOVE STATE TO CONVERT-IT.

    DIVIDE CONVERT-IT BY 999 GIVING TEMP REMAINDER TRACK-KEY.
```

However, it might still occur that more than 10 social security numbers translate to the same track. System/370 Job Control Language permits one to code DCB = (OPTCD = E,LIMCT = *tracks*) on the DD statement for a direct file to extend the search some number of tracks. Thus if LIMCT = 10 is coded and a track is full, the system will look at the 9 following tracks for available space to write the record. Likewise with a read, COBOL will search up to the number of tracks to find a record when LIMCT is coded. The LIMCT for the read must be at least as large as that in the write or records will not be found that have been written in the file. The higher the LIMCT value is set, the more use of the storage space there is, but the longer it takes to read and write records. If the LIMCT were set to the number of tracks in the file, reading the file to see if a record is *not* in the file would require reading all the records in the file.

When records are written, COBOL places them in the next available space on the track, or on the next several tracks if LIMCT is coded. No check is made for duplicate record keys, and so several records having the same record key can be written on the same or following tracks. Only the first record can then be read with random access. The subsequent records with duplicate record keys can be read sequentially, or randomly by deleting the preceding records. Direct files, for better or worse, differ from relative and indexed files in that they may contain records with duplicate keys.

A. Specifying Direct Files

The following statements specify direct files.

```
FILE-CONTROL.

      SELECT file-name ASSIGN TO DA-D-ddname

                  RANDOM
                  SEQUENTIAL

      ACCESS IS _ _ _ _ _ _

      ACTUAL KEY IS key.

   □  □  □

FD  file-name

   RECORD CONTAINS number CHARACTERS

      [BLOCK CONTAINS is omitted because the records are unblocked.]

   LABEL RECORDS STANDARD.
```

```
01   record.

     □  □  □

WORKING—STORAGE SECTION.

01   key.

     05   track—key          PIC S9(5) COMP.

     05   record—key.

          10   delete—byte   PIC X.

          10   rest—of—key   PIC (1 to 254 characters).
```

The *key* may be defined in the FILE-CONTROL, WORKING-STOR-AGE, or LINKAGE section. If defined in the FILE-CONTROL section, it cannot be contained in the record for which it is the key. The *track-key* contains the relative track number, with a value of zero for the first track, and a maximum value of 65,535 in System/370. The *record-key* contains data that uniquely identifies the record. A value of HIGH-VALUES in the *delete-byte* denotes a dummy record.

B. Creating Direct Files

1. Sequential Creation

The entire file must be written when it is created sequentially, and its size cannot be increased thereafter. Space can be reserved to allow new records to be inserted by writing dummy records (F records only), or by leaving unfilled tracks. The remaindering method of computing the track key from the record key cannot be used when the file is created sequentially. Direct files are created sequentially as follows.

```
SELECT file—name ASSIGN TO DA—D—ddname

   ACCESS IS SEQUENTIAL

   ACTUAL KEY IS key

   TRACK—LIMIT IS tracks.
```

> [The TRACK-LIMIT clause specifies the number of tracks to format when the file is closed. The tracks must be an integer literal. If TRACK-LIMIT is omitted, COBOL formats only up to the last track written, and any following tracks are unusable. They can be released by coding RLSE in the SPACE parameter of

the DD statement. By coding TRACK-LIMIT = 100, tracks 51 to 99 would
be formatted when the file is closed if track 50 was the last track written.]

□ □ □

```
OPEN OUTPUT file-name.

MOVE relative-track-number TO track-key.

MOVE value TO record-key.

WRITE record FROM identifier

    INVALID KEY imperative-statement.
```

If the *track-key* contains a relative track number less than the next
available track, it is ignored and COBOL writes the record in the next
available track and returns this value in the *track-key*. If *track-key* contains a value larger than the next available track, the intervening tracks are
filled with dummy records for fixed-length records and available space for
V, U, and S records. Hence the *track-key* can be initialized to zero, and
COBOL will fill each track in turn as the records are written. Alternatively,
the user can set the *track-key* to a value to leave available space. This is
the only way of leaving available space for V, U, and S records. It also
writes dummy records for F records, or the user can insert them himself
by moving HIGH-VALUES to the first byte of the *record-key*. When the
file is closed, the relative track number of the last track written is stored in
the *track-key*.

If the user does not supply the track key, there is no way to compute the
track key from the record key. This means that if COBOL supplies the
track key, the user must somehow save the track key and record key to be
able to later retrieve records.

The following System/370 JCL statement is required to create a direct
file sequentially. There are many other forms, but the following is typical.

```
//GO.ddname  DD  DSN=file-name,DISP=(NEW,CATLG),DCB=DSORG=DA,

//   UNIT=device,VOL=SER=pack,SPACE=(TRK,(primary),RLSE)
```

2. Random Creation and Writing

For new files (DISP = NEW coded in the DD statement), the entire file is
formatted when the file is first opened. For F records, it is filled with
dummy records. For V, U, and S records, all the space is made available.

```
SELECT file-name ASSIGN TO DA-D-ddname

ACCESS IS RANDOM

ACTUAL KEY IS key

TRACK-LIMIT IS tracks.
```

[The TRACK-LIMIT clause is used for multivolume files to force secondary allocations on the first volume. If omitted, the secondary allocations go on the second volume even if there is available space on the first volume.]

□ □ □

```
OPEN OUTPUT file-name.

MOVE relative-track-number TO track-key.

MOVE value TO record-key.

WRITE record FROM identifier

    INVALID KEY imperative-statement.
```

The records may be written in any order. The INVALID KEY phrase is executed if a track key is presented outside the range of formatted tracks or if a track is full. The DCB=(OPTCD=E,LIMCT=*tracks*) may be coded on the DD statement to permit COBOL to look for available space on the following tracks. If a record is written with a record key that already exists on the track, it is written anyway, resulting in duplicate record keys. The duplicate record cannot be retrieved except by reading the file sequentially or by deleting the previous records with the same key. The following System/370 JCL statement is required to create a direct file randomly. There are other forms, but the following is typical.

```
//GO.ddname DD DSN=file-name,DISP=(NEW,CATLG),

//   UNIT=device,VOL=SER=pack,

//   SPACE=(TRK,(primary,secondary),RLSE),

//   DCB=(LIMCT=tracks,OPTCD=E,DSORG=DA)
```

C. Reading Direct Files

1. Sequential Reading

```
SELECT file-name ASSIGN TO DA-D-ddname

  ACCESS IS SEQUENTIAL

  ACTUAL KEY IS key.


□ □ □

OPEN INPUT file-name.

READ file-name INTO  identifier

  AT END imperative-statement.
```

Records are read in the order that they are stored, and dummy records are also read. The ACTUAL KEY clause is optional, and if coded, COBOL stores the record key in the *record-key* data item. (The track key is not stored.) ACTUAL KEY should be coded so that the record key is returned because the delete-byte in the record key is the only way to detect dummy records.

The following System/370 JCL statement is required to read a direct file sequentially. There are other forms, but the following is typical.

```
//GO.ddname   DD   DSN=file-name,DISP=SHR,DCB=DSORG=DA
```

2. Random Reading

Records may be retrieved in any order with random reading by specifying the track key and record key. If $DCB=(OPTCD=E,LIMCT=tracks)$ was coded when the file was created, it should also be coded when retrieving records so that COBOL will look on successive tracks when necessary.

```
SELECT file-name ASSIGN TO DA-D-ddname

  ACCESS IS RANDOM

  ACTUAL KEY IS key.


□ □ □

OPEN INPUT file-name.

MOVE relative-track-number TO track-key.
```

```
MOVE value TO record-key.

READ file-name INTO identifier

    INVALID KEY imperative-statement.
```

Dummy records are not read. The INVALID KEY phrase is executed if the record is not found or if it is a dummy record. The following System/ 370 JCL statement is required to read a direct file randomly.

```
//GO.ddname  DD  DSN=file-name,DISP=SHR,DCB=DSORG=DA
```

3. Random Updating

Files opened for I-O may be read, written, and updated. DCB=(OPTCD= E,LIMCT= *tracks*) should be coded if specified when the file was created.

```
                              DA-W-ddname
                              DA-D-ddname

    SELECT file-name ASSIGN TO _ _ _ _ _ _
```

[DA-W is coded to replace records with the REWRITE statement, and DA-D is coded to replace with the READ/WRITE statements.]

```
    ACCESS IS RANDOM

    ACTUAL KEY IS key.

□ □ □

    OPEN I-O file-name.
```

The DA-W and the DA-D in the SELECT clause are identical except for replacing records. DA-W is more efficient for replacing records by allowing the REWRITE statement to replace records. DA-D replaces records with the READ/WRITE statements. The WRITE statement replaces records if the record has just been read; otherwise it adds the record.

When DA-W is coded in the SELECT phrase records are replaced by the REWRITE statement as follows.

```
    MOVE relative-track-number TO track-key.

    MOVE value TO record-key.

    REWRITE record FROM identifier

        INVALID KEY imperative-statement.
```

The record is found and replaced. The INVALID KEY phrase is executed if the record cannot be found. When DA-D is coded in the SELECT, records are replaced by reading the record and then writing the record.

```
MOVE relative-track-number TO track-key.

MOVE value TO record-key.

READ file-name INTO identifier

    INVALID KEY imperative-statement.

WRITE record FROM identifier

    INVALID KEY imperative-statement.
```

The record is replaced only if the record is found when it is read and if no I/O statement intervenes between the previous READ; otherwise the record is added.

New records can be added for either DA-W or DA-D as follows, presuming that either space or dummy records are available.

```
MOVE relative-record-number TO track-key.

MOVE value TO record-key.

WRITE record FROM identifier

    INVALID KEY imperative-statement.
```

The record is added even if a record with the same record key already exists on the track. The INVALID KEY phrase is executed if space is not available to store the record or if the track key is outside the limits of the file. Records are marked as deleted by setting the delete-byte to HIGH-VALUES and rewriting the record. The records are not physically deleted, but they can no longer be read randomly.

Records can be read randomly for either DA-W or DA-D as follows.

```
MOVE relative-track-number TO track-key.

MOVE value TO record-key.

READ file-name INTO identifier

    INVALID KEY imperative-statement.
```

The INVALID KEY phrase is executed if the record is not found or if it is a dummy record.

The following System/370 JCL statement is required to update direct files randomly.

```
//GO.ddname   DD   DSN=file-name,DISP=OLD,

//   DCB=(LIMCT=tracks,OPTCD=E,DSORG=DA)
```

The remaindering method of computing relative track addresses works well, but has some unfortunate side effects. What if despite the user's best planning the file runs out of space? One can increase the LIMCT parameter to allow the system to look forward onto more tracks to store the record, with some degradation in performance, but this is only a stopgap measure. One can allocate more space and recreate the file from a sequential backup copy, but the relative track address computed from the remaindering method depends on the number of tracks allocated to the file, and if 20 programs read this file, they would all have to be changed to compensate for the larger number of tracks. Also, the remaindering method depends on knowing the number of records that can be stored on a track. If a file residing on a 2314 disk pack is moved to a 3330 disk pack, the 3330 has a larger track, and fewer tracks need to be allocated to contain the file. But again the method of storing and retrieval depends on knowing the number of tracks allocated, and all programs that depend on this knowledge must be changed.

None of these problems are insurmountable, but neither are they trivial. If a production program runs out of disk space, there is generally a rush to get it running again—the worst possible time to have to change many programs. It is a problem best avoided. The user should allow for growth by estimating how large the file will grow—adding perhaps 20 to 50% extra. But unfortunately a method of providing for growth that requires someone to be wise enough at the beginning of a system implementation to know how large a file will ultimately grow is apt to disappoint. One way to avoid the problem is to use indexed files rather than direct. They allow for growth, although they are slower for random access than are direct files.

III. INDEXED FILES

The record keys in indexed files are a part of the record, each record must have a unique record key, and the records are stored in the file in ascending order based on this key. For example, a personnel file might have the person's name as the record key. The file could be read sequentially to process the records for each person in the file, one at a time in alphabetical order. Records can also be accessed randomly by specifying the record key so that the record for SMITH could be read by presenting SMITH as the record key. The file can also be positioned at a point in the file other than the first record in the file to begin sequential processing. Thus one could position the file to the record for SMITH, and sequentially read all the following records. A generic key can also be specified to position the file. The *generic key* consists of a character-string, and the file is positioned to the first record to match the characters specified. Thus one could position the file to the first record with a key beginning with 'S', or 'SM', or 'SMI'.

A major advantage of indexed files is that records can be added or deleted. With sequential files, records can be added or deleted only by rewriting the entire file, and records cannot be added to direct files unless dummy records have been inserted to allow room. Indexed files are slower to read sequentially than are sequential files, and slower to read randomly than are direct files. How much slower depends on the implementation, but in the past the processing speed has been relatively slow. There are several options that one can use to increase the processing speed, and if one is going to the effort to create an indexed file, one might just as well do everything possible to increase the processing efficiency.

There are two types of indexed files on System/370, an older type termed *ISAM* (Indexed Sequential Access Method), and a newer type termed VSAM (Virtual Storage Access Method). *VSAM* corresponds to the latest ANS Standard. The COBOL statements differ somewhat between VSAM and ISAM. VSAM is generally more efficient than ISAM. (Not only is ISAM inefficient for a single application program, but it can also degrade the performance of the entire operating system of large multiprogramming computers by tying up the I/O channels.)

Records in both ISAM and VSAM files can be blocked. ISAM files can have only fixed-length records whereas VSAM records may be fixed or variable length. The blocking for ISAM files is specified in the BLOCK CONTAINS clause. The system handles all blocking for VSAM files, and the user cannot specify the blocking. As for sequential files, blocking for indexed files reduces the number of interblock gaps, conserving mass storage. Unlike sequential files, blocking for indexed files does not necessarily increase the I/O efficiency. It does when the file is processed sequentially, but not when it is processed randomly. For random access, it is less efficient to bring in an entire block of records rather than just one unblocked record. Because the access is random, it is unlikely that the next record to be accessed would be in the same block as that of the last record brought in.

Space for ISAM files can be allocated in three separate areas, an *index area* to contain the index, a *prime area* in units of cylinders to contain the records in the file with a portion of each cylinder reserved to contain overflow records, and an *independent overflow area* to contain more overflow records. The three separate areas are allocated by coding three separate DD statements. Alternatively, one can imbed either the index or overflow area in the prime area by omitting the corresponding DD statement. ISAM files cannot be given secondary space allocations.

The space allocation for VSAM files is even more complex. A special catalog must be created to be used by all VSAM files, and then separate user catalogs may also be created. A large amount of space, often an entire disk pack, is then allocated to VSAM, and this space is later subdivided and allocated to individual user files. The VSAM space may have up to 15 secondary allocations, and the user files may each obtain up to 123 secondary allocations out of the VSAM space.

Indexed files must be created sequentially. When the indexed file is created, the user writes the records ordered on their keys in blocks, and the system maintains a separate index containing the key of the last record written in each block. Records are retrieved randomly by searching the index to find the block containing the record, and then searching the block for a record with a matching key. Indexed files can also be updated by replacing, adding, or deleting records. Records are replaced by overwriting the old record. The method of adding and deleting records is different between ISAM and VSAM.

ISAM records are stored on tracks ordered on their record keys. When a record is added, it is inserted in place, and the remainder of the records are moved down on the track. Records forced off the end of the track are stored in an overflow area, with pointers inserted in the track to point to the overflow records. The cylinder overflow area is filled first, and when it becomes full, the independent overflow area is filled. The records stored in the overflow areas are unblocked. This, along with the time required to trace the overflow records down through the pointers linking them together, makes processing the file inefficient when many records are placed in the overflow area. The files must sometimes be reorganized by copying them sequentially to remove all the records from the overflow areas and place them on the prime area tracks.

When records are deleted from an ISAM file, they are not physically removed, but are marked as deleted by setting the first byte of the record to HIGH-VALUES. (The first byte should be reserved for the delete-byte.) This means that deleted records still occupy storage space. The deleted records are physically deleted only when the file is copied (because dummy records are not read sequentially) and when the dummy record is forced off the end of the track by a record being added. This can present a security problem because unwanted records are not physically deleted from the file.

The records in a VSAM file are stored in control intervals. A *control interval* is similar to a block in that it contains several records, but it also contains free space. The system selects an efficient control interval size based on the I/O device's track size and the file's record length. When the file is created, free space can be specified in two ways. First, a percentage of each control interval can be left free, and a percentage of the total control intervals can also be left for free space.

The index area also consists of the same control intervals. As the file is created, the key of the last record stored in each control interval, along with a pointer to the control interval containing the record, is stored in the index control interval. The system creates as many levels of index control intervals as needed. When an index control interval is filled, another control area is allocated, and a higher-level index control interval is created to point to the two lower level control intervals. When this higher-level control interval is filled with pointers, a higher-level control interval is again created. This continues for as many levels as needed. The lowest-level group of control intervals is termed the *sequence set*, and it points to all the control intervals containing data records.

VSAM files are reorganized as they are updated. When a record is deleted, all the records following it are moved down in the control interval, increasing the free space. When a record is added, the record is inserted where it belongs in the control interval, and the records following it are moved down, collapsing the free space at the end of the control interval. If there is not enough free space to contain the new record, a *control interval split* occurs. A new control interval is allocated, and records moved off the original control interval so that both the old and new control interval now contain free space. The indexes are then updated. The overflow records are thus stored in the same blocked format as the original records. The result is that VSAM files seldom require a separate reorganization.

When indexed files are updated, the records are written into the file and the pointers are updated. If the program abnormally terminates when the file is opened for OUTPUT, I-O, or EXTEND, the file may become unusable because the pointers may not get updated. This is a serious problem if the user does not have a backup. This generally requires that one back up the file at some point and save all the transactions entered until a new backup is made.

A. Specifying Indexed Files

The following statements are required to specify indexed files.

ISAM:

```
FILE-CONTROL.

    SELECT file-name

    ASSIGN TO DA-I-ddname

            RANDOM
            SEQUENTIAL

    ACCESS IS _ _ _ _ _ _

    RECORD KEY IS record-key

    NOMINAL KEY IS source-key.
```

- *record-key.* 1 to 255 character key. Must be contained within the record area of the file.
- *source-key.* Same format as the *record-key.* Used to randomly access or position the file. Must be in WORKING-STORAGE.

VSAM and the ANS Standard:

```
FILE-CONTROL.

    SELECT file-name

    ASSIGN TO ddname

    ORGANIZATION IS INDEXED

            RANDOM
            DYNAMIC
            SEQUENTIAL

    ACCESS IS _ _ _ _ _ _

    RECORD KEY IS record-key

    PASSWORD IS password

    STATUS IS status.
```

- *record-key.* 1 to 255 character key. Must be contained within the record area of the file.
- *password.* Optional. A PIC X(8) data item containing the password. Not in the ANS Standard.
- *status.* Optional. A 2-character data item into which the file status is stored at the completion of each I/O statement. The error codes are listed in Table 4 in Chapter 13.

```
I-O-CONTROL.

    APPLY CORE-INDEX ON file-name
```

[Optional. Causes the highest level of the index to be kept in memory for processing efficiency, at the expense of some additional memory.]

```
APPLY REORG—CRITERIA TO re—org ON file—name.
```

[Optional. When combined with DCB = OPTCD = R, statistics are stored in the *re-org* data item when the file is closed, enabling one to better determine when to reorganize the file. The *re-org* data item must be defined in WORKING-STORAGE as shown here.]

`FILE—SECTION.`	`FILE—SECTION.`
`FD  file—name`	`FD  file—name`
`    RECORD CONTAINS` `       number CHARACTERS`	`    RECORD CONTAINS` `       number CHARACTERS`
`    BLOCK CONTAINS number RECORDS` [The block size must be specified; BLOCK CONTAINS 0 cannot be coded.]	[BLOCK CONTAINS is omitted.]
`    LABEL RECORDS STANDARD.`	`    LABEL RECORDS STANDARD.`
`01  record.`	`01  record.`
`    05  delete—byte PIC X.`	
`    05  record—key PIC X(1 to 255).` [*record-key* may be placed anywhere within the record.]	`    05  record—key PIC X(1 to 255).` [*record-key* may be placed anywhere within the record.]
`    05  rest—of—record PIC ...`	`    05  rest—of—record PIC...`

```
WORKING—STORAGE SECTION.

77  source—key              PIC X(1 to 255).
```

[The *source-key* cannot be described within the record in the record area for the record of which it is the key.]

```
01  re—org.
```

[Needed only if **APPLY CORE-INDEX** or **APPLY REORG-CRITERIA** are coded.]

```
    05  cyl—overflow        PIC S9(4) COMP.
```

[Number of cylinder overflow areas that are full.]

```
    05  ofl—tracks          PIC S9(4) COMP.
```

[Number of tracks available in the independent overflow area.]

```
    05  ofl—activity        PIC S9(8) COMP.
```

[Number of records read or written in the overflow area.]

The ANS Standard also has an ALTERNATIVE RECORD KEY clause coded as follows:

```
SELECT file-name

   ASSIGN TO ...

    ACCESS IS ...

   RECORD KEY IS ...

   ALTERNATIVE RECORD KEY IS alternative-record-key
      WITH DUPLICATES ...

   STATUS IS ...
```

The ALTERNATIVE RECORD KEY clause causes one or more additional indexes to be created to contain alternative record keys. The WITH DUPLICATES clause is optional and indicates that there may be records with duplicate alternative record keys. This facility is not in System/370 COBOL, but VSAM supports alternative keys, and so they may be added to System/370 COBOL.

Alternative keys allows files to be inverted on some key. If the term *inverted* is unfamiliar, the concept is not. Consider a telephone book. The primary index would be the names of people. One could invert the file using the telephone numbers as the alternative key so that one could look up a person's name given his telephone number. Since several people may have the same telephone number, the WITH DUPLICATES clause would be needed. A library is an even more familiar example of an inverted file. Libraries maintain card catalogs with the book titles as the primary key. They then invert the file on the author so that a book can be retrieved by either its title or author.

Alternative record keys are a significant feature. They give COBOL the facility for inverting files, a facility generally found only in some generalized data base management systems.

B. Creating Indexed Files

Indexed files are created sequentially. The VSAM catalog and space allocation must be done with a separate IBM-supplied utility program. Space for ISAM files is allocated by JCL statements. The files are created by writing the file sequentially, presenting the records in ascending order on the record key.

ISAM: VSAM and ANS Standard:

```
SELECT file-name                        SELECT file-name
  ASSIGN TO DA-I-ddname                    ASSIGN TO ddname

  ACCESS IS SEQUENTIAL                     ORGANIZATION IS INDEXED

  NOMINAL KEY IS source-key               ACCESS IS SEQUENTIAL

  RECORD KEY IS record-key.               RECORD KEY IS record-key.


  □  □  □                                 □  □  □


OPEN OUTPUT file-name.                   OPEN OUTPUT file-name.

WRITE record FROM identifier            WRITE record FROM identifier

  INVALID KEY                             INVALID KEY
    imperative-statement.                   imperative-statement.
```

The INVALID KEY phrase is executed if the *record-keys* are not in ascending sort order.

1. Space Allocation for ISAM Files

The System/370 JCL statement for ISAM files has many options. One can set up independent cylinder, index, and overflow areas by coding separate DD statements. When allocated with separate DD statements, the file cannot be cataloged with the DISP=(NEW,CATLG) parameter, but must be cataloged with an IBM-supplied utility program. The following DD statements allocate an ISAM file with three separate areas.

```
//GO.ddname   DD   DSN=file-name(INDEX),DISP=(NEW,KEEP),
```

[The INDEX area must be allocated first, followed by the PRIME and OVFLOW. The INDEX area contains the index to the cylinders containing the records.]

```
//   UNIT=device,VOL=SER=pack,SPACE=(CYL,cylinders,,CONTIG),
```

[*cylinders* is the number of cylinders to allocate. CONTIG is optional and causes contiguous cylinders to be allocated for faster access.]

```
//   DCB=(KEYLEN=length,RKP=position,DSORG=IS,
```

[KEYLEN specifies the length of the key in byfes, and RKP specifies the relative byte position (0 to *n*) of the *record-key* in the record.]

```
//   OPTCD=YM,CYLOFL=tracks,NTM=tracks)
```

[OPTCD = Y in combination with CYLOFL specifies the number of tracks to allocate on each cylinder for overflow records. This area is filled before the independent overflow area is filled. OPTCD = M in combination with NTM specifies the number of tracks to allocate to each level of the cylinder index. Up to three levels may be created.]

```
//   DD   DSN=file-name(PRIME),DISP=(NEW,KEEP),
//        UNIT=device,VOL=SER=pack,
```

[The PRIME area is defined next and contains the records. The PRIME and OVFLOW areas need not be on the same pack as the INDEX, but they must be on the same type of device.]

```
//   SPACE=(CYL,cylinders,,CONTIG),DCB=*.GO.ddname
```

[The DCB parameters for each area must be the same. The referback copies them from the first statement to ensure that they are the same.]

```
//   DD   DSN-file-name(OVFLOW),DISP=(NEW,KEEP),
//        UNIT=device,VOL=SER=pack,
```

[The OVFLOW area contains the independent overflow area.]

```
//        SPACE=(CYL,cylinders,,CONTIG),DCB=*.GO.ddname
```

The file can now be cataloged with an IBM utility program.

```
//STEP2   EXEC PGM=IHEPROGM
//SYSPRINT  DD   SYSOUT=A
//DD1  DD   UNIT=device,VOL=SER=pack,DISP=SHR
```

[The device and pack containing the INDEX are must be specified.]

```
//SYSIN DD *
   CATLG DSNAME=file-name,VOL=device=pack
```

The DD statement required to retrieve the file is coded as follows.

```
//GO.ddname   DD   DSN=file-name,DISP=SHR,DCB=DSORG=IS
```

If the file is not cataloged, the following DD statement is required.

```
//GO.ddname   DD   DSN=file-name,DISP=SHR,DCB=DSORG=IS,
//   UNIT=(device,P),VOL=SER=(pack,pack,pack)
```

[The UNIT = (*device*, P) indicates that several packs may be used concurrently. The packs containing the INDEX, PRIME, and OVFLOW areas must be listed. If they are all on the same pack, code VOL = SER = *pack*.]

The index, prime, and overflow areas can also be allocated with a single DD statement, and the space for the index and overflow is suballocated out of this area. This also allows the file to be cataloged in the DD statement.

```
//GO.ddname  DD  DSN=file-name(PRIME),DISP=(NEW,CATLG),
```

```
//   UNIT=device,VOL=SER=pack,
```

```
//   SPACE=(CYL,(cylinders,,index),,CONTIG),
```

[*cylinders* is the number of cylinders to allocate, and *index* is the number of cylinders to reserve for the index area.]

```
//   DCB=(KEYLEN=length,RKP=position,DSORG=IS,
```

```
//   OPTCD=YM,CYLOFL=tracks,NTM=tracks)
```

[CYLOFL specifies the number of tracks to allocate on each cylinder for overflow records. NTM specifies the number of tracks to allocate to each level of cylinder index.]

The file is then retrieved as follows.

```
//GO.ddname  DD  DSN=file-name,DISP=SHR,DCB=DSORG=IS
```

2. Space Allocation for VSAM Files

The first step in creating a VSAM file is to define the VSAM catalog, although this is usually done by the installation.

```
//STEP1  EXEC  PGM=IDCAMS
```

```
//SYSPRINT  DD  SYSOUT=A
```

```
//VOL  DD  UNIT=device,VOL=SER=pack,DISP=OLD
```

[This statement points to the pack that is to contain the catalog.]

```
//SYSIN  DD  *
```

```
   DEFINE MASTERCATALOG( -
```

[The – indicates that the card is continued.]

```
   NAME(catalog-name) FILE(VOL) VOLUME(pack) -
```

[Name the catalog and the pack that is to contain it.]

```
   RECORDS(primary secondary) -
```

[Give the number of records which the primary and secondary areas are to contain. Up to 15 secondary allocations will be made if necessary.]

```
MASTERPW(password) UPDATEPW(password) READPW(password))
```

[The passwords are all optional, and are one to eight characters. MASTERPW is the master level password, UPDATEPW the password for reading and writing, and READPW the password for reading only.]

After the master catalog is created, user catalogs may be created. Although not required, they can speed up access by limiting the number of catalog entries. They also make the files more exportable, as the user catalog can be copied with the file. User catalogs are created like the master catalog, except that the DEFINE statement is coded as follows.

```
DEFINE USERCATALOG( -
   NAME(catalog-name) FILE(VOL) VOLUME(pack) -
   RECORDS(primary secondary) -
   MASTERPW(password) UPDATEPW(password) READPW(password)) -
   CATALOG(master-catalog-name/password)
```

[The *password* is optional, and is coded only if MASTERPW was coded for the master catalog.]

If a user catalog was specified, a JOBCAT or STEPCAT DD statement must be coded for each job or step that uses the catalog. JOBCAT applies to an entire job, and STEPCAT to a single job step, similar to the JOBLIB and STEPLIB DD statements. The JOBCAT follows the JOB statement, and the STEPCAT follows the EXEC statement.

```
//TEST#9 JOB (5542,30),'A JOB',CLASS=A

//JOBCAT  DD  DSN=catalog-name,DISP=SHR

//STEP1  EXEC  PGM= ...

//STEPCAT  DD  DSN=catalog-name,DISP=SHR
```

After the catalogs have been created, a large amount of space is allocated to be used by several VSAM files. This is done with the following job step.

```
//STEP1 EXEC  PGM=IDCAMS

//SYSPRINT  DD  SYSOUT=A
```

```
//SPACEDD  DD  UNIT=device,VOL=SER=pack,DISP=OLD
```

[This DD statement points to the pack upon which the space is to be allocated.]

```
//SYSIN  DD  *

    DEFINE SPACE( -

                              RECORDS
                              TRACKS
                              CYLINDERS

    VOLUMES(pack) FILE(SPACEDD) _ _ _ _ _ (primary secondary) -
```

[VOLUMES specifies the pack upon which the space is to be allocated. The primary and secondary areas can be allocated in units of cylinders, tracks, or records. Up to 15 secondary allocations are made as needed.]

```
    RECORDSIZE(average maximum)      )
```

[RECORDSIZE must be coded if the space allocation is made in units of RECORDS.]

```
    CATALOG(catalog-name/password)
```

[CATALOG specifies the catalog to contain the entry. The /password is optional and is coded only if MASTERPW was coded for the catalog.]

The final step is to suballocate a portion of the space to an individual file.

```
//STEP1  EXEC  PGM=IDCAMS

//SYSPRINT  DD  SYSOUT=A

//SYSIN  DD  *

    DEFINE CLUSTER(  -

    NAME(file-name) VOLUMES(pack) INDEXED -

    RECORDS(primary secondary) RECORDSIZE(average maximum) -
```

[Specify the number of records the primary and secondary areas are to contain. Up to 123 secondary allocations are made as needed. Specify the average record and maximum record size; they will be the same for fixed-length records.]

```
    FREESPACE(internal-pct total-pct)  -
```

[Specify the percentage of free space within each control interval (internal-pct), and the percentage of total control interval to be reserved for free space (total-pct).]

```
KEYS(length position) -
```

[Specify the *length* of the record key, and its relative byte *position* (0 to *n*) in the record.]

```
UPDATEPW(password) READPW(password) ATTEMPTS(0)) -
```

[The update and read passwords are optional and specify the passwords for updating and reading. ATTEMPTS(0) should be coded if either UPDATEPW or READPW is coded.]

```
CATALOG(catalog-name/password)
```

[The */password* is optional and is required only if MASTERPW was coded for the catalog.]

Once the file has been created, the following DD statement suffices to access the file.

```
//GO.ddname   DD   DSN=file-name,DISP=SHR
```

ISAM files can be extended by coding DISP=(MOD, . . .) on the DD statement, and then opening the file for output as normal. VSAM files require the same in the DD statement, but must in addition be opened for EXTEND rather than OUTPUT.

VSAM:

```
OPEN EXTEND file-name.
```

C. Reading Indexed Files

1. Sequential Read

Indexed files are read in ascending order of the record keys. ISAM dummy records are not read; VSAM and the ANS Standard have no dummy records.

ISAM, VSAM, and ANS Standard:

```
ACCESS IS  SEQUENTIAL
```

□ □ □

```
OPEN INPUT file-name.
```

```
READ file-name INTO identifier

    AT END imperative-statement.
```

2. Positioning for Sequential Access

The START statement positions the file to a specific record. Files can be positioned several times, either forward or backward.

ISAM: VSAM and ANS Standard:

```
ACCESS IS SEQUENTIAL                 ACCESS IS SEQUENTIAL

   □  □  □                              □  □  □

        I-0                                  I-0
        INPUT                                INPUT

OPEN _ _ _ file-name.                OPEN _ _ _ file-name.

MOVE value TO source-key.            MOVE value TO record-key.

START file-name                      START file-name

    INVALID KEY                          INVALID KEY
        imperative-statement.                imperative-statement.
```

[The record is located whose *record-key* is equal to the *value*. The INVALID KEY phrase is executed if no record is found in the file matching the *value*.]

[The record is located whose *record-key* is equal to the *value*. The INVALID KEY phrase is executed if no record is found in the file matching the *value*. In the ANS Standard, the *record-key* may be an *alternative-record key*. If so, the file is positioned to this *alternative-record-key*, and if the file is later read sequentially, it is read in the order of the alternative record keys.]

The comparison can be made to an *identifier*. Only the number of characters in the *identifier* is used in the comparison. This gives the facility for generic keys.

ISAM:

```
START file-name
```

```
record-key = identifier

INVALID KEY imperative-statement.
```

VSAM and ANS Standard:

```
                            ⟨
                            =
START file-name KEY _⟩_ identifier

     INVALID KEY imperative-statement.
```

The file is positioned to the first record whose *record-key* is equal to (=), less than (<), or greater than (>) the value contained in the *identifier*. The INVALID KEY phrase is executed if no record is found in the file meeting the specified condition. If the record is found, the next READ statement will read the found record.

3. Random Read

Indexed files are read randomly by specifying the *record-key* of the record to be read. Dummy records are read in ISAM files. This is surprising because dummy ISAM records are not read sequentially, but are read randomly. Dummy records do not exist in VSAM or the ANS Standard.

ISAM: VSAM and the ANS Standard:

```
    ACCESS IS RANDOM                        ACCESS IS RANDOM

  □ □ □                                   □ □ □

  OPEN INPUT file-name.                   OPEN INPUT file-name.

  MOVE value TO source-key.               MOVE value TO record-key.

  READ file name INTO identifier          READ file-name INTO identifier

    INVALID KEY                             INVALID KEY
      imperative-statement.                   imperative-statement.
```

In the ANS Standard, the records may be retrieved on an *alternative-record-key* as follows:

```
MOVE value TO alternative-record-key.

READ file-name INTO identifier

    INVALID KEY imperative-statement.
```

4. Sequential Updating

Files can be opened for I-O to update them sequentially by rewriting the
last record read. The WRITE statement is used for ISAM and the RE-
WRITE statement for VSAM and the ANS Standard.

ISAM: VSAM and ANS Standard:

```
ACCESS IS SEQUENTIAL           ACCESS IS SEQUENTIAL

   □ □ □                           □ □ □

OPEN I-O file-name.            OPEN I-O file-name.

READ file-name                 READ file-name
   INTO identifier                INTO identifier

   AT END                         AT END
      imperative-statement.          imperative-statement.

WRITE record                   REWRITE record
   FROM identifier                FROM identifier

   INVALID KEY                    INVALID KEY
      imperative-statement.          imperative-statement.
```

The INVALID KEY phrase is executed if no previous record has been
read. Records can also be deleted sequentially by deleting the last record
read using the WRITE statement in ISAM and the DELETE statement in
VSAM and the ANS Standard. ISAM records are only marked as deleted
by setting the delete-byte to HIGH-VALUES; VSAM and the ANS
Standard physically remove deleted records from the file.

ISAM: VSAM and ANS Standard:

```
ACCESS IS SEQUENTIAL           ACCESS IS SEQUENTIAL

   □ □ □                           □ □ □

OPEN I-O file-name.            OPEN I-O file-name.

READ file-name                 READ file-name
   INTO identifier                INTO identifier

   AT END                         AT END
      imperative-statement.          imperative-statement.
```

```
MOVE HIGH-VALUES              DELETE file-name
     TO delete-byte.
                                 INVALID KEY
WRITE record                       imperative-statement.
     FROM identifier

INVALID KEY
   imperative-statement.
```

The INVALID KEY phrase is executed if a previous record has not been read.

5. Random Updating

In ISAM, the TRACK-AREA clause should be coded in the SELECT clause when randomly updating files. TRACK-AREA improves the efficiency by holding an entire track in memory, allowing the records on it to be updated in memory. But more importantly, the contents of the NOMINAL KEY are unpredictable after a WRITE if TRACK-AREA is not coded.

ISAM:

```
SELECT file-name ASSIGN TO DA-I-ddname

   ACCESS IS RANDOM

   RECORD KEY IS record-key

   NOMINAL KEY IS source-key

   TRACK-AREA IS number CHARACTERS.
```

The literal integer *number* must be a multiple of 8 and be equal to or greater than the track size plus one record. For example, a 100-byte record stored on a 2314 track containing 7294 bytes equals 7394, which is rounded up to 7400 to be divisible by 8.

Records are written, updated, deleted, and read randomly by opening them for I-O.

ISAM: VSAM and ANS Standard:

```
ACCESS IS RANDOM            ACCESS IS RANDOM

 □ □ □                       □ □ □

OPEN I-O file-name.         OPEN I-O file-name.
```

Writing:

```
MOVE value TO source-key.        MOVE value TO record-key.

WRITE record                     WRITE record
     FROM identifier                  FROM identifier

   INVALID KEY                      INVALID KEY
      imperative-statement.           imperative-statement.
```

The INVALID KEY phrase is executed if the record already exists in the file.

Updating:

```
MOVE value TO source-key.        MOVE value TO record-key.

REWRITE record                   REWRITE record
      FROM identifier                   FROM identifier

   INVALID KEY                      INVALID KEY
      imperative-statement.           imperative-statement.
```

The INVALID KEY phrase is executed if the record does not exist in the file.

Deleting:

ISAM records are marked as deleted by setting the delete-byte to HIGH-VALUES; VSAM records are physically deleted from the file, as they are in the ANS Standard.

```
MOVE HIGH-VALUES                 MOVE value TO record-key.
     TO delete-byte.

MOVE value TO source-key.        DELETE file-name

REWRITE record                     INVALID KEY
      FROM identifier                 imperative-statement.

   INVALID KEY
      imperative statement.
```

The INVALID KEY phrase is executed if the record does not exist in the file.

Reading:

```
MOVE value TO source-key.        MOVE value TO record-key.

READ file-name                   READ file-name
     INTO identifier                  INTO identifier

INVALID KEY                      INVALID KEY
     imperative-statement.            imperative-statement.
```

In the ANS Standard, records may be read directly based on the *alternative-record-keys* as follows.

```
                         MOVE value TO
                              alternative-record-key.

                         READ file-name
                              INTO identifier

                         KEY IS
                              alternative-record-key

                         INVALID KEY
                              imperative-statement.
```

The INVALID KEY phrase is executed if the record does not exist in the file. VSAM and ANS Standard files can be specified to have DYNAMIC access, which permits them to be accessed sequentially or dynamically, depending on the I/O statement. That is, after a record is located by a random read, the records following it can be read sequentially. Another random read can then be issued to switch back to random access.

VSAM and ANS Standard:

```
                    ACCESS IS DYNAMIC

                    □  □  □

                    OPEN I-O file-name.
```

The VSAM and ANS Standard READ, WRITE, REWRITE, and DELETE statements access the file randomly just as they do for ACCESS IS RANDOM. The READ NEXT statement may be interspersed with these statements to read the file sequentially from the current file position. The file is positioned for sequential reading by the following statements.

- OPEN.   Positions the file to the first record.
- START.   Positions the file to the first record meeting the specified condition.
- READ.   Positions the file to the record following the record read.

The WRITE, REWRITE, and DELETE statements have no effect on sequential reading. The READ NEXT statement has the following format.

VSAM and ANS Standard:

```
READ file-name NEXT
     INTO identifier

AT END
     imperative-statement.
```

The record is read from the current file position, and the file is positioned to the next record so that it can be read by a subsequent READ NEXT. The AT END phrase is executed if there are no more records in the file.

This concludes the discussion of relative, direct, and indexed files. They are more complex than sequential files, may be slower to process, and result in difficult backup problems. Because of this, neither relative, direct, nor indexed files should be used unless a sequential file proves untenable. The chapter that follows describes the communications facility, and because it is rarely used, the reader might elect to skip this chapter and go to the concluding chapter that goes beyond COBOL.

EXERCISES

1. Describe several applications in which relative, direct, and indexed files might each be used.

2. Write a program to read a deck of cards containing a charge number in columns 1 to 6, and create a relative file. Then write a program to read in each transaction in random order that contains a charge number in columns 1 to 6. Validate each charge number by looking it up in the relative file. Print an error message on the transaction if the charge number is not found in the file.

3. Repeat Exercise 2 for a direct file. Assume that the charge number can be any alphanumeric characters.

4. Repeat Exercise 2 for an indexed file. Assume that the charge number can be any alphanumeric characters.

5. Assume the same file described in Exercise 2. However, the card trans-actions are to be used to update the file. Assume that column 7 of the trans-actions contains a D to delete the record in the file, an A to add the card transaction to the file, and an R to replace the record in the file with the transaction. Any other character in column 7 is in error. Print an error message if the record to be deleted or replaced is not in the file, or if a transaction to be added already exists in the file. Do this exercise for either relative, direct, or indexed file organization.

6. Write a program to sequentially backup and restore the file described in Exercise 2.

REFERENCES

1. "Introduction to IBM Direct-Access Storage Devices and Access Methods," Student Text GC20-1649, IBM Corporation, Poughkeepsie, N. Y., 1976.

2. "OS/VS2 Access Method Services, GC26-3841, IBM Corporation, Poughkeepsie, N. Y., 1976.

3. "IBM OS/VS COBOL Compiler and Language Programmer's Guide," SC28-6483, IBM Corporation, Poughkeepsie, N. Y., 1974.

4. "IBM System/360 Operating System Full American National Standard COBOL Compiler and Library, Version 3 Programmer's Guide" SC28-6437, IBM Corporation, Poughkeepsie, N. Y., 1971.

5. V. Y. Lum, P. S. T. Yuen, and M. Dodd, "Key-to-Address Transform Techniques: A Fundamental Performance Study on Large Existing Formatted Files," *Communications of the ACM*, Vol. 14, No. 4, April 1971, pp. 228–239.

eighteen

COMMUNICATIONS FACILITY

The communications facility is provided on some compilers to receive and send messages between a COBOL program and one or more terminals. An on-line reservation system is an example in which many terminals might be connected to a single computer. The messages from the terminals occur randomly and at relatively slow speeds because people cannot type fast compared to a computer's speed. However, several terminals could request a reservation at the same time. This is not bad luck; queuing theory tells us that if items enter a queue randomly, they will often enter in clusters. (This explains why there never seems to be a line in the supermarket checkout stand until one enters it.)

Because the computer cannot process all the requests simultaneously, and it would not be acceptable to take the first and ignore the remainder, the messages are queued. The operating system does this, and the COBOL program receives the messages from the queue rather than directly from the terminal. Likewise when the COBOL program sends messages, it writes them into a queue so that the program need not wait for the message to be slowly typed out on the terminal. The operating system synchronizes the input queue by sending the completed input messages to the COBOL program, and synchronizes the output queue by accepting messages sent from the COBOL program and later transmitting them to the terminals. The queues are served in first-in, first-out order, so that the oldest messages are processed first. This is shown in Figure 12.

The communications facility is a complex and difficult application for the operating system. It is closely associated with the computer's operating

428

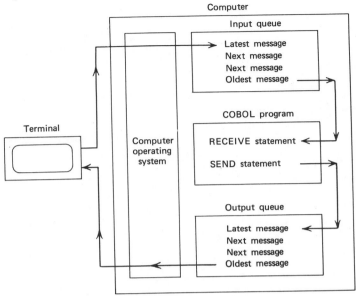

FIGURE 12. Message queues.

system and hardware. Consequently, there are differences in implementations. This chapter describes the System/370 implementation where it differs from the ANS Standard.

The messages in the queues may be retained in memory or queued on direct-access storage, all transparent to the COBOL program. The queues may also be divided into one to four hierarchical levels. For example, a four-level hierarchy for our reservation system might have the state as the first level, the county as the second level, the cities the third level, and the district as the fourth level. In System/370 COBOL, one must write an assembler language Message Control Program (MCP) to serve as the interface between the operating system and the COBOL program.

To write a communications application, first define the input and output queues in the COMMUNICATION SECTION in the COBOL program. The interface consists of a structure into which the operating system places information about the number of messages, the time when the latest message was received or sent, and the message length. Within the Procedure Division, the RECEIVE statement moves the latest message to the program and removes it from the input queue. The SEND statement transmits a message from the program and places it in the output queue. In the ANS Standard, the ACCEPT statement determines the number of messages in the input queue, the ENABLE statement enables a specific terminal to send messages, and the DISABLE statement cuts off the connection to a specific terminal.

The following items are required for the communications facility.

WORKING—STORAGE SECTION.

LINKAGE SECTION.   [If any.]

COMMUNICATION SECTION.

CD entry.   [To define the input and output queues.]

REPORT SECTION.   [If any.]

PROCEDURE DIVISION.

    RECEIVE statement.   [To retrieve messages.]

    SEND statement.   [To send messages.]

    ACCEPT MESSAGE COUNT statement.

[To retrieve the number of messages in the input queue. The MESSAGE FOR condition in System/370 COBOL serves this purpose.]

    ENABLE statement.   [To enable a terminal; not in System/370 COBOL.]

    DISABLE statement.   [To disable a path to a terminal; not in System/370 COBOL.]

I. MESSAGE INPUT

The following entries are required to receive messages from a terminal.

COMMUNICATION SECTION.

CD input—cd—name FOR INPUT

[The *input-cd-name* names an 87-character area used to contain data related to the input queue. The area is initialized to spaces.]

[All of the following items are optional.]

QUEUE IS queue

[*queue*, automatically defined as PIC X(12), contains the symbolic name of the input queue. The symbolic name is a ddname in System/370.]

SUB—QUEUE—1 IS subqueue—1

[*subqueue-1*, automatically defined as PIC X(12), contains the symbolic name of any level 1 input queue. The symbolic name is a ddname in System/370.]

SUB-QUEUE-2 IS subqueue-2

[*subqueue-2*, automatically defined as PIC X(12), contains the symbolic name of any level 2 input queue. The symbolic name is a ddname in System/370. SUB-QUEUE-1 must be defined if SUB-QUEUE-2 is defined.]

SUB-QUEUE-3 IS subqueue-3

[*subqueue-3*, automatically defined as PIC X(12), contains the symbolic name of any level 3 input queue. The symbolic name is a ddname in System/370. SUB-QUEUE-2 and SUB-QUEUE-1 must be defined is SUB-QUEUE-3 is defined.]

MESSAGE DATE IS date

[*date* is automatically defined as PIC 9(6), and the RECEIVE statement stores the date of the message in the form yymmdd.]

MESSAGE TIME IS time

[*time* is automatically defined as PIC 9(8), and the RECEIVE statement stores the time of the message in the form hhmmsstt; tt is hundredths of a second.]

SOURCE IS source

[*source* is automatically defined as PIC X(12), and the RECEIVE statement stores the symbolic name of the terminal or blanks if the terminal is not known to the system.]

TEXT LENGTH IS length

[*length* is automatically defined as PIC 9(4), and the RECEIVE statement stores the length of the message in it.]

END KEY IS end-key

[*end-key* is automatically defined as PIC X, and the RECEIVE statement stores values in it to indicate whether a complete message was transmitted.]

'3'	[End of group.]
'2'	[End of message.]
'1'	[End of segment. Can occur only if RECEIVE SEGMENT is coded.
'0'	[Less than a complete message or segment was received.]

[If two or more conditions occur, the highest number is stored so that an end of group and end of message results in a three being stored.]

```
STATUS KEY IS status-key
```

[*status-key* is automatically defined as PIC XX, and the result of any RECEIVE, ACCEPT, ENABLE INPUT and DISABLE INPUT statement is stored in it. The values are described further on in this chapter.]

```
QUEUE DEPTH IS count.
```

[*count* is automatically defined as PIC 9(6), and the MESSAGE FOR condition or the ACCEPT statement stores the count of the messages in the input queue. MESSAGE COUNT must be coded in place of QUEUE DEPTH in the ANS Standard.]

The final result is a record implicitly described as follows.

```
01   input-cd-name.                                    Byte position.

    05   queue          PIC X(12).                     1

    05   subqueue-1     PIC X(12).                     13

    05   subqueue-2     PIC X(12).                     25

    05   subqueue-3     PIC X(12).                     37

    05   date           PIC 9(6).                      49

    05   time           PIC 9(8).                      55

    05   source         PIC X(12).                     63

    05   length         PIC 9(4).                      75

    05   end-key        PIC X.                         79

    05   status-key     PIC XX.                        80

    05   count          PIC 9(6).                      82
```

The CD statement may be followed by one or more records to redefine the 87-byte area. For example, the following could be coded to redefine the MESSAGE DATE.

```
01   CD-1.

    05   FILLER         PIC X(48).

    05   DISSECT-TIME.

        10   HH         PIC XX.

        10   MM         PIC XX.

        10   SS         PIC XX.

    05   FILLER         PIC X(33).
```

To receive the messages, first move the symbolic queue names to the QUEUE, SUB-QUEUE-n identifiers for the queues from which to receive messages; move spaces to the unused queue identifiers. In System/370, the symbolic queue name is the name of a DD statement.

```
MOVE 'ddname' TO queue.
```

```
MOVE 'ddname' TO subqueue-n.
```

[For needed queues.]

```
MOVE SPACE TO subsqueue-n.
```

[For unwanted queues.]

The RECEIVE statement is coded as follows.

```
                         MESSAGE
                         SEGMENT

   RECEIVE input-cd-name _ _ _ _ INTO identifier

       NO DATA imperative-statement.
```

Characters are transmitted from left to right into *identifier*. If the message is smaller than *identifier*, *identifier* is not padded out with blanks. If the message is longer than *identifier*, *identifier* is filled, *end-key* is set to zero, and subsequent RECEIVE statements can receive the remainder of the message. If the program terminates before a complete message is transmitted, the remainder of that message is undefined, but the remaining messages in the queue are undisturbed.

RECEIVE SEGMENT receives a message segment. A *segment* is a portion of the message, and is implementation dependent. Some terminals have a segment key that inserts a special control character to delimit a segment, and the RECEIVE statement transmits the message up to the control character.

RECEIVE MESSAGE transmits a complete message. If the record contains segments, the segment control character is transmitted as part of the message as illustrated in the following diagram.

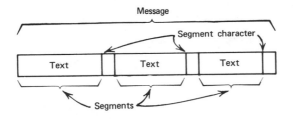

The optional NO DATA phrase is executed if the queue is empty. If it is not coded and the queue is empty, program execution is suspended in the RECEIVE statement until a message is placed in the input queue. The following items in the *input-cd-name* are also set by the execution of the RECEIVE statement.

- MESSAGE DATE
- MESSAGE TIME
- SOURCE
- TEXT LENGTH
- END KEY
- STATUS KEY

At the completion of the RECEIVE statement, the STATUS KEY is set as follows.

- '00'.   Message received with no errors. A message is received only if this code is set.
- '20'.   Invalid queue.
- '21'.   Insufficient storage for statement execution.
- '29'.   I/O error.

The ANS COBOL ACCEPT MESSAGE COUNT statement and its System/370 equivalent, the MESSAGE FOR condition, stores the number of messages in the input queue into MESSAGE COUNT (ANS Standard) or QUEUE DEPTH (System/370 COBOL). The symbolic queue names must first be moved to QUEUE through SUB-QUEUE-3 as necessary before executing the statement.

ANS Standard:

```
ACCEPT input-cd-name MESSAGE COUNT.
```

System/370 COBOL:

```
IF MESSAGE FOR input-cd-name

    THEN ...
```

      [The condition is true if there are messages in the input queue.]

```
IF NOT MESSAGE FOR input-cd-name

    THEN ...
```

      [The condition is true if there are no messages in the input queue.]

Most COBOL compilers stop evaluating logical expressions with the first condition that is not true, and the expressions that follow are not evaluated. This saves needless evaluation, but the QUEUE DEPTH is stored only if the MESSAGE FOR condition is evaluated. This is illustrated in the following expression in which the QUEUE DEPTH is not stored if A is not equal to B.

```
IF (A = B) AND (MESSAGE FOR CD-1)

    THEN ...
```

The problem is solved in this instance by placing the MESSAGE FOR condition first.

```
IF (MESSAGE FOR CD-1) AND (A = B)

    THEN ...
```

At the completion of the statement execution or the condition evaluation, the STATUS KEY is set as follows.

- '00'. No errors, MESSAGE COUNT or QUEUE DEPTH set. They are set only if this condition is returned.
- '20'. Invalid queue name.
- '21'. Insufficient storage for statement execution.
- '29'. I/O error.

II. MESSAGE OUTPUT

The following statements are required to send messages to a terminal.

COMMUNICATION SECTION.

CD output-cd-name FOR OUTPUT

[The *output-cd-name* names an area used to contain data related to the output queue. The area length is $10 + 13(n)$ where n is the number of destinations defined following. Usually there is only one destination, and the length is 23 bytes.]

[Each of the following clauses is optional.]

DESTINATION COUNT IS count

[*count*, automatically defined as PIC 9(4), contains a count of the number of destinations as specified in the DESTINATION TABLE to which the message

is to be sent. System/370 COBOL permits only one destination, and this clause
may be omitted.]

TEXT LENGTH IS length

[*length* is automatically defined as PIC 9(4), and prior to the execution of the
SEND statement, must be set to the length of the message to be transmitted.]

STATUS KEY IS status-key

[*status-key* is automatically defined as PIC XX, and the result of any SEND,
ENABLE OUTPUT, or DISABLE OUTPUT statement is stored.]

DESTINATION TABLE OCCURS n TIMES INDEXED BY index

[This clause defines a table of destinations in which each destination contains an
ERROR KEY and a DESTINATION. System/370 COBOL permits only one
destination, and this clause may be omitted.]

ERROR KEY IS error-key

[*error-key*, automatically defined as PIC X, is set by the SEND, ENABLE OUT-
PUT, and DISABLE OUTPUT statements as follows.]

'0'   [Destination know.]

'1'   [Destination not known, message not
sent.]

DESTINATION IS destination.

[*destination*, automatically defined as PIC X(12), contains the symbolic name of
the terminal to which the message is to be sent.]

The final result is a structure implicitly defined as follows.

                                                      Byte position:

```
01  output-cd-name.

    05  count          PIC 9(4).                    1

    05  length         PIC 9(4).                    5

    05  status-key     PIC XX.                      9

    05  table OCCURS n TIMES INDEXED BY index.

        10  error-key     PIC X.                   11

        10  destination   PIC X(12).               12
```

The CD may be followed by one or more records to redefine the area. The following redefinition assumes that there is only one destination.

```
01   CD-OUT.

     05   FILLER            PIC X(11).

     05   TERMINAL-NAME     PIC X(12).
```

The SEND statement sends messages to specified terminals. First, the message length must be stored in TEXT LENGTH, the number of destinations, if more than one, must be stored in DESTINATION COUNT, and the symbolic terminal names must be stored in DESTINATION.

```
MOVE number TO length.

MOVE 'terminal-name' TO destination.

SEND output-cd-name FROM identifier.
```

The leftmost *number* of characters of the message as specified in *length* are transmitted from *identifier*. The message is not actually transmitted until all segments are sent as indicated by sending an end-of-message or end-of-group indicator. The start of each message begins in the leftmost character position of a new line on a line-oriented terminal. If the message is longer than the line on the terminal, it is continued on the next line.

The following form of the SEND also transmits the end of group, end of message, or end of segment indicators.

```
SEND output-cd-name FROM identifier

          EGI
          EMI
          ESI
          code

     WITH _ _ _.
```

- EGI. End-of-group indicator. Indicates that all messages are terminated and implies EMI.
- EMI. End-of-message indicator. Indicates that the complete message has been sent and implies ESI. The message is not transmitted until EMI is sent.
- ESI. End-of-segment indicator. Indicates that a segment is being transmitted.

- *code.* An identifier described as PIC 9 with values as follows.
  - 0. Null indicator. Used to send a portion of a segment.
  - 1. Same as ESI.
  - 2. Same as EMI.
  - 3. Same as EGI.

The WITH phrase may be omitted to send a portion of a segment. The FROM phrase may be omitted to send only the indicator. The results of the SEND execution are stored in the STATUS KEY as follows.

- '00'. No errors, message is sent. No message is sent unless this code is returned.
- '20'. Destination unknown.
- '21'. Insufficient storage for statement execution.
- '22'. No output queue defined.
- '50'. The TEXT LENGTH is set to a value greater than the length of the identifier.
- '60'. The TEXT LENGTH was set to zero, or the FROM phrase was omitted. This is not an error condition.

Although not provided in System/370 COBOL, the ANS Standard controls the line spacing of a line-oriented terminal with the ADVANCING phrase, similar to the ADVANCING phrase in the WRITE statement used to control the spacing of the printer.

```
SEND output-cd-name FROM identifier

       EGI
       EMI
       ESI
       code

   WITH _ _ _

   AFTER           PAGE
   BEFORE          number LINES

   _ _ _ _ ADVANCING _ _ _ _ _ _ _.
```

The indicated spacing is done BEFORE or AFTER the message is printed. The *number* may be a integer literal or identifier.

III. ENABLE/DISABLE STATEMENTS (Not In System/370)

The ENABLE/DISABLE statements enable or disable the path between the queue and a terminal. The statements are not a part of System/370 COBOL, but are a part of the ANS Standard. If required, the paths are enabled as follows.

```
        OUTPUT
        INPUT
        INPUT TERMINAL

ENABLE _ _ _ _ _ _ _ cd—name WITH KEY password.
```

If required, the paths are disabled as follows.

```
        OUTPUT
        INPUT
        INPUT TERMINAL

DISABLE _ _ _ _ _ _ _ cd—name WITH KEY password.
```

- INPUT TERMINAL. The path to the terminal specified in the SOURCE clause of the *input-cd-name* is enabled or disabled.
- INPUT. All paths specified by the QUEUE through SUB-QUEUE-3 clauses in the *input-cd-name* are enabled or disabled.
- OUTPUT. All paths named in the DESTINATION clause of the *output-cd-name* are enabled or disabled.
- *password*. A 1 to 10 character literal or identifier containing a password built into the system.

Upon completion of the ENABLE or DISABLE statement, the STATUS KEY is set as follows.

- '00'. No error, action completed. The paths are enabled or disabled only if this code is returned.
- '20'. For OUTPUT, DESTINATION IS unknown. For INPUT, a *queue* or *sub-queue* is unknown. For INPUT TERMINAL, the *source* is unknown.
- '30'. For OUTPUT the DESTINATION COUNT is invalid.
- '40'. The *password* is invalid.

This completes the communications facility, and all of the COBOL language features have been discussed. The next chapter goes beyond COBOL into some broader programming areas.

nineteen

BEYOND COBOL

This chapter contains a collection of topics that are not a part of the COBOL language, but are a part of programming. They include production computing, efficiency, maintenance, programming for change, reading programs, and testing and debugging. Techniques for these have been discussed throughtout the book where they apply to individual language statements, and they are brought together here for a complete discussion.

I. PRODUCTION COMPUTING

Many computer programs are written to be run only once to solve a particular problem. However, this is not the world of COBOL. It is not a good language for quick, one-time programs, but it is an excellent language for production programs. Most COBOL programs are run repeatedly in production after they are written. This is perhaps the most significant fact about COBOL, and the one that makes it difficult for many in computing to understand and appreciate it. The production environment of COBOL leads to many considerations, some not at all obvious.

The program will exist for a long time, and the environment will change. The operating system will change, the compiler will change, and a new version of the ANS Standard may even change COBOL itself. The I/O devices will change, as will the computer. The requirements will change. Laws will change; new information will be legally required, and old information will be legally prohibited. The users will change, as will the organization.

Latent errors will come to life. A single run of the program might not discover some errors, but when the program is run often, those latent errors will occur. Most programs contain errors that lie dormant until a particular combination of data brings them to life. The longer the program's life, the more that can go wrong with the program.

The program must run on schedule. A schedule must be prepared, input must be coordinated, and conditions that would affect the schedule must be anticipated. Errors require immediate attention, and the pressures are intense.

Information is retained. This is an enormously complicating factor because errors are cumulative. When an error introduces bad data in a file, correcting the program does not correct the error. The file must be purged of the bad data. Also, other programs will be affected if they read the file with bad data.

Someone else will run the program. The organization may set up a separate run group to collect the input, schedule the runs, submit the job, and check and distribute the output. The run group must know how to run the job and keep track of files. They must also be able to tell if the program ran successfully, and they must know what to do if the run was unsuccessful.

Someone else will modify the program. The original programmer may be reassigned or even leave the company. Someone completely unfamiliar with the program must locate errors and make modifications.

Someone else will read the output. Reports must be carefully formatted with row and column titles and page headings. It is not enough to just print the information; it must be organized and presented so as to be clear.

Sheer volume will cause problems. The program may run too long, the files may be too large, and too much may be printed. A production program may encounter limitations in memory size, CPU time, elapsed running time, tape and disk capacity, and lines of output. You must consider backup and recovery. The volume will tend to grow over time, and this may suddenly cause the program to stop running if the maximum capacity is exceeded.

II. EFFICIENCY

Efficiency permeates computing. Programming classes emphasize it, and techniques for improving efficiency are learned long before techniques for writing correct and easily modified programs are mastered. The typical programming class problem requires the solution to be coded in as few statements as possible, but rarely with as much clarity as possible. Besides teaching habits that are hard to break, writing a program in the fewest number of statements is not necessarily efficient.

Efficiency was critical early in programming when the storage was small, the CPU relatively slow, and the I/O devices equally limited. It made no difference if a program was clear if it would not fit on the computer. Many of these restrictions have now been eased. New computers and virtual storage systems provide large amounts of storage, CPUs are an order of magnitude faster, and so are tapes and disk. Why then worry about efficiency?

We need to worry about efficiency for three reasons. First, the operating system's consumption has kept pace with the increased hardware capacity so that the amount of computer available to work on a program is heavily diluted. The computing power of large computers is further diluted because many programs are run concurrently, and a single program receives only a portion of the computer's resources. Second, most computer systems charge for use of the computer's resources, and if fewer resources are used, the job will cost less. If you can cut a $200 job down to $50, that is $150 saved, and it is irrelevant that such a job might have cost $1000 to run 10 years ago. The final reason is to guard against Parkinson's law—that the size of the program will expand to use all the computer's resources. Constraints still exist, but perhaps it is good that they do because they give discipline to programming. People tend to get sloppy when things are too easy.

Still, efficiency is less important than it was 10 years ago, and this gives us the opportunity to be selective and intelligent in our approach. All installations have their tale of a person spending weeks to optimize a program that is run only once. This is not intelligent. Nor is it wise to mount an effort to optimize a program whose biweekly run cost is $2. Even if the run cost were cut to zero, the cost of optimizing would exceed the savings.

The first step in efficiency is to decide what you want to make efficient. Efficiency, as measured by the run cost, will generally depend on some combination of CPU, memory, and I/O. These items may conflict. Increasing the blocking factor to reduce the number of I/Os can cost more in memory. However, the three may interact in surprising ways. One application used an indexed file for editing, and the program ran slowly. It was changed to read the indexed file into a table, and a binary search was then used for the editing rather than random access. This saved I/O as expected, CPU time rather surprisingly, and memory totally unexpectedly. (The random-access routines required more memory than storing the table.) This points out something else; the results of optimizing can be unexpected. Unless there is some means of measuring the results, optimizing can increase the run cost.

We often optimize in the wrong place—at the detail level where the results are rarely measurable instead of at the design level where the results can be significant. For example, one may labor long over whether it is more efficient to open all files with a single open statement or several open statements. This may or may not save a few microseconds in a computer run, but files are generally opened only once in a computer run, and this is bound to have little effect on the cost. One may neglect to increase the blocking factor of the files which might cut the run cost in half.

Begin optimizing during the design. Programs cost little to change there, but they are expensive to change after they have been coded. Bad design cannot be rescued by efficient coding. The best way to optimize is to eliminate something entirely. This saves designing, programming, documenting, and run costs. For example, do not sort a file that is already in the proper sort sequence.

Program simply and clearly, with an eye toward efficiency so that a separate effort is not required for optimization. It generally requires no more effort to program for efficiency than to program in any other way. If any significant inefficiencies occur, they are likely to be localized to a few places within the program, and you can concentrate on these. Often 90% of the program's execution time is concentrated in 10% of the statements.

Concentrate your effort where there will be a payoff, as in the 10% of the statements that constitute 90% of the run time. Do not attempt to optimize the compilation of the program with techniques such as using as few blanks as necessary and crowding many statements onto a line. Such savings are both insignificant and counterproductive. To save compilation time, reduce the number of times that you must recompile the program by writing it correctly and finding as many errors as possible in each test run.

Optimize where there is repetition, such as in loops, in processing high-volume transactions, and in programs that are run often. Do only what is necessary within a loop, and move all statements outside it where possible. For example, if COMPUTE A = B + C appears within a loop and the values of B and C do not change, move the COMPUTE outside the loop. But do not sacrifice clarity for efficiency. If the table element X (YEAR + 2) appears within a loop and the value of YEAR does not change, a data item could be defined to contain the value of YEAR + 2 computed outside the loop. However, this requires another data item, which is undesirable, and X (TEMP) loses some of the meaning of X (YEAR + 2).

Use an optimizing compiler if one is available. Good optimizing compilers will define a temporary data item as a subscript for the X (YEAR + 2). The optimizing compiler requires no effort, and you need not sacrifice clarity. It should not be used for testing because it compiles slower than the ordinary compiler, but it can be used to recompile the production version of the program.

Think about the effort that the computer must expend, and do not force it to do unnecessary work. For example, COMPUTE A = B * 4 / 2 forces an unnecessary division that can be eliminated by coding COMPUTE A = B * 2. Choose the data type that is the most efficient and minimize conversion. Use PIC X whenever data is not used in computations, COMP for integer counters, and System/370 COMP-3 for most other cases. Use the REDEFINES to minimize the movement of data and as an alternative to the STRING and UNSTRING statements. Use a binary search wherever possible in searching a table.

Do not waste memory. However, if the computer has a fixed memory or region size allocated to each program and the program fits in the computer, nothing is gained by expending effort to conserve storage. If the run cost depends on the amount of memory used, you might try to optimize memory, although it is often not worth the effort because memory is the hardest resource to optimize; its requirements are usually fixed.

Some things may have no effect on the run cost, but may affect the efficiency of the operating system. For example, if several files are being written consecutively onto the same tape, each close will rewind the tape to the load point. Then when the next file is opened, the tape will be spaced forward to the proper position on the tape. It is unlikely that this would be reflected in the computer system's charging equation, but as a matter of professional pride, do not let this happen. The CLOSE WITH NO REWIND solves the problem by leaving the tape positioned to where it was when the close was issued.

The cost of I/O depends primarily on the blocking and to a lesser extent on the record size. Block as high as permitted within the constraints of storage and the I/O device. Tape files can be blocked up to 32,676 bytes in System/370, and the amount of storage is generally the limiting factor. A block size of 10,000 bytes requires 20,000 bytes of storage if there are two buffers. Disk files should be blocked to a full track or to some fraction of a full track.

Sorts are a heavy user of I/O. Eliminate any redundant sorts. If a job consists of sorting a file, selecting records, and then producing a report, select the records first, sort them, and then generate the report to reduce the number of sorted records. Do not be foolish in saving I/O. It saves I/O to compile parameters into a program rather than reading them in from control cards, but it costs little to read a control card. It might take 100 years of reading in a control card to equal the cost of one compilation to change a parameter built into the program.

Assuming that a program runs at an acceptable cost, it will still be necessary to change it. Changing an existing program is termed maintenance, and it is the subject of the next section.

III. MAINTENANCE

A computer program cannot wear out, and from this one might assume that maintenance is not required for computer software as it is for hardware. But, surprisingly, computer software has exactly the same characteristics as hardware and does require maintenance. The reasons are several. First, no computer program of any size can be tested for all possible combinations of data, and there will be undetected errors that can be triggered by new data. Then, although the computer program does not change, the environment does. Perhaps a new department is added and the department table overflows. Perhaps the company opens a field office in another state that has a state income tax and the payroll system must be changed. Perhaps a file being written on tape will no longer fit on a single tape reel. All of this requires maintenance. The computer, its operating system, or the COBOL compiler may also change, which may either introduce new errors or bring to light old, dormant errors in the program.

Maintenance on computer programs is a constant need, as it is for hardware. Because computer programs are not subject to physical wear, they may not require preventive maintenance. However, some installations collect several changes and schedule them together, and the result is much like scheduling preventive maintenance. Some installations go even further and actually do preventive maintenance on systems with structured walkthroughs and programs that read the master files and validate each field to ensure that bad data has not crept in.

Unfortunately, maintenance has little status in programming. Many programmers view maintenance as being only slightly higher in status than hog butchering. And yet when maintenance is considered to be important, it does not carry this stigma. For instance, a surgeon does maintenance and even works with his or her hands, but the importance of this maintenance gives it a high status. Programming maintenance is often as important to a company as the surgeon is to the patients. There is no alternative to getting the payroll out on time. There is no alternative to producing the billing reports on schedule. The demands of these systems are relentless. Yet, without skilled and motivated people in key roles, the payroll could be late, and the billing system might someday stop running.

Many managers probably wish that programming maintenance would go away. However, this should not affect the importance of those assigned to it. Companies are realizing that they often spend more on maintenance than on the development of new systems, and that if they are not willing to pay for the maintenance, the money spent on development is a waste. They have also seen the impact that good and bad computer systems can have on the very life of companies.

There are several benefits to the professional programmer in doing maintenance. It provides an opportunity to learn both good and bad practices and to distinguish between them. It also gives a person feedback on systems design. Some system designers never learn about their mistakes by revisiting the project. In the rush to meet deadlines and stay within budget, much is sacrificed, and the result is often a product that is developed more or less on time and within budget, but which costs an inordinate amount to maintain over its life. If systems designers and implementers were forced to see and correct their mistakes, we would have better systems.

During the next 10 years, maintenance programming will probably be the fastest growing part of programming. It will grow faster than development because all the old systems must be maintained in addition to the new ones that are developed. It also seems that new systems require more maintenance than the old ones they replace. Perhaps this is because they are more complex or because the old system has been shaken out whereas the new system is loaded with undiscovered errors, but maintenance does not disappear with new systems.

Maintenance includes fixing errors and making modifications. When an error is discovered or a change is requested, the programmer must locate the necessary materials, including the source listing, source programs, file descriptions, test data, test JCL, and documentation. Then he must make the change, test it, update the documentation, and place the new version of the program in production.

The first step in maintenance is to locate the materials. The programmer should be provided with some means of locating them and making sure that they are current. Sometimes changes are made to old versions of source program with unfortunate results. Once the program change is made, the testing is similar to that of a new program, except that there is now real data with which to test. You must also be more on guard against side effects. Correcting an error does no good if it introduces another error. The trickiest part of maintenance is in implementing the change. It should be done with little risk and disturbance. Often you can make a parallel run with the new program version to ensure that it is working properly with real data.

Maintenance changes must not be allowed to destroy the integrity of the design. Do not try to minimize the effort with quick and dirty changes whose cumulative effect is often to make a program unmaintainable. Modifications should be as carefully thought out as the original design.

Some formal control must usually be established for maintenance. This allows changes to be evaluated, assigned priorities, and scheduled. It also gives the people doing maintenance a way of measuring their progress, and lets managers know what they are doing. Control must also be established over the source program, listing, documentation, and run libraries. This is critical when the efforts of several people must be coordinated.

Maintenance in systems that retain data in files must account for the bad data that may remain in the files after the error is corrected in the program. For example, if a program improperly added an employee's current salary to the year-to-date total, the program can be corrected, but the employee's W2 income tax form will still be wrong at the end of the year unless the data in the file is corrected.

When making changes, leave a record of who made the change, when it was made, and what was changed. Perhaps the best place to do this is in the REMARKS section of the program. Comment cards within the program can also indicate the specific change. This information helps if some other error crops up because one can tell what was changed, but do not try to use this history as program documentation. It is too difficult to read through pages of changes, some of which may supersede others, to learn what a program is supposed to be doing today.

Good error messages and an audit trail are also essential in maintenance. They can tell what caused an error, and what data was involved. The error messages should tell the following.

- What the error is.
- The transaction and field within the transaction in error.
- The severity of the error. (Catastrophic, serious, warning, or simply a note.)
- What the program will do with the error. (Assume a value for the field, reject the transaction, or terminate the program.)
- What, if anything, should be done outside the program. (Perhaps increase a table size and recompile.)

There are four major categories of errors, and the program should be written to anticipate each.

- Catastrophic error. The program cannot continue execution. There should be very few errors of this type. For example, a person missing from the payroll file might be thought to be catastrophic, but it may be better to continue processing the payroll so that everyone else gets paid, and then write the check for the person by hand. An out-of-date payroll file would be a catastrophic error. A program should never abnormally terminate. Conditions that would cause abnormal terminations, such as processing nonnumeric data when numeric data is expected, should be detected by the program with appropriate error messages printed.

- Serious error. A transaction must be corrected before the run can be successful or the data accepted. A person missing from the payroll file might be a serious error.

- Warning. The data looks wrong and is not accepted, but it may actually be valid. A transaction entered with a salary of $100,000 might result in a warning. There must be a means of overriding the warning if the transaction is verified as correct.

- Note. The data is accepted, and an informational message is printed. This is more of a "you told me to let you know when this happened" thing than an error. An employee receiving overtime might merit a note.

An audit trail is also essential for maintenance. The audit trail consists of listings of all data read and written by the program, and telling the progress of the program's execution. Some of the audit trail may consist of the files themselves if programs are available to print their contents. Alternatively, one might print all the transactions read or written by the program if there are few, or print the transactions on request if there are many. The latter is handy for debugging, but less useful in production because once the program is run and an error is discovered, it is too late to request an audit trail from the program unless it is rerun. Programs should always print at least the following.

- Number of records read and written for each file.
- Number of records selected if there is selection logic.
- Any relevant totals, such as the total dollar amount of the transactions read or written.
- The progress of the program's execution through its major phases. As a minimum, print when the program begins and ends execution.

Perhaps the greatest aid in maintenance is to write programs that are easy to change. The next section describes techniques for this.

IV. PROGRAMMING FOR CHANGE

Programming is much easier if you know beforehand what to program. This is the basis of top down design and programming, and the alternative of waltzing into something and immediately starting to program is unthinkable, although it is often done. However, the only time when you can know completely what is to be programmed beforehand is when you have just finished programming it. Unfortunately, most systems are not immediately reprogrammed after they are completed, and for those that are, the person who wrote the first version is usually not invited to write the next.

Although the ideal is to know in full detail what should be programmed, in practice you cannot for several reasons. First, programming requires a complete specification of the details, with nothing left ambiguous. Humans have a high tolerance for ambiguity, and many questions that must be answered will not be raised until one sits down to code. (This was an early and unexpected side benefit of programming. The detail required to program a solution had never been required before, but to program the solution, the detail had to be obtained.)

Another reason for change is that the end user cannot know in full detail what is needed. You must elicit from the user all the known requirements, but not until receiving the reports for some period of time will he or she really know in full detail what is wanted. This is not a communications problem. Managers who program often write their own little systems for themselves, and these systems go through iterations just as they do when the end user and the programmer are different people.

Write the program with change in mind. Some try to achieve this by incorporating every conceivable requirement. But a program that has attempted to incorporate every conceivable situation would be a monster to change. Anyway, it is usually not the conceivable changes that give problems, but the inconceivable ones. The tradeoff between being comprehensive and being flexible is difficult, but do not confuse the two by choosing one and assuming you have the other. They usually conflict.

The best way to make programs easy to change is to write clear, understandable programs, and to drive the program with data as much as possible. For example, in a billing program it would be bad to code the prices as constants directly in the Procedure Division statements. Not only are they hard to find when they must be changed, especially if a price appears in several places in the program, but the program must be recompiled to make the change, and this is a slow maintenance task. If the rate is parameterized as a data item and assigned an initial value, it is easy to find, there is only one place in which the price must be changed, but the program must still be recompiled. The best way is to read the price in from a control card. Then to change a price, only this card needs to be changed, and the program can be left intact.

Minimize the impact of outside forces. Never read in a table without checking to see that the table does not overflow. In reading any file, be prepared to handle an excessive number of records or no records at all. Programs should also be protected against incorrect data. Validate the input data before accepting it.

Safety factors are used in engineering designs so that each component can withstand greater forces than the maximum expected. Computer programs should also have safety factors built into them to accommodate greater growth than expected. Each file and transaction in the system should have some unused space that is carried as filler so that if new data is required in the file or transaction, there is space for adding it without recompiling all the programs that read it.

V. READING PROGRAMS

Reading programs for debugging and maintenance is an important skill. For debugging, you will probably be familiar with the program because you wrote it, but for maintenance you may know nothing about the program. Begin by trying to understand in general what the program does. A user's manual, if one exists, is perhaps the best source. There may be an overview in the program documentation, and the introductory remarks section in the program is another source. A systems flow chart or a JCL listing also tells a great deal about the program.

The next step is to identify the input and output; what is read and written. If you know what goes into a program and what comes out of it, you can make some fairly accurate assumptions about what must be going on inside the program. Get samples of the input and reports, if possible; study file layouts, input forms, and even keypunch instructions. Locate the files used within a COBOL program by looking at the FILE SECTION where they must all be listed.

At this level, the understanding depends on the documentation that is available. Do not depend only on formal documentation; use whatever is available. Talk to the people who receive the output of the program and who prepare the input. They often know more about the program than anyone if the original programmer is not available. Although they may not know programming, they know what the program does and they can often answer detailed questions from their long experience that might take days to discover by pouring over the code.

Now we are ready to read a program. It is an actual program, not a good one, but typical, and we shall use it as an example of how to read a program. It is not a structured program, but this will be typical of most programs you will read. First, look at the Identification Division.

```
00001          IDENTIFICATION DIVISION.

00002          PROGRAM-ID.    PAYYE.

00003          REMARKS.

00004      *    THIS PROGRAM COPIES THE PAY FILE AND EXCLUDES THOSE PERSONNEL
00005      *    RECORDS WHICH ARE NOT NEEDED IN THE NEW FISCAL YEAR.  RECORDS
00006      *    ARE NOT NEEDED FOR THE NEW FISCAL YEAR IF THE PERSON IS
00007      *    INACTIVE, DOES NOT HAVE A COST IN THE COST FILE, AND DOES
00008      *    NOT APPEAR AS A PERSON RESPONSIBLE FOR A PROJECT IN THE
00009      *    PROJ FILE.

00010          ENVIRONMENT DIVISION.

00011          CONFIGURATION SECTION.

00012          SOURCE-COMPUTER. IBM-370.

00013          OBJECT-COMPUTER. IBM-370.
```

The remarks are useful, and from them we can expect there to be four files: the PAY file in, the PAY file out, a COST file, and a PROJ file. The main loop within the program is probably controlled by reading the PAY file. Next look at the INPUT-OUTPUT SECTION which lists the files.

```
00014          INPUT-OUTPUT SECTION.

00015          FILE-CONTROL.

00016              SELECT IN-PAY-FILE        ASSIGN UT-S-PAY.

00017              SELECT IN-COST-FILE       ASSIGN UT-S-COST.

00018              SELECT IN-PROJ-FILE       ASSIGN UT-S-PROJ.

00019              SELECT OUT-PAY-FILE       ASSIGN UT-S-PAYOUT.
```

The FILE SECTION lists each file, and as we expected, there are four files. Evidently IN-PAY-FILE is the PAY input file, IN-COST-FILE is the COST file, IN-PROJ-FILE is the PROJ file, and OUT-PAY-FILE is the PAY file written out. Next, we shall look at the Data Division and the FILE SECTION where the files are further described.

```
00020          DATA DIVISION.

00021          FILE SECTION.

00022          FD  IN-PAY-FILE

00023              BLOCK CONTAINS 0 RECORDS

00024              RECORD CONTAINS 80 CHARACTERS

00025              LABEL RECORDS ARE STANDARD.

00026      *****  PAY FILE RECORD LAYOUT.  RECORD LENGTH = 80.

00027      *****  RELATIVE BYTE POSITION IN COLUMNS 73-77.

00028          01  PAY-RECORD.

00029              04  PAY-KEY.

00030          *                                      RECORD KEY.

00031                  10  PAY-EMP-ID          PIC X(9).

00032          *                                      PERSONS ID

00033              05  PAY-NAME       PIC X(25).

00034          *                              PERSONS NAME.

00035              05  PAY-ORGP       PIC X(3).

00036          *                              ORG OF PERSON.

00037              05  PAY-SALARY     PIC S9(9)V9(2).

00038          *                                  ANNUAL SALARY IN DOLLARS.

00039              05  PAY-STATUS          PIC X(1).

00040          *                                  PERSONS STATUS.

00041          *                                  A-ACTIVE- I-INACTIVE.

00042              05  PAY-DATE-UPDATED    PIC X(6).

00043          *                                  DATE RECORD LAST UPDATED.

00044          *                                  YYMMDD.

00045              05  FILLER         PIC X(25).

00046          *                              AVAILABLE SPACE.

00047          FD  IN-COST-FILE
```

```
00048                RECORD CONTAINS 80 CHARACTERS

00049                BLOCK CONTAINS 0 RECORDS

00050                LABEL RECORDS ARE STANDARD.

00051        *****  COST FILE RECORD LAYOUT.  RECORD LENGTH = 80.

00052        *****  RELATIVE BYTE POSITION IN COLUMNS 73-77.

00053        01   COST-RECORD.

00054             05   COST-KEY.

00055                  10 COST-EMP-ID          PIC X(9).

00056        *                                       ID OF PERSON.

00057             05   COST-CHG        PIC X(4).

00058        *                                 CHARGE NUMBER.

00059             05   COST-OBJ        PIC X(3).

00060        *                                 OBJECT CODE OF PERSON.

00061             05   COST-TO-DATE.

00062        *                                 CUMULATIVE AMOUNTS TO DATE

00063                  10 COST-AMT       PIC S9(9)V99.

00064        *                                 DOLLAR AMOUNT EXCLUDING FRINGE

00065        *                                 AND OVERHEAD

00066                  10 COST-DAYS      PIC S9(9)V99.

00067        *                                 DAYS WORKED.

00068                  10   COST-FRINGE  PIC S9(9)V99.

00069        *                                 DOLLAR AMOUNT OF FRINGE.

00070                  10   COST-OVERHEAD PIC S9(9)V99.

00071        *                                 DOLLAR AMOUNT OF OVERHEAD.

00072             05   COST-DATE-UPDATED  PIC X(6).

00073        *                                 DATE RECORD LAST UPDATED.

00074        *                                 YYMMDD

00075             05   FILLER          PIC X(14).

00076        *                                 AVAILABLE SPACE.
```

```
00077          FD  IN-PROJ-FILE

00078              BLOCK CONTAINS 0 RECORDS

00079              RECORD CONTAINS 80 CHARACTERS

00080              LABEL RECORDS ARE STANDARD.

00081      *****  PROJ FILE RECORD LAYOUT.  RECORD LENGTH = 80.

00082      *****  RELATIVE BYTE POSITION IN COLUMNS 73-77.

00083          01  PROJ-RECORD.

00084          05  PROJ-KEY.

00085          *                                    RECORD KEY

00086              10  PROJ-CHG          PIC X(4).

00087          *                                CHARGE NUMBER.

00088              05  PROJ-CHG-TITLE   PIC X(25).

00089          *                              PROJECT TITLE.

00090              05  PROJ-ACT-TYPE    PIC X(1).

00091          *                              ACTIVITY TYPE.

00092          *                              D-DIRECT

00093          *                              I-INDIRECT

00094              05  PROJ-PERSON          PIC X(9).

00095          *                              ID OF PERSON RESPONSIBLE.

00096              05  PROJ-AMOUNT      PIC S9(9)V9(2).

00097          *                              TOTAL CONTRACT AMOUNT.

00098              05  PROJ-START-DATE.

00099          *                              CONTRACT START DATE.

00100              10  PROJ-START-YR   PIC 9(2).

00101              10  PROJ-START-MO   PIC 9(2).

00102              10  PROJ-START-DAY  PIC 9(2).

00103          05  PROJ-END-DATE.

00104          *                              CONTRACT END DATE.
```

```
00105                    10  PROJ-END-YR      PIC 9(2).

00106                    10  PROJ-END-MO      PIC 9(2).

00107                    10  PROJ-END-DAY     PIC 9(2).

00108                05  PROJ-ACTIVE-FLAG     PIC X(1).

00109        *                                   ACTIVE FLAG.

00110        *                                   A - ACTIVE.

00111        *                                   I - INACTIVE.

00112                05  PROJ-DATE-UPDATED    PIC X(6).

00113        *                                   DATE RECORD LAST UPDATED.

00114        *                                   YYMMDD.

00115                05  FILLER               PIC X(11).

00116        *                                   AVAILABLE SPACE.

00117        FD  OUT-PAY-FILE

00118            BLOCK CONTAINS 0 RECORDS

00119            RECORD CONTAINS 80 CHARACTERS

00120            LABEL RECORDS ARE STANDARD.

00121        01  OUT-PAY-REC.

00122                05  OUT-PAY-KEY          PIC X(9).

00123                05  FILLER               PIC X(71).
```

From this we can tell that all the files are sequential. The record descriptions are well documented, and we can easily tell what the files contain. Now let us look at the WORKING-STORAGE SECTION which will describe other data items used within the program.

```
00124        WORKING-STORAGE SECTION.

00125        01  FILLER COMP SYNC.

00126                05  IN-COUNT     PIC S9(4) VALUE 0.

00127                05  OUT-COUNT    PIC S9(4) VALUE 0.

00128                05  DROP-COUNT   PIC S9(4) VALUE 0.
```

```
00129          01  FILLER.

00130              05  PROJ-TABLE-SIZE PIC S9(4) COMP SYNC VALUE 1000.

00131              05  PROJ-TABLE OCCURS 1000 DEPENDING ON PROJ-TABLE-SIZE

00132                  INDEXED BY PROJX PIC X(6).
```

IN-COUNT, OUT-COUNT, and DROP-COUNT are evidently counters, and we might guess that they count the PAY records read, dropped,
and written. The PROJ-TABLE is a variable-size table, and we shall have
to see how it is used. There are no input/output records described in
WORKING-STORAGE, and so the READ INTO form cannot be used.
The data is processed in the buffers. As we read the program, we should
keep this in mind for the potential problems it can cause. Now let us look
at the Procedure Division.

```
00133          PROCEDURE DIVISION.

00134          A10-BEGIN.

00135              OPEN INPUT IN-PROJ-FILE.

00136              SET PROJX TO 1.

00137          A20-READ-PROJ.

00138              READ IN-PROJ-FILE AT END GO TO A30.

00139              MOVE PROJ-PERSON TO PROJ-TABLE (PROJX).

00140              SET PROJX UP BY 1.

00141              GO TO A20-READ-PROJ.

00142          A30.
```

The program begins with a paragraph name. We need to know if this is
the start of a loop and how control gets back to A10-BEGIN. For this,
we need the cross-reference list of paragraph names.

PROCEDURE NAMES	DEFN	REFERENCE	
A10-BEGIN	000134		
A20-READ-PROJ	000137	000141	
A30	000142	000138	
B10-READ-PAY	000150	000163	000167

B20—DROP—PAY	000160			
B30—KEEP—PAY	000164	000153	000155	000159
C10—LEVEL—COST	000168	000154	000173	
C20—EXIT	000174	000154	000169	000172
D10—END	000175	000151		

A10-BEGIN is not used, and so the beginning code does not start a loop, but is executed only once. The first statement following A10-BEGIN opens the IN-PROJ-FILE. Then we set PROJX to 1. PROJX indexes the PROJ-TABLE, and so we can expect to store values in it. Next we pass through the A20-READ-PROJ label, and we might expect this to be the start of a loop. Again the cross-reference list tells us that only statement 141 refers to it, and it is apparent that it is a loop to read IN-PROJ-FILE. The file is read, and on encountering an end-of-file we go to A30. (We also note that this is the only way we can get to A30.) PROJ-PERSON from IN-PROJ-FILE is stored in PROJ-TABLE with PROJX used as the index. Then we set PROJX up by 1 and go to A20-READ-PROJ to read the next record. We do not know the sort order of IN-PROJ-FILE, and we must check to see if there is an assumption of a sort order when PROJ-TABLE is used.

Now we should examine the extreme cases within the loop. What happens if IN-PROJ-FILE is empty? We will immediately go to A30 with PROJX set to 1. Notice that we always go to A30 with PROJX set to 1 greater than the number of records read. We should keep this in mind because it is a potential source of error. Now look at the other extreme when more than 1000 records are read. There is no check to see if the table overflows, and this is a potential error that should be corrected. We might now expect the program to search for the person's employee ID in the PROJ-TABLE rather than by reading the PROJ file. Now let us see what happens next in the program.

```
00143          SET PROJX DOWN BY 1.

00144          SET PROJ—TABLE—SIZE TO PROJX.

00145          CLOSE IN—PROJ—FILE.

00146          OPEN INPUT IN—PAY—FILE.

00147          OPEN INPUT IN—COST—FILE.

00148          OPEN OUTPUT OUT—PAY—FILE.
```

PROJX is set down by 1 because it contains one more than the number of records read. Then PROJ-TABLE-SIZE, the item that controls the size of PROJ-TABLE, is set to PROJX. This appears correct, but it contains a potential error. If IN-PROJ-FILE contains no records, PROJX will contain one, and setting it down by 1 yields a value of zero, but zero is not a valid value for an index. (Indexes often lead to errors such as this.) We can correct the error by first setting PROJ-TABLE-SIZE to PROJX, and then subtracting 1 from it.

The next statement closes the IN-PROJ-FILE. Lines 135 to 145 encompass the statements to read records from IN-PROJ-FILE into PROJ-TABLE, and we might set them off with comments. Next, we open the IN-PAY-FILE and IN-COST-FILE for input and the OUT-PAY-FILE for output. Now to read some more of the program.

```
00149             MOVE LOW-VALUES TO COST-EMP-ID.

00150             B10-READ-PAY.

00151             READ IN-PAY-FILE AT END GO TO D10-END.

00152             ADD 1 TO IN-COUNT.

00153             IF PAY-STATUS = 'A' GO TO B30-KEEP-PAY.

00154             PERFORM C10-LEVEL-COST THRU C20-EXIT.
```

First, we move LOW-VALUES to COST-EMP-ID. It is not apparent what this is for, and we shall have to see. The programmer may not have realized it when he placed the MOVE here, but if it had preceded the open for IN-COST-FILE, it would be in error. COST-EMP-ID is in the record area, and there is no record area until the file is opened. Quirks such as this are the reason that it is bad to read and write from the record area.

Next, we pass through the B10-READ-PAY label and read IN-PAY-FILE. Since IN-PAY-FILE is the master file, we would expect B10-READ-DAY to be the start of the main loop of the program. We note from the cross-reference list that we can get back to here from statements 163 and 167. Let us remember this when we examine those statements. On encountering an end-of-file, we go to D10-END where we would expect the program to be terminated. If an end-of-file is not encountered, we add 1 to IN-COUNT. We expected IN-COUNT to count the IN-PAY-FILE records, and apparently it did. Since we have not moved an initial value to IN-COUNT, we should check to see that it is assigned an initial value in the WORKING-STORAGE section. On checking, we see that it is assigned a value of zero, as are OUT-COUNT and DROP-COUNT. The next IF statement goes to B30-KEEP-PAY if the PAY-STATUS is 'A'. We are to keep records whose pay status is 'A', and so B30-KEEP-PAY should write out the record. Let us look at the B30-KEEP-PAY paragraph.

```
00164          B30-KEEP-PAY.

00165              WRITE OUT-PAY-REC FROM PAY-RECORD.

00166              ADD 1 TO OUT-COUNT.

00167              GO TO B10-READ-PAY.
```

We write the OUT-PAY-REC from PAY-RECORD. We are writing the output record from the record area; is this permitted? It turns out to be correct, but it is a bad practice. Then we add 1 to OUT-COUNT, which we know has an initial value of zero, and this confirms our belief that OUT-COUNT counts the OUT-PAY-FILE records. Next, we go to B10-READ-PAY to read the next record. This GO TO is one of the two references to B10-READ-PAY. Now let us get back to the main line of the code where we perform C10-LEVEL-COST THRU C20-EXIT. Let us see what this paragraph does.

```
00168          C10-LEVEL-COST.

00169              IF COST-EMP-ID NOT < PAY-EMP-ID GO TO C20-EXIT.

00170              READ IN-COST-FILE AT END

00171                  MOVE HIGH-VALUES TO COST-EMP-ID,

00172                  GO TO C20-EXIT.

00173              IF COST-EMP-ID < PAY-EMP-ID GO TO C10-LEVEL-COST.

00174          C20-EXIT. EXIT.
```

First, we compare the COST-EMP-ID of the IN-COST-FILE with the PAY-EMP-ID of the current IN-PAY-FILE record. If it is not less than (greater than or equal to), we go to C20-EXIT and exit the paragraph. Otherwise we read in the next IN-COST-FILE record, and if an end-of-file is encountered, move HIGH-VALUES to COST-EMP-ID and go to C20-EXIT to exit the paragraph. The first time we enter C10-LEVEL-COST, COST-EMP-ID contains LOW-VALUES, and this will cause the first IN-COST-FILE record to be read. Now it is clear why we moved LOW-VALUES to COST-EMP-ID: to force the first record to be read.

If an end-of-file is not encountered, we check to see if the COST-EMP-ID is less than the PAY-EMP-ID, and if so, we go to C10-LEVEL to read another record. In essence, we read IN-COST-FILE until we have a record whose key is equal to or greater than the key of the current IN-PAY-FILE record. Moving HIGH-VALUES to COST-EMP-ID ensures that the first IF statement in the C10-LEVEL-COST paragraph will immediately go to C20-EXIT without attempting to read more records. Now let us get back to the main line of code following the PERFORM.

```
00155                   IF PAY-EMP-ID = COST-EMP-ID GO TO B30-KEEP-PAY.

00156                   SET PROJX TO 1.

00157                   SEARCH PROJ-TABLE

00158                       WHEN PAY-EMP-ID = PROJ-TABLE (PROJX)

00159                           GO TO B30-KEEP-PAY.

00160               B20-DROP-PAY.

00161                   ADD 1 TO DROP-COUNT.

00162                   EXHIBIT NAMED PAY-KEY.

00163                   GO TO B10-READ-PAY.
```

We return from the C10-LEVEL-COST paragraph with the next IN-COST-FILE record equal to or greater than the current IN-PAY-FILE record, or HIGH-VALUES if there are no more IN-COST-FILE records. Then if the PAY-EMP-ID of the IN-COST-FILE record equals the COST-EMP-ID of the current IN-PAY-FILE, we go to B30-KEEP-PAY to keep the record. This is correct, but notice the assumptions that the program makes about the order of the IN-PAY-FILE and the IN-COST-FILE. They must both be in ascending order on the PAY-EMP-ID and COST-EMP-ID, respectively. The program does not check the sort orders, and this too is a potential source of error. What if there are duplicate records in IN-PAY-FILE or IN-COST-FILE? We do not know if they are permitted, but the logic will work correctly if they exist. This is comforting.

If the PAY-EMP-ID does not equal the COST-EMP-ID, we set PROJX to 1 and search the PROJ-TABLE sequentially for an entry equal to PAY-EMP-ID. Since it is a sequential search, the program makes no assumption about the order of PROJ-TABLE, and duplicate entries will not cause a problem. If PAY-EMP-ID is found in PROJ-TABLE, we go to B30-KEEP-PAY to keep the record. If not found, we pass through the unused B20-DROP-PAY label, add 1 to DROP-COUNT, display the key of the record dropped, and go to B10-READ-PAY to read the next record.

This is the second place from which we go to B10-READ-PAY, and we have looked at all the statements in the loop. The statements to read the IN-PAY-FILE encompass statements 146 through 174, and we should enclose them in comments to show their beginning and end. The last thing is to look at D10-END, where we go when there are no more IN-PAY-FILE records to read.

```
00175          D10-END.

00176               DISPLAY 'PAY IN  =' IN-COUNT.

00177               DISPLAY 'PAY OUT =' OUT-COUNT.

00178               DISPLAY 'PAY DROP=' DROP-COUNT.

00179               CLOSE IN-PAY-FILE.

00180               CLOSE OUT-PAY-FILE.

00181               CLOSE IN-COST-FILE.

00182               STOP RUN.

00183          *** END OF PROGRAM ***
```

We display the count of records in, out, and dropped. Then we close the three files and stop the run. This concludes the program. We have read the entire program, and it appears to be correct, although we did discover some potential errors. Notice how invaluable the cross-reference listing was to reading the program. This was a small program, but the same techniques apply to large ones.

As you read a program, you will encounter important data items, such as tables, flags, and counters. If the names do not adequately describe their contents, note where the items are declared and your assumption of their use. Again the cross-reference listing is essential to find all the places in the program where they are used to see if your assumptions are correct, and whether they are reused for some other purpose. When you are sure what they contain, insert a comment where they are defined to explain their use.

Often at a particular place in the program, you will want to know what value a data name contains. By using the cross-reference listing to find all references to the data name, and by knowing the major flow of control, you can usually discover what value the data name contains. Let us use the cross-reference listing to verify that IN-COUNT counts the IN-PAY-FILE records. The cross-reference listing tells where it is defined, and where it is used.

DATA NAMES	DEFN	REFERENCE	
IN—COUNT	000126	000152	000176

[It is defined in statement 126.]

```
00125              01  FILLER COMP SYNC.

00126                  05  IN—COUNT        PIC S9(4) VALUE 0.
```

[It is used in statement 152.]

```
00151              READ IN—PAY—FILE AT END GO TO D10—END.

00152              ADD 1 TO IN—COUNT.
```

[It is also used in statement 176.]

```
00175              D10—END.

00176              DISPLAY 'PAY IN  =' IN—COUNT.
```

IN-COUNT is used only to count IN-PAY-FILE records, and the count is displayed at the end of the program. As you read a program, annotate the source listing as you discover things. Later, you should insert some of these annotations as comments in the program so that the next time the program is read it will be easier. These comments are often the best of all comments because they tell the reader what was not obvious when you read the program.

As you read the program, look closely for errors. Just because the program has run correctly does not mean that there are no errors. We found several potential errors in the program we just read. The following items suggest things that should be checked.

- In a division, look for a possible division by zero or a loss of precision. Look for expressions such as A * (B / C) that should be changed to (A * B) / C.
- In a nested IF statement, look for a misplaced period.
- In an arithmetic expression, check the accuracy, especially if it contains a division.
- Look at the compiler error listing because there may be error or warning messages. This is especially important when you recompile an old production program because a new compiler may discover previously undetected errors, or there may be changes in the language since the last compilation. If you are link editing to place a load module in a library, check the linkage editor listing to ensure that the module was added or replaced correctly.

- Be suspicious of logical statements. If NOT and OR appear in the same logical expression, it is likely to be coded wrong.
- Look for exceptional conditions for which there is no detection. If items are stored in a table, check to see that the table does not overflow. Check for indexes having the potential of being set to a zero value or a value larger than the table they index.
- Look for off-by-1 errors. In the PERFORM VARYING, check that the loop executes the proper number of times. A PERFORM VARYING X FROM 1 BY 1 UNTIL X = 10 executes the loop 9 and not 10 times as one might at first expect.
- Identify each file, where it is opened, read or written, and closed. Note any assumptions the program makes about the file's order.
- If you discover an error, do not be mislead into believing that it is the last error. That makes it even more likely that there are more errors.

VI. DEBUGGING AND TESTING

Debugging consists of attempting to discover the cause of known bugs and fixing them. Testing consists of running the job to discover unknown bugs. Debugging and testing consume an inordinate amount of the program development time, often around 50%.[1]

Programmers are often accused of not testing enough, especially when bugs are discovered in production. However, testing cannot be exhaustive, and undiscovered bugs will always remain in production programs. Testing can only prove the presence of errors; it cannot prove their absence. Dijkstra[2] points out that to check all possible combinations in multiplying two numbers might take 10,000 years on a computer, and Boehm[1] notes that a simple flow chart with two loops and a few IF statements would take 2000 years on a modern computer to follow all the possible paths. Since testing cannot be exhaustive, one can only test up to the point where the potential cost of undiscovered bugs is less than the cost of additional testing. Unfortunately, this crossover point is never clear. In practice, testing is a bad place to try to save money.

The amount of testing can be reduced by checking only a few values, and assuming that the program will work for all values. For example, if the computer adds 10 and 20 correctly, we can safely assume that it will add 5 and 10 correctly. However we might not so safely assume that it will add 5 and 1000 correctly because the resultant item may be too small to contain the result. Hence we should include the extreme values in our testing. If a computation is tested for the smallest, the largest, and a representative value, we can assume that it is correct, even though there are an infinite number of values that have not been tested. We can ensure that the values will be within the allowable range by editing the input data.

Debugging and testing should begin during the design. Design the system and the programs to be easy to test. For example, three separate programs that each runs $\frac{1}{2}$ hour are easier to test than one gigantic program that runs for $1\frac{1}{2}$ hours. Start with a test plan for the program or system. You may even go so far as to generate test data before the programming begins. Writing the test data before you write the program also forces you to think up the exceptional cases before you begin programming. In effect, this allows you to do your desk checking while you are writing the program. The test data should be expandable to enable new situations to be tested, but the old test data should be retained to ensure that old errors do not creep back in.

Although it may be hard to generate test data, it is even harder to verify it. The program's authors often do a poor job of finding errors because they do not expect to find them. Seeing that so much of the program did work to produce any output at all they sometimes assume that the numbers must be correct. If someone else verifies the output, he or she will make fewer assumptions about the results being correct, and since there is only the output to verify, a better job of verification will result. The end users are perhaps the best people to do this verification because they usually know what the numbers mean. They can also catch specification errors in which the program is doing what the programmer intended, but in which the intent is not what is wanted.

Validating the test runs also serves to debug the specifications. They too may be wrong or may not be what the users want. Often when users are given a fully tested first version of a report, they will say something like "These numbers don't look right. Did you exclude the field offices?" No, you did not because the users did not tell you to, and even though it was their fault, the report is still wrong. They may have seen a mock-up of the report, perhaps even with representative numbers, but after they receive the report with real data they may want changes. This is a major reason why programs take longer to implement than planned. Those last few "minor" changes seem never to end, and they are often difficult changes to make. Some discipline must be imposed on the user so that the changes are not unending.

Testing usually goes in three phases—unit testing to test each individual program or subroutine, system testing to test several programs and their interactions, and the final testing with real data. Each phase will turn up new errors. The final testing with real data is the most important because it is here that the unanticipated situations will turn up.

Errors range in seriousness. The least serious errors are those that are discovered, and the most serious are those that are undiscovered. Compilation errors are not serious because the compiler always catches them. They can be minimized by desk checking, but it is wasteful to spend the painstaking effort to eliminate all compilation errors because the compiler is better at catching them than are humans. Abnormal terminations are not serious during testing because they too are always discovered. Abnormal terminations are serious in production runs, but not as serious as undiscovered errors in production runs that contaminate the data.

Errors may be undiscovered because they do not show themselves with the test data or because they are overlooked. The latter can be overcome by more careful checking, but to detect errors that do not manifest themselves with the test data or even with real data, the best tool is desk checking. Exhaustive desk checking is wasteful in catching compilation errors because the compiler will catch them. Save your effort to catch logical and arithmetic errors that are not found by the test data. The structured walk-through is a variation on this in which several people go through a program as a group. This is an excellent debugging tool, although often hard to arrange.

Desk checking consists of reading the program statement by statement to see if it works properly and to detect potential errors. The preceding section on reading a COBOL program illustrated desk checking. Desk checking can also thwart many errors in production programs caused by the environment. It is difficult to generate test cases to tell when a tape reel will be exceeded, when a disk file will overflow, or when the time limit will be exceeded. It is difficult to test a hardware error, an operator error, or operating system errors. With desk checking, you can foresee these errors and determine how the program can recover from them.

Debugging brings out some interesting aspects of our human nature. You may not see these quirks in yourself, but if you ever have the opportunity to do consulting where programmers bring you their problems, you will quickly spot them. As humans, we do not expect to make errors, and we are always amazed when they occur in our programs. Programmers often fail to see even the error messages produced by the program or the operating system. "It didn't run. There must be a hardware problem or something wrong with the operating system." Well yes, there could be, but 99 times out of 100 the problem is in the person's program. You would also be surprised at how often programs run with no problem, and then fail when run again with no change made. "It worked last time, and I didn't change anything. Oh yes, I did make one trivial change, but that couldn't have done anything. Oh my goodness, I just didn't think about the OPEN when I moved the WRITE there." You quickly learn that test runs are never made without something being changed.

Debugging is a little like detective work. First, establish that there was an error and get concrete evidence of it. Then look at what happened in the program, and also what did not happen. For example, a program might terminate while searching a table, indicating that the table contained bad data. But the table was read in from a file, and the same termination would have occurred when the data was moved to the table if the bad data had been in the file. This might lead you to check to see if you are searching beyond the current end of the table; perhaps the table size was set incorrectly. If a report produces bad output, look at where the output is bad and where it is good.

Look for clues as to what went wrong and what the program was doing when the error occurred. Look at the CPU seconds consumed, the I/O performed, the output produced, the completion codes issued by the operating system, and any error messages. Look at the data. Was the program changed recently, or were there changes made in the data? Was anything special done for this run? All of these can give an indication of what the program was doing and what caused the problem.

Next, make some assumptions about what must be causing the error, and track these down. Just because you discover an error, do not stop. It may not be the error for which you are looking, or there may be more errors. If you have a particularly perplexing problem, find someone with whom you can discuss the problem. Often you will discover the cause while you are describing the problem to them. If not, they may catch some obvious things that you overlooked, or they may make suggestions on how to locate the cause of the error.

Compilers can help in detecting errors. If a program terminates, they can tell where in the program the termination occurred, the files that are open, and the last input and output records transmitted for each file, preferably in a formatted dump. This is usually enough to track down all except the most difficult errors. (Unfortunately, not all compilers provide these.) These debugging tools are excellent because they are passive, requiring no programming effort. They can also be left in production programs. Debugging compilers can give additional help by checking for invalid subscripts and other error conditions. They can also reformat the listing to place a single statement on a line and indent structures and conditional statements to show the hierarchy.

Beyond this, you may have to trace the execution of the program and print out the values of important data items as the program executes. The problem with these debugging tools is that they require effort, they may introduce errors themselves, and they also require rerunning the program. Some compilers provide special debugging statements that can be inserted in a separate packet to make them easy to remove. In practice, such features are seldom used; perhaps because they are not a part of the ANS Standard (The ANS Standard does have a debugging module), because they must be learned, because they must be coded, and because they may generate voluminous output that is unrelated to the error.

Try to do your debugging at the source level, the level at which you program. If you must look at the machine language code generated by the compiler or look at hexadecimal or octal storage dumps, debugging is an order of magnitude harder. Storage dumps should be used only as a last resort because they take so long to read and they are so far removed from the way we think about programming. Storage dumps may be necessary to locate difficult errors, especially if the compiler does not provide you with adequate debugging information. But often a problem that takes half a day to find from reading a storage dump can be located in a few minutes by just thinking about what must be causing the problem. Your most important debugging tool is your reasoning.

One final word on testing; test all program changes however trivial. There are just too many things that can go wrong to forgo testing. The following example from a real situation is typical. To reduce the run cost of a program, the blocking factor was increased. Later a separate program that read the file failed. The programmer discovered that the BLOCK CONTAINS clause specified the blocking, which no longer matched that of the file. To prevent the problem from recurring, the programmer changed the statement to BLOCK CONTAINS 0 RECORDS and recompiled the program, but this resulted in a compilation error. The original programmer had coded the SAME AREA clause, and BLOCK CURTAINS 0 cannot be coded when SAME AREA is coded. (The SAME AREA clause should never be used because it causes obscure problems like this.)

The programmer removed the SAME AREA clause and the program compiled with no errors, but then it terminated when it was run—the increased blocking required more memory. The region size was increased in the JCL, and the program was run again. Again it failed, this time because the new region size was larger than that allowed by the installation for the job class. The job class was changed, but now the schedule had to be revised because the new job class gave slower turnaround. Ultimately, the old blocking factor was restored, and all the programs were changed back. For the programmer under pressure to get a program running again, these problems are an exquisite form of torture.

This chapter has emphasized that errors may exist in any program, even one that has run correctly in production for years. This does not mean that we should accept or tolerate errors, but only that we must acknowledge that they can exist. This is a large part of the battle in debugging because if you expect errors to be present, you will look for them and find a surprising number. But if you do not expect errors to exist, human nature is such that you will never find them.

REFERENCES

1. Dr. Barry W. Boehm, "Software and its Impact: A Quantitative Assessment," *DATA-MATION*, May 1973.
2. O. J. Dahl, E. W. Dijkstra, and C. A. R. Hoare, *Structured Programming*, Academic Press, Inc., London and New York, 1972.

appendix A

COBOL RESERVED WORDS

ACCEPT
ACCESS
ACTUAL
ADD
ADDRESSING
ADVANCING
AFTER
ALL
ALPHABETIC
ALPHANUMERIC
ALPHANUMERIC-EDITED
ALSO
ALTER
ALTERNATE
AND
APPLY
ARE
AREA
AREAS
ASCENDING
ASSIGN
AT
AUTHOR

BASIS
BEFORE
BEGINNING
BLANK
BLOCK
BOTTOM
BY

CALL
CANCEL
CBL
CD
CF
CH
CHANGED
CHARACTER
CHARACTERS
CLOCK-UNITS
CLOSE
COBOL
CODE
CODE-SET
COLLATING

COLUMN
COM-REG
COMMA
COMMUNICATION
COMP
COMP-1
COMP-2
COMP-3
COMP-4
COMPUTATIONAL
COMPUTATIONAL-1
COMPUTATIONAL-2
COMPUTATIONAL-3
COMPUTATIONAL-4
COMPUTE
CONFIGURATION
CONSOLE
CONTAINS
CONTROL
CONTROLS
COPY
CORE-INDEX
CORR

CORRESPONDING	DEPTH	FILE-CONTROL
COUNT	DESCENDING	FILE-LIMIT
CSP	DESTINATION	FILE-LIMITS
CURRENCY	DETAIL	FILLER
CURRENT-DATE	DISABLE	FINAL
CYL-INDEX	DISP	FIRST
CYL-OVERFLOW	DISPLAY	FOOTING
C01	DISPLAY-ST	FOR
C02	DISPLAY-n	FROM
C03	DIVIDE	
C04	DIVISION	GENERATE
C05	DOWN	GIVING
C06	DUPLICATES	GO
C07	DYNAMIC	GOBACK
C08		GREATER
C09	EGI	GROUP
C10	EJECT	
C11	ELSE	HEADINGS
C12	EMI	HIGH-VALUE
	ENABLE	HIGH-VALUES
DATA	END	HOLD
DATE	END-OF-PAGE	
DATE-COMPILED	ENDING	I-O
DATE-WRITTEN	ENTER	I-O-CONTROL
DAY	ENTRY	ID
DAY-OF-WEEK	ENVIRONMENT	IDENTIFICATION
DE	EOP	IF
DEBUG	EQUAL	IN
DEBUG-CONTENTS	EQUALS	INDEX
DEBUG-ITEM	ERROR	INDEX-n
DEBUG-LINE	ESI	INDEXED
DEBUG-NAME	EVERY	INDICATE
DEBUG-SUB-1	EXAMINE	INITIAL
DEBUG-SUB-2	EXCEEDS	INITIALIZE
DEBUG-SUB-3	EXCEPTION	INITIATE
DEBUGGING	EXHIBIT	INPUT
DECIMAL-POINT	EXIT	INPUT-OUTPUT
DECLARATIVES	EXTEND	INSERT
DELETE	EXTENDED-SEARCH	INSPECT
DELIMITED		INSTALLATION
DELIMITER	FD	INTO
DEPENDING	FILE	INVALID

IS	NEXT	PROCEED
	NO	PROCESS
JUST	NOMINAL	PROCESSING
JUSTIFIED	NOT	PROGRAM
	NOTE	PROGRAM-ID
KEY	NSTD-REELS	
	NUMBER	QUEUE
LABEL	NUMERIC	QUOTE
LABEL-RETURN	NUMERIC-EDITED	QUOTES
LAST		
LEADING	OBJECT-COMPUTER	RANDOM
LEAVE	OBJECT-PROGRAM	RD
LEFT	OCCURS	READ
LENGTH	OF	READY
LESS	OFF	RECEIVE
LIBRARY	OMITTED	RECORD
LIMIT	ON	RECORD-OVERFLOW
LIMITS	OPEN	RECORDING
LINAGE	OPTIONAL	RECORDS
LINAGE-COUNTER	OR	REDEFINES
LINE	ORGANIZATION	REEL
LINE-COUNTER	OTHERWISE	REFERENCES
LINES	OUTPUT	RELATIVE
LINKAGE	OVERFLOW	RELEASE
LOCK		RELOAD
LOW-VALUE	PAGE	REMAINDER
LOW-VALUES	PAGE-COUNTER	REMARKS
	PASSWORD	REMOVAL
MASTER-INDEX	PERFORM	RENAMES
MEMORY	PF	REORG-CRITERIA
MERGE	PH	REPLACING
MESSAGE	PIC	REPORT
MODE	PICTURE	REPORTING
MODULES	PLUS	REPORTS
MORE-LABELS	POINTER	REREAD
MOVE	POSITION	RERUN
MULTIPLE	POSITIONING	RESERVE
MULTIPLY	POSITIVE	RESET
	PRINT-SWITCH	RETURN
NAMED	PRINTING	RETURN-CODE
NATIVE	PROCEDURE	REVERSED
NEGATIVE	PROCEDURES	REWIND

REWRITE
RF
RH
RIGHT
ROUNDED
RUN

SA
SAME
SD
SEARCH
SECTION
SECURITY
SEEK
SEGMENT
SEGMENT-LIMIT
SELECT
SEND
SENTENCE
SEPARATE
SEQUENCE
SEQUENTIAL
SERVICE
SET
SIGN
SIZE
SKIP1
SKIP2
SKIP3
SORT
SORT-CORE-SIZE
SORT-FILE-SIZE
SORT-MERGE
SORT-MESSAGE
SORT-MODE-SIZE
SORT-OPTION
SORT-RETURN
SOURCE
SOURCE-COMPUTER
SPACE
SPACES
SPECIAL-NAMES

STANDARD
STANDARD-1
START
STATUS
STOP
STRING
SUB-QUEUE-1
SUB-QUEUE-2
SUB-QUEUE-3
SUBTRACT
SUM
SUPERVISOR
SUPPRESS
SUSPEND
SYMBOLIC
SYNC
SYNCHRONIZED
SYSIN
SYSIPT
SYSLST
SYSOUT
SYSPCH
SYSPUNCH
S01
S02

TABLE
TALLY
TALLYING
TAPE
TERMINAL
TERMINATE
TEXT
THAN
THEN
THROUGH
THRU
TIME
TIME-OF-DAY
TIMES
TO
TOP

TOTALED
TOTALING
TRACE
TRACK
TRACK-AREA
TRACK-LIMIT
TRACKS
TRAILING
TRANSFORM
TYPE

UNEQUAL
UNIT
UNSTRING
UNTIL
UP
UPON
UPSI-0
UPSI-1
UPSI-2
UPSI-3
UPSI-4
UPSI-5
UPSI-6
UPSI-7
USAGE
USE
USING

VALUE
VALUES
VARYING

WHEN
WHEN-COMPILED
WITH
WORDS
WORKING-STORAGE
WRITE
WRITE-ONLY
WRITE-VERIFY

ZERO	+	**
ZEROES	−	⟩
ZEROS	*	⟨
	/	=

appendix B

ANSWERS TO
SELECTED EXERCISES

Every computer problem usually has several correct solutions, each one perhaps better than the others judged by a particular criterion. A solution may be tightly coded to be very efficient, but it may be complex and in-flexible and may make the program difficult to debug and maintain. One thing is clear—any acceptable solution must give correct results. They must be correct not merely with a set of test data, but with the wide range of values and unexpected data that may occur in real situations.

Chapter 4

1.

```
MOVE 1 TO A, B.                  A = 1, B = 1

ADD B TO A.                      A = 3, B = 2

MULTIPLY B BY A.                 A = 6, B = 2

DIVIDE A BY 5 GIVING C           A = 6, B = 2, C = 1, D = 1
   REMAINDER D.
```

11.

```
PERFORM LOOP1 VARYING X FROM 1 BY 1 UNTIL X > 9.

IF (B > 6) OR (B < 0)

    THEN PERFORM INNER-PART

    ELSE IF B > 3

            THEN ADD 1 TO G

            ELSE IF C = 0

                    THEN PERFORM INNER-PART

                    ELSE MOVE ZERO TO D

                         ADD 1 TO B

                         ADD 1 TO F.


    □  □  □


LOOP1.

    MOVE ZERO TO A (X).

**** EXIT

INNER-PART.

    MOVE ZERO TO E.

    ADD 1 TO F.

    IF (X + Y) NOT > 0

        THEN ADD 1 TO G.

**** EXIT
```

14.

```
MULTIPLY A BY 2.
```
[The 2 must be an identifier.]
```
ADD '125' TO B.
```
[An alphanumeric literal cannot participate in an arithmetic expression.]

```
DIVIDE BUDGET-REMAINING BY PERIODS-REMAINING.
```

[From the context of the names, PERIODS-REMAINING will contain zero in the last period, resulting in a division by zero.]

```
MOVE ZERO TO A, B, C.
```

[Should be a comma rather than a period after B.]

```
COMPUTE A = B * C ROUNDED.
```

[Should be COMPUTE A ROUNDED = B * C.]

```
IF A = 2 = B
    GO TO START.
ELSE GO TO DONE.
```

Should be coded as:

```
IF A = 2 AND B
GO TO START
ELSE GO TO DONE.
```

Chapter 5

6.

One ought to ask what the basis is for measuring productivity. What is measured? What are the units of measurement? What is the basis for the comparison? What caused the increase in productivity? Could something other than the listed techniques have caused part or all of the postulated increase in productivity? For example, one might have selected only the top programmers for the experiment, and they might have been affected by the Hawthorne effect. The Hawthorne effect occurs when the results on an experiment are influenced by watching it. If people know they are being watched to see if they do better, they will do better because they know they are being watched rather than because variables are changed in the experiment.

It is impossible to predict accurately what would occur if programmer productivity was increased tenfold. At one extreme, 9 out of 10 programmers might be laid off. At another extreme, the programming population might produce 10 times the number of computer programs they do now. There are social and technical considerations to these extremes, and in the entire spectrum in between.

Chapter 6

3.

```
COMPUTE E = A * D.
```

   [A converted to COMP-3 and then to COMP-1. A * D COMP-1 intermediate
   result converted to COMP-2 and stored in E.]

```
COMPUTE A = D * B * C.
```

   [B and C converted to COMP-1. COMP-1 intermediate result converted to
   USAGE DISPLAY and stored in A.]

```
ADD 1 TO C.
```

   [Conversion depends on compiler. Literal constants in System/370 are COMP-3,
   and so the 1 would be converted to COMP and be added to C.]

```
MOVE B TO A.
```

   [COMP-3 converted to USAGE DISPLAY.]

4. Results shown are for System/370 COBOL.

```
COMPUTE A = 3.5.     A = 3
COMPUTE A ROUNDED = 3.5.      A = 4
COMPUTE B = 1254.6 * 3.3235 / 6.43229 + 12.1136.
   1254.6 (4V1) * 3.3235 (1V4) = 4169.6631 (5V5)
   4169.6631 (5V5) / 6.43229 (1V5) = 648.23928 (10V5)
   648.23928 (10V5) + 12.1136 (2V4) = 660.35288 (11V5)
   660.35288 (11V5) stored in B as 660.352 (6V3)
MOVE 12.211 TO B.       B = 12.211 (6V3)
COMPUTE B = B / 4.395 * 6.4 + 7.1135.
   12.211 (6V3) / 4.395 (1V3) = 2.778 (9V3)
   2.778 (9V3) * 6.4 (1V1) = 17.7792 (10V4)
   17.7792 (10V4) + 2.778 (1V3) = 20.5572 (11V4)
   20.5572 (11V4) stored in B as 20.557 (6V3)
```

```
COMPUTE A = (12 + .1) / 7.
  12 (2V0) + .1 (0V1) = 12.1 (3V1)
  12.1 (3V1) / 7 (1V0) = 1.7 (3V1)
  1.7 (3V1) stored in A as 1 (4V0)
COMPUTE A = (12 / 7) + .1.
  12 (2V0) / (1V0) = 1 (2V0)
  1 (1V0) + .1 (0V1) = 1.1 (2V1)
  1.1 (2V1) stored in A as 1 (4V0)
```

Chapter 7

1.

```
A - 'Obbbbb'
B - compilation error
C - 'ABC'
D - '121212'
E - 'bbbbb123'
F - 'ABCbbb'
G - '000000'
```

3.

```
01  TITLES     PIC X(200).
01  COUNT-IT   PIC S9(5) COMP.

    □ □ □

    MOVE ZERO TO COUNT-IT.
    INSPECT TITLES TALLYING COUNT-IT FOR ALL 'ABCD'
                                        ALL 'EFG'.
      [Or:]
    EXAMINE TITLES TALLYING ALL 'ABCD'.
```

```
MOVE TALLY TO COUNT-IT.

EXAMINE TITLES TALLYING ALL 'EFG'.

ADD TALLY TO COUNT-IT.
```

Chapter 8

3.

The technique is termed *rippling a character*. A single character is moved to the first position of an identifier, and then the identifier is moved to itself, one character position beyond the first character. On some computers, this propagates the character through the entire identifier. This is efficient, but it is an abominable practice. First, it is not clear that all that code simply moves blanks to the identifier. Second, it violates the ANS Standard, and does not work on many computers. It works in System/360 computers, but does not work on System/370 computers.

Chapter 9

3.

```
01  SOMETHING.

    05  ISUB      PIC S9(4) COMP.

    05  TABLES    PIC S9V9(4) COMP-3

                  OCCURS 200 TIMES INDEXED BY IX.
```

Unordered, count 3.6257 entries:

```
MOVE ZEROS TO COUNT-IT.

PERFORM A10-COUNT-IT

   VARYING ISUB BY 1 FROM 1

   UNTIL ISUB > 200.

   □ □ □

A10-COUNT-IT.

   IF TABLES (ISUB) = 3.6257

      THEN ADD 1 TO COUNT-IT.
```

Unordered, see if 0.07963 is in table:

```
SET IX TO 1.

SEARCH TABLES

   AT END DISPLAY '0.07963 NOT IN TABLES'

   WHEN TABLES (IX) = 0.07963

        DISPLAY '0.07963 IS FOUND IN TABLES'.
```

Ordered, see if 2.1537 is in table:

```
SEARCH ALL TABLES

   AT END DISPLAY '2.1537 NOT IN TABLES'

   WHEN TABLES (IX) = 2.1537

        DISPLAY '2.1537 IS FOUND IN TABLES'.
```

5.

Chapter 16 contains an example showing how to write a program to sort a table.

Chapter 11

5.

```
WORKING-STORAGE SECTION.

01   ISUB        PIC S9(4) COMP.

01   TABLE-TOTAL PIC S9(9)V99 COMP-3.

LINKAGE SECTION.

01   THING.

     05   ITS-SIZE   PIC S9(4) COMP.

     05   TABLES     PIC S9(5)V999 COMP-3

                     OCCURS 0 TO 500 TIMES

                     DEPENDING ON ITS-SIZE.

     05   TABLE-MIN  PIC S9(5)V99 COMP-3.

     05   TABLE-MAX  PIC S9(5)V99 COMP-3.

     05   TABLE-AVG  PIC S9(5)V99 COMP-3.
```

```
PROCEDURE DIVISION USING THING.

A10-BEGIN.

     MOVE ZEROS TO TABLE-TOTAL.

     MOVE -99999.99 TO TABLE-MAX.

     MOVE 99999.99 TO TABLE-MIN.

     PERFORM B10-PROCESS-TABLE

       VARYING ISUB FROM 1 BY 1

       UNTIL ISUB ) ITS-SIZE.

     COMPUTE TABLE-AVG = TABLE-AVG / ITS-SIZE.

 A20-RETURN.

     EXIT PROGRAM.

**** EXIT

 B10-PROCESS-TABLE.

     ADD TABLES (ISUB) TO TABLE-TOTAL.

     IF TABLES (ISUB) ) TABLE-MAX

         THEN MOVE TABLE (ISUB) TO TABLE-MAX.

     IF TABLES (ISUB) ( TABLE-MIN

         THEN MOVE TABLES (ISUB) TO TABLE-MIN.

**** EXIT
```

Chapter 13

3.

```
     SELECT FILE-IN ASSIGN TO UT-S-FILEIN.

       □ □ □

  FD  FILE-IN
       RECORDS CONTAINS 33 CHARACTERS
       BLOCK CONTAINS 0 RECORDS
       LABEL RECORDS STANDARD.
```

```
01  REC-IN     PIC X(33).

WORKING-STORAGE SECTION.

01  IN-REC.

    05  IN-PROJ     PIC X(4).

    05  IN-NAME     PIC X(25).

    05  IN-OHD      PIC S9(5)V99 COMP-3.

01  IN-DUP-PROJ    PIC X(4).

01  IN-NO-DUP      PIC S9(4) COMP.


    □ □ □

    OPEN INPUT FILE-IN.

    MOVE LOW-VALUES TO IN-REC,

                      IN-DUP-PROJ.

    MOVE ZEROS TO IN-NO-DUP.

    PERFORM A10-READ-ALL

       UNTIL IN-REC = HIGH-VALUES.

    CLOSE FILE-IN.

    DISPLAY 'NUMBER OF DUPLICATES: ', IN-NO-DUP.


    □ □ □

A10-READ-ALL.

    READ FILE-IN INTO IN-REC

       AT END MOVE HIGH-VALUES TO IN-REC.

    IF IN-REC NOT = HIGH-VALUES

       THEN PERFORM B10-CHECK-RECORDS.

**** EXIT

B10-CHECK-RECORDS.

    IF IN-PROJ ⟨ IN-DUP-PROJ

       THEN DISPLAY 'RECORD OUT OF SORT:',
```

```
                    DISPLAY IN REC
          ELSE IF IN-PROJ = IN-DUP-PROJ
                    THEN DISPLAY 'DUPLICATE PROJECT NUMBER:',
                         DISPLAY IN-REC
                         ADD 1 TO IN-NO-DUP.
          MOVE IN-PROJ TO IN-DUP-PROJ.
**** EXIT
```

8.

The program will work improperly if either the MASTER-IN or TRANS-IN files are out of sequence or if they contain duplicate records. Section VIII in this chapter is essentially a solution to this problem.

Chapter 14

1.

```
    MOVE 23658.97 TO W.           'bbb$23,658.97bb'

    MOVE -2 TO W.                 'bbbbbbbb$2.00CR'

    MOVE .01 TO W.                'bbbbbbbbb0.01bb'

    □ □ □

    MOVE 26531 TO X.              'bbb26,531'

    MOVE -4 TO X.                 'bbbbbbbb4'

    □ □ □

    MOVE -16 TO Y.                '-***16'

    MOVE 327 TO Y.                'b**327'

    MOVE -823845 TO Y.            '-23945'

    □ □ □
```

```
MOVE 35278.6 TO Z.              '$bbbb35,278.60'

MOVE -247.96 TO Z.              '$bbbbbb-247.96'

MOVE ZERO TO Z.                 'bbbbbbbbbbbbbb'
```

Chapter 15

4.

```
INPUT-OUTPUT SECTION.

FILE-CONTROL.

    SELECT RPT-FILE ASSIGN TO UT-S-FILEOUT.

DATA DIVISION.

FILE SECTION.

FD  RPT-FILE

    RECORD CONTAINS 133 CHARACTERS

    BLOCK CONTAINS 0 RECORDS

    LABEL RECORDS STANDARD

    REPORT IS SQRT.

WORKING-STORAGE SECTION.

01  LEFT-NUM    PIC S9(4)V9(5) COMP-3.

01  RIGHT-NUM   PIC S9(4)V9(5) COMP-3.

01  LEFT SQRT   PIC S9(4)V9(5) COMP-3.

01  RIGHT-SQRT  PIC S9(4)V9(5) COMP-3.

01  LINE-CTL    PIC S9(4) COMP.

REPORT SECTION.

RD  SQRT

    PAGE 54 LINES

    HEADING 1

    FIRST DETAIL 5.
```

```
01  TYPE PAGE HEADING.

    05  LINE 1.

        10  COLUMN 30  PIC X(21) VALUE 'TABLE OF SQUARE ROOTS'.

        10  COLUMN 50  PIC X(4) VALUE 'PAGE'.

        10  COLUMN 55  PIC ZZ9 SOURCE PAGE-COUNTER.

    05  LINE 3.

        10  COLUMN 1   PIC X(19) VALUE 'NUMBER SQUARE ROOT'.

        10  COLUMN 45  PIC X(19) VALUE 'NUMBER SQUARE ROOT'.

01  DTL-LINE TYPE DETAIL LINE PLUS 1.

    05  COLUMN 1       PIC ZZZ9 SOURCE LEFT-NUM.

    05  COLUMN 8       PIC ZZZ9.99999 SOURCE LEFT-SQRT.

    05  COLUMN 45      PIC ZZZ9 SOURCE RIGHT-NUM.

    05  COLUMN 52      PIC ZZZ9.99999 SOURCE RIGHT-SQRT.

PROCEDURE DIVISION.

A00-BEGIN.

    OPEN OUTPUT RPT-FILE.

    INITIATE SQRT.

    PERFORM B10-PRINT-PAGE

        VARYING LINE-CTL FROM 1 BY 100

        UNTIL LINE-CTL ) 1000.

    TERMINATE SQRT.

    CLOSE RPT-FILE.

    STOP RUN.

B10-PRINT-PAGE.

    PERFORM C10-PRINT-LINES

        VARYING LEFT-NUM FROM LINE-CTL BY 1

        UNTIL LEFT-NUM ) LINE-CTL + 50.
```

```
**** EXIT

  C10-PRINT-LINES.

       COMPUTE RIGHT-NUM = LEFT-NUM + 50.

       COMPUTE LEFT-SQRT = LEFT-NUM ** 0.5.

       COMPUTE RIGHT-SQRT = RIGHT-NUM ** 0.5.

       GENERATE DTL-LINE.

**** EXIT
```

Chapter 16

1.

```
FILE-CONTROL.

       SELECT SORT-FILE ASSIGN TO UT-S-SORTWK.

       SELECT SORT-IN ASSIGN TO UT-S-SORTIN.

       SELECT SORT-OUT ASSIGN TO UT-S-SORTOUT.

DATA DIVISION.

FILE SELECTION.

SD   SORT-FILE.

01   SORT-REC.

     05   SORT-KEY-1      PIC X(8).

     05   SORT-KEY-2      PIC X(12).

     05   FILLER          PIC X(60).

FD   SORT-IN

     RECORD CONTAINS 80 CHARACTERS

     BLOCK CONTAINS 0 RECORDS

     LABEL RECORDS STANDARD.

01   IN-REC      PIC X(80).

FD   SORT-OUT

     RECORD CONTAINS 80 CHARACTERS
```

```
    BLOCK CONTAINS 0 RECORDS

    LABEL RECORDS STANDARD.

01  OUT-REC      PIC X(80).

PROCEDURE DIVISION.

A00-BEGIN.

    SORT SORT-FILE

         ON ASCENDING KEY SORT-KEY-1

         ON DESCENDING KEY SORT-KEY-2

         USING SORT-IN

         GIVING SORT-OUT.

    STOP RUN.
```

5.

Sort the number as follows:

- Leftmost digit in descending order.
- Second digit in descending order.
- Third digit in ascending order.

index

Index